THE IMPERIAL WAR MUSEUM BOOK OF THE

SOMME

'We are on the eve of a great battle,
probably the greatest of the many great encounters
of the greatest war the world has ever seen.'

Captain George McGowan
Brigade Signals Officer, 90th Infantry Brigade
24 June 1916

'... this, the greatest of all battlefields'

Lieutenant-Colonel C.H. Ommanney,
83rd Brigade, Royal Field Artillery,
The Somme, 10 September 1918

OTHER BOOKS BY MALCOLM BROWN

Scapa Flow
(with Patricia Meehan)

Tommy Goes to War

Christmas Truce
(with Shirley Seaton)

A Touch of Genius:
The Life of T.E. Lawrence
(with Julia Cave)

The Letters of T.E. Lawrence
(Editor)

Secret Despatches from Arabia,
and Other Writings by T.E. Lawrence
(Editor)

The Imperial War Museum
Book of the First World War

The Imperial War Museum
Book of the Western Front

The Imperial War Museum
Book of 1918: Year of Victory

MALCOLM BROWN

THE IMPERIAL WAR MUSEUM BOOK OF THE

SOMME

PAN BOOKS

in association with
The Imperial War Museum

First published 1996 by Sidgwick & Jackson

First published in paperback 1997 by Pan Books

This edition published 2002 by Pan Books
an imprint of Pan Macmillan Ltd
Pan Macmillan, 20 New Wharf Road, London N1 9RR
Basingstoke and Oxford
Associated companies throughout the world
www.panmacmillan.com

ISBN 0 330 49206 3

Copyright © The Imperial War Museum and Malcolm Brown 1996

The right of The Imperial War Museum and Malcolm Brown to be identified as the
authors of this work has been asserted by them in accordance
with the Copyright, Designs and Patents Act 1988.

All rights reserved. No part of this publication may be
reproduced, stored in or introduced into a retrieval system, or
transmitted, in any form, or by any means (electronic, mechanical,
photocopying, recording or otherwise) without the prior written
permission of the publisher. Any person who does any unauthorized
act in relation to this publication may be liable to criminal
prosecution and civil claims for damages.

1 3 5 7 9 8 6 4 2

A CIP catalogue record for this book is available from
the British Library.

Typeset by CentraCet Limited, Cambridge
Printed and bound in Great Britain by
Mackays of Chatham plc, Chatham, Kent

This book is sold subject to the condition that it shall not,
by way of trade or otherwise, be lent, re-sold, hired out,
or otherwise circulated without the publisher's prior consent
in any form of binding or cover other than that in which
it is published and without a similar condition including this
condition being imposed on the subsequent purchaser.

IN MEMORY OF

PRIVATE W.G. BROWN, RAMC,

WHO CAME BACK,

AND OF

PRIVATE E.V. RADCLIFFE, ROYAL WELSH FUSILIERS,

WHO DID NOT

Contents

LIST OF ILLUSTRATIONS

SECTION ONE

1. The 'Leaning Virgin' of Notre Dame de Brebières, Albert, September 1917 (Q 11676)

2. The 'Leaning Virgin' no more; the ruins of the Albert Basilica in August 1918 (Q 11203)

3. Captain Harold Yeo, who wrote of the first British attack on the Somme: 'The whole affair is a great success, and our sacrifices aren't going to be in vain.' (IWM Docs)

4. Private Archie Surfleet, who wrote of the Somme: 'The very name conjures up a picture of miserable wastes, mud and devastation.' (HU 35917)

5. Captain Alfred ('Bill') Bland, 22nd Manchesters; killed in action, 1 July 1916. (Courtesy Mr Richard Bland, Mrs Margaret Mace)

6. Captain Charles ('Charlie') May, 22nd Manchesters; killed in action, 1 July 1916. (Courtesy Mr H.E. Karet)

7. Private Arthur Wrench, who wrote in November 1916: 'It strikes me there is not much glory these days in dying for your country.' (IWM Docs)

8. Lieutenant Alan Lloyd MC, Royal Field Artillery, killed in action on the second anniversary of the outbreak of war, 4 August 1916. (HU 59399)

9. Lloyd in civilian happiness with the wife he married in September 1914. (HU 59400)

10. The rough-hewn cross made by Lloyd's servant, Gunner Manning, for his officer's first, temporary grave. (HU 59401)

ACKNOWLEDGEMENTS

Since this book represents the fulfilment of a twenty-year-old ambition, it is fitting that my list of acknowledgements should begin with those who introduced me to the subject of the Somme and who assisted me in making my earliest attempt at telling the story recounted in this book. Thus I should like to record my great gratitude to the late Rose Coombs and to her doughty companion in field research, Mike Willis, in whose company I had my first sight of the former Western Front on Remembrance Sunday 1975, at a moving commemoration service held at the massive Canadian Memorial on Vimy Ridge. Rose was at that time engaged in compiling her classic guidebook *Before Endeavours Fade*, and I was subsequently gratified, if surprised, to find myself unexpectedly an extra in one of her photographs of Delville Wood. Next I must express my very special thanks to Martin Middlebrook, who not only inspired my interest and my imagination with his outstanding book *The First Day on the Somme*, but also conducted me on an unforgettable, week-long exploratory visit to the Somme battlefield in that same November of 1975. I recall that the sun which had shone on our arrival rapidly gave way to an all-enshrouding fog, in which the temperature dropped out of sight and visibility was reduced to a matter of yards. Yet I can imagine no better initiation, for the gaunt winter trees and the crosses of cemeteries loomed like ghosts in the mist, while areas of preserved battleground such as that at Beaumont Hamel, with its zigzag trench-lines, its shell holes and its rusted screw-pickets stuck oddly in the turf, seemed almost to take on the aspect of the actual, original Western Front. Even the cold contributed, for it made one realize how fortunate one was to be able to retreat at nightfall to a warm hotel, an excellent meal and a bottle of wine, while the soldiers of the Somme had no option but to stay out in that strange, dangerous wilderness however grim the conditions.

What those conditions were like was brought home to me in a tide of correspondence which followed an appeal I subsequently made in the *Radio Times* for material of all kinds – letters, diaries, documents, drawings, photographs – in order to help me to present the story of the Somme on television. The mass of material brought in by that appeal not only contributed substantially to the enrichment of my TV documentary, *The Battle of the Somme*, first transmitted on 29 June 1976, it also became the foundation of my subsequent book *Tommy Goes to War*. So my next acknowledgement is to those who kindly responded to that appeal, and I am glad to report that some of the material sent to me in 1976, for which there was no space in my previous efforts, is at last being published in this book in 1996. My gratitude also goes to the BBC which commissioned the documentary, and to those who worked on it with me, notably Leo McKern, who presented it with ardour, conviction and skill, himself striding the terrain like a ghost telling the story of what had happened in those memorable fields.

All this led in due time to my present association with the Imperial War Museum, this being the third book that I have written on the First World War using their material and with their support. So I am pleased to record my deep gratitude to that institution, of which I have now been a virtual honorary member for almost eight years, with the full support initially of its former Director-General, Dr Alan Borg, and latterly of its present one, Robert Crawford. To their names I must also add that of Dr Christopher Dowling, who has throughout been in charge of the Museum's dealings with the publishers. With regard to the central matter of research, I wish to record my very warm thanks to Roderick Suddaby and all the members of his Department of Documents (now my colleagues since it is in their offices that I have been allowed habitation): Nigel Steel, Simon Robbins, Stephen Walton and Penny Bonning, not forgetting David Shaw and Wendy Lutterloch. Next my thanks go to the Department of Printed Books, with particular gratitude to Mary Wilkinson and Sarah Paterson, and also to James Taylor who in a free-lance capacity translated some important documents for me from the German. The Department of Photographs has as ever been most helpful in the provision of illustrations. Very special thanks must go to Peter Simkins, the Museum's senior historian, and to his colleague – himself the author of a most valuable book on the Somme to which Peter wrote an excellent Introduction – Chris McCarthy, who kindly read the manuscript and offered me much valuable advice and wisdom, and also suggested some most welcome corrections. A third sharp-eyed reader of the text was Roderick Suddaby. I am deeply indebted to these gentlemen, feeling that if a book can pass the scrutiny of three such wise men it cannot be too far from some approximation to the truth. A fourth reader to whom I am most grateful, and who has retrieved my manuscript from numerous verbal hazards, is my wife Betty, to whom I apologize for the general state of chaos to which the domestic scene always seems to deteriorate in the final stages of the completion of a book.

Mention should also be made of the Commonwealth War Graves Commission, whose staff are always most courteous and patient in the answering of enquiries. I would like to express my gratitude to the Commission for its help over many years and am particularly pleased to be able to publish an account, in the book's final chapter, which shows some of its earliest representatives already carrying out their vital, dedicated task on the Somme long before the region was finally released from the shackles of war.

I have been conscious throughout the many months of research and writing of the enthusiastic support of my publisher, William Armstrong, the founder of this series of Imperial War Museum books, and I am proud to be able to add another volume to the long list of titles under the imprint of Sidgwick & Jackson with a bearing on the Great War, which included, far back, *1914 and Other Poems* by Rupert Brooke and (mentioned in the text of the present volume) F.W. Harvey's *A Gloucestershire Lad at Home and Abroad*. My warm thanks go to him, and also to those who have seen the book through its editing and production stages, notably Carey Smith and Peter Hull, whose wise and sympathetic guidance has done much to improve its text and texture, thereby enhancing a quality I value above all else, its readability.

Finally, I wish to record my profound gratitude to those whose vivid and memorable accounts I have been privileged to use to provide the basic material of this history. Their names, and the names of the copyright holders who have kindly allowed me to quote from their writings, appear in the Index of Contributors. (I should add that my dealings with some copyright holders have been far from perfunctory, in that I have been the recipient of much friendly, even if at times vigorous, advice, and have also been entrusted with a number of priceless family photographs.) In several cases, copyright holder and writer are, remarkably, the same person, still thriving eighty years after the event. It gives me special pleasure, therefore, to salute Mr Norman Edwards, Mr Norman Collins, Mr George Harbottle and Herr Ernst Jünger, gallant participants in this drama in the early part of the century, but, it is good, and important, to add, enemies no more.

Some Definitions

SOMME: A Department of northern France, part of the ancient French province of Picardy, with a short coast-line on the English channel, crossed east-west by the River Somme. Principal towns are Amiens (the capital), Abbeville, Montdidier and Péronne. Area 6156 square kilometres; population approx. 500,000.

SOMME: A river of northern France, 246 kilometres in length, which rises near St. Quentin and flows to the sea by Amiens and Abbeville.

BATTLE OF THE SOMME: A major battle of the First World War lasting from July to November 1916.

SECOND BATTLES OF THE SOMME: Official, but rarely used, name for the fighting in the Somme region from 21 August to 3 September 1918.

'ON THE SOMME': A formula with a special resonance among battle sectors of the Western Front war. Men fought in France, in Flanders, in the Ypres Salient, at Passchendaele, at Arras, at Verdun, but 'on the Somme'.

'ANOTHER SOMME': The nightmare scenario widely feared by politicians and strategists since 1916.

SOMME: French noun, feminine. Sum, amount; sum of money. *Payer la forte somme*, to pay top price. *Tout fait somme*, everything counts. *Somme toute*, when all is said and done.

SOMME: French noun, masculine. Nap, snooze. *Faire un somme*, to take a nap. *Ne faire qu'un somme, dormir d'un somme*, to sleep without a break; to sleep the night through.

FOREWORD

A SUBJECT OF CONTINUING CONTROVERSY

'THE SOMME WAS JUST SLAUGHTER,' affirmed a survivor of the great 1916 battle, a former officer, in a letter written in 1976. I quoted him in the 60th anniversary television documentary, entitled *The Battle of the Somme*, which I made for the BBC that year. I also quoted as an opposite verdict the claim made by Charles Carrington in his classic *A Subaltern's War*: 'The Somme battle raised the morale of the British Army. Although we did not win a decisive victory there was what matters most, a definite and growing sense of superiority over the enemy, man to man.... We were quite sure that we had got the Germans beat: next spring we would deliver the knock-out blow.'

I used these contrary voices to show what I believed, and believe still, to be the case, that, in a sense, the Battle of the Somme did not end when it closed down in late 1916, in that the argument over its conduct and cost, and its outcome, continued. Indeed, it continues even now, with no prospect of there ever being a generally accepted verdict. It is a subject which, in contemporary jargon, will run and run. In one other respect, however, the two voices have an important element in common, in that they represent hindsight views, opinions delivered in retrospect – in the first case sixty years after the event, in the second case thirteen.

The nature of the evidence used in this book is different in that – apart from a small number of clearly signalled instances – it is contemporary. This is the Somme as it was seen *at the time*, by men who did not know as they wrote how the war would develop, or whether they themselves would survive it; indeed, a substantial core of those quoted here did not. These are the thoughts of soldiers involved in great events without the privilege of knowing the outcome, to whom the prospect of looking back at the web in which they were then caught must have seemed infinitely remote, beyond imagining.

It might be argued that there is a weakness in this approach, in that anything written down while the conflict was in full flood around the writer must by definition be so partial and particular, so lacking in any kind of perspective, or alternatively so anodyne and bland, as to be of little historical value. I have not found this to be the case. On the contrary, contemporary writings are often sharply focused, full of energy and adrenalin, strongly informed with forthright views firmly held.

But, it will be asked, what about the censorship to which letters from the front were regularly subjected? Strange as it might seem, fear of censorship seems not to have been quite so inhibiting a factor as has generally been assumed. Names of units and of places were the first casualty at the censor's hand; attitudes and sentiments, even descriptions of fighting, appear to have been allowed through rather more easily – the example quoted in Chapter 5 of a letter 'torn by censor' (see page 110) is notable principally for its rarity. More, while ordinary correspondence was censored locally, letters could occasionally be sent in special green envelopes which were subject only to random spot-checks at the base. Men often took a chance with their 'green envelopes', knowing the likelihood of their being picked out for scrutiny was very small. (My previous book, *The Imperial War Museum Book of the Western Front*, included the interesting case of a soldier who took advantage of his 'private letter' – as he called it – to describe the killing of prisoners during the Second Battle of Ypres in 1915.) Another way of outwitting the censor was to have letters taken across the Channel for posting by comrades going on leave. Diaries, of course, were subject only to their writer's personal censorship; since these were, strictly speaking, forbidden documents anyway, their owners would tend to be of the kind that would be prepared to write frankly about their experiences.

Being away from the front in the home country – usually known as 'Blighty', a term of great resonance for the fighting soldier, part paradise, part never-never land, part (in Housman's famous phrase) 'blue remembered hills' – allowed the greatest freedom of all. Hence perhaps the most outspoken letter in this book, that of 23 August 1917 by Private Willie Robins of the South African Brigade quoted in Chapter 15 (see pages 300–1) Hence also this example from October 1916, admittedly not from a letter or a diary – the stock-in-trade of this book – but from an article published by a Sergeant of the 22nd Battalion of the Manchester Regiment (also known as the 7th Manchester Pals), recovering in England after being wounded in the opening attack on the Somme. He is addressing the British public, which appears to him to have no comprehension of the reality of what is happening at the front in its name, to have lost any sense of idealistic purpose, and to be interested only in assessing the great battle taking place in France in terms of future political and economic advantage:

> You speak lightly, you assume that we shall speak lightly, of things, emotions, states of mind, human relationships and affairs, which are to us solemn or terrible. You seem ashamed, as if they were a kind of weakness, of the ideas which sent us to France, and for which thousands of sons and lovers have died. You calculate the profits to be derived from 'War after the War', as though the unspeakable agonies of the Somme were an item in a commercial proposition.

He is merciless in attacking the new, fashionable concept of the time: attrition, the theory which saw assurance of ultimate victory in the fact that the Allies had a longer suit in manpower than Germany and Austria-Hungary and were therefore in the end bound to win. Shrewdly choosing a cricket metaphor for his punch-line, he denounces '*The Times* military expert's hundredth variation on the theme that the abstruse science of war consists in killing more of the enemy than he kills of you, so that whatever its losses – agreeable doctrine – the numerically preponderant side can always win, as it were, by one wicket.'

Admittedly this Sergeant of the 22nd Manchesters – a battalion which will figure prominently in this book – was a very unusual figure: the Balliol-educated future professor of economic history and writer, R.H. Tawney. But he is worth quoting in that he shows that serious thoughts about the Somme were possible during the actual battle, and because he introduces some of the assumptions and arguments which have been part of the equation of the Somme ever since.

He did, however, *publish* his views; and both the article quoted, 'Some Reflections of a Soldier', and a second essay originally published in August 1916 about the first day of the Somme, were subsequently gathered into a book, *The Attack, and Other Papers*, which appeared in 1953. By contrast, the great majority of those whose evidence is presented in this book have *not* been published heretofore; their often superb and powerful writings are given public space here for the first time. They are, as it were, messengers from the front whose reports have at last got through. They may not write with quite the polemical force of a Tawney producing a journalistic article; but they offer much that is extremely well expressed and communicate in terms which people of the present generation should have no difficulty in understanding. Most importantly of all, they do not speak with one voice; they display a wide range of thoughts, views and opinions, from a wholehearted belief in the war to a downright loathing of it. There is every kind of gradation, from extreme fervour to angry disenchantment.

It is this mix of rich if often contrary voices, indeed, which more than any other factor justifies this book. This is now an old story from the distant, teenage years of the century, but the evidence of these hitherto unheard witnesses makes it, I believe, as fresh, and as disturbing, as the crises that fill the headlines as the century moves towards its close.

By way of a sample in advance, here is a voice from the sceptical end of the spectrum: an extract from a letter written to his mother in early January 1917 by a Private Eric Blore, member of No 31 Kite-Balloon Section of the Royal Flying Corps. One canard that has long exasperated me is that which assumes that no ordinary soldier could turn a decent sentence or say anything other than that he hoped that everybody at home was in the pink as it left him at present. For an ordinary private, Blore had a sense of style as sophisticated as that of any of his superiors in rank, and with a caustic wit thrown in. A conscript, so that one need not expect from him the high-flown sentiments of the volunteers of 1914, he had arrived on the Somme just after the 1916 battle had finally closed down:

I'm allowed to state that we are in the Somme area and although I'm not 'writing this by the light of bursting shrapnel' still I'm about a twopenny bus ride from the trenches. The shrapnel, however, occasionally gets here for nothing, which so excites it that it bursts from sheer joy not far away. The prevalent discomfort at the moment is the mud which clings like poor relations and breeds twice as fast. It's burlesque simply. The roads are a swilling bath of filth which splashes the tree tops and the moon. No habitation is immune and men and horses pass one another like plasticine models and without a glance of recognition or concern. There's something amazingly commonplace in the whole huge drama; and something amazingly dramatic in the commonplaceness of it all. Anyway it's *all* very silly. I went up in our balloon the other day and had a look at the turmoil from the only clean spot in France. I wasn't very impressed. The air is apparently pricked with little bursts of light – rather like a starry sky in which the stars take it in turn to come out for a fraction of a second. Up and down, thousands of feet above the line but still amongst the flashes, float our aeroplanes like lonely swallows.

Yesterday we started bombarding the Huns which we are still continuing to do with the result that sleep is about as rare as strawberries. One might be living in a huge drum which a thousand savages are beating with a hundred different kinds of hammers. Sometimes – quite often in fact – one savage in particular takes a running kick at the vellum. *That* is a huge gun only a few hundred yards away. Otherwise I'm enjoying myself!

Blore was clearly no stranger to irony, so it can be assumed that there was no hint of 'cheero, chin-chin, tickled to death to go' in his final statement; rather there is a suggestion of the wry resignation of someone whose safety-valve in an inhuman situation not of his making is to make mockery of it. He would remain a member of that band of men who, whatever their views of the basic reasons for the war, always maintained a sharply independent, critical attitude in relation to the philosophy, and the methods, by which it was fought.

For the high patriotic school, there could be no better spokesman than Captain Harold Yeo, of the 9th Battalion, King's Own Yorkshire Light Infantry, 21st Division, an eager, stalwart, 'thrusting' officer *par excellence*. This is from the letter to his mother of 6 July 1916, in which he described the events of six days earlier, the catastrophic first day of the Battle of the Somme, but for him a day of rich achievement, even of glory:

Since I last wrote to you a lifetime of experience has come my way. Last Friday night this brigade toed the line, and at 7.30 next morning set off to make our appointed dent in the Hun line – which we did.

The actual gain we got was his first line system for about 1500 yards on a little bit of front immediately north of Fricourt. We consolidated that, i.e. made it a reasonably firm stepping stone for our successors, and on Monday night we came back to bivouac, our sorrow for all those who went up but did not return with us being counterbalanced by the pride in their noble deaths, and all having a feeling of hard earned satisfaction.

It rained that night so that the two hours sleep was a little disturbed, but when we boarded the train which took us away, we never saw such looks of content. We ran slowly through, along the banks of the Somme (with a lavish display of pickelhaubes hung out of the windows) and eventually came to the beautiful village where we now are. After a good sleep and wash, we are now setting to work to put our house in order, tell frantic lies to American War correspondents, exchange yarns, and, if many generals say it to us, we shall begin to think we are 'some' fellows. The whole affair is (not *was* please) a great success, and our sacrifices aren't going to be in vain.

In my previous book, I gave prominent place to a young officer of the Somme who felt that there were two sides to the war being fought there, which he defined as 'the mud and the stars'. He saw both the horror and the heroism – the sheer awfulness of so much that was taking place, and the character and tenacity with which men were facing their ordeal – as inevitable parts of the Somme experience. Clearly this is reflected in the quotations given at the start of this Foreword, as it is also in those from the writings of Tawney, Blore and Yeo. The story which follows cannot really be understood unless it is accepted that these were the essential concomitants of the campaign on the Somme.

Perhaps this point should be amplified in view of the fact that, in spite of numerous efforts by various historians in this field, the Somme is still almost universally seen as a symbol of *absolute* horror and *total* futility. Some recent highly successful novels and non-fiction studies have taken this pillorying of the Somme (and other such battles) as virtually axiomatic. A significant consequence of this view – understandably bolstered by the famous case of the denunciation of the war by the poet Siegfried Sassoon (himself a hero of the Somme battle) and by the anti-war writings of Wilfred Owen, Robert Graves and others – is a kind of instinctive retrospective pacifism, a mixture of horror and pity so potent that it inspires the urge to cry out (as Sassoon himself did in 1917 in his poem 'Attack'), 'O Jesus, make it stop!' The character of the Somme fighting is seen as so appalling and the losses it entailed so unimaginably huge that decent, civilized people find themselves, as it were, angrily demanding that it should be called off, for the sake of the wretched victims duped into fighting it.

The advantage of researching what the alleged victims wrote *at the time* is that they don't seem to have seen things that way. Even those who clearly deplored the brutal, inhuman aspects of the Somme – and there are not a few of such persuasion in this book – believed that there was no option other than that of carrying on with the fighting. They might not like the practice, but there was little argument as to the principle. After all, the Germans were occupying French and Belgian soil and had to be removed. It was no more possible to say 'let them stay where they are and let's all go home', than it was to condone the occupation of a much greater part of Europe a generation later during the war of 1939–45. There was also a gut feeling that having got into the game, they might as well win it; they hadn't signed up to get beaten. More, while the Germany of Kaiser Wilhelm II was not in the same league for evil and extremism as the Germany of Hitler and the Nazis, the prospect of a continent dominated by the autocratic empires of Germany and Austria-Hungary was clearly not one that appealed to the populations of the

Western democracies, whether rich man in his castle or fighting man in his trench.

Throwing in the towel not being an option, the soldiers of 1914–18 (on all sides, because the enemy also believed firmly in his cause) swiftly acquired an amazing resilience and fortitude, which meant that the task assigned them was not abandoned, however daunting it might seem, but stoically persevered with until a satisfactory conclusion was reached. In an eloquent essay on 'Europe on the Eve of the First World War' Sir Michael Howard has written of the men who would fight in that conflict: 'None knew what they were marching towards, and any romantic notions they had about war shredded to pieces the moment they came under artillery fire. But they adjusted to the ordeal with astonishing speed and stoicism. It was indeed because they adjusted so well that the ordeal lasted for as long as it did.'

Perhaps a caveat should be added in case this statement might seem to suggest that all Western Front soldiers were motivated at all times by high political ardour and a vision of a rejuvenated continent cleansed of autocracy. There were undoubtedly many such, and many who genuinely enjoyed their war, but for the majority the prime motivation was to come through in one piece. 'Après la guerre' was the universal dream, a phrase well described as 'magical' by those masters of Great War slang, Brophy and Partridge, for its encapsulation of that 'secret sentiment' common to almost everybody, a 'longing for survival and for the return of peace'. The men at the front knew the familiar jingle that you couldn't make omelettes without breaking eggs (see Rifleman Percy Jones's pre-battle comment on page 58), but they hoped they might not be one of the eggs that would have to be broken. Private Arthur Wrench, of the 51st (Highland) Division, dismayed at some of the horrors of the Somme fighting in November 1916, undoubtedly spoke for many when he wryly commented: 'It strikes me there is not much glory these days in dying for your country.' In fact, if you could do your bit, and then retire with reasonable honour from the field, that was an extremely attractive option, possibly the best option of all. Hence the widespread lust for a 'Blighty' wound (a wound sufficiently serious to get you back home but not serious enough to endanger your health), which was undoubtedly a stronger motivation for many than the lust for glory.

Even volunteer officers of proud battalions were not immune to such beguiling thoughts. In July 1916 Captain Arthur Roberts of the Civil Service Rifles wrote to a girl-friend who had told him that she was about to sail from America to England: 'You don't know how everyone out here would envy you. I don't much as a matter of fact because I am quite content: but out here it is fashionable to sigh for Blighty.' Yet Roberts and those to whom he was referring knew what they were there for and duly played their part in the September offensive on the Somme, and many – Roberts included – never did get home.

A second corollary of the 'horror/futility' view is a tendency to assume that all commanders, indeed almost everybody in authority at this time, from politicians to battalion COs, were by definition uncaring butchers, happy to wave long casualty lists in the air like so many scalps or trophies, or, in political terms, useful symbols of national virility. They are assumed to have taken little care of, and to have had virtually no consideration for, the cannon-fodder troops at their disposal. They are also deemed to have been incapable of learning any lessons, even to have been interested in the possibility of improving their performance.

There certainly were generals of that kidney (most of whom ended up being sent back home), but even in such cases it is important to place them in the context of the time. The possibility of a major conflict in Europe had been in the air for years. There had been a widespread assumption that when it came it would be short; there had also been a widespread acceptance that it would be nasty and brutish. As Sir Michael Howard states in the essay already quoted, it was believed that 'in any future war, armies would have to endure very heavy losses indeed ... Avoidance of casualties was seen as no part of the general's trade, and willingness to accept them was regarded as a necessity for commander and commanded alike. Into the literature of pre-war Europe there crept the word which was to become the terrible leitmotiv of the coming conflict: "sacrifice"; more particularly, "the supreme sacrifice".'

With such a culture already in place (feeding the philosophy of the military commanders of *all* the belligerent nations, not just the British), it is a matter of high credit that there were those who looked beyond the prescribed parameters of twentieth-century war and searched for ways of avoiding its seemingly inevitable tragedies. A notable example featured in this book is Major-General Ivor Maxse, who, far from despatching the troops of his 18th (Eastern) Division casually 'over the top' on the Somme, trained them most scrupulously for action and was eager to try every possible means of advantaging them so that when they attacked they would do so in the best possible circumstances. (Significantly, a biography of him has recently appeared under the title *Far from a Donkey*, a harking-back to the much quoted description attributed to a German source in the First World War that the 'English soldiers' fought 'like lions' but were 'led by donkeys', a tag now thought to have originated in relation to the French armies defeated in the Franco-Prussian War of 1870–71.)

Also evident from the present book is that whatever questions might remain over the conduct of the Somme battle in 1916, its two leading architects on the British side, Sir Douglas Haig and Sir Henry Rawlinson, had acquired a much more 'modern' grasp of the practice of warfare by the time they fought their second Somme campaign two years later. Further, Haig should be credited not only with being clear-sighted but also with showing undeviating determination with regard to the task facing the Allies once they were committed to a land war with the best fighting force of the continent, Germany. As early as March 1915 he stated: 'We cannot hope to win until we have defeated the German Army', and he never wavered from that view. He certainly believed (though he would not have put it in such terms) that the British in the end had gone through a crucially successful learning-curve in that he wrote in his final despatch of 21 March 1919: 'It is in the great battles of 1916 and 1917 that we have to seek the secret of our victory in 1918.'

All this having been said, it is an entirely legitimate response to feel a sense of dismay, even of outrage, at the fate of those who went to their deaths, or to a lifetime of disablement or aftershock, on the Somme. To visit the cemeteries of that haunted battlefield (the Commonwealth War Graves Commission acknowledges as many as

240 cemeteries in the 1916 area alone) is to risk being overwhelmed by a feeling of grief not made less potent by the fact that it all happened so many decades ago; while for my own part I have met enough survivors who carried scars throughout the rest of their lives to be aware that no argument about the political or military pluses and minuses of the Somme should be thought in any way to invalidate their experience or undermine their perception. May this also be said about the witnesses quoted in these pages.

This book is not only about the great battle of 1916; it aims to cover a larger canvas, that of the Somme throughout the war. There was fighting there in every year from 1914 to 1918, and the Germans only withdrew from the area in the final stages; the Somme is therefore a useful metaphor, 'a macro microcosm' as it were, of the whole conflict. Deliberately, however, the two 1918 chapters are less detailed, more impressionistic than those dealing with the events of 1916, which inevitably provide the book's prime subject.

Unlike my two previous books published under the name of the Imperial War Museum, which were thematic in approach, this one is presented as a continuous chronological narrative. In a sense, it is almost a *war novel*, with a range of characters coming and going, some reappearing after many months, others falling by the wayside through wounding or death, or through simply being transferred to other theatres. It is also different in format, with more emphasis on text and less on illustration. The Museum is especially rich in first-hand evidence relating to the Somme, in the wake of which – indeed, largely as a result of which – it was founded in 1917, and it has therefore been decided to give this material maximum space. One thing the book is not: a full strategic history – there are plenty such, and here, intentionally, the military background is sketched in lightly, giving, it is hoped, sufficient overall information for the reader to appreciate the experiences and thoughts of the officers and men who occupy the foreground. These figures in a memorable and haunting landscape – the Somme is certainly that – are the true heroes of this tale.

By far the greater part of the evidence used here comes from one remarkable source: the Department of Documents of the Imperial War Museum, with its many hundreds of collections of first-hand material, the amassing of which still continues, so that some of the material in the book only arrived in the department while it was being researched. These collections have been the principal seed-corn of all three of my Imperial War Museum volumes. A second very valuable source is the Museum's Department of Printed Books, i.e. its library, which has been of particular help for the important, and I believe most necessary, chapters on the German experience of the Somme and on Somme humour. For illustrations, of course, I have turned primarily to the rich resources of the Department of Photographs, though there are also a number of photographs of soldiers quoted drawn from their individual collections in the Department of Documents, and, as stated in the Acknowledgements, some photographs have come from private sources.

A point worth emphasizing, especially in relation to the Department of Documents, is that the material to which I have had access, because of the way it has been collected, cannot be schematic, being by definition – to use a phrase which had a strong resonance a generation or so ago – a random harvest. The reader will not find, therefore, an across-the-board representation of the experience of the Somme. Certain well-known aspects are thinly covered; for example, the subject of the 'Pals' battalions – those locally raised units in which whole groups of men, from factories, football clubs, even churches, enthusiastically enlisted in 1914 with dire consequences for their communities when the casualty lists came through two years later – principally because evidence relating to them tends to be collected in regional archives rather than being gathered into a national museum. On the other hand, many new, unexpected aspects will be given their place for the first time.

A further important point should be made. It is because the Imperial War Museum has been the basic provider that the book bears its title, but it must be strongly underlined that this does not mean that it represents or embodies in any way an authorized IWM 'view' about the Battle of the Somme. There is no such thing, nor has there been any attempt in the case of this or of any of the other IWM books that I have produced to impose any attitude or enforce any doctrine. As stated in the Acknowledgements, I have shown my manuscript to a number of IWM experts in this field whose knowledge and understanding of the subject I greatly respect and have asked for their comments, but this does not imply that the book bears any kind of 'imprimatur'. I have been as free to pick and choose, to be as prejudiced or unprejudiced, as any other historian approaching such a theme, though it would be foolish indeed to pay no heed to the results of much thoughtful and responsible study. I wish to state this unequivocally because it might be assumed that the very title implies that the book will express an 'establishment' justification – a cover-up, as it were – of the Somme in all its aspects, particularly its controversial ones. It will not aim to do so, nor on the other hand will it try to impose any opposite viewpoint. I have myself been engaged with the subject of the Somme for twenty years: far too long for me to be able to take a simplistic attitude either 'pro' or 'con' this great episode in our history. Indeed, the more one attempts to infiltrate the mind-set of those caught up in it, at all levels from trench to headquarters château, from ally to enemy, the more it becomes impossible to believe that there is one truth, one correct interpretation, in relation to the Battle of the Somme. There were many Sommes – some heroic, some splendid, some ghastly, some tragic, some neither one thing nor the other; as many, indeed, as there were people involved.

In this book, therefore, it is those who were there who make the running; their views, or lack of views, or mix of views, are of the essence. This book's aim above all is to give these men their chance to be heard. In short, it is their Somme rather than anyone else's which it is all about.

*   *   *

In conclusion, a word should be said about the two former soldiers to whose memory I have dedicated this book. The first, Private W.G. Brown RAMC, was my own father; he marched through the Somme region in early 1918 and came hurrying back with the rest of his 59th (North Midland) Division in March, brushing the edge of the old Somme battlefield as they moved westwards in rapid retreat. Although as a minister of religion he was essentially a man of peace, talks with him in my childhood and after helped to awaken my long interest in the Great War. He died in 1978 as my first book on this subject was in process of publication. The second, Private E.V. Radcliffe, 16th Battalion, Royal Welsh Fusiliers, my mother's favourite cousin, lost his life somewhere in the Somme region in April 1918. As was the case with not a few Western Front fatalities, the circumstances of death were never clearly established, pleas by his parents in local newspapers and elsewhere producing no definite news. His body was never found and his name is engraved on the Memorial to the Missing of the Somme of 1918 at Pozières. These were minor players in the drama of the Somme, along with the vast majority of the many thousands who took part in it, but I am pleased to single them out for honourable mention in this way.

MALCOLM BROWN
January 1996

MAPS

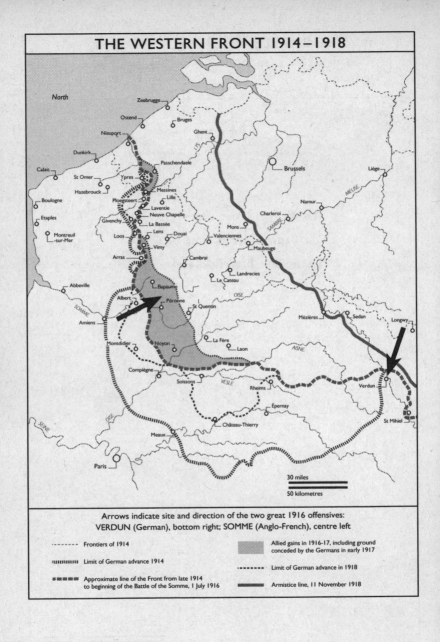

THE WESTERN FRONT 1914–1918

North

Zeebrugge
Ostend
Bruges
Nieuport
Ghent
Dunkirk
Passchendaele
Brussels
Liège
Calais
St Omer
Ypres
Hazebrouck
Messines
Lille
Namur
Boulogne
Ploegsteert
Laventie
Charleroi
Etaples
Givenchy
Neuve Chapelle
La Bassée
Mons
Montreuil-sur-Mer
Loos
Lens
Douai
Valenciennes
Vimy
Maubeuge
Arras
Cambrai
Abbeville
Bapaume
Landrecies
Albert
Péronne
Le Cateau
Amiens
St Quentin
Mézières
Sedan
Longwy
Montdidier
Noyon
La Fère
Laon
Compiègne
Verdun
Soissons
Rheims
St Mihiel
Épernay
Château-Thierry
Meaux
Paris

30 miles
50 kilometres

Arrows indicate site and direction of the two great 1916 offensives:
VERDUN (German), bottom right; SOMME (Anglo-French), centre left

- - - - - - -   Frontiers of 1914

▪▪▪▪▪▪▪▪   Limit of German advance 1914

✳✳✳✳✳✳   Approximate line of the Front from late 1914
to beginning of the Battle of the Somme, 1 July 1916

[shaded]   Allied gains in 1916–17, including ground
conceded by the Germans in early 1917

- - - - - -   Limit of German advance in 1918

▬▬▬▬▬▬   Armistice line, 11 November 1918

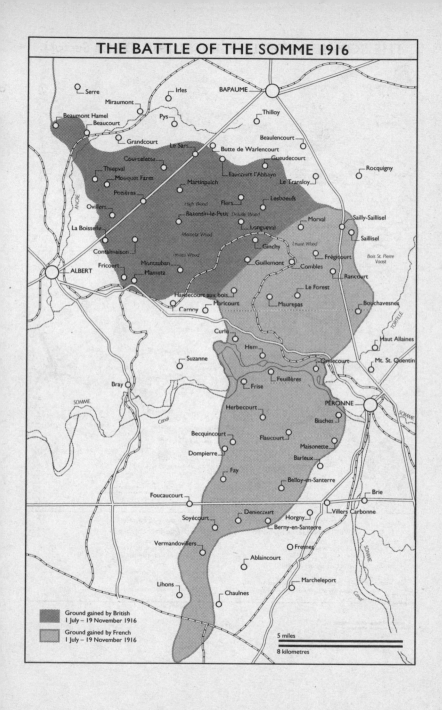

THE BATTLE OF THE SOMME 1916

Serre
Irles
BAPAUME
Miraumont
Thilloy
Beaumont Hamel
Pys
Beaucourt
Grandcourt
Beaulencourt
Le Sars
Butte de Warlencourt
Courcelette
Gueudecourt
Rocquigny
Thiepval
Eaucourt l'Abbaye
Mouquet Farm
Martinpuich
Le Transloy
Pozières
High Wood
Flers
Lesboeufs
Ovillers
Bazentin-le-Petit
Delville Wood
Morval
Sailly-Saillisel
La Boisselle
Longueval
Saillisel
Mametz Wood
Leuze Wood
Ginchy
Bois St. Pierre
Contalmaison
Trones Wood
Vaast
Montauban
Guillemont
Frégicourt
ALBERT
Fricourt
Combles
Mametz
Rancourt
Hardecourt aux bois
Le Forest
Bouchavesnes
Carnoy
Maricourt
Maurepas
Curlu
TORTILLE
Hem
Haut Allaines
Suzanne
Omiecourt
Mt. St. Quentin
Feuillères
Bray
Frise
SOMME
Herbecourt
PÉRONNE
Canal
SOMME
Biaches
Becquincourt
Flaucourt
Maisonette
Dompierre
Barleux
Fay
Belloy-en-Santerre
Foucaucourt
Brie
Deniécourt
Villers Carbonne
Soyécourt
Horgny
Berny-en-Santerre
SOMME
Vermandovillers
Fresnes
Ablaincourt
Lihons
Marcheleport
Chaulnes
Canal

Ground gained by British
1 July – 19 November 1916
Ground gained by French
1 July – 19 November 1916

5 miles

8 kilometres

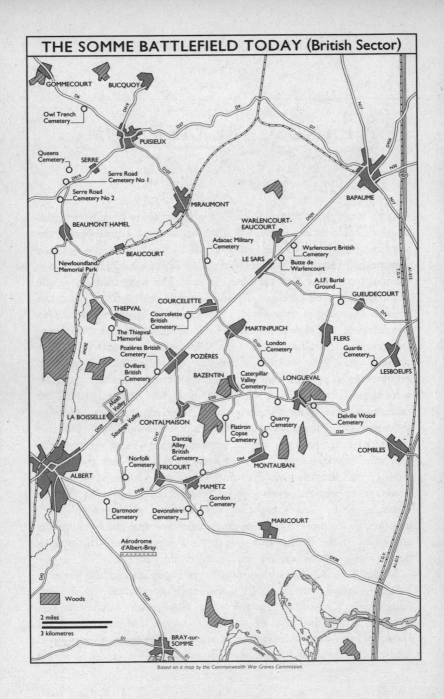

THE SOMME BATTLEFIELD TODAY (British Sector)

GOMMECOURT
BUCQUOY
Owl Trench Cemetery
PUISIEUX
Queens Cemetery
SERRE
Serre Road Cemetery No 1
Serre Road Cemetery No 2
MIRAUMONT
BAPAUME
BEAUMONT HAMEL
WARLENCOURT-EAUCOURT
Adaoac Military Cemetery
Warlencourt British Cemetery
BEAUCOURT
LE SARS
Butte de Warlencourt
Newfoundland Memorial Park
A.I.F. Burial Ground
GUEUDECOURT
COURCELETTE
THIEPVAL
Courcelette British Cemetery
MARTINPUICH
London Cemetery
FLERS
Guards Cemetery
The Thiepval Memorial
Pozières British Cemetery
POZIÈRES
BAZENTIN
LESBOEUFS
Ovillers British Cemetery
Caterpillar Valley Cemetery
LONGUEVAL
LA BOISSELLE
Mash Valley
Sausage Valley
CONTALMAISON
Flatiron Copse Cemetery
Quarry Cemetery
Delville Wood Cemetery
COMBLES
Dantzig Alley British Cemetery
Norfolk Cemetery
FRICOURT
MONTAUBAN
ALBERT
MAMETZ
Gordon Cemetery
Dartmoor Cemetery
Devonshire Cemetery
MARICOURT
Aérodrome d'Albert-Bray

Woods

2 miles

3 kilometres

BRAY-sur-SOMME

Based on a map by the Commonwealth War Graves Commission

CHAPTER ONE

A LANDSCAPE LIKE HOME

THERE WAS SOMETHING familiar and attractive about the landscape of the Somme. After the grim squalors of Flanders and the dispiriting drabness of the industrial sector of Lens and Loos, the Somme had an air to which the men in khaki could relate. It was French, but it was also curiously British. The long folds of gentle chalkland; the well-groomed woods like shadows on the skyline; the streams sparkling in the valleys; the meandering country roads. This was 'abroad', but it was not, somehow, alien. Of course there were differences: Christ-figures hanging from roadside crucifixes, gaunt churches in a style so strange that one officer called it Byzantine, monuments to wars of which the Tommies knew nothing. The fields were larger than in Britain, with a notable lack of hedgerows; and the farmsteads were quite distinctive, with their single-storey buildings arranged into a defensive square, within which stood that inevitable mound of steaming dung which could announce a farm's presence to the nose almost before it was evident to the eye. But this was a country that invited rather than repelled and in which there was much to appreciate, even enjoy. Wild flowers bloomed by the roadside; crops flourished; this was a place at ease with itself, comfortable, remote from the great highways and the busy towns and cities. If the British had to fight in a foreign field, this was as decent and companionable a one as they could wish for.

In April 1916, after three months at Houplines in the Franco-Belgian border country, G.F. Ellenberger, a subaltern of the 9th King's Own Yorkshire Light Infantry (fellow-officer of Captain Yeo already quoted, and also of the future writer and historian, Basil Liddell Hart), found himself clambering down from a lorry in a landscape so fresh and appealing that as soon as he could he wrote an almost lyrical essay describing his reactions. Titled simply 'Arrival on the Somme', it is the only document of its kind in his numerous papers; this is its keynote first paragraph:

> We fell in on the road and moved off: it was almost dawn and gradually through the damp mist we could make out what nature of country it was to which we had come. The poplar-lined pavés straight-stretching across the continuous plains of the North were a thing of the past; the road on which we were wound up and down following the valley on our left, on the other side of which the country rose again in delightful hills; in the bottom of the valley flowed the Somme; the land we were traversing recalled the downs of Hampshire, its chalky slopes undulating and covered with coarse grass, and here and there dotted with dark copses and small woods. It was a sumptuous new world in the morning mist, seeming almost as if it were home to which we had come from the flat mud of Flanders.

There would be many others who saw a similarity between the Somme country and the southern English shires. The Prime Minister's son, Raymond Asquith, who would die there, described the area to his wife on his first sight of it as 'a rolling down country, rather like the uplands of Hants or Wilts'. John Buchan, in a book about the 1916 battle published before the year was over, wrote of the Somme's modest tributary, the Ancre, that it 'is such a stream as may be found in Wiltshire, with good trout in its pools'. Even a South African, Private Willie Robins, in a letter to his family in June 1916, could state that in parts it 'is very much like England', (though he added that 'it can't touch Home for beauty' and saw hints of Africa in its areas of bush and low grassy hills). Lieutenant Charles Carrington, coming out of action in the first month of the fighting, declared of the village where his battalion was on rest that 'it might be Kent if it wasn't Picardy. Poppies, cornflowers, deep green lanes, wide rolling downs, all the same [as England] except that France has long and bluer distances and wider expanses of open country.' He added, wryly: 'It's fine country for fighting in, but finer for Peace and Quiet.'

Yet peace and quiet was not what they had come for and after the battle was over there would be other verdicts from the men who fought there, such as this from the diary of Private Archie Surfleet, for whom the very name of the Somme now 'conjured up a picture of miserable wastes, mud and devastation'. 'Surely', he wrote, 'no place could be more trying to patience, temper and comradeship.' And more than a landscape was changed in that encounter of 1916. The German, Ernst Jünger, would later write: 'Chivalry here took a final farewell. It had to yield to the heightened intensity of war, just as all fine and personal feeling has to yield when machinery gets the upper hand. The Europe of today appeared here for the first time on the field of battle ...' For the soldier-poet David Jones, the Somme provided a kind of seismic fault: 'From then onward things hardened into a more relentless, mechanical affair, took on a more sinister aspect ... The period of the individual rifleman, of the "old sweat" of the Boer campaign, the "Bairnsfather" war, seemed to terminate with the Somme battle. There were, of course, glimpses of it long after – all through in fact – but it seemed never quite the same.' Yet also something was made, if out of a fierce fire: their first effort there was disastrous for the British, yet as a recent historian, the former Sandhurst lecturer Paddy Griffith, has convincingly claimed, it represented for them 'a very significant "changing of gear" – however graunchingly the synchromesh may have been strained by the experience.' Writing in similarly positive terms in 1979, Colonel Victor Stewart, who had fought on the Somme in 1916 as a subaltern of the Royal Garrison Artillery, summed up his feelings by stating: 'I am only disappointed at the result of the Somme battle by the number of men killed. There was no loss of morale, only the wish to meet the enemy and we would show them.'

Given such interpretations the Somme can be seen as representing the start of a new maturity and of a remarkable progress. Neither for the British, nor, indeed, for the other participants, nor for the location where the fighting took place, would things ever be the same again. In short, the Somme did not end as it had begun.

It had 'begun', in fact, long before the British came there. The Germans had marched through the area in the first weeks of the war. In late August 1914, only days after engaging with the retreating British at Le Cateau, the IV Reserve Corps of General von Kluck's First Army had advanced rapidly from the east, over-running

Albert and Amiens before swinging south in the direction of Paris. There were some fierce local encounters which planted the earliest of what would eventually become a huge crop of military cemeteries across the whole region. But the stalwart resistance of the French on the Marne stopped the Germans in their tracks and they fell back, settling on a line which they would hold for most of the next two years. That line put them firmly athwart the Somme country.

They established their positions with great deliberateness and efficiency, because they were determined to stay in them; there was to be no further retreat. Since the decision was theirs as to where they should entrench, they had first choice of terrain, and they chose well, usually siting themselves so that their opponents were forced to accept less advantageous ground which they, the Germans, could overlook and dominate. The chalk soil enabled them to prepare strongly-constructed trench systems, of which elaborate, virtually indestructible dugouts formed an essential feature. As one German officer who fought there, Leutnant F.L. Cassel, later described them (in a memoir written first in German and then translated by the author into English): 'Nearly all dugouts were 18–20 steps deep, i.e. like two storeys of a house. They had an earth cover of *circa* 3 metres. Most were connected with each other or had two exits. We had,' he added, 'no presentiment', clearly implying that with such well executed defences the Germans felt that what they had they could hold. In effect, what had been created was a kind of vast linear fortress, almost a fortress-city, barely visible at ground level except for the barbed wire which guarded it, but up to forty feet in depth and – by virtue of a strong second system of defence linked by communication trenches to the first – up to 3,000 to 5,000 yards from front line to rear; a fortress designed to stand a prolonged siege, including the worst that modern artillery could throw at it, and only to be taken with extreme difficulty and at high cost. A third line lay several miles further back. Indeed, on a front of over 450 miles, from Flanders to the Swiss frontier, there was no better defensive ground than that provided by the country of the Somme.

What the Allied troops, across the other side of No Man's Land, could actually see was no mean barrier either. As the British

Commander-in-Chief, General Sir Douglas Haig, would graphically describe it in his despatch on the 1916 battle: 'The front of the trenches in each system was protected by barbed wire entanglements, many of them in two belts forty yards broad, built of iron stakes interlaced with barbed wire, often almost as thick as a man's finger.' They for their part found themselves in trench lines which were far less fortress-like, for they were meant to be temporary defences only. The Germans were occupying territory not their own, from which the Allies had every intention of ousting them. The French and British, therefore, had no deep dugouts; instead there was the usual trench system which, with variations according to the nature of the terrain, had been established everywhere else along the Western Front – strictly temporary defences to be left behind at the earliest opportunity, when the time was ripe to drive the invader back to whence he had come. There was, in fact, a deliberate policy not to make them seem permanent in case this sapped the offensive spirit of the troops who inhabited them.

The French faced the Germans at first, but on 18 July 1915 a new British army – the Third – was formed and by early August four divisions had taken over a seventeen-mile sector to the north of the River Somme. Now the British found themselves opposite a skein of fortified villages woven into the German defensive system, the names of which would become famous, though only after they had been destroyed. The point was well made at the time by a young volunteer infantry officer, Lieutenant E.F. Chapman, in a letter written in the second month of the Somme battle, on 8 August 1916: 'These little places have had rather a strange fate. When they existed, no one had ever heard of them. Now that they have ceased to exist, they are household names.'

Gommecourt, Serre, Beaumont Hamel, Thiepval, Ovillers, La Boisselle, Fricourt, Mametz, Montauban: they have all been rebuilt, largely, it must be said, in the same dour, unattractive style of the originals; certainly they seem little different from other villages of the area which were spared. One notable landmark has been replaced entirely: where at Thiepval a château stood on a high bluff overlooking the valley of the Ancre, there now rises the huge imperial arch designed by Sir Edwin Lutyens in memory of the missing of the

Somme. But that was far in the future as the British began to acquaint themselves with their new sector in the summer of 1915.

Curiously, only a minority among them ever saw the river which gave the area its name. If much of the Somme country had British resemblances, the same could not be said of the Somme itself, for this was in style a very un-British river; no strong flowing Thames or Severn or Tyne, rather a wayward wandering thing, wide in places but frequently diverting into substantial lakes – *étangs* – fine for boating or fishing, and usually surrounded by tangled woods of great beauty, with here and there a château peering over the treetops or making an elegant surprise appearance in a roadside clearing. Most British troops were on the rolling chalk-folds to the north, with the Somme's tributary, the Ancre, as their local, private river. The Ancre too had its lakes, if smaller ones, often overlooked by lines of lacy trees, and in peacetime, like the Somme itself, reflecting the forms of immobile, cigarette-smoking fishermen.

One other feature of the British sector of the Somme front requires special mention. The base-town of the British sector was Albert, barely a mile and a half from the front line. It had been a place of pilgrimage since the Middle Ages following the finding by a shepherd of a 'miraculous' statue of the Virgin Mary in a nearby field. The late nineteenth century had seen an attempt to enhance its appeal by the construction of a new church, the huge red-brick basilica of Notre Dame de Brebières, completed in 1897. Its massive tower had been capped with a gilded statue of the Virgin and Child, the former holding the latter high above her head by way of offering her infant Son to God the Father. The plan to turn Albert into a kind of Lourdes of the north, had been less than successful – given the well-known attractions of southern France, this otherwise undistinguished Somme township was scarcely a natural draw for visitors – but it had given the place this notable legacy. Dramatic enough in its original conception, the war made it even more so. There was a widespread soldiers' belief that shell fire spared crucifixes – not always justified in fact – but certainly it did not spare the 'Golden Virgin' of Albert; or then again perhaps it did. On 15 January 1915 a German shell dislodged the statue, so that instead of standing tall and triumphant as its creators intended, it now hung weirdly over the square below in the attitude of a frozen fall, as though miraculously held in the act of plunging to the ground. The result was a bizarre, almost macabre sight which inevitably caught the eye of the countless soldiers marching through the town.

For the majority of Britons, one might have thought, nothing could be more alien and strange, but in the event the Tommies virtually naturalized it, adopted it, made it their own. The 'Golden (or 'Leaning' or 'Hanging') Virgin' became a symbol, almost a mascot, of the Somme, rather as the ruined Cloth Hall became a symbol of that other famous sector, the Ypres Salient. Having 'acquired' it, they wove a superstition around it, that when the statue fell, as sooner or later it inevitably would, the war would come to an end.

Such ideas enshrined the pipe-dream of many, if not most, of the soldiers who went to or from the front under the shadow of Albert's unique landmark, or indeed by any of the other routes that took them into or out of the trench lines. They knew what they were there for, but even at this early stage the general, earthy view was that they would have no objection if circumstances allowed them to finish their business, pack up and return to their normal lives; in other words, if the Leaning Virgin fell, they would not have too many objections. Private Sidney Appleyard of the Queen Victoria's Rifles, one of the first British units to come to the Somme, encapsulated this attitude in an account of his journey there from the battalion's previous posting near Ypres, in a letter forwarded to his family by a fellow soldier going home on leave. 'We all have one great ambition,' he wrote, 'to see Germany smashed, and then have the time of our lives upon our return home.'

The Golden Virgin was visible from miles around, as its replacement is today. To the north-east from the basilica's tower could be seen a main road heading with Roman straightness from the edge of Albert towards – a dozen miles off – the German-occupied town of Bapaume. This road would become the central axis of the British effort on the Somme. It crossed the two front lines at the village of La Boisselle and then continued through or not far from another series of villages which, like those already named, would become part of the fabric of the campaign to come: Pozières, Contalmaison,

Bazentin, Longueval, Guillemont, Ginchy, Martinpuich, Flers, Les-boeufs, Courcelette, Le Sars. In doing so it passed over the open plateau on which the later stages of the Somme battle was fought. Beyond Le Sars lay another landmark which would become part of the story and which would draw English comparisons, the Butte de Warlencourt: an antique burial mound which Charles Carrington would describe as looking like a smaller version of Wiltshire's Silbury Hill.

But such places were not yet part of the agenda as from mid-1915 the area behind the Allied lines resounded to the beat of marching boots as the British battalions came slogging down the roads from the railheads, sometimes fortifying their courage with a song, some-times too weary to do anything other than fix their eyes grimly on the boots of the man just ahead. This theme would have many variations over the next months, especially after the decision was made at a conference in Chantilly in December 1915 that the major Allied initiative on the Western Front in the following year would be a joint Anglo-French attack on the axis of the Somme river. If for the British 1914 had been the year of Mons, the Aisne and First Ypres, and 1915 had been the year of Neuve Chapelle, Festubert, Second Ypres and Loos, 1916 would be the year of the 'big push' on the Somme.

CHAPTER TWO

BUILD-UP TO 'THE PUSH'

AT THIS STAGE of the war the Somme was a quiet sector; as in the case of a number of other areas held by the French a 'live and let live' philosophy had prevailed there since the armies had entrenched in late 1914. Whatever view thrusting military theorists might take of unofficial understandings between enemies, they were not unreasonable in view of the sheer length of that part of the Western Front for which the French were responsible; it was simply neither possible nor desirable to maintain a high offensive spirit along the whole of a trench zone more than 300 miles in extent.

The period between the advent of the British and the opening of the 1916 offensive did not greatly change the Somme's peaceful reputation. The 48th (South Midland) Division which arrived there in August 1915 and saw little serious fighting for many months, won the soubriquet of the 'Goalkeepers', on the grounds that they hadn't been in a battle, they had just held the line. However, certainly for those in the forward trenches, life was far from uneventful. Even in relatively 'cushy' sectors the British were in favour of making their presence felt with aggressive action, which inevitably produced a response in kind from the other side of No Man's Land. There were thus frequent flurries of hostility, with a trickle of fatalities which, in the case of troops still new to the mores and rigours of trench life, could deliver severe blows to morale. It would take time to become inured to the concept of the death of comrades as a regular adjunct of service on the Western Front.

It should be added that though this philosophy of constant harassment of the enemy was very much part of the prevailing ideology, it was not meant to be applied in every situation and without regard to cost. In March 1916, at a time when such 'minor operations' (so-called) represented virtually the only available means of discomfiting the Germans, Haig put his name to a statement encouraging discrimination and forbearance in their implementation. 'The possession of a few acres of ground of no importance,' he wrote, 'for tactical or other reasons can have no influence on the course of the war, which must be decided by the defeat of the enemy's forces.' He was even prepared to accept the abandonment of a portion of the line deemed to be of little value if this could be combined with inflicting maximum casualties on the enemy at minimum cost to the British. Nevertheless, many small initiatives of dubious worth went ahead, often because it seemed to the commanders or Staffs which devised them that it was safer and wiser to err on the opposite side from caution. It has been estimated that the combined total of casualties produced in small-scale hostilities between 19 December 1915 and 30 June 1916 was 5,845 officers and 119,296 other ranks. The Germans were, it should be stressed, also substantial contributors to the mix, in that they mounted numerous such initiatives on their own account. 'Economical strategy, after all,' as John Terraine has written in discussing this subject, 'does require the enemy's concurrence.'

Private Sidney Appleyard (already quoted in the previous chapter), of the Queen Victoria's Rifles, at this stage part of 5th Division, kept a detailed diary which offers a revealing snapshot of the Somme experience in this early phase. His battalion moved between billets at Bray-sur-Somme and trenches at Carnoy, to the south of the British sector. These are extracts from his entries for the first half of September:

9th September. We took over the fire trench from B. Company – at this point we had to supply a listening post about 40 yards in front of our lines. It is a very nerve-racking job as we could hear the Germans digging and talking.
11th September. Captain Holmes of B. Company was hit and we have just heard that he has died. He was a fine officer, but a bit of a dare-devil. Stand-to, digging and listening post all night. During our second shift on listening post a sniper hit the earth in front of the post and one shot went so close to Wilding that I thought it had gone through him.

12th September. There is heavy bombardment on our right and left. About 9 p.m. a big explosion occurred on our left and large sheets of flame leapt into the air – I think we blew up one of the German saps. There was rapid fire all along the line after this.

13th September. A QUIET DAY

14th September. I have a very sad occurrence to relate. A sniper kept on hitting the front of our dugout and I held up my hat to try him – to prove what a good shot he was he put a bullet through it. Sergeant Coulter, aggravated by the disturbance, went to our second line to snipe back, but from this expedition he did not return for he was shot through the head and died instantly. This has upset us tremendously as we looked up to him and admired his coolness and pluck. He came out with the Battalion last November, and from the way he acted we thought his life must be charmed. Everybody was very quiet this evening and there was no singing or joking.

That same evening, 14 September, some new arrivals from 'Blighty' who had just joined the 11th Battalion of the Welsh Regiment, 22nd Division, moved into trenches for a period of instruction at Maricourt – at the extreme southern point of the British sector, with the French to their immediate right. 'There was very little doing except for sniping,' wrote Private W. A. Rogers in his diary, commenting with a hint of bravado on the spatter of bullets which came 'whizzing across the road' as they waited to enter the communication trench leading to the front line that 'no one seemed to mind'. Next morning, however, after standing-to at 5 a.m., he found himself being instructed as to the severe risks from sniping and the necessity of taking appropriate precautionary action. 'It was not safe to look over the parapet,' he noted, 'so we used a periscope. The sergeant of the Devons who were occupying the trenches told me that they had three periscopes smashed by a sniper in one day.'

Their first experience of real action came a week later, though Rogers and his comrades were little more than enthralled spectators:

Tuesday 21st September. Things were quiet during the day and I went on duty in an advanced post 40 yards from the trenches of the enemy. I was on from 6 p.m. to midnight. The South Wales Borderers were on our left and at 10.30 the Germans blew up a

mine and attempted to rush their trenches. They were received
with a fusillade of rifle and machine–gun fire. Our artillery
commenced to send shells over our heads into the German
trenches. As a rule the trenches are not shelled when so close
together but this was an exception. The enemy replied with their
huge guns and trench mortars and a heavy bombardment took
place which lasted fully 35 minutes. Our artillery fire was truly
magnificent. Some shrapnel, bursting just over our heads, sent its
bullets forward and did a tremendous amount of damage, while the
shells of the French 75 mil. guns shattered the trenches until the
ground represented a honeycomb. The ground was shaking with
the concussion of the shells, and all our boys were quivering with
excitement. It was our first real baptism of shell fire, but not one
man flinched from his duty and had the word charge been merely
whispered I think every man would have done so without a second
thought.

I think our artillery can honestly claim a victory for this night's
work, as the Germans ceased fire before we did, and soon
everything was quiet save for the occasional burst of a machine-
gun or some sniper having a shot at some usually imaginary object.
The remainder of my turn on duty soon ended and I went into the
fire trench to get some sleep.

Sleep was not an option, however, for any members of the
battalion on the following night:

Wednesday 22nd September. I had an easy day and at 6 p.m. went
into another post 40 yards from the enemy, but with my own
platoon. Our engineers were sapping towards the enemy trenches
and they were doing ditto. I was on duty at 10.15 p.m. when one
of the engineers looking frightfully scared came running up from
the sap, and said the Germans were under us and would probably
blow up their mine during the night. This was anything but
cheerful news but there was nothing to be done, as the advance
post had to be held until the last minute. We all had to stand to
and stood, expecting to be blown up at any minute. Our nerves
were on edge, and we started at the slightest sound. The night was
deathly quiet, as though all were waiting and no-one knew what to
expect. If only the artillery had fired or something had happened,
it would have brought us back to earth. As it was we could do

nothing but think, and of course as is usual under such circs. our thoughts turned to home. This of course did not improve matters and as hour after hour stole by we began to think they would not explode the mine that night. At last, after what seemed to us years, dawn began to break across the sky and we breathed a sigh of relief as we thought of what we had gone through during the night.

It seemed, the engineer told us afterwards, that the Germans had struck water and he had mistaken the beating of the pumps for the sound of men beating down the earth with shovels around the charge. This is called tamping and the explosion loses half the effect unless well tamped. Of course we were all relieved at the news but that did not recompense us for the night we had just gone through. *Thursday 23rd September.* We all had a rest, most of us needed it too as we felt run down after such a night.

Rogers' battalion was not to remain long on the Somme; in mid-October his division was withdrawn and despatched by train and boat to the new theatre opening in the other end of Europe at Salonika (where the principal enemy, following their joining the war in September 1915 on the side of Germany and Austria-Hungary, would be the Bulgarians). The two nights described provided the most memorable experiences of their brief stay, though Rogers himself nearly became a victim in early October when attempting to make the post he was occupying in front of the trenches more secure with a few extra sandbags. 'The snipers were soon busy,' he wrote, 'and a sniper put three shots into a sandbag while I was placing it on the parapet.' He survived intact, however, as he also did the following day when a shell struck the parapet quite close to his post. He noted: 'I kept a piece of the shell as a souvenir.'

One highly visible consequence of even the relatively low level of warfare pertaining at this time was already apparent: the serious damage to property; the Albert basilica was not the only notable edifice to receive the early attention of the German guns. Private Robert Cude, a battalion runner of the 7th East Kent Regiment, 18th (Eastern) Division, was much moved by the devastation inflicted on the small château at Bécourt, a hamlet some three kilometres south of Albert. Built in a gentle wooded valley which was dead ground to the German trench lines, it had nevertheless been found by their artillery and reduced to a ruin. In late September Cude noted:

> Sleep in the family vault of the Comte de Valmont, in company with three other Runners, and 7 closed Coffins. Slept well for all that however. This Château has been a beautiful place and situated in very nice surroundings, in the heart of a wood, from which it derives its name. Remains of several houses around. It is a sorry spectacle but I am getting used to it. Such a sight does not impress us now, as it would have done 2 months ago, nevertheless a lump forms in our throats when we consider what the place was like, and what it is like now.

Another phenomenon to reveal itself in these first months was – Somme mud. This would become legendary in 1916 but even in 1915 it inflicted its miseries and exacted its toll. This is Cude's summing up of several days in November after working on the construction of trenches in the vicinity of La Boisselle – an entry which also reflects the long-standing gripe of the infantryman, that being officially out of the line did not mean the longed-for rest away from the danger zone; instead it often entailed back-breaking work right in it:

> Relieved by W. Kents on Nov. 16th and plod back to Dernancourt. Might mention that owing to the abnormal rains the trench and cubby holes are caving in. We have 2 or 3 killed by suffocation. Next 6 days we get 'fed up' right to the neck. Nothing but fatigues to and from Line. Working on building dugouts which cave in before they are finished. As fast as you can dig a hole it fills with water. This is carried almost to excess, for day and night it carries on, and as a relief instead of rest, they have to sweep the roads which is a mass of mud. On either side of roads about here, there are ditches, and these are soon overflowing with mud and filth. God help any unfortunate chap who loses the road at night. Still, we are learning a trade all right that is one thing.

Mud and bad conditions did not deter either side from mounting patrols or raids. On 21 November a German patrol was captured by troops of the Queen Victoria's Rifles; it had approached a listening post in front of the British trenches, had been spotted and met with a hail of fire. Lance-Corporal Appleyard (he had just been promoted) described what followed, in an unsparing account written for his brother which was not submitted to the censor but, as in the case of an earlier account already quoted, delivered by a friend going home on leave. The account also reveals, as in the case of Private Rogers, the soldierly proclivity shared by all sides and all or most ranks in the war – the desire in whatever circumstances to acquire souvenirs:

Corporal Stone with Borrow [a soldier who spoke good German] went out to the Listening Post to find the German patrol, three in number, severely wounded. Borrow spoke to them in their own language and at the same time disarmed them, while the remainder of us carried in the wounded men, which was a difficult bit of work. The German I carried in was still alive and in great agony, and I assisted the stretcher-bearers to bind him up. He had two bad wounds, one in the side and another in the chest, and a large quantity of blood was soaked up in his clothing. After binding him up, we managed to carry him into a dugout, and made him as comfortable as possible.

Although our deadly enemies, one could hardly help sympathising with this chap, for the weather was intensely cold and he must have been chilled to the bone, for his wounds prevented him from moving a muscle. He kept on groaning, and from what I gather from Borrow, he said '*Jesus, Jesus, ich kann es nicht mehr aushalten*', meaning 'Jesus, Jesus, this is more than I can stand!' The other two men were in a more pitiful condition than the first – one received four wounds and when he landed in the trench his insides fell out, and the other was shot through the mouth and died almost immediately.

I then strolled off along the communication trench to find all sorts and conditions of men, all very excited and asking one another what souvenirs they had obtained. I then realised that I had forgotten to get a keepsake for myself, so I went back to the dying German, and got Borrow to ask him for his hat, which he decided to give me on condition that I obtained something warm for his head. This I did, and he passed over his cap which of course I considered my property, but much to my disgust the Officers collected all the souvenirs, as they were Government property. This man died about 6 a.m. after Borrow had obtained a fair amount of information from him.

Appleyard clearly felt his brother was owed some further explanation for what might seem a somewhat callous attitude, for he continued: 'This patrol was obviously after blood, for they carried bombs, and when they found they had been located they fixed swords. All this will no doubt surprise you, for you must have thought it a frequent occurrence for us to see and capture Germans, but you can take it from me that Mr. Fritz is very careful and never shows himself until night time and the only opportunity of seeing him one has is in a charge, and up to the present I have not had the pleasure, and am not anxious to get mixed up in one.'

If not in a charge, there was always the opportunity of confronting the enemy in a raid. Appleyard was involved in one a few weeks later, mounted in spite of what those involved thought to be most unsuitable conditions: '15–16 December: Although the weather is so bad I volunteered for a bombing patrol – in my opinion it is ridiculous to carry out raids at this time for we have quite enough hardships in the line without looking for trouble from Fritz. While on this patrol the Battalion on our right sent out a large party without giving us a warning and the German artillery opened fire, and there was also rapid fire from their own trenches which made things very unpleasant indeed.'

Some days later a larger-scale effort was mounted, the intention being to attack an enemy strong-point heavily fortified with machine-guns. The raiding party consisted of a Lieutenant Eccles, in command, four sergeants and seven riflemen, of whom Appleyard was one. The object was to crawl through the two lines of enemy wire guarding the strong point and bomb along the parapet. Unfortunately the front was bathed in the glow of a brilliant moon. This is Appleyard's less than enchanted account of what followed:

19–20th December. We started out at 5 a.m. and it was so light that I mentioned the danger to Lieut. Eccles, but he said we must go. We reached the enemy wire and the first party crawled through, but Mr Eccles got caught up and stepped over the wire. This roused the sentry who started shouting at the top of his voice and opened fire. I threw a bomb at him and immediately it exploded they opened fire on us. My word, I thought my last day had come when I heard the bullets striking the wire over my head. As soon as the firing stopped I threw another bomb in the direction of the machine-gun and heard no more out of it until we got away from the wire, and we think my bomb must have killed the team. By this time the Huns were really roused and bombs were falling all around us. My blood was up and I threw all the bombs I had and some of Corporal Eames's, when Lieut. Eccles told us to cut for it. He said Marriott and Bland were killed and Thorpe wounded. Eames got Thorpe through the wire and between us we got him back. It was a disastrous night's work, for our casualties were 2 killed and 5 wounded. I had a small piece of bomb in my hand.

When he transcribed his diary fifty years later, Sidney Appleyard commented that everybody had been deeply concerned at the prospect of undertaking so ambitious an action on a clear moonlit night: 'Lieut. Eccles was a brave and ambitious officer, but we all felt he should have postponed the raid.' He also recalled Private Marriott saying before they left, 'Some of us will have two blankets when we return to Bray'. He added: 'Poor chap, he never thought the extra blanket would be his.'

Eccles was awarded the Military Cross; Corporal Eames was given the Distinguished Conduct Medal. Appleyard's diary records that next day, back in their billets at Bray, he and some of his comrades went to an entertainment put on by the 5th Division concert party, 'The Whizz Bangs' – all part of the process of initiation into the strange diversities of a soldier's life on the Somme, 1915.

* * *

With 1916 the pace of war began to quicken as many new divisions, a substantial number of them straight from Britain, came to the area of the Somme. Now was the time for members of the Kitchener 'New Army' battalions to face the implications of the commitment they had made when they flocked to the colours in the euphoric atmosphere of the summer of 1914.

There could be no greater contrast than the attitudes expressed in the writings of two officers of 22nd Battalion, The Manchester Regiment, 7th Division, a New Army unit known to its members as the 7th Manchester Pals: Captain Alfred 'Bill' Bland and Captain

Charles 'Charlie' May. Both married men with children, Bland with two sons, May with a new born baby girl, they did not hide themselves from the prospect ahead but approached it from radically different viewpoints.

Bill Bland, at thirty-four, was the older of the two, and had had time enough to start an academic career. After an education at Christ's Hospital and Queen's College, Oxford, he had co-authored a text-book on political economy with R.H. Tawney, and a third author, P.A. Brown, which had been published in 1914. Now both he and Tawney were in uniform in the same battalion, the latter remaining in the ranks while Bland swiftly rose to the status of company commander. The war turned him overnight, it would seem, from scholarly reseacher into archetypal cheerful soldier, exultant and elated at the thought of adventure and the prospect of fighting for King and Country. On the day he landed in France in November 1915 he had written to his wife, Violet (also known as Lettie): 'Dear, I am extraordinarily happy, simply bursting with riotous spirits. The one thing lacking is shell fire. I shall not achieve the real thrill till I get within sound of the guns and the phut-phut of the rifle and the glorious ping of the bullet that whirrs past like a singing whipcord. This is not blather. I mean it. This is not a summer holiday, but it's a gloriously exciting picnic.' A fortnight later, under twenty-four hours from his first taste of the front line, his mood was virtually that of an excited child: 'What does it feel like? Picture yourself at a seaside resort, arriving at night, and hearing the sea but not seeing it. That's how I feel tonight. Calm, happy, merry even, *very* merry, with a rich sense of a new experience to follow immediately.'

On 18 February 1916, having had actual experience of trench life, if admittedly at a relatively unstressful period, he wrote in even more exuberant terms:

Darling, I can't bear you to be unhappy about me. Don't be grey and old, my darling. Think of the *cause*, the cause. It is England, England, England, always and all the time. The individual counts as nothing, the common cause everything. Have faith, my dear. If only you will have faith in the ultimate victory of the good, the true and the beautiful, you will not be unhappy even if I never return to you. Dear, if one's number is up, one will go under. I am

here, and I shall either survive or not survive. In the meantime, I
have never been truly happier.

He added in a brief postscript, clearly wishing to disabuse his wife
of any preconceptions about the alleged ardours of Western Front
life: 'Hardship be damned! It's all one long blaze of glory.' Bland
was clearly a soldier for whom Horace's dictum 'Dulce et decorum
est pro patria mori' – 'it is sweet and fitting to die for one's country'
– was not, as Wilfred Owen would later call it, the 'old lie'.

By contrast, Charlie May, aged twenty-seven, by profession an
engineer, a former Yeomanry territorial, and now like Bland a
company commander, saw the prospect of battle in a far less
glamorous light. Writing on 29 January in the diary which he kept
throughout his time in France, and which he cast in the form of one
long, continuous monologue to his wife, Bessie, he commented, drily:

> One is supposed to have, as a soldier going into action, no other
> desire than some high-souled ambition to do or die for his country.
> Reality I am afraid falls far short. We go because it is right and
> proper that we should. But I do not think there is one high souled
> one amongst us. On the contrary we are all rather bored with the
> job, the thought of the bally mud and water is quite sufficient to
> extinguish keenness, and we are all so painfully ordinary that we
> think of leave more than we do of the nobleness of our present
> calling. When one is tired and unwashed I think one is legitimately
> entitled to refuse to feel noble, if one so desires.

It would seem from this that Bland, than whom no one, to judge
by his letters, could be more 'high-souled', clearly cannot have
paraded his ardent views. Though as captains in different companies
he and May would not have been in continuous contact, May would
surely have been aware if Bland had spoken as he wrote. But then it
would not have been within the accepted code to utter aloud the
high-flown sentiments which Bland confided to his wife, any more
than it would have been acceptable for May to admit the mood of
unmartial disillusion he described in his diary, also for his wife's eyes
only. Both men would continue privately to discuss and mould their
attitudes to the ordeal to come over the following weeks and months
as the prospect of battle grew closer.

One other young officer who thought deeply about the prospects ahead, and whose attitude came between the extremes expressed by Bland and May, was Second Lieutenant W.P. 'Billy' Lipscomb, a subaltern of the 1st Dorset Regiment, 32nd Division – like Captain Bland, a 'Hostilities Only' officer who had enlisted under the pressures of the mood of 1914. His confidante was not a wife but a young actress, Vera, whom he longed to marry, but whose free spirit made her elusive, unconvinced, hard to persuade; in the end he achieved his ambition, but there was much uncertainty at this time. There is therefore a bracing vigour about Lipscomb's letters to her; she was no easy touch, and – though we have only his letters from which to judge, hers not having survived – clearly not susceptible to any facile patriotism. No doubt, however, he must have assumed that even her sceptical mind would have been diverted when he recorded what for him was a side-splitting moment during his battalion's slow railway journey to the front in January 1916: 'Oh, one more choice remark! Coming along all night the station names are very illegible. "I can't see the name of the place," said one of the men, "oh there it is . . . 'Dames!' " – shrieks of joy.'

Before that Lipscomb had already gauged the mood of the crowd with whom he found himself in France and gone along with it; he wrote this on 16 January: 'Everybody is quite happy, nobody wants to be a hero and everybody wants to keep alive as long as they can which seems a healthy outlook.'

In a further letter of 22 January he noted a conspicuous lack of a desire for glory among those he had met who had already undergone trench experience: 'All the subs and people in the line are praying for the soft squidgy wound in the shoulder (or elsewhere) to take them to Blightie [sic] – Blightie is all they talk about.'

The widespread desire for a Blighty wound – conventionally spelt this time – surfaced again in a letter some weeks later in March 1916, after having obtained a closer view of the realities of trench life: 'A Sergeant who had been out 12 months got a stray bullet in his wrist this morning and he's as pleased as punch over it – hopes it will turn out a blighty case!' He then went on to show a sympathy with the other ranks, in this case the bottom-of-the-rung private soldier, not always to be found among the more privileged officer class: 'Don't wonder they long for home, weeks in the trenches and then when you get out say at 10 pm they are on fatigue work at 7 am next morning. They really do have a hard time – 1/- a day for it all and pay for everything they lose of their kit. No wonder they make remarks about Navvy battalions and A.S.C. [Army Service Corps], 30/- and £2–2–0 a week and no danger at all, and not overworked.'

Yet Lipscomb could spring to the defence of the cause when, as seems to have happened in April 1916, Vera commented scathingly on the validity of the reasons which kept her lover and so many others in a situation of risk and danger in France. He had sent her a clutch of – in his view – aptly named flowers gathered in the vicinity of the trenches and they had not been well received. He answered her criticism in some heat:

> Certainly there is a contrast between wild forget-me-nots growing under the feet of wild men doing wilder things, but that doesn't mean as you suggest that it is all senseless dear. If you look round you will see I believe that this war has accomplished more than years of preaching and theory of right living would do. In place of individual and rather selfish existence we have cohesion and a very primitive bond that was very lacking before. I mean the desire and the need for co-operation and self-protection. And for your own sex it has done more than many years of Mrs Pankhurst would have done. Which just shows the old old story that an ounce of practice will outweigh and prove anything to such a fathead as a nation usually is, sooner than tons of talk.

'Practice' of a particularly challenging kind was by now not far off, and the battalions training on the Somme front were well aware that they were very likely to be involved in it.

* * *

The fact that a famous battle was fought on the Somme is so much part of the accepted culture that it almost seems a matter of inevitability that it should have taken place there. It is as though it was an arena prepared, a stage assigned by destiny for one of the greatest of twentieth-century encounters. 'Cushy' one year, a crucible of horrific sacrificial fighting the next: it all seems part of the preordained game-plan of the First World War. Yet if one contemplates the military and strategic potential of this part of Picardy, one rapidly comes to the conclusion that it was virtually non-existent. Where was the industry, where were the railheads, where were the lines of communication? It was as though a battle was fought on a vast prairie, with more prairie stretching in every direction beyond. There has been much criticism of the British concentration on the Ypres area, which, after all, produced the Somme of 1917, that other famous symbol of Great War frightfulness, Passchendaele. But at least in Flanders there were strategic targets: major cities, railheads, and – not far off – submarine pens from which U-boats sailed to contribute to the highly successful campaign against Allied shipping. By contrast, the Somme was virtually a fight for fighting's sake alone.

The reason for the battle taking place there was, in fact, political, and the motives behind it were, largely. national. The French were already committed to mortal combat with the Germans, and they wanted to make sure the British got into similar grips with the enemy as soon as possible. The best way to ensure this was to mount an offensive side by side. The Somme was where the two Allies joined. QED: the offensive should take place on the Somme. This is perhaps as good an introduction as any to the following account of the political and military chess-match which preceded the launching of the Battle of the Somme.

* * *

Over the winter of 1915–16 there were numerous developments in the forward thinking about the possibilities of further military action on the Western Front. At Chantilly on 29 December 1915 the principal item on the agenda had been the proposal by the French commander-in-chief, General Joffre, that a massive combined Franco-British offensive, on a front of sixty miles, should be launched in the Somme region. This was put to the newly appointed British commander-in-chief, General Sir Douglas Haig, who had taken over from Field Marshal Sir John French on 19 December. However, before Haig could make a formal reply to this gargantuan scheme, on 20 January Joffre, who had been warned by his government against incurring further huge losses, came to British GHQ with a somewhat less ambitious proposal in terms of commitment, though also much less attractive in its actual concept. He proposed to have five smaller French offensives planned by the end of April, to be preceded about 20 April by an attack by the British on at least 20,000 yards of the Somme front. This would be a subsidiary attack to those to be mounted by the French, the idea of it being to wear out the enemy and draw and exhaust his reserves; in French vocabulary this would be a *bataille d'usure* – an attritional battle, which was not intended to produce an advance by the British, rather intended to facilitate a significant forward move by the French. Joffre also proposed a further *bataille d'usure* to be mounted elsewhere by the British in May. Haig demurred, claiming that such attacks, designed to produce no positive result, would be bad for the morale both of his troops and of his public at home, and would also be regarded – if there were no appreciable changes in the maps over which the experts of all nations regularly pored – by neutral countries as Allied defeats. He suggested that a succession of raids might achieve a similar effect without running the risk of bad publicity.

Basically Haig was not persuaded that an advance on the Somme was the best option anyway; he believed there would be more profit in an offensive in Flanders, where (as already argued), there were practical gains to be made, whereas the open downland of Picardy was merely ground to be won: a territorial scalp, as it were, but not one with strategic significance. If, however, this was the ordained area for the next confrontation with the enemy – as junior partner in the land war, Britain had ultimately to go along with French decisions – then Haig favoured the idea of a simultaneous attack as originally conceived. By 14 February after further discussion and correspondence the Franco-British offensive astride the Somme was back on the table, with a date in the vicinity of the end of June or beginning of July as a likely time for its launch.

In recording this phase of the war the British Official Historian would state unequivocally that 'the decision of the French Commander -in-Chief to make the main offensive of 1916 astride the Somme seems to have been arrived at solely because the British would be bound to take part in it.' He would continue, with unusual vehemence:

The reasons advanced by General Joffre will hardly bear examination. It was certainly true that the sector had for long months,
about twenty, been a quiet one; but that it was so had merely given
the Germans time to elaborate their defences. The phrase that 'the
ground is in many places favourable to the development of a
powerful offensive' would have applied equally well to almost any
part of the front, although it might be argued that the good ground
observation rendered possible by the open rolling country of
Picardy was a distinct asset when compared with the more
restricted vistas of French Flanders. But against this possible
advantage had to be set the fact that, owing to the number of
villages and to the facility with which deep dugouts could be
excavated in the chalk, the sector was particularly strong for
defence, in fact might be considered the strongest. The French
plans for the offensives of 1916 had had a definite strategic basis
... The Somme offensive had no strategic object except attrition
... Even a complete breakthrough, unless carried very far, would
not have led to an interruption of the main German
communications ...

A further factor was to make itself felt before February was out.
On the 21st the Germans attacked the fortress city of Verdun in
eastern France. A massive attritional battle began which would grind
on through most of 1916, drawing ever more French troops into its
maw, and radically affecting the Franco-British plans for the Somme.
The battle to come would still be an Allied affair, but the British
would have to play the principal hand.

To fulfil their assigned task, the British now had available a
recently established army, the Fourth, which had come into existence
in January. The process of making a new army was less formidable
than it might sound. It required the creation of an administrative unit
of approximately a hundred headquarters staff, to which corps and
divisions were assigned according to the requirements and exigencies
of the campaign. Command of the new army was given to Lieutenant-General Sir Henry Rawlinson, whose career had been held back
by his unhappy relations with Haig's predecessor as commander-in-
chief, Field Marshal Sir John French. Rawlinson now joined four
other army commanders – Monro, Plumer, Allenby and Gough –

who between them commanded a total of twelve corps consisting of thirty-eight infantry and five cavalry divisions, though it should be added that Gough's Reserve Army was only in process of formation at this time. Rawlinson would have at his disposal an army of approximately half a million men made of five corps and sixteen divisions. This would be the prime British weapon on the Somme, though Allenby's Third Army would also play an important role in the opening phase of the offensive, as would Gough's Reserve Army (ultimately to be renamed the Fifth) in its later phase.

* * *

Meanwhile more and more British troops were arriving on the Western Front; indeed, by the time the Somme battle opened, the British Expeditionary Force – the BEF – would have expanded to a force of one and a half million men. Many new units fresh from Britain entrained for the Somme front, while others were moved there from the hard-fought sectors further north. Second Lieutenant Frank Wollocombe came with the 9th Devons of 7th Division in February. On the 7th he wrote cheerfully to his father: 'Sorry not to have written before, but we have been shifting. We came here on Saturday. It is a very blissful part after our old haunts, especially in the matter of mud. We are having beautiful weather on the whole: an early spring, so the Boches will be able to do their push soon if they like!'

Next day he was eagerly spying out the land with an officer colleague; he noted in his diary: 'I explored in the trenches with Adams all the morning and found fine views of the Boche trenches for miles: rather different to the old flat country in the north. Fricourt, through which their line runs, is a pretty village which looks practically undamaged.'

He was soon recording more warlike events, however, if only on a relatively small scale:

February 13th. One of the Borders was killed outside our billet last night. Our Divisional Artillery have been getting to work in their old style this afternoon: this part has certainly warmed up in the last week. At about 5.30 the Boche began shelling Bécordel.

Sergeant Atkins was hit by a H.E. I saw and ran over, but he was already dead. It had gone into his forehead and was sticking out at the back of his head. He is a very great loss.

The trench world was a notorious breeding-ground for rumours – that there had been a great sea-battle off Southampton, that the Kaiser had been shot dead by the Crown Prince – while sightings of spies were so frequent that just occasionally some of them had to be genuine. Thus Wollocombe in a further entry under 13 February:

Lewis and Sandoe were up here for working party. After dinner I went out and took over and sent them to have some dinner. Just before they came back (I was right down on the left) an Officer came up and spoke to the men. He then went on to the right. They called out that there were no more men up that way. He took no notice so they began to wonder, not recognising him as one of their Officers, and called out 'Who are you?' He took no notice and darted off through a gap. Search went on for hours but he could not be found. He was caught a few days later by the Gordons. There are several spies about here – one pair dressed as a Border Lance Corporal and man. I had a chase the other night after an Officer whom a man of mine suspected, but I couldn't find him.

Sergeant Robert McKay of the 109th Field Ambulance arrived with the 36th (Ulster) Division in March. His first taste of the Somme country was far from benign, since his party of sixty or so officers and men set off on the last lap of their journey in blizzard conditions. A man of considerable education who would later become a university professor, McKay described events in an eloquent diary which would be his vade-mecum until the end of the war:

March 4th. We were on parade at 7.0 a.m. and had to stand over one and a half hours before the officers were ready. A fierce snow storm was raging the whole time and the men were numb before ever the march started. The route was along a road on a plain devoid of trees and hedges. The wind was driving the snow with bitter violence against one side of the face until feeling left it numb. The snow on the road was up to our knees and we were wet through. One lad called Chambers lay down in the snow, and would have lain there until the water-cart went over him, only a Staff-Sergeant pulled him out of the way. He was only one of several who fell out. Williamson absolutely refused to go any further, and I stopped along with him. He saw a hay stack some little distance away from the road and we made for it. After floundering through the snow, falling and rising we finally found the hay stack only to find we were worse off than we were on the road. After a short rest and with a good deal of coaxing, I got him enticed out onto the road again and we finally reached our destination about 4 p.m.

For McKay the destination was the main dressing station in the village of Mailly-Maillet, one of the largest villages in the Somme rear area and one subject to frequent German shelling, though the British artillery was always on hand to fire back: 'Garrison guns were in position behind our dressing station and every time the guns fired the old building shook. This is the first time I ever heard the screech of a shell.'

His diary was somewhat sparse during his first weeks on the Somme. He noted 'heavy frost' on the 6th, a 'fairly heavy bombardment at night' on the 7th, while 'some snow; aeroplanes over every day, both British and German' was his entry for the 10th. On the 19th, he reported, correctly though without comment: 'Two deserters of the 15th Royal Irish Rifles shot in Mailly-Maillet today, Sunday'. A move shortly after to the advanced dressing station at Mailly-Maillet's near-neighbour, Auchonvillers ('Ocean Villas' to the troops), which had received a great deal of attention from enemy gunfire, produced a more eloquent reaction:

This is the first wrecked village which I have seen. There is scarcely a roof on any house in the place. From the house cellar where we are stopping, at the back we can see quite plainly our own front line and then the enemy's and further back the village of Beaumont Hamel.

We are not allowed to go down the main road by day, as enemy snipers have a clear view of it, and sometimes they turn a machine-gun on parts under their observation. The walls which are standing appear to be a continual eye-sore to the Germans, and especially is this the case with the Chapel remains, which consist of one side wall and part of a gable. Every day the enemy throws over a few shells at the Chapel.

Between Auchonvillers and the line lay a communication trench, one of many such vital umbilical connections giving access to the front line from the rear area. McKay scrutinized it carefully from the point of view of a medical man whose task it would be to evacuate wounded along it, perhaps under fire or in darkness. Looking back on his unit's use of it in their brief time in this sector – they would soon move elsewhere – he would write:

This was about seven feet deep and from three to three and a half feet wide, the bottom of the trench being paved with brick which had been obtained from the ruins in the village. Owing to the wintry weather and the continual usage, many of the bricks were turned up on their edge making it difficult to keep one's feet. Imagine what it was to carry a patient down this at night; the entire length of the trench would be about half a mile, but only ten or twelve yards in any one part of it straight. In some places there were shell-holes too – three feet deep and filled with water, and the only plan of passing them was to walk right through them, because if a person stepped on the side of the hole, the soil gave way and they generally came down. Trench boots were served out to us but they only made matters worse; the soles being rubber, a person could obtain no grip in the mud at all. On one particular night a stretcher party was taking a patient down, and one man named Jackson, from Dublin, took his trench boots off and walked it in his stockinged feet, and this was through six or seven inches of snow and mud.

The communication trench was entered by a sunken road leading out of Auchonvillers and it debouched at a point three hundred yards behind the front line called White City – so named because it consisted of a number of dugouts excavated out of the white chalk. (This would later have its place in cinematic history in that it was from there that possibly the most famous image of the first day of the battle was filmed, the massive explosion of the mine at Hawthorn Ridge.) At this point McKay's unit had a squad of half a dozen men on permanent duty in a dugout shared with a company of signallers. If not of the depth and scale of the dugouts built by the Germans, this was nevertheless no mean construction: 'The one we occupied was sixty feet long by eight or nine wide and six high. The roof consisted of a layer of trees six to eight inches in diameter laid close together and smaller branches above them, all being covered with three feet of clay and chalk.'

After this first baptism the Ulsters were withdrawn for a time of rest at Verrennes, following which they moved to the part of the line east of the River Ancre with which they would become permanently associated. McKay wrote on 20 April:

Along with W. Foreman, D. Neill and J. Williamson, I went up to the Regimental Aid Post of the 10th Inniskilling Fusiliers. We continued up to Paisley Dump and then entered a communication trench which was cut through a wood. The ground on our left falls steeply down to the river and swamp, on the far side of which lies the village of Mesnil and a little further on Hamel. Dugouts were scattered all through the wood. At night the wood is swept by enemy machine-gun fire. Here the Germans hold all the dominating positions, the strongest of which is Thiepval village.

Thiepval would be a target for the first day on the Somme and would be the scene of much hard fighting in which the Ulsters would play a most valiant part, but would stubbornly resist seizure until many weeks into the campaign.

*   *   *

The distinguished soldier who would make the greatest contribution of all to the capture of Thiepval was by this time well established on the Somme and already preparing vigorously for the battle to come. This was Major-General Ivor Maxse, who had commanded the 1st (Guards) Brigade from 1910, had gone to France with the BEF in 1914 and had then returned, in October that year, to take command of the 18th (Eastern) Division, a division of Kitchener's New Army. Well known for his inspiring personality and with a reputation as an outstanding trainer of troops, he was to mould the 18th Division into a formidable fighting force. It had sailed for France in July 1915 and had soon established itself on the Somme; Private Cude of the 7th Buffs, already quoted, was one of its members. It was assigned to the southern part of the Somme front, where it would face the German lines between Mametz and Montauban, with 30th Division to its right. These two divisions were part of XIII Corps, commanded by a famously successful soldier in the person of Lieutenant-General W.N. Congreve VC. Beyond 30th Division the French Sixth Army under General Fayolle held the line to the Somme and beyond.

From the report which he would later compile about his division's part in the opening phase of the battle, it is clear that Maxse was not for sitting back and waiting supinely for orders from elsewhere. He knew where his men would ultimately have to go and he set to work to do everything he could to support their progress. Point 11 of his report begins: 'Commencing in March we started to dig eight Russian Saps from our trenches across No Man's Land and by the 1st July they were all within 20 yards of the German trenches.'

A Russian sap was a trench built forward just below ground level which could be easily and swiftly opened up at the required moment. Another major pre-battle effort was the running out of an underground gallery to a position forty feet below Kasino Point, one of a number of 'particular localities and strong points' in the German defences which Maxse saw as requiring special attention. Here a mine would be planted, to be blown just before the attack, thus removing 'what must otherwise have proved a serious menace to our advance across No Man's Land'. This was one area at least where the British would go into action in the best possible conditions.

CHAPTER THREE

COUNTDOWN TO ZERO

AS THE SPRING WORE ON, there was growing awareness that the time for the great offensive was rapidly approaching. Many felt the impulse to express their thoughts about the challenge which would face them, either in the confines of a diary or the more public display of a letter.

On 31 May Second Lieutenant Billy Lipscomb, having observed the elaborate ritual of a French funeral in the village where he was billeted, wrote to his actress friend Vera:

> By the way, *don't* be downhearted if you don't hear for some days if there is anything big on because the first lorries to be cut off are the post lorries if they are needed for transport. Sit tight and hang on and hope, and never, never, never wear black if you get the chance, dear (this isn't a moody sentiment dear, it's just a passing thought) for after all, there's nothing appalling about the fact. Pain I object to strongly, but t'other thing – well, I refuse to think of it as a calamity, even a personal one – so if it ever comes to that – think of me, miss me, but be at peace with me. I think what has put this idea into my head again is the parade the entire village makes of mourning. Horses, plumes and the entire village of about 350 in deepest black – of all the mid-Victorian slush. Possibly I'd pass sober black clothes, but the females in black British veils – Gurr-rrr!
>
> This is a cheerful document – yes it is, if one can write and think cheerfully about *these* things, then one has – what did the good lady say in 'Fanny's First Play' – the happiness that comes from within.

Meanwhile Captain Charlie May's entries grew ever more out-spoken and passionate as the weeks passed by and the huge scale of the coming offensive became more apparent. By now everybody was fully aware that though there might be great gains, there would also be great losses. Success would only be achieved through much sacrifice. He wrote on Saturday 17 June:

> I must not allow myself to dwell on the personal – there is no room for it here. Also it is demoralising. But I do not want to die. Not that I mind for myself. If it be that I am to go, I am ready. But the thought that I may never see you or our darling baby again turns my bowels to water. I cannot think of it with even the semblance of equanimity.
>
> It may well be that you will only have to read these lines as ones of passing interest. On the other hand, they may well be my last message to you. If they are, know through all your life that I loved you and baby with all my heart and soul, that you two sweet things were just all the world to me.
>
> I pray I may do my duty, for I know, whatever that may entail, you would not have it otherwise.

*   *   *

Steadily the build-up for the push continued. Units of all kinds now came to the Somme to create the organizational base required for the launch and maintenance of a major offensive. The spearhead might be provided by the artillery and infantry, but there was also need for engineers, miners, signallers, specialists in gas warfare, camouflage, or anti-aircraft defence, plus the pilots and observers of the Royal Flying Corps who would assist the artillery and carry the air war to the enemy. Training camps had to be opened and manned, medical and veterinary services to be got in place, postal and printing services to be established, schemes for the digging of massed graves and registration of burials to be devised. Most importantly, the problem of supply had to be tackled, so that the troops could be fed and armed and the guns furnished with the mass of ammunition with which it was intended to make the coming attack irresistible. Transport vehicles of all kinds filled the roads while light railways were hurriedly constructed to assist in the transporting of *matériel* to remoter parts of the front. Not entirely to their pleasure, infantry-men out of the line could find themselves drawn into assisting in this work. Private Bernard Stevenson of the 1/7th Sherwood Foresters, 46th (North Midland) Division, Territorial Force, wrote to his mother on 7 June:

> We were only two days in the half-ruined village which is still shelled intermittently but in that brief period I managed to get in the way of one of the most tiring jobs I have ever had the misfortune to meet. We fell in, a party of 50 at 7 p.m., marched three or four kilometres to where a new railway is being constructed (by the English of course) and there climbed up on the top of trucks full of coal waste or ballast. After a run up the line for another two 'kilos' we were set to work to unload them with shovels. Before the dawn had broken we had disposed of twenty-two large sized wagon loads, each wagon containing tons of the stuff. Then we had to march back to billets. You never saw such a state as we were in. Faces were black or streaked with dust as any collier fresh from the pit. Indeed there was coal dust in our eyes and ears as well.

A new arrival from Britain, Lance-Corporal Sam Chandley, who was to join the 1/5th Cheshires at Hébuterne, where it was serving as pioneer battalion to 56th (London) Division, saw another aspect of the preparations for battle while awaiting his posting at the base at Rouen. He noted in his diary: 'The camp here is right out of the town and situated at the top of a hill. Hospitals galore which are all empty for the advance which is about to start. All the old Bully-beef tins are used to make foundations for roads and I even saw one side of a hospital made up of old biscuit tins.'

Attempting to give his mother, in a letter written after the push had begun, some idea of the work necessary for launching and maintaining so major an offensive, Captain Harold Yeo, who had been released from his battalion, the 9th King's Own Yorkshire Light Infantry, to carry out temporary staff work at 64th Brigade Headquarters, offered the following thumbnail description:

> To go into the preparations in detail would be tedious, but to realize them you should understand that the trenches have to be adapted for holding large numbers of men immediately prior to the assault: dumps of food, water, rifle ammunition, bombs, grenades, and other things have to be prepared so that they can go

forward at once [when] success is obtained. I had the job of making those dumps and it was no end of a task. Guns of all shapes and sizes had meanwhile arrived and been put in position: conferences as to orders held: peeps taken from all angles at the promised land.

* * *

Achieving this high state of readiness was the result of a huge amount of intensive work carried out over many weeks. One aspect of the Somme too easily neglected is the fact of the sustained and very largely effective performance of the personnel who put into place the vast infrastructure which allowed the offensive to be launched in the first place. The 'Staff' – the butt of innumerable jokes throughout the war – were rarely congratulated when successful, and almost always abused when they were not. They would shortly be the object of much forceful, if somewhat unfocused, attack, while by contrast those in high command would seem too remote, too high in fact, for meaningful criticism. They would also in due course – particularly in the case of staff officers attached to regiments – be accorded a mixed review by the official historian for their work in the subsequent campaign, for which one important reason was that there were not enough trained officers for the task in hand and that too many of them had to 'learn the duties of their branch in the heat of battle'. Yet the staff work that *preceded* the battle has been adjudged worthy of very high praise. In what had become by this time not so much a conventional army as a vast, complex *society* spread from Flanders to the Somme – with all the extra difficulties of functioning overseas and of a 'work force' under constant threat of death or injury – there were bound to be numerous mistakes and misjudgements; but there is no doubt that by the time the Somme attack was launched a huge and daunting challenge of organization had been met. It was also a *new* challenge, for there had been nothing on this scale before. The point has been well made by General Sir Anthony Farrar-Hockley: 'Viewing this gigantic administrative problem in retrospect, what is remarkable is not that there were minor muddles, shortages and delays, but that almost everything was ready for the men and their gear when they arrived, and complete for the moment of assault when it came.'

At the time a similar judgement was affirmed in a letter written not long before the 'push' began, by Captain George McGowan – himself a staff officer, being Brigade Signals Officer of 90th Infantry Brigade, in 30th Division, but one whose role was to be close to the battle, not in a situation of out-of-range remoteness behind the lines. (Indeed, he was proud that his duty was at Brigade Headquarters, that is, virtually in the battle zone, as opposed to Divisional Head-quarters, to which a colleague of his who had shown signs of wilting under the strain had been despatched, where he would be relatively far from bullets or shells in anger.) What allowed McGowan to praise the work of the staff so freely was the fact that he had newly returned from England, and therefore could not be thought to be patting himself on the back:

> When I got back from leave a fortnight ago I was amazed to see what rapid strides had been made in preparation for a struggle, that when I left the line to go on leave, I and many others believed could not possibly take place before August, but where there's a will there's always a way and the powers that be suddenly decided to hustle things. The roads leading to the front line were packed from early morning to early morning with transport stretching for miles back, bringing ammunition and stores. Working parties were hard at it day and night trench digging, cable burying, laying waterpipes, digging gun pits and dugouts and carrying out scores of other fatigues necessary to ensure success.
>
> After I got back we had a week amongst such turmoil, then we as a brigade left the line by train for the training area. There is a large area here, mapped out with trenches, representing no man's land, the Boche trenches beyond, and a plan of the village of Montauban, which we are to capture and hold, all to scale as obtained by aerial photographs. Trenches, streets etc. are marked with names that we shall christen them when we get across there, and here the Bde goes en bloc each day, to practise step by step (in accordance with the timetable fixed for the actual day) our part in the big offensive.

McGowan was enthused by the effort and enthusiasm going into the push, and he was well aware of its significance. 'I'm sure that if any troops hold on we shall, for we know we shall be playing before a crowded house, with great issues at stake.' He also told his parents, not without pride: 'We are on the eve of a great battle, probably the greatest of the many great encounters of the greatest war the world has ever seen.'

*   *   *

In brief outline, the great attack would be carried out as follows. Operations would begin with a sustained artillery bombardment on the enemy's positions to last several days. These days would be named respectively U,V,W, X and Y. On Z Day – the intended date of the infantry's 'over the top' advance – along a front of eighteen miles five corps of General Sir Henry Rawlinson's Fourth Army and the right-hand corps of General Sir Edmund Allenby's Third Army would mount a concerted attack, from Maricourt in the south to Gommecourt in the north, with a gap in the offensive between the two Army fronts. The function of the Third Army's action would be diversionary: that is, it was to inflict as much damage and draw as much enemy attention as possible, while the move forward, the actual 'push', was to be made by the Fourth Army. To the south, the French would contribute five first line divisions to the offensive from their positions astride the River Somme.

Eighteen British divisions would be involved, of which fourteen would attack in the first line. Of these fourteen divisions eleven were from Kitchener's New Armies or from the Territorial Force, 'two legions of amateurs,' as the historian Cyril Falls would describe them, 'about to engage a first-class army still leavened with professional peace-trained soldiers. Here stood the flower of Britain, drawn from all classes of the community but on the average the best of all. Though the first universal service act was nearly six months old these men were volunteers with hardly a conscript in their ranks.' In even grander phraseology, Winston Churchill would hail these men as 'a young army, but the finest we have ever marshalled; improvised at the sound of the cannonade, every man a volunteer, inspired not only by love of country but by a widespread conviction that human freedom was challenged by military and Imperial tyranny.'

Not all leading generals thought well of these civilian soldiers, but one who did was Major-General Maxse, who had direct experience of training some of them. 'The New Divisions', he wrote in his post-battle report, 'can be relied upon to do as well as the Old ones provided they understand what is required of them, and they do even better when they are also given reasons for dispositions.' He endorsed this judgement at numerous conferences, 'at which captains and officers above that rank freely gave their opinions'. Moreover, 'we took into our confidence the 64 section commanders of all battalions, gave them the *reason* for their positions in our forming up trenches and drilled them to move from their positions direct to their objectives in the enemy's lines. Thus all ranks started with some idea of what they were to do, a conviction that their pals also knew what to do and a complete absence of any fear of being left in the lurch by them.' This was a general who was a far cry from the popular concept of a donkey leading lions to their deaths.

* * *

On 13 June, Lieutenant-Colonel H.C. Rees, who had served for fourteen months as staff officer in 38th Division, came back from leave in England to find that he had been promoted to the rank of Brigadier-General. The GOC of 94th Brigade, 31st Division, had gone sick and Rees was to take over from him in temporary command. On the 14th he set off by car for the Somme, going first to the Headquarters of VIIIth Corps to report to its GOC, Lieutenant-General Sir Aylmer Hunter-Weston, who took him to his room and immediately plunged into expounding the scheme for the attack to be undertaken by his brigade. This would be on the German strong point at Serre. 'I took my coat off and listened in my shirt sleeves,' Rees noted in his diary, 'as Hunter-Weston insisted on a tailor converting my uniform to that of a brigadier at once'. Thus began Rees's brief association with a brigade largely consisting of 'Pals' battalions from the North of England who were to face a tragic baptism in the forthcoming attack.

There was no question, Rees found, that the plans for the coming offensive had been most elaborately prepared – the briefing for his brigade alone ran to seventy-six pages of close typing – and every effort made to ensure that they were fully understood. After being

shown them by a fellow brigadier, General Hore Ruthven, whom he
had met in 1914 during the First Battle of Ypres, he went back to
Hunter-Weston who made him run over with a map what he had
managed to pick up. Then, having borrowed Hore Ruthven's best
hat, he set off for the Headquarters of 31st Division to meet his
divisional commander, Major-General Wanless O'Gowan, dined
there, and then went to the Headquarters of his brigade, to meet the
officer who had taken temporary command until Rees's arrival,
Colonel Richman, CO of the 11th East Lancs. On the following day
he met the COs of the remaining battalions and was given a tour of
the trenches in front of Serre.

Rees later noted that 'a great spirit of optimism prevailed in all
quarters', but he for his part soon found himself less than happy with
his brigade's situation and prospects. His men would have to advance
across 700 yards of No Man's Land up 'a decided rise', the summit
of which was 'obviously a point of observation of great value [to the
enemy]. The village itself, although a good deal knocked about, was
quite recognizable as such, roofs of houses being visible among the
trees with which it was thickly planted.' There was one other factor
which he found disturbing. His brigade was at the northern extreme
of the main attack; beyond lay ground over which no advance would
be made, and beyond that lay the Gommecourt sector, the target of
the diversionary attack to be mounted by Third Army. Rees noted
with some concern: 'Our advance up the slope to the village was in
full view from the north, from the German salient of Gommecourt.'

He realized that when the bombardment began before the battle
the enemy could hardly fail to know the extent of the expected
attack, and would thus be able to bring especially heavy fire-power
to bear on his sector. He was sufficiently disturbed by this to suggest
to the Corps Commander that a number of dummy assembly
trenches might be constructed in the area between the two attacks to
deceive the enemy and draw his artillery on to it. 'Hunter-Weston
congratulated me on the idea,' he later commented, 'but whether it
was put into execution or not, I don't know.'

This was not the only matter on which he felt bold enough to
challenge his Corps Commander: 'One of my criticisms of the
general plan of operations was that the time allowed for the capture

of each objective was too short. I had a severe argument with Hunter-Weston before I induced him to give me an extra ten minutes for the capture of an orchard, 300 yards beyond the village of Serre. I was looked upon as something of a heretic for saying that everything had been arranged for except the unexpected, which usually occurs in war.'

Rees meticulously continued with his preparations, condensing and simplifying the mass of corps instructions into clear and precise orders for the units under his command.

* * *

At forty-six, Captain Harry Bursey of the Royal Horse Artillery was a veteran among the junior officers of the British Army. He had run away to enlist in 1888 and had served in the ranks in India, where he had achieved the distinction of being a tent-peg lance medallist and champion. Commissioned on the outbreak of war and sent to a different foreign field, he now found himself on the Somme in charge of an artillery ammunition column. Some days before the opening of the battle he began a diary, in a large lined exercise book, which he filled with detailed and often eloquent entries for several weeks and then as suddenly desisted, adding only a few later notes and then, apparently, closing the book entirely. He looked forward in confident anticipation to the coming offensive, but at the same time he had no facile enthusiasm for it. It was a necessary duty for the good of Europe, but it could only be undertaken at great cost. His experience had not made a military zealot of him; on the contrary, there is a remarkable sensitivity in his writing, and a deep sympathy for the many young men who would be called upon to suffer in the weeks ahead.

He began breezily enough, however, his first entry being dated 21 June:

It is fourteen months since I landed in France and at a very late date I take up my pencil to give a record of my doings. It will not be retrospective which is a pity, for the world will never know what it has lost. (Ahem)

I purpose setting down here when occasion – and the wily Hun – allows, a short and modest record of my doings with the Army in France in this, the greatest war the world has ever seen. God grant it may be the last. The sights one sees out here are quite sufficient to warrant that wish. It is a war which we knew must come. Two years before war broke out I advocated conscription, in a passage of arms in the *Birmingham Gazette* with a person signing himself '73'. I said that the huge armies Austria and Germany were amassing rendered it imperative. When I say it I mean 'conscription', I also said that conscription would come. The war I predicted came to pass and in its train conscription. But there was one thing I didn't know. And that was that I would take part in it as an officer!

But so it is, and here I am in a dugout at the foot of a hill in the Bois des Taille, near the river Somme, on a very hot day in June, commencing a recital of my doings, which will as I have already stated be set down here in modest fashion, as becomes an old warrior who ran away from home 28 years ago and joined the Army. And never once regretted doing so. All things work together for good etc. we are told and up to the present this has been so with me. What the future has in store I do not know. But I hope to meet it with a smile, even if the end comes. What better end than that of a soldier laying down his life for his country and so I look to the future without fear and trust that, all being well, I shall live to tell the story of my doings out here, in years to come.

Here I am on the right flank of the British Army, next to the French. The sights one sees here are just wonderful. Guns, guns and more guns. From a machine-gun to a 17″. What are they here for? Ah, now you are coming to it. They are here for 'The Day'. The day we have looked forward to for many weary months, the thoughts of which have helped to cheer us when we have been soddened by rain and our bodies numbed by the bitter cold.

And it is coming soon. Will we get through I do not know. But we will try. I can realize all that it means. Dying and dead lying together on the blood soddened ground. Wounded men biting the grass beneath them in their agony. Others, happily unconscious, babbling of days gone by ere their spirit passes to the great beyond. Cheers of victory. Many a cheer ending in a sob as a bullet lays the cheerer low.

I know it all. And it is all in front of us. Many a bright eyed boy laughing on this 21st day of June, will ere many days are past be laid beneath the sod. That is what 'the day' means. But it means something else too. It means the liberation of Europe from a mad tyrant, William II of Germany. God grant that our arms may be successful.

The next day's entry produced a total change of tone, in the light of an unexpected foretaste of the suffering he had predicted:

June 22nd 1916. I have wondered many times why I commenced this book yesterday. Within half an hour after I had penned the above lines I had had the most terrible experience of my life. Truly might I say 'O, my prophetic soul'. I had gone with the horse lines where my drivers were cleaning harness when the Huns commenced shelling my section. Four 2.9″ shells burst over us before we started to move and then we made for a wood 200 yds away. Four more shells of the same calibre came and the last one burst right in the centre of the group in which I was standing. We heard it coming and threw ourselves down on the ground. The noise of the burst was appalling. I sprang up at once and as I did so a gunner of mine with bubbles of bloody foam issuing from his mouth, fell at my feet. I could see he was mortally hit. Eleven more lay on the ground. Only the sergeant major, Lieut Nicholson and myself escaped scot free of the group in which we were standing. Poor Waterman died almost instantaneously. Another gunner died in half an hour shot through the liver. Half were severely wounded and a few with slight wounds. We quickly got doctors and had their wounds dressed and sent the men away in a motor ambulance.

I do not know how the S-Major, Nicholson or myself escaped. According to all accepted rules of gunnery we should all have been dead men. One can only be thankful.

So today two poor blood-stained bodies have been lowered into Mother Earth. For them the fight is o'er, the battle won. And the guns are sounding their requiem. Death comes but fighting still goes on.

His entry for 23 June carries a message which everybody on the British side knew in their bones was the case; that the Germans were fully aware of the purpose of the huge build-up of men and *matériel* on the Allied side:

The morning is beautifully fine. Guns are very quiet. Everyone is making preparations for the coming advance. The Huns put a board up yesterday in their front line trenches and on it was pinned a paper with the following. 'We know you are going to attack. Kitchener is done. Asquith is done. You are done. We are done. In fact we are all done'.

It did not convey much to us. Of course they know the attack is taking place. It is impossible to hide great columns of guns, men, horses and motor lorries, such as have been moving to the firing line during the last fortnight.

Kitchener had indeed been 'done' by this time; on 6 June he had sailed off from Scapa Flow for a visit to Russia in the cruiser HMS *Hampshire*; the ship had struck a mine off the west coast of Orkney and had gone down leaving only a handful of survivors, of whom the Secretary of State was not one. The news shocked the nation, and in particular it shocked the troops of Kitchener's Army. 'It was as bad as having lost a battle', was one soldier's comment. It was an attitude shared by many.

* * *

The preliminary bombardment before the offensive began on Saturday 24 June. There was, as it turned out, precisely one week to go to the opening of the battle, but at that time the general assumption was that the attack was only five days away, the intended date for it being Thursday the 29th. Ironically, since the first day on the Somme is now remembered as a day of almost continuous sun, bad weather, which impeded artillery observation, was the principal cause of the postponement.

Lieutenant-Colonel Ronald Fife, commanding officer of the 7th Green Howards, 17th (Northern) Division, kept a detailed diary throughout this period and his entries for the last days before battle contain frequent references to adverse weather conditions. 'Our camp a swamp after yesterday's rain,' he wrote on the 24th, there having been 'a violent thunderstorm at 3.45' on the 23rd. On the 26th: 'Heavy thunderstorm about 3.30 turned camp into a lake.' Going out late that night from their Fricourt trenches to billets at Ville, the battalion was fortunate enough to be put up in houses and barns; 'luckier than the W. York [i.e. the 10th West Yorks, a sister battalion in 50th Brigade], who had to pitch tents on sodden ground.' The 27th began with 'a showery morning', while his entry for the 28th opened: 'Heavy rain in early morning and trenches in an awful state.' It was not until the 29th – by which time the attack had been delayed to 1 July – that he could write: 'A fine morning.' The weather of the first phase of the Somme had arrived.

Thunder and rain, however, were minor concerns as he concentrated on the serious matter of preparing for the attack; the progress of the bombardment was also a subject for frequent notice and assessment:

> *24th June.* In the evening after dinner walked with Cotton [his second-in-command] towards Albert to watch the bombardment which began today. The spectacle was rather disappointing and compared unfavourably with similar scenes round Ypres.
> *25th June.* Spent practically the whole morning writing my orders for the attack on 29th. I made them as short as possible but they are still very long. I don't think I have left out anything. In the afternoon Brigadier-General Glasgow took me in a motor to a conference at 7th. Division Hd.Qrs. General Glasgow has nominated me to command the 50th Bde. in the event of his becoming a casualty during the attack, and Major-General Pilcher [GOC of Fife's 17th Division] has approved of this.
>
> Artillery fire very violent all day. Heard that our aeroplanes have shot down 3 German observation balloons today. At present there are 13 of our balloons up and none of theirs to be seen.

On the 26th he recorded the observation of another standard pre-battle ritual: 'Battalion paraded at 9.30 am with the W. Yorkshire. General Pilcher made a speech wishing us good luck in the attack.' Later he rode with Major Cotton to high ground to the south of Méaulte 'from which we had a good view of the bombardment. While we were there we saw gas and smoke clouds rolling from our front across the Boche trenches. Our shelling seemed to be both heavy and accurate.'

* * *

'Well, all the long period of toil and preparation and vast accumulation of resources has at last come to its consummation,' wrote Second Lieutenant Jocelyn Buxton, an officer of 2nd Battalion, The Rifle Brigade, who was now attached to the Machine Gun Corps, to his father on that same day, Monday 26 June. 'Two days ago at 4 o'clock in the morning began the bombardment which now and until the day of assault rages with varying intensity along miles of the front on either side. Events will now work out so rapidly that in many ways it is a definite relief that the weeks of waiting and preparation are behind us.'

Buxton's aim was to write what he called 'a sort of diary letter of events', to be sent home 'the last day before "the ball opens".' In the end he did not quite achieve this, but one long letter to his father and three shorter ones to his mother provide a virtual equivalent. Together they give a moving insight into the mind of a sensitive, intelligent young man of little more than twenty trying to balance his own acute anxieties against the potential gain for which the forthcoming battle was being fought. He had no illusions as to the nature of the ordeal he was facing. In an earlier letter he had written of the coming attack that 'when its purpose has finally been attained peace will truly feel like Heaven after Hell'; now he elaborated his thoughts, though with the reassuring disclaimer that there was little time to dwell on them in the flurry of preparing for action:

> One guesses that it is all going to be very huge and hideous – this great effort – one knows in a vague way too the still more unfathomably terrible meaning of it afterwards to countless waiting and watching homes on our side – and on theirs – but frankly and mercifully it is impossible in the general activity to dwell on that side. And it is best I feel sure just to keep hold of the faithfulness of God and share in the cheerfulness which is clear to every one and which is chiefly due to the confidence that this effort will be a success and bring peace quickly.

Buxton was opposite Thiepval, behind which lay the village of Pozières, 'our objective in this sector'. In his letter of the 26th he described the sight of Pozières under bombardment, as seen the previous morning:

For 10 minutes all possible guns hurled shells on to the place which could be seen among the trees about 3000 yards away across an intervening dip. It was not long before it was all swathed in brown and yellow smoke. Meanwhile our innumerable trench mortars had been doing persistent work on the German front line and wire. They have unlimited reserves of ammunition and from the rapid-firing 11-pounders they range to huge 200-pound sort of aerial torpedoes; their apparent effort was terrific. On this day the German retaliation was more marked but it came in rapid bursts and not continuously like ours. There were still long intervals when no answer came from them. It is obvious that they are anxious about their supply of ammunition and are waiting to gauge the magnitude of our intent and for the opening of the attack. One can imagine that the German generals opposite are having to think furiously.

In the afternoon of the 26th he went up to a vantage point near the front line 'to take a general survey of things'; returning to the headquarters he wrote this memorable and moving description:

From here I could see the maze of lines extending to both sides, following the rise and fall of the downs. On the left the opposing trenches bent back and then rose up to a crest and disappeared; on the right I could follow the line which went in a vague sweep right down to the Somme at Bray. But it was a hazy evening and I was only able to trace out the lines by the thick murky smoke which everywhere spurted up in spouts of yellow, or grey, or brown (according to the light or the explosive) and then spread away into wide smudges. All the while at different points the air above was spattered with multitudinous white wisps of shrapnel. It was indeed an immense and terrible sight and it seemed especially so when I turned round, to the beautiful contrast behind me. Long green ridges thick with cornfields along their lower slopes with here and there bright dashes of colour – the gold of the mustard or bright scarlet of the poppy. And all these gentle hills which were bright blue at the horizon towards which the sun was hastening, enfolded lovely wooded valleys and pretty villages set in the more secluded folds. This was a view far more wonderful and dear in its beauty and peace and it seemed that with all that wilful crashing and panting of guns it would remain for long a veiled vision to us, in its full meaning and message of smiling peace, because it was all so

insecure while the passions and ambitions of men continued to
find vent in mutual slaughter.

Another young officer who was much struck by the loveliness of
nature in that final week before battle was Captain Ronald Wilson of
the 1/4th Yorks and Lancs. He was very near to Buxton, his 49th
Division being in reserve in the area from Authuille Wood to the
Ancre, with (as his battalion's history notes) 'Thiepval as the key of
the situation'. Writing on the same day, the 26th, he informed his
'dearest parents': 'The country is very beautiful and there are flowers,
red, yellow and blue everywhere. I have never seen such gorgeous
natural colouring as some of the fields give. Here and there bits of
them are absolutely one mass of scarlet with poppies.'

But his mind was also firmly on the events to come. A man of
strong religious faith, he also told them: 'We had a quiet little
communion service this evening led by a Wesleyan padre. Just 5 of
us out in a field. There would have been more there I know but
many no doubt could not get off for it.' His letter concluded: 'Please
pray specially for us. But don't mention anything to anyone else.
With my very best love to all. Ron.'

Buxton's and Wilson's letters were duly despatched. Neither
attempted the type of letter, of which there were many written in
that final week, which was only to be opened in the event of the
writer's death. Second Lieutenant G.F. Ellenberger wrote one, which
now survives as a literary curiosity, since he survived the battle and
the war, so that the letter was never required. It is, however, worth
quoting at some length, because it is a classic of its kind, expressing
immaculately the sentiments of the gilded young men of his generation. It is dated 25 June, the second day of the great bombardment:

My very very dearest Mother
    I feel I ought to write to you all something in the nature of a
farewell in case I should not return to you from this war.
    You'll understand the difficulty I have in writing a letter that
you will not read till I am no more, and that though there is so
much that I should like to say, it is exceedingly hard to say it.
    I will begin by trying to explain what have been my feelings
ever since I came out here, but more pronounced now than before.

I believe I do not fear death – at least I hope not and tell myself I do not; but I am a coward, for I do fear pain. I will not dwell on the idea of receiving some horrible wound; but worse than all, I believe, I fear causing you to suffer pain – pain which I know would be mental rather than physical, and for that reason the greater. So if there is any afterlife in which we can still take notice of and interest in the things that happen in this world, nothing would cause me greater trouble than to see you, after my death, stricken down by grief. Of course I know the measure of your sorrow would be the measure of your love for me – and so I do not ask that you should not grieve for me, only that you should not be overcome and dominated by your grief.

All I can do myself is to assure you that I have gone into this great adventure loving you with all my heart and with all my soul, further that the great love which I have for you has kept me straight – has almost been my God. I cannot tell you what my feelings are on religion – I do not yet know myself – all I can say is that I am not a Christian in the true sense of the word, but I am also not an atheist. I believe in some good God – more I cannot say, or, at any rate, write.

I know nothing – what mortal really knows anything? – of a future life; but I trust that we shall in some state hereafter all meet again.

Others put serious 'last thoughts' into ordinary letters in which a range of other subjects were discussed. One such was Captain George McGowan. As an officer at Brigade Headquarters, he was less likely to become a casualty than the infantryman going over the top, but, he warned his parents in a letter of 24 June, 'very often the back of the front is worse than the actual front and in any case I shall be out amongst it, you may be sure. Of course for your dear sakes I will not be needlessly reckless, but on the other hand I've not the least intention of wrapping myself in cotton wool.' As for certain unavoidable possibilities: 'If I am to be wounded or killed before the war is over, I'd much prefer it to happen at a time like this, when there's a big issue at stake, rather than be knocked hors de combat by a stray bullet or a bit of shrapnel when there's really nothing doing.'

* * *

Like Captain Wilson, Corporal Norman Edwards of the 1/6th Gloucesters, 48th (South Midland) Division, who chronicled his war in a series of tiny pocket diaries, went to a service on Sunday 25 June, though for his battalion this was a formal church parade. 9.15 was the assigned time for the Church of England men, while the Nonconformist service which he attended was at 11.30. 'Unfortunately,' he noted, 'the Chaplain didn't turn up but the C. of E. man came across and gave us an address.' His main comment for the day, however, concerned the artillery bombardment, which speeded up during the afternoon until it was 'almost what I expected it to be like, one continuous roar.'

Later, in the evening, he and his comrades were delighted to receive what he called 'some jolly good news, that our aeroplanes had gone across and dropped incendiary bombs on the three German balloons on our front and exploded them.' He added: 'I bet the German Generals across there have got the wind up and I couldn't help feeling sorry for the poor beggars in their front line. As the night came on the bombardment grew heavier and we fairly bumped 'em across.'

* * *

On the other side of No Man's Land the 'poor beggars' cowered in their dugouts as the massive bombardment ground on. The following is from a later account by a young German Jewish medical officer (with an English-sounding name), Stephen Westman, who was in the German lines to the south of Beaumont Hamel – not far from the sector where Buxton noted the contrasts between the landscapes of war and peace on 25 June:

> On June 24, 1916, the British gunners opened up and their fire increased in intensity, combined with fierce gas attacks. For seven days and seven nights the ground shook under the constant impact of light and heavy shells, and in between the bombardments gas alarms were sounded, and we could hardly breathe. Our dugouts crumbled, tumbled on top of us, and our positions were razed to the ground.
>
> Again and again we had to dig ourselves and our comrades out of masses of blackened earth and splintered wooden beams. Often

we found bodies crushed to pulp, or bunks full of suffocated soldiers. The 'drum-fire' never ceased. No food or water reached us. Down below, men became hysterical and their comrades had to knock them out, so as to prevent them from running away and exposing themselves to the deadly shell splinters. Even the rats panicked and sought refuge in our flimsy shelters; they ran up the walls, and we had to kill them with our spades.

Leutnant F.L. Cassel, 99th Infantry Reserve Regiment, in the German line at Thiepval, wrote a similarly vivid account of the experience of being under that sustained week-long bombardment:

The fire never stopped. It goes on through all day and the whole night, the men detailed to get the food come back without. The field kitchen has not arrived and we have to do without warm food. Battalion reports that all the base quarters have had heavy fire, that Bapaume has been bombarded with 38 cm calibre and even heavier, and that Division and Corps command had to be moved and a number of villages had to be evacuated. Many lines of communication are cut.

On the 4th or 5th day it became obvious that the fire was directed on to the first and second line trenches, and it began to be very uncomfortable. It was not very pleasant in the trench, too much hardware flying about. We were tired too and slept as much as one could. The noise of the barrage (*Das Trommelfeuer*) was too monotonous and so prevented sleep for overtired people. There was only one harassing question. Could one rely on the sentries? They stood on the top steps of the dugout and had to watch lest the fire was changed to the rear, and had to look in quieter moments across the ramparts whether the enemy was coming across. Day long, night long, for ten full days! And not all men are heroes, so from time to time one had to go up to see whether the sentries did their duty.

By and by we became the target of the heaviest calibre, to our cost. The English were damned cautious. They wanted to be sure of overkill. Nobody should be alive when their infantry left their trenches.

* * *

That such was the intention was made clear to many soldiers on the British side in the last days before the push. Indeed, it was the accepted doctrine, to question which in any way was not permitted. The position was later clearly stated by the official historian: 'It was ... impressed on all, at conferences and other times, both by Sir Douglas Haig and General Rawlinson – to use the words of the latter at a conference of corps commanders – that "nothing could exist at the conclusion of the bombardment in the area covered by it", and the infantry would only have to walk over and take possession.' He added, ironically: 'Much the same had been said by the commander of the German Fifth Army before the assault at Verdun.'

The defence of Verdun was still in progress after more than four months of brutally hard fighting.

It was because of this confidence among the British High Command that the attacking troops were instructed not to rush, lightly armed, for the enemy lines; instead, in line abreast, heavily loaded with the necessary equipment for occupying the presumed-to-be empty German trenches, they would march across No Man's Land when the whistle blew for zero hour as if on parade. Commanders at all levels passed on the reassuring deductions of their superiors to the waiting troops. Expressing what was probably a widespread attitude, Corporal Arthur Hubbard of the London Scottish, in the 56th London Division opposite Gommecourt, had written home before the bombardment had begun: 'I hope the battle doesn't come off myself, if it does I am sure our artillery will give them a nice time before we arrive over in their trenches. I don't suppose we shall find many of them stay behind to tackle us.'

Yet undoubtedly there were those who, even if they kept their thoughts to themselves, doubted whether it would all be quite so easy. Rifleman Percy Jones, Queen's Westminster Rifles, also part of the 56th (London) Division at Gommecourt preparing to take part in the diversionary attack at Gommecourt, noted in his diary on 26 June:

> General Snow and his staff are busy telling us that we shall have practically no casualties because all the Germans will have been killed by our artillery barrage. This is nothing like the truth! The

fact is that this attack is based entirely on the supposition that there will be no Germans left alive to oppose us. On paper the plans are A1, but if the Germans obstinately refuse to die and make way for us, our scheme will become impractical.

The men keep very cheerful, and spend most of the time in heated arguments over the details of the attack, waving maps in each other's faces, and drawing fresh diagrams on the room walls with their bayonets. As I have already mentioned we mostly hold the view that the plans have been based entirely on the supposition that our artillery barrage will have killed all the Germans within about three miles of Gommecourt. We know, however, that the Germans have dugouts 40 feet deep, and I do not see how the stiffest bombardment is going to kill them all off. Nor do I see how the whole of the enemy's artillery is going to be silenced. Also, if we do get through Gommecourt Wood and the 46th Div have failed to meet us, we shall be left in the air, with open flanks – a most unenviable position. Still, our duty is plain enough – to go on until somebody stops us.

Nor were such doubts only the preserve of the lower ranks; commanding officers could also have their grave anxieties. One such was Lieutenant-Colonel E.T.F. Sandys of the 2nd Middlesex (see later in this chapter, page 60). Another was the newly promoted Lieutenant-Colonel E.K. Cordeaux, whose 10th Lincolns, a 'Pals' battalion known as the 'Grimsby Chums', were to attack in the vicinity of La Boisselle. He wrote on 27 June to his wife from his château headquarters at Bécordel: 'The noise is terrific. I wonder what the little fledgling swallows in their nest above my head think of it all; they will be deaf for the natural term of their lives. I wonder what the effect is on the Boche, well we shall soon know, but I am inclined to think their dugouts are too deep for him to have suffered much.'

There was, however, nothing that could be done, except to hope and pray: 'We are in God's hands and the road that he will have us travel may be beset with trials and much sorrow but it is the best for it is his choice. There will be millions of anxious hearts at home just now; I trust all may go well, we shall do our best.'

Elsewhere, confidence was high and, or so it seemed, with good reason. Also on the 27th, Captain McGowan told his parents of a visit he had made to his sector of the front – the extreme right of the line, next to the French – to see for himself how the Germans were getting on: 'They aren't half getting it hot. I had a peep at Montauban over the parapet today and could hardly recognize it. All familiar prominent features had disappeared. The artillery won't half be enjoying themselves. In fact everyone with time to spare chooses some point of observation to watch the target practice.'

Two days later he wrote in similarly upbeat mood: 'The intelligence reports which reach us from the line are most cheering. Our guns along the whole of the front appear to be doing excellent work. May they only have unlimited ammunition to continue and the task of the infantry will not be a hopeless one, quite the reverse.'

There were important factors supporting McGowan's confidence. One was that 30th Division, like its neighbour, Maxse's 18th, was prepared to make its own dispositions in the matter of the method of attack. As has been stated (see page 30), Maxse's troops would go forward through Russian saps in the opening advance; they would not be part of the fatal ceremonial parade across No Man's Land which pertained in so many other sectors. Moreover, at the time of the attack the barrage in this sector would be most intelligently employed; it would, arguably, be the first use by the British of a 'creeping' barrage – that is, one that advanced at a carefully pre-arranged pace so that the infantry could follow behind a moving curtain of fire. The author, or rather the adapter, of this concept was a Major Alan Brooke, Brigade-Major, Royal Artillery, in 18th Division. He took the idea from a French Colonel Herring whom he had escorted round the 18th Division sector in March, and developed it into a system supported by clear maps and fire orders which was applied successfully on 1 July and later became standard practice. This officer had a striking future ahead of him as Lord Alanbrooke, Chief of the Imperial General Staff in the Second World War.

* * *

Here and there were men who, as the ordeal approached, felt they simply could not cope. Writing on 29 July Corporal Arthur Hubbard of the London Scottish in 56th Division opposite Gommecourt reported a case which he had witnessed of a self-inflicted wound:

> I was 20 yards from one of the Kensingtons, 13th London Regiment, last week, when he shot himself through the foot just to get back to England out of it. Of course, he will get about 84 days field punishment after the wound has healed up. I went over and fetched assistance to him and extracted the empty case out of his rifle, what a feeling he will have later on if it takes a long time to heal up, and to know he had done it himself, but still he is not the only one that has done likewise.

* * *

Lieutenant Billy Lipscomb, whose 1st Dorsets were just to the south of Thiepval, was now in a mood of high elation. He wrote to Vera on 25 June:

> By the time you get this you will know by the papers what is going on here I expect. I hope the British Army is off this time for good. At present from our cornfield we can see nothing but huge clouds of smoke on the ridges – we have been letting them have it for two days without a moment's pause and haven't finished yet. If I get through this there *will* be some letters to write.
>
> Anyhow we are all delighted it's coming at last – pray we roll the Hun up. I don't think there is any military secret in all this – the Hun *knows* all about the bombardment, he ought to, he's getting it in the neck.
>
> Lordy, it is a sight at night.
>
> Times worth living in, Vera.

When Captain Bill Bland, opposite Mametz, wrote to his wife on 26 June, he was still in his usual breezy mood, and, it would seem, no longer concealing his exuberance from his colleagues with the great day so near:

> It's a marvellous war, with these thousands of miles of Trench system. If only we can smash it all in, and get out in the open, the war might suddenly collapse this year. I am afraid this is too optimistic, though at the present time I am *outwardly* blatantly optimistic. The true English spirit of deliberate self-depression and self-deprecation has to be countered.

We are all a most happy family, everybody doing his best to help everybody else, none of us expecting too much, but all ready to do our part of the job, minimising the obstacles to the men, but considering them carefully enough in our thoughts and conversation.

By the time this reaches you, the sun ought to be rising a fraction earlier upon us – a new vista, one hopes, fresh woods and pastures new, a slaughtered dragon, a monster laid low. Our Manchester lads are in good form today, burnt brown, eager and keen. I love 'em.

Three days later, however, on 29 June he wrote a letter in which perhaps for the first time one can see the hint of a question, of an alternative viewpoint: a hope for high success, but the hope too that it might not be required of him to drink the ultimate cup in gaining it: 'You say you have passed through *your* Gethsemane. You are always more and more wonderful to me. I am not so resigned. The conflict between communal duty and individual desire is never absolutely at rest in my heart. I want *both all* the time.'

But there was also an acceptance that this could be a final farewell: 'Give my lads such a lot of hugs from me and thank them for their dear long letters, which are beautifully written and spelt. God bless *you*.'

By contrast, Captain Charlie May had now fully prepared himself for battle, and writing on the same day could state: 'We are all agog with expectancy, all quietly excited and strung to a pitch but unhesitatingly I record that our only anxiety is that we will do our job well. That is but natural. This is the greatest thing the battalion or any of us have ever been in.'

Lieutenant-General Hunter-Weston chose 29 June to address the members of Brigadier-General Rees's 94th Brigade, poised to attack opposite Serre. 'It was a magnificent speech,' the latter wrote of the occasion, 'and obviously strongly impressed the men. As far as the men were concerned, they were convinced they could beat any number of Germans, and, if they had had a chance, I have no doubt they would have done so. We had been informed on several occasions that the enemy had only 55 guns north of the Ancre, a statement about which I was a trifle sceptical at the time; my scepticism was fully justified as the enemy were reported on the 3rd of July to have no less than 66 batteries in action behind Serre alone.'

For the moment, the British troops were more aware of their own guns' performance than of the potential threat from the enemy's. 'Day cloudy and showery, bombardment continues,' wrote Sergeant McKay of the 36th (Ulster) Division opposite Thiepval, also under the date 29 June, beginning a vivid description of the awesome battering being carried out by the British artillery on the German defences with the courageous assistance of airmen of the Royal Flying Corps:

> Our aeroplanes scouting over the German lines all day and flying very low. As one watched, an aeroplane would fly back over our own lines, a signal would be dropped to the artillery and a salvo of shells would fall on some particular part of the enemy's line. As many as nineteen shells bursting at one time could be counted on a stretch of about 500 yards front. On some point a very heavy shell would burst, and a column made up of earth, stones, water and perhaps part of a machine-gun emplacement or barbed wire entanglements was projected into the air to a height of sixty or seventy feet. Smaller columns were rising and falling on all the enemy's line under observation, and the whole side of Thiepval Wood resembles a district of hot springs or innumerable miniature volcanoes.

Major Walter Vignoles, second-in-command of the Grimsby Chums, found the effect of the bombardment on the German lines not so much menacing as curiously beautiful. He wrote to his wife on 29 June: 'The enemy's trenches look very pretty sometimes in the sunlight, our shells bursting over them in yellow, black or white puffs, many of the trenches covered with a bright yellow weed, while between the heavy white lines of chalk marking the principal trenches, there are frequently large fields of brilliant scarlet poppies.'

Like his commanding officer, he had been concerned about the fate of the swallows in the battalion's Bécordel headquarters, but now felt sure that they would survive: 'The swallows' anxieties over their families will soon be over: one family got on the wing yesterday, and one sweet little fellow was picked up by one of the men; I suppose he was tired. Anyway he flew away as soon as he was released.'

* * *

Over the four days before the assault raiding parties from Major-General Maxse's 18th (Eastern) Division penetrated enemy lines to see what damage had been done to their front trenches and wire by the bombardment, to capture prisoners and 'procure identifications'. These operations met with varying success, as Maxse would later describe: 'In some places the raiding parties penetrated to the support line and even further before meeting any enemy, while in others the parties were held up at the front line and could get no further, but, on the whole, much valuable information was brought back as a result of four successful night raids, two of which spent a couple of hours exploring the enemy's trenches.

About 8 p.m. on 29 June, 8th Company, 6th Bavarian Infantry Regiment, received orders to relieve troops of the 62nd Infantry Regiment in the front line in the vicinity of Montauban. Commanding no 3 Platoon was Leutnant Josef Busl. On the previous night, according to his account in the Regiment's official history, he had 're-established communications with the front line by means of a patrol and under the heaviest artillery fire.' The situation was no better on the 29th–30th as, after receiving provisions in the quarry at Montauban, they moved slowly forward: 'The company reached the position at 5.30 a.m. after an extremely exhausting march through heavy artillery and M.G. fire. This had been hit by constant fire, and the trenches were in places demolished, the sniper posts being scarcely of any use. The platoon had use of only 3–4 dugouts.'

The Bavarians were not, however, for giving up in such circumstances: 'Although our men were exhausted due to the continuous overexertions and privations, the necessary clear-up started immediately. On the evening of the 30th another dugout was crushed with the loss of eight men. As far as rations were concerned only coffee could be fetched owing to the constant heavy fire.'

It is an intriguing thought that some of Maxse's raiders going east and Busl's party making its way west must have been very close in these last hours before the opening attack.

* * *

Friday, 30 June: the battle would begin on the following morning, 1 July, at 7.30 a.m. Along an eighteen-mile front the attacking battalions of the British Fourth and Third Armies would go 'over the top' in accordance with the master plan.

Everywhere those assigned to taking part in the attack prepared themselves for action. This was what they had looked forward to and trained for, but the prospect, now that it was immediate, was daunting. For some it was too much; Lieutenant-Colonel Fife of the 7th Green Howards, noted in his account of the day: 'An officer's servant of C Company found to be drunk, having got hold of some rum. Provost-Sergt stowed him away in a small dugout, into which he was thrust head first, like the dormouse into the teapot. The entrance was then closed with sandbags!'

On a more elevated note, many who had not written pre-battle letters previously felt the need to do so. One officer wrote one – full of high sentiment and and heroic abnegation – which would be published, anonymously, in a newspaper in Britain before July was out. (From his reference to the loss of forty years, it would seem he was aged thirty, adding up to the standard three score years and ten.) Like Second Lieutenant Ellenberger's already quoted, it caught the romantic-cum-sacrificial mood common to many young officers, and doubtless some men, at this time:

I am writing this letter to you just before going into action tomorrow morning about dawn.

I am about to take part in the biggest battle that has yet been fought in France, and one which ought to help to end the war very quickly.

I never felt more confident or cheerful in my life before, and would not miss the attack for anything on earth. The men are in splendid form, and every officer and man is more happy and cheerful than I have ever seen them. I have just been playing a rag game of football in which the umpire had a revolver and a whistle.

My idea in writing this letter is in case I am one of the 'costs', and get killed. I do not expect to be, but such things have happened, and are always possible.

It is impossible to fear death out here when one is no longer an individual, but a member of a regiment and of an army. To be killed means nothing to me, and it is only you who suffer for it; you really pay the cost.

I have been looking at the stars, and thinking what an immense distance they are away. What an insignificant thing the loss of, say, 40 years of life is compared with them! It scarcely seems worth talking about.

Well, goodbye, you darlings. Try not to worry about it, and remember that we shall meet again really quite soon.

This letter is going to be posted if . . . Lots of love

From your loving son.

In the event the 'if' was to become a reality, and the letter would be published, like so many others, as a gesture of family commemoration.

By contrast, opposite Gommecourt Rifleman Percy Jones devised a letter which showed a similar concern for his family but from which he deliberately excluded all high-flown emotion. He copied it into his diary at the end of an entry more concerned with his pre-battle musings than with the activities of the day. Earlier, in March, before moving to the Somme, he had written warmly of some of the young lads of the company, singling out for particular praise one Billy Green: 'Billy Green is only eighteen, but he has more heart than many a full-grown man. No matter how much water there may be in the trenches, or how many shells drop on the ration party, you can always hear Billy's laugh. Life in mud and water is apt to get on anyone's nerves, but there is always something to smile at if Billy is about. I remember Newnham once saying to me at Ypres, "If anything happens to that boy, I really don't know how I shall keep going." And so say all of us.'

Now once again he expressed the hope that, whatever took place, Billy Green might be spared; Green seems to have become, and not for Jones alone, a symbol of the best of new British youth:

30th June, 1916

We met in the little café last night and sang the old songs, perhaps for the last time. We are good friends, true friends, because the trials of trench life have made us know one another, because we have held money, food, shelter and clothing in common and shared all that we have had. We hope to meet again in a day or two, but it is quite plain that in the meantime, some of us will have 'gone west'. You cannot have an omelette without breaking eggs, and we shall not take Gommecourt Wood without taking lives. Who will go? Who can say? I have only one wish: that nothing may happen to Billy Green. He is only eighteen, he is always cheerful, he can always make others cheerful, and that is the sort of man we want in the trenches.

After careful consideration I have written the following letter, which, while I hope it will not alarm anyone at home in the event of all going well with me, will, if the worst happens, let them know I thought of them to the last.

'We have marched up to the little village of St. Armend, about three miles from the trenches. Here we are billeted in a ruined house, which a 12 inch gun in the back garden shakes every time it fires.

'I received the books, for which many thanks. Now that I am on this subject, I take the opportunity of thanking you very much indeed for all the books and parcels you have sent while I have been out here, and for the long and frequent letters I have received. Perhaps you people at home don't know what letters mean to a man in the trenches, but I can assure you that correspondents such as I have had make life out here 100% better. I am afraid I have been rather slack in answering letters, so when you meet any of my friends, please apologize for me and say that I know I have always had better pals than I deserved. Goodbye and good luck to all.'

Also on 30 June Captain Bland sent a brief message to his wife: 'My darling. All my love for ever. Alfred.' Enclosed with the note was a pressed flower – a forget-me-not.

* * *

Captain May's last before-battle message was yet to come; he would write it the following morning. But on the evening of the 30th he sought out his closest friend in the battalion, the adjutant, Captain F.J. Earles, and told him that he had a strong presentiment that he might not come through the next day's attack. If that were the case, he asked him, would he look after his wife and child? Earles assured his friend that he would do all he could to answer his request.

For another young married officer, Lieutenant Alfred Bundy, 30 June was only his third day at the front. He had arrived in France as

recently as 15 June, had passed several days of monotonous training
at the 'Bullring' at Etaples and on the 28th began a nineteen-hour
train journey via Calais, Dunkirk and Béthune which finally depos-
ited him at Albert at 8 p.m. After a meal in a YMCA hut, which he
pronounced 'excellent', he and several other officers were taken by
transport wagon to the battalion headquarters of the 2nd Middlesex.
'Arrived 11 p.m.,' he noted in his diary, adding: 'Shell fire terrific.
Understand we're for it. Am told our attack starts tomorrow.
Strangely enough, I'm not a bit nervous.'

The 2nd Middlesex, in 8th Division, were almost at the very centre
of the British front, at La Boisselle. They were due to make their
attack across an exposed piece of No Man's Land nicknamed 'Mash'
Valley (in deference to a nearby sector known as 'Sausage', since the
Germans frequently had an observation or 'sausage' balloon overlooking it) where they would be advancing into a salient defended
by the enemy on three sides. The battalion CO, Lieutenant-Colonel
E.T.F. Sandys, had spent many hours since the bombardment began
in observing its effect on the German barbed wire, and had become
convinced that it was not being cut and that therefore his men would
be marching into almost certain disaster. He had passed his doubts
to his brigade commander but they had not been heeded, being
contrary to the optimistic mood mandated from the High Command.
He seems to have refrained from communicating his anxieties to
those around him because there was no hint of such apprehensions
in Bundy's account of 30 June, though he did report the cautious
views of one of his fellow officers. His description might have been
duplicated in any officers' dugout almost anywhere along the British
front line:

> Out at 4 a.m. to get a glimpse of scene. Bombardment still more
> intense but very little from German lines. Air full of acrid fumes,
> dawn stabbed in all directions by gun flashes. Very lights like a
> continuous firework display. Take tour of duty 5 a.m. and talk to
> men. We attack tomorrow but it is freely stated there will be no
> resistance. Our 'drum' fire has been going on for three or four days
> and the German lines appear to have been pulverized. Surely
> nothing can live there. Off duty 7. Hunt announces Zero at 5.30
> tomorrow and doesn't believe 'it will be so easy'. Laid down and

THE 'LEANING VIRGIN' OF NOTRE DAME DE BREBIÈRES

Left: Through an Albert window, September 1917.

Below: The 'Leaning Virgin' no more. The ruins of the Albert Basilica in August 1918.

CAPTAIN HAROLD YEO
(photographed as Lieutenant-Colonel), who, despite the heavy losses suffered in the first British attack on the Somme on 1 July 1916, wrote to his mother: 'The whole affair is a great success, and our sacrifices aren't going to be in vain.'

PRIVATE ARCHIE SURFLEET
who wrote when the battle was over: 'The very name of the Somme conjures up a picture of miserable wastes, mud and devastation. Surely no place could be more trying to patience, temper and comradeship.'

CAPTAIN A. E. 'BILL' BLAND   CAPTAIN C. C. 'CHARLIE' MAY

During the build-up to the battle, Bland wrote to his wife: 'If only you will have faith in the ultimate victory of the good, the true and the beautiful, you will not be unhappy even if I never return to you.' May wrote to his: 'I do not want to die. If it be that I am to go, I am ready. But the thought that I may never see you or our darling baby again turns my bowels to water. I cannot think of it with even the semblance of equanimity.' Both officers were killed on the first day.

PRIVATE ARTHUR WRENCH
who wrote in his diary in November 1916:
'It strikes me there is not much glory these days
in dying for your country.'

LIEUTENANT ALAN LLOYD

Killed in action on the second anniversary of the outbreak of war, 4 August 1916. The officer who was with him when he was fatally hit wrote to Lloyd's father: 'Your son was a very good soldier and a most valuable trained artilleryman. It is the prospect of meeting again his sort that makes one contemplate calmly one's own future in this War.' He is pictured here with his much loved motor-car, a 'D.F.P.', known to the family as 'Damn Fool Purchase'.

Below: Alan Lloyd *(left of frame)*, in civilian happiness – probably on a wartime leave – with the wife he married in September 1914, and whom he adored. His younger brother, Eric, later a distinguished doctor, is pictured right.

Left: The rough-hewn cross made by Lloyd's servant, Gunner Manning, for his first, temporary grave; still a prized possession in the Lloyd family.

Below: Photograph and burial details as sent to the family by the Director of Graves Registration. Lieutenant Lloyd's permanent headstone includes most of Gunner Manning's admiring epitaph, only leaving out the final words 'A True British Hero'.

Director of Graves Registration & Enquiries.

Begs to forward as requested a Photograph of the Grave of :—

Name *Lloyd. M. C.*

Rank and Initials *Lieut. A. S.*

Regiment *Royal Field Artillery*

Position of Grave *Dartmoor Cemetry.*

near Bécordel.

Nearest Railway Station *Bécordel,*

via Albert.

All communications respecting this Photograph should quote the number *(8/10513.)* and be addressed to:—

Director of Graves Registration and Enquiries,
War Office,
Winchester House,
London, S.W.

Owing to the circumstances in which the photographic work is carried on, the Director regrets that in some cases only rough Photographs can be obtained.

"COPYRIGHT FULLY RESERVED."

'THE HAPPY HERO'

The last letter of Second Lieutenant
Eric Lever Townsend, Civil Service Rifles,
died of wounds 16 September 1916;
privately published, price one shilling.
'We shall live for ever in the results of our
efforts. We shall live as those who by
their sacrifice won the Great War.'

THE
HAPPY
HERO

Written before Battle:
a young soldier's letter
to his parents.

ERIC·LEVER·TOWNSEND

Frontispiece to the booklet; a sketch portrait
of Second Lieutenant Townsend.

September 8, 1916.

DEAREST MOTHER AND
FATHER,

*You are reading this
letter because I have gone
under.*

*Of course I know you will
be terribly cut up, and that it
will be a long time before you
get over it, but get over it you
must. You must be imbued
with the spirit of the Navy
and the Army to "carry on."*

7

The first page of Second Lieutenant
Townsend's letter.

LIEUTENANT GEOFFREY FILDES

who felt his fear evaporate when finally he went 'over the top' in late September, 1916. 'With a sort of gasp I became a man again. As soon as I began to move I felt my horrible mid-day nightmare slipping from my mind . . . Mortal men had gone through this before me, I reflected, so where they had gone would I follow with all my resolution.'

MAJOR-GENERAL SIR IVOR MAXSE

(photographed as a Lieutenant-General), commander of the highly successful 18th (Eastern) Division on the Somme. 'The system in the Division is to tell subordinates as much as possible of impending operations long before they occur . . . It is better to risk information leaking out through captured prisoners than to run the greater risk of ordering infantry over the parapet unacquainted with what they are expected to do or where they are to go.'

THE BROTHERS ROBINS

of the South African Infantry Brigade; Private Willie Robins, killed in action 23 March 1918, aged 21. Private Percy Robins, killed in action 12 April 1917, aged 19. Frontispiece to the bound typescript of their letters home.

slept till 10 a.m. then excellent breakfast of bacon and coffee. Left letter for Kitty with Quartermaster for posting if anything happens to me.

Bundy seems to have approached the final hours with a certain philosophical calm, but for many they were the worst part – or so it seemed. Waiting, moving forward through the night, anxious questions being asked about the passage of time, thoughts of the past racing through the mind, of the people at home, fears for the future, hope against hope that the promised success would be delivered, that all would be well, that there would be no shell or bullet with one's number on it. 'Blighty or death' was one soldier's alternatives for the day to come, while, writing in his Regimental Aid Post in the Ancre valley, Sergeant McKay noted that 'tension in the cellar was high during the night. An occasional man slept, but this was rare and, although most of the men were awake, there was more or less silence in the cellar which was most unusual.' Sometimes, however, the silence was broken incongruously by voices with more than a hint of bravado, such as those heard on the 56th Division front at Gommecourt by a young private of the 1/7th Middlesex, A.L. Atkins. He would later write:

> On the night of 30th June our battalion was moved back a little way into reserve trenches and another battalion took our place in the front line ready to go over the top at dawn next day. As they passed us on their way to take up their positions, they were all lustily singing a sentimental song of the period, which was not only pathetic but, as it transpired, was also prophetic. It went thus:
>
> > Break the news to Mother, tell her there is no other.
> > Tell her not to wait for me for I'm not coming home.
>
> In the case of most of them, how true that turned out to be! Since then, to hear that song again has always brought a lump to my throat.

* * *

At last dawn broke across the Somme front, with just a hint of mist in the valleys and the prospect of a fine summer's day to come. The weather would later be described by Second Lieutenant Siegfried

Sassoon, brave soldier and among the most famous of war poets, as 'of the kind commonly called heavenly'. One soldier writing sixty years after the event expressed his thoughts thus: 'It was really a pity to have a war on July 1st, for in all my time in France it was the most beautiful day we had. The sky was cloudless and the sun shone. The skylarks were singing as they flew heavenwards, and unknown to them thousands of our soldiers were on their way there too.'

Some days previously, Second Lieutenant Charles Carrington, then acting adjutant of the 1/5th Battalion, Royal Warwickshire Regiment, 48th (South Midland) Division, who were in the gap between the Third and Fourth Armies, had said to his CO while conversing in the mess, 'I wonder what this battle will be called in history.' 'The Battle of the Somme, I suppose', the Colonel had promptly replied. 'Why, I don't know,' the young officer had mused, 'for the Somme was twenty miles away.' History shows that the Colonel's hunch was a correct one.

CHAPTER FOUR

THE FIRST DAY:
THE FOURTH ARMY FRONT

Am just going to try and write a few impressions of my first big engagement, for we're within a very few minutes of what is to be the beginning of the end of German culture.

WITH THIS SENTENCE Lieutenant E. Russell-Jones, commander of the 30th Division Trench Mortar Battery, in front of Maricourt, at the junction between the French and British sectors, began the one-day diary which he kept during the morning and early afternoon of 1 July 1916. He felt reasonably confident of success, though he also had serious anxieties about his own capacity to cope with the baptism of fire to come:

> For seven whole days our guns have been pounding the enemy's line, and now on the early morning of the eighth day, the attack is about to take place.
>
> Our little battery has done its share in preparing the way for the infantry. Most days we have fired with excellent results, though I'm sorry to say not without casualties to ourselves.
>
> We were up at 2 a.m. this morning and at 3.45 a.m. set off for our positions. Dawn was just breaking and a heavy mist hung over everywhere, shutting out any view of the lines. As we came up communication trenches there were hundreds of infantrymen lying about in all kinds of old corners, some even stretched out on the bare trench boards, sound asleep and sublimely unconscious to the sounds of war, which even at that early hour were making themselves heard. Just a few salvos from an 18 pndr battery, then some of our big guns, their shells sounding for all the world like an express train rounding a curve at top speed, now a battery of

those wonderful French guns the 75s opens fire and drowns everything in their uproar. We'd got close up to the trenches proper by this time and distant objects were coming into view. Right ahead could be seen the tall trees surrounding the village which we are to take today. An aeroplane could be heard buzzing away in the distance. Fritz tries several shots at him but they were all far away from their mark.

I'm sitting in a tiny little dugout which is just about splinter-proof but no more, surrounded by dozens of our bombs and ammunition boxes, waiting for the next 35 minutes to pass as quickly as it can, for at the end of that time we open fire and keep it up for 65 minutes, just to put the wind up Fritz before the assault.

War is a curious business, and very well for those who like it, but I must say I am no lover of the game. At the moment I feel pretty rotten and hate myself for it, for when one has such splendid fellows under one as I have, one feels one's deficiencies very much, but here we are and we've all got to see it through now, so all there is to do is to stick it to the end as well as possible.

A little over a mile to the west of Russell-Jones's 30th Division, on the 7th Division front facing Mametz, Captain Charlie May of the 22nd Manchesters was also at work on his diary; he found time to write a substantial entry in it that morning. Originally one of the most reluctant of soldiers, he had now so repressed or mastered his fears and questionings as to seem almost one of the most dedicated. At the least, he had convinced himself that he was not only ready, but even eager, for the attack to begin:

1.7.16. 5–45 am.
We marched up last night. The most exciting march imaginable. Guns all round us crashed and roared till sometimes it was quite impossible to hear oneself speak. It was, however, a fine sight and one realized from it what gun power really means. Fritz, of course, strafed back in reply causing us some uneasiness and a few casualties before ever we reached the line. The night passed noisily and with a few more casualties. The Hun puts a barrage on us every now and then and generally claims one or two victims.

It is a glorious morning and is now broad daylight. We go over in two hours time. It seems a long time to wait and I think, whatever happens, we shall all feel relieved once the line is launched. No Man's Land is a tangled desert. Unless one could see it one cannot imagine what a terrible state of disorder it is in. Our gunnery has wrecked that and his front-line trenches all right. But we do not yet seem to have stopped his machine-guns. These are pooping off all along our parapet as I write. I trust they will not claim too many of our lads before the day is over.

This is a significant as well as a poignant description in the light of what was to happen that day as at last, at 7.30 a.m., the long expected 'big push' began, for the German machine-guns would claim many victims over the following hours. But the first major moves were by the British as, in the words of Captain Harold Yeo of 9th King's Own Yorkshire Light Infantry, about 6 a.m. 'the final anger' – the last barrage before battle – 'broke out and the air just throbbed with sound.' This would increase in intensity and then at the last moment extend its range to focus on the German reserve line, thus allowing the attacking battalions to advance on the enemy's front-line trenches without fear of 'friendly fire' from their own guns.

The 9th KOYLIs were on 21st Division's front some two miles north of May's Manchesters. Yeo mingled with the men who were to take part in the attack, in which he himself was not to be involved, and found them 'very cheery, and wondering if another Minden Day would have to be added to the institutions of the regiment, for July 1st instead of August 1st' – a reference to an action in 1759 in which English, Hanoverian and Brunswick forces won a notable victory over Britain's present ally, the French.

'Just before the guns were to lift,' Yeo's account continues, 'our people began creeping out to the attack and the earth rocked with two enormous mine explosions, one on either flank only a short distance away.'

These were the so-called Lochnager mine near La Boisselle just to their north, and the Triple Tambour mine just south of them opposite Fricourt, which like the two other mines in this southern sector – Y Sap mine just north of La Boisselle and the Maxse's Kasino Point mine to their west between Mametz and Montauban – were fired at 7.28, two minutes before zero hour. This gave the attacker the opportunity to exploit the explosion while not allowing the defender

time to react. In the northern sector, however, between Beaumont
Hamel and Serre, the Hawthorn Ridge mine, by the decision of the
corps commander, Lieutenant-General Hunter-Weston, was fired at
7.20, thus giving the Germans ample time to make ready for the
advancing British. This error, for such it was, undoubtedly, was
compounded by the decision to lift the barrage from the German
front line at the same time. In this manner a mine seventy-five feet
deep, over 1000 feet long, and packed with 40,600 pounds of
ammonal, which the Royal Engineers' 252nd Tunnelling Company
had taken weeks of precise and dangerous work to construct, was
blown to much dramatic effect but to little practical purpose. On the
contrary, the Germans were given so much warning that the British
attack was about to be launched that at zero hour they were poised
and ready.

*   *   *

Promptly at 7.30 to the blowing of innumerable whistles by their
officers the assault troops rose from their advanced positions or
climbed from their trenches and set out across what Captain May
had aptly named the 'tangled desert' of No Man's Land. Captain
Yeo, in the letter already quoted, watched in admiration: 'And then
you saw the most wonderful sight imaginable: rows of steel-hatted
people with bayonets fixed going slowly forward, over the German
parapets and onwards. This was to be seen from where we were
(about 50 yards behind) with smoke and morning mist enveloping
them a short way ahead.'

'Going slowly forward'; the tactic of the slow walk across No
Man's Land to enemy trenches assumed to be empty of living
defenders was now to be put to the test. It was found to be wanting.
Within seconds, it seemed, the machine-guns whose destructive
capacity Captain May feared were pouring streams of bullets into the
advancing battalions. This, from F.L. Cassel's memoir, is the story of
the 1 July attack as seen through German eyes:

> More than a week we had lived with the deafening noise of the
> battle, and we knew that this went on not only in our sector but
> northwards almost as far as Arras and southwards as far as Péronne.

Dull and apathetic we were lying in our dugouts, secluded from life but prepared to defend ourselves whatever the cost.

On 1 July, at 7.30 am, the shout of the sentry 'They are coming!' tore me out of apathy. Helmet, belt, rifle and up the steps. On the steps something white and bloody, in the trench a headless body. The sentry had lost his life by a last shell, before the fire was directed to the rear, and had paid for his vigilance with his life. We rushed to the ramparts, there they come, the khaki-yellows, they are not more than twenty metres in front of our trench. They advance fully equipped slowly to march across our bodies into the open country. But no boys, we are still alive, the moles come out of their holes. Machine-gun fire tears holes in their rows. They discover our presence, throw themselves on the ground, now a mass of craters, welcomed by hand-grenades and gun fire, and have now to sell their lives themselves.

For the German medical officer, Stephen Westman, this was his memory of the day:

On the morning of July 1st the British gunners directed their fire on our rear positions and their armies went over the top in solid formations ... They did not expect anybody on the other side to have survived the bombardment. But German machine-gunners and infantrymen crawled out of their holes, with inflamed and sunken eyes, their faces blackened by fire and their uniforms splashed with the blood of their wounded comrades. It was a kind of relief to be able to come out, even into air still filled with smoke and the smell of cordite. They started firing furiously, and the British had frightful losses. Their advance, on our part of the front, was not more than a mile or so, and then the whole mighty offensive came to a halt. The British and French generals had not yet learned that it was useless to let human beings run against machine-gun and intense infantry fire, even after 'softening up'.

For those observing from the British side there were sights which would impress themselves indelibly on the memory. The anonymous author of a manuscript account of the part played in the Great War by the 1/1st Welsh Heavy Battery (Territorial Force) wrote this about the opening attack on the Somme:

Thousands went down that day. I saw from my Post the first wave of troops scrambling out of their Trenches, in the early morning sunlight. I saw them advancing rapidly led by an officer, the officer reached a hillock holding his sword on high. Flashing it in the sunlight, he waved and sagged to the ground. His men undaunted swept up the mound to be mown down on reaching the skyline, like autumn corn before the cutter. Their story belongs to History, but I have witnessed their deeds with my own eyes, and the sights of that July morning will be ever before me.

* * *

For the 2nd Middlesex in Mash Valley on the front of 8th Division, 1 July proved a day of total disaster, as the tragic scenario feared by their commanding officer duly came to pass. Their task that morning was to cross a vast stretch of No Man's Land overlooked by the enemy on three sides, at the end of which, should they get that far, they would almost certainly find themselves confronted by uncut barbed wire. The newly arrived Lieutenant Alfred Bundy was one of few officers of the battalion to survive unhurt at the end of their hopeless attack; shortly afterwards he wrote this account of the course of events:

Went over top at 7.30 a.m. after what seemed an interminable period of terrible apprehension. Our artillery seemed to increase in intensity and the German guns opened up on No Man's Land. The din was deafening, the fumes choking and visibility limited owing to the dust and clouds caused by exploding shells. It was a veritable inferno. I was momentarily expecting to be blown to pieces. My platoon continued to advance in good order without many casualties and until we had reached nearly half way to the Boche front line. I saw no sign of life there. Suddenly however an appalling rifle and machine-gun fire opened against us and my men commenced to fall. I shouted 'down' but most of those that were still not hit had already taken what cover they could find. I dropped in a shell hole and occasionally attempted to move to my right and left but bullets were forming an impenetrable barrier and exposure of the head meant certain death. None of our men was visible but in all directions came pitiful groans and cries of pain.

I began to suffer thirst for my water bottle had been pierced with a bullet. After what seemed hours of waiting I was almost tempted to take a chance and crawl back in daylight. I was dreading the dark for I thought I should lose my sense of direction in my distraught condition. I finally decided to wait till dusk and about 9.30 I started to crawl flat on my stomach. At times I made short wild dashes and finally came to our wire. The Boche were still traversing our front line trenches and as I lay waiting for strength to rush the final few yards sparks flew from the wire continuously as it was struck by bullets. At last the firing ceased and after tearing my clothes and flesh on the wire I reached the parapet and fell over into our trench now full of dead and wounded. I found a few of my men but the majority were still out and most were dead. Came across my Company Commander Hunt who was almost insane. Took charge of 'C' Company of about 30 men!

The 2nd Middlesex casualty figures for 1 July were 23 officers and 517 men, a total of 540. There would be one other linked fatality some weeks later, when the battalion's commanding officer, Lieutenant-Colonel E.T.F. Sandys, bitterly remorseful as to his failure to do more on behalf of his men, committed suicide in a London hotel.

* * *

To the north of 8th Division, facing Thiepval village, was 32nd Division, among its constituent units the 1st Dorsets, the battalion of Lieutenant Billy Lipscomb. They were among the many battalions which lost a commanding officer that day, their Lieutenant-Colonel J.V. Shute being wounded in the course of the morning so that their second-in-command had to come hurrying up from battalion headquarters to take over. Next day Lipscomb wrote a letter to his friend Vera which did not quite reflect the full picture of events: 'As it will soon be published I think I can tell you that we've lost 20 officers (nearly all wounded) on the first day, other ranks 500 out of 800 – bad luck isn't it? Know nothing of what has happened but hear other divisions have done well and got right through.'

But two days later when he wrote a second letter he had had time to get a wider perspective on what had happened and – not to put too fine a point on it – he was angry:

Well, they've taken us out of it for a bit and we expect to be away for a bit until we get drafts up and re-form. I'm back with the battalion and am looking after a Coy – at present it numbers 70 instead of 250 or so, but it will be made up shortly. When we meet don't mention the word 'Staff' to me or I shall be ill. Somebody ought to be hung for this show, and the day following was the most utterly futile I've ever seen. The chief fault is that the General Staff sit behind and look at maps of trenches and say 'if that is taken so and so will happen', but it doesn't, for trenches are impossible things to judge from maps – oh there's a host of things one could talk about on this theme . . .

I suppose they could court-martial me for criticism of superior officers, but I don't care if they do – we've only got about 4 of the officers left who were with us when I joined and all the rest are just out and not very good.

This is a rotten letter but we are naturally a bit 'down' at present, though of course this is only a local setback and we can't expect to overrun a Boche line when he has had 18 months to fortify it and *has* fortified it too.

To the north of 8th Division, however, attacking to the left of Thiepval, the 36th (Ulster) Division, succeeding where numerous other divisions failed, penetrated deep into enemy territory. Their leading battalions found the wire well cut and they pushed through to the German reserve trench some 500 yards beyond a formidable system of trenches – a veritable bastion in the German line – known as the Schwaben Redoubt, achieving a brilliant advance of nearly a mile. This was the most dramatic advance in the northern half of the British attack. Unfortunately, the inability of other divisions to keep up with them against the unexpectedly fierce German retaliation, together with the fact that as the day wore on they were in increasing risk of running out of bombs and small-arms ammunition, meant that they had no alternative but to relinquish the ground gained. Their success did not prevent them from acquiring a massive list of casualties, indeed one so enormous that the sense of loss engendered on 1 July 1916 would leave a permanent scar on the psyche of the province. The diary of the Field Ambulance Sergeant, Robert McKay, provides a vivid commentary of the course of events:

The 11th, 13th, 8th, 9th, 10th, 15th and 14th Royal Irish Rifles along with the 9th, 10th and 11th Inniskilling Fusiliers carried all before them, though they had suffered terribly in the assault trenches. These troops penetrated into the enemy's third line. Some even managed to reach the fourth line. All these, however, were under enfilade fire from the trenches untaken at Beaumont Hamel. Twelve men with an officer found themselves in a portion of the third line, the Germans being on their right and left flanks. They held on until our troops again swept forward, but by then only five of the twelve remained and these were all wounded. When our men entered the enemy's trenches many of them surrendered, and after 12 o'clock noon from Hamel we could see prisoners racing across no man's land under heavy fire from their own guns. At first it appeared as if the enemy were counter-attacking, but it soon became obvious that none of the Germans were carrying arms. Had our reinforcements been up at this time, the infantry would have had little difficulty in taking the enemy fourth line.

McKay's concern was with the plight of the wounded and he and his comrades were soon heavily engaged: 'Men were continually crawling in out of no man's land and dropping into the trench.' More and more came in throughout the day, for if the initial German response was severe, it was if anything even more destructive as the hours went by: 'From 2 o'clock p.m., the Germans rained shells of every description on the ground they had lost, and also on Thiepval Wood and our communication trenches – whizz-bangs, high explosives, five-nines, tear shells and stink shells of all kinds. The stretcher-bearers were working in shirt and trousers, tunics being discarded. The smell of the stink shells was nauseous, and as one of our men said "The Germans were throwing over everything but shite".'

* * *

If Cassel and his comrades at Thiepval had seconds in which to bring their machine-guns into operation, at Hawthorn Ridge near Beaumont Hamel their fellow countrymen had had ten minutes, following the premature explosion of the mine. They had made good use of that time and were well prepared when the whistles blew in the British front line and the tiny figures began to appear en masse in

No Man's Land. 'Ahead of us,' wrote the historian of one of the German regiments involved, 'wave after wave of British troops were crawling out of their trenches and coming towards us at a walk, their bayonets glistening in the sun.' The troops in their sights were the 2nd Royal Fusiliers and the 16th Middlesex, who would respectively lose 561 and 522 in casualties out of, in each case, an attacking force of approximately 800.

This sector later was the setting for one of the most tragic events of the day, the virtual annihilation of the one battalion of the then colony of Newfoundland. Sent into action as part of a second wave attack by 29th Division that was doomed before it began, the 1st Newfoundland Regiment lost twenty-six officers and 658 men, a total of 684: a figure exceeded only in the case of one other unit, the 10th West Yorks of the 17th (Northern) Division.

To the north of the Hawthorn Ridge, still in the area alerted by the mine explosion at 7.20, two Territorial battalions of the 48th (South Midland) Division – attached for the attack to 4th Division – advanced at zero hour along the line of the Serre road, to emerge from the day with extremely high losses, if not quite so high as in the case of the battalions just named. These were the 1/8th and 1/6th Battalions of the Royal Warwickshire Regiment; between them their casualty list would run to 1,060 names, of which 588 were members of the 1/8th. Both battalions lost their commanding officers, Lieutenant-Colonel Innes of the 8th being killed while Lieutenant-Colonel Franklin of the 6th was wounded. The following is from the diary account of the day by Private Sidney Williamson of the 1/8th battalion. One famous saying in relation to the numerous Pals battalions who suffered badly on 1 July was that they were two years in the making and ten minutes in the destroying. This could also have been said of 1/8th Warwicks:

> It was a lovely bright morning, but the feelings of the men were tense. We had breakfast at 5.0 a.m., afterwards the officers were going round to see all the men and have a talk with us. The shelling was terrific and the Germans started to shell our lines. At 7.20 a mine was exploded under the German trenches. An officer detailed me and another soldier standing by me to carry forward with us a box containing a signalling lamp. At 7.30 a.m. whistles were blown

and the attack started. What did I see! To the left as far as Gommecourt and to the right as far as Beaumont Hamel, lines of soldiers going forward as though on parade in line formation. Just 'over the top' the soldier helping me with the box stopped and fell dead. I had to go on but without the box. Lt Jones was the next officer I saw to fall, then CSM Haines was calling for me, he had been wounded. I reached the first German line and dropped into it where there were many German dead. The battlefield was nothing but shell holes and barbed wire, but now I noticed many dead and dying, and the lines of soldiers was not to be seen. With no officers or NCO near I felt alone and still went forward from shell hole to shell hole. Later Cpl Beard joined me and he asked me to hold down a ground signalling sheet so that he could get a message to the observing aeroplane flying overhead. He asked for 'MORE BOMBS' and the Pilot of the aeroplane asked 'Code please'. This was flashed back and the aeroplane flew away.

Things were now getting disorganised and at this point we could not go any further. The machine-gun fire was deadly. And our bombs had all been used up. The Colonel of the Seaforths came up and took charge of all the odd groups of men belonging to various Regiments. He told us to dig ourselves in and eventually there must have been 50 or 60 men at this spot, and it all started from the one small shell hole Cpl Beard and myself were first in.

Now there was a lull in the fighting till 3.0 p.m. At one time a shout went up that we were surrounded by Germans, but they were Germans running from the dugouts in the first line and giving themselves up. I do not think they made it.

Williamson himself finally made his own escape from No Man's Land that evening: 'With Cpl Beard we started to get back to our lines shell hole by shell hole, but we soon got parted. I managed to reach the British lines at 7.30 p.m., but the sight that met my eyes was terrible. Hundreds of dead soldiers were everywhere, and the Germans kept up their heavy shelling. Met Sam and Bob Patterson in the trench, the only two of my own Battalion. Stayed in the British trench all night.'

* * *

Opposite Serre on the front held by the 31st Division Brigadier-General H.C. Rees, 500 yards behind the front line, had gone through various emotions as the attack of his brigade went in. The 94th Brigade consisted entirely of Pals battalions: the Accrington Pals, the Sheffield City Battalion, and the 1st and 2nd Barnsley Pals; other Pals battalions in the division included the Leeds, the 1st and 2nd Bradford, the Durham Pals and the Hull Commercials. In this sector the final bombardment had been much shorter and, as further south, British intentions had been announced by the early blowing of the Hawthorn Ridge mine less than a mile away. Rees's diary describes what he saw:

Ten minutes before zero our guns opened an intense fire. I stood on top to watch. It was magnificent. The trenches in front of Serre changed shape and dissolved minute by minute under the terrific hail of steel. Watching, I began to believe in the possibility of a great success, but I reckoned without the Hun artillery. This ten minutes intense bombardment combined with the explosion of twenty tons of dynamite under the Hawthorn Redoubt near Beaumont Hamel must have convinced any enemy observer that the attack was in progress and, as our infantry advanced, down came a perfect wall of explosives along the front trenches of my Brigade and the 93rd. It was the most frightful artillery display that I had seen up to that time and in some ways I think it was the heaviest barrage I have seen put down by the defence on any occasion.

At the time the barrage became really intense, the last waves of the attack were crossing the trench I was in. I have never seen a finer display of individual and collective bravery than the advance of that brigade. I never saw a man waver from the exact line prescribed for him. Each line disappeared in the thick cloud of dust and smoke which rapidly blotted out the whole area. I can safely pay a tribute also to the bravery of the enemy, whom I saw standing up in their trenches to fire their rifles in a storm of fire. They actually ran a machine-gun out into No Man's Land to help repel the attack.

I saw a few groups of our men through gaps in the smoke cloud, but I knew that no troops could hope to get through such a fire. My two staff officers, Piggott and Stirling, were considerably surprised when I stopped the advance of the rest of the machine-gun company and certain other small bodies now passing my Hqtrs. It was their first experience of a great battle and all that morning they obviously found it impossible to believe that the whole brigade had been destroyed as a fighting unit.

Later on, news came in of great successes further south, of the capture of Fricourt [this was not correct] and a great advance by the French, south of the Somme. This cheered us up a little. We reorganised the remnants of the Brigade to defend our own front line. The two leading battalions were annihilated and the two supporting battalions had lost heavily, but of some 2600 men who were launched to the attack, very few returned. I had only some 550 men left, as far as I could find out.

Rees's diary account lays no blame on his Corps Commander, but it is clear from his analysis that the fact that, as he had anticipated, the enemy could safely ignore the dead ground between the main and the diversionary attacks had been fully exploited, The Germans had taken advantage of the situation to make a special artillery effort in this sector. Rees paid credit to the 'skilful assembly of the enemy of a great mass of guns between Serre and Puisieux undetected by us and the concentration of all these guns on a comparatively small, but most important, stretch of front'. Elsewhere, he commented, the Germans had not put so much emphasis on their big guns. 'In front of Beaumont Hamel, on the lower ground, the hostile artillery fire was not excessively violent. On this frontage, the Huns reckoned on the stopping power of large numbers of machine-guns in concrete emplacements and his confidence was justified by events.'

* * *

What of the fate of other battalions whose stories have been featured in this narrative?

Lieutenant-Colonel Cordeaux's Grimsby Chums had had a disastrous day, having suffered heavily in their attack in Sausage Valley to the south of La Boisselle. Irregularity in the distance between the two front lines meant that they had further to go than the battalions on their right while being exposed to fire from three sides, in particular from a formidable German strong point known as 'Sausage

Redoubt', the northern face of which virtually flanked their advance. They had attacked with the 11th Suffolks following on but within two minutes of zero hour, before they had cleared their front trench, they had been raked by machine-gun fire. The Lincolnshires lost 15 officers and 462 other ranks, the Suffolk battalion 15 officers and 512 other ranks. An artillery officer who walked the ground later found 'line after line of dead men lying where they had fallen', indicating the discipline and steadiness with which they had advanced.

A tribute to the Chums' gallant but doomed performance has survived among the papers of one of the battalion's officers, Major C.H. Emerson, in the form of a letter sent to Colonel Cordeaux on 5 July by his brigade commander, Brigadier-General R.C. Gore (though it should be pointed out that Gore seems to have had an exaggerated picture of the battalion's actual achievement in the matter of the penetration of enemy lines). In terms that must have been matched many times in letters of condolence and encouragement following the great Somme attack, Gore wrote:

> Will you please express to your Battalion my admiration of their fearless conduct in the Battle on July 1st. Having to start further back than the two right Battalions they had to bear the brunt of the machine gun fire during their advance across the Sausage Valley. They never wavered but pressed forward, their ranks were too thin, as their casualties show, to gain their final objective though they got well into the German lines and assisted in holding for two days the exposed left flank which became the pivot of the successful advance of the Divisions on our right.
>
> No troops could have done better and it was no fault of theirs that they did not reach their allotted objective.

A letter of 2 July by Cordeaux's second-in-command, Major Walter Vignoles, offers a touch of light relief in an otherwise depressing story. He was wounded early in the action and had to withdraw to seek medical attention. On his way down he was ribbed by soldiers coming up to the line, with shouts of 'Wot Cheer matey! got a Blighty?' from a group of Tommies, while a sergeant called out, 'I see you're smilin' now you've got a Blighty'. (Having 'gone over' wearing a private's uniform with only his major's crown visible, he was taken for an ordinary soldier but made no objection.) As he went through Albert there was something else to gladden the heart: 'At a shop near the church, a man and his wife were giving drinks of lemonade to the wounded as they passed. I was very glad of it, as it was very hot, and I was beginning to feel the effect of the long walk. Everything was peaceful in Albert, though the guns were still at work, but I didn't notice them much.'

He made his way to a hospital, where his wound was dressed, and an orderly gave him a bowl of Bovril, and he was offered the inevitable, and welcome, cigarette.

* * *

What, meanwhile, of the 22nd Manchesters, and Captains Bland and May? The battalion had made substantial progress together with the 1st South Staffordshires, crossing No Man's Land – only 100–200 yards wide at their point of attack – and overrunning the German front line. However, severe machine-gun and rifle fire from Mametz village and a German communication trench known as Dantzig Alley inflicted heavy casualties on the companies as they moved on across more open ground. Nevertheless by 7.45 they had advanced about seven hundred yards and by 8 a.m. some of the Manchesters had reached a German point known as Bucket Trench not far short of their target, while the leaders of the Staffordshire regiment were entering Mametz. Sadly, however, the machine-guns which Captain May had reported as 'pooping along the parapet', in what proved to be his diary's final entry, *did* claim many members of the battalion, and May was among those who fell. Captain Bland was also killed that day. Sergeant R.H. Tawney's account of the attack provides what is almost certainly a glimpse of Bland that morning just before zero hour. 'My Captain,' he wrote, 'a brave man and a good officer, came along and borrowed a spare watch from me. It was the last time I saw him.' However different they had been in their attitudes to the challenge before them, Bland and May were united in their fate. Later they would share the same burial place, which would take its name from the communication trench from which so much lethal fire had poured on their battalion that morning – Dantzig Alley military cemetery, Mametz.

The 22nd Manchesters suffered almost 500 casualties that day; eighteen officers, of whom ten were killed, and 472 men, of whom 120 were killed and 241 wounded, while 111 were missing. The battalion 'ceased to exist in any recognizable form.' Tawney himself suffered a so-called Blighty wound; it was while recovering in England that he published the outspoken criticism of civilian attitudes already quoted (Foreword, page xxi).

Captain Bland's widow never remarried. Captain Earles in due time made good his promise to his friend Captain May and married his widow, Bessie, proving a genial step-father to May's much loved daughter, Pauline. Both Bland and May are still held in the highest regard by their families.

* * *

A battalion which came out of the opening offensive on the Somme with a remarkable story to tell was the 9th KOYLIs, 21st Division. It was their advance which had so moved their own officer, Captain Yeo, that for him it was 'the most wonderful sight imaginable'. It was their fine spirit after a day of some success but at very high cost which would inspire the eloquent description of a battalion after battle given pride of place in the Foreword to this book (Foreword page xxiv.)

Among those whom Captain Yeo saw advancing so splendidly towards the enemy were two junior officers of the battalion, Lieutenant B.L. Gordon and Second Lieutenant G.F. Ellenberger, both of whom would shortly provide memorable accounts of what happened after they disappeared into the enveloping mist and smoke. Their reports have perhaps a special value in that they show that the British were giving as well as taking that day, and that amid the inevitable, indeed literal, 'fog of war' there were numerous minor dramas as handfuls of men fought for advantage in small worlds of their own.

Gordon's account, written on 4 July, makes clear that the KOYLIs attacked from two starting-off points, with B and D companies advancing from the front-line, while A and C companies moved off from a 'Russian sap' of the kind favoured by Major-General Maxse. Gordon was with B company. A and C companies climbed out of their Russian sap at 7.25 and began to crawl forwards towards the German trench. This produced an immediate response from the Germans: 'Instantly the enemy put up a thick shrapnel barrage; most of the shells burst between our own front line and the Russian sap; but many fell short of the latter. At the same time his parapet became lined with machine-guns and riflemen. At 7.29 a.m. I led my wave forward from the front-line trench. There was no gas (we had used that on a previous day); but the smoke from the shells was as dense as a Scotch mist.'

One other interesting variation on the general pattern is evident from Gordon's account. If, as Yeo's description suggests, the KOYLIs began 'going slowly forward ... with bayonets fixed', they soon resorted to other means under the impact of enemy fire:

> The advance was by crawling and by rushes from shell hole to shell hole. The noise was deafening and the German machine-gun fire was terrible. Just before reaching the Russian sap, I was struck on the chin by a bit of shrapnel. When I reached the Sap, I lay down and looked into it. I saw the CO, Colonel Lynch, who said, 'Hullo, Gordon, are you hit?' I put up my hand to my chin, and found it was covered with blood. The Colonel then began to get out of the Sap. He was killed by a shell almost immediately afterwards. I crossed the Russian Sap, and pushed on. By this time our waves were jumbled together, and, owing to the smoke, it was difficult to keep direction.
>
> Advancing through the machine-gun fire and shrapnel barrage was hellish, and our losses were heavy. I passed poor Walker's body; he had been killed by a machine-gun, I think. I saw two Germans firing it over their parapet.
>
> After a few more minutes, which seemed ages, I reached the German front trench. Several 'B' Company men joined me, and I sat in a shell hole while one of them bandaged my chin, which was cut and bruised, and bleeding freely.

Despite his wound and the extreme anxieties and tension of the situation, Gordon was able to include in his report a clear description of the state of the German front line after a week of severe attention from the British artillery:

Although our bombardment had failed to knock out the enemy
machine-guns, its effect on the trenches had been very great. For
the most part, they were entirely knocked in – one long succession
of shell holes; brown craters mainly, for the soil is thick. Now and
then one came to an enormous white crater, caused, I believe, by
our trench mortars. These were 10 or 20 ft deep, and as many yards
across. In consequence they penetrated beneath the brown soil,
and threw up masses of the chalk which lies beneath.

In places one came to a bit of 'pukka' trench, almost untouched.
This was comparatively rare. The German machine-guns and
infantry must have been preserved owing to their deep dugouts.
These were numerous and elaborate, most of them 30 or 40 feet
below ground level, with two or three entrances. The enemy wire
entanglements had everywhere been completely destroyed by our
artillery.

Looking at his map while his chin was being bandaged, Gordon
realized that he had strayed to the right, towards Fricourt, into the
area of the Somerset Light Infantry. He therefore decided to switch
direction, and with about half a dozen of 'B' Company, one or two
Somersets and a Durham private (the 'Faithful Durhams', as he called
them, were in support to the KOYLIs), was crossing the tangle of
shell holes which marked the position of a former German trench,
when they found themselves in a flurry of action:

We suddenly came upon about a dozen Germans, about 10 or 12
yards off. They fired at us with rifles. I whipped out my revolver
and fired several rounds, and some of my men also fired. One of
the Germans dropped; and suddenly my 'Faithful Durham' rushed
forward shouting 'Come on boys, the ——s are on the run'. The
enemy would not face the bayonet. We captured the wounded
man, and one other, who threw down his rifle and held up his
hands; the rest fled. The prisoners belonged to the 111th (Reserve)
Bavarian Regiment. I led my party along what was left of the
trench, and soon came to the entrance of a deep dugout. Down this
I threw a Mills bomb; I heard a 'noise within', and heard groans,
and cries of 'Mercy!' I shouted 'Come out!' in English, and, after a
moment, a thin and haggard man, covered with blood, rushed out,
holding up his hands. Several of my men were about to stick him
with their bayonets, but he had been badly wounded in the face,

and was unarmed, so I stopped them. Seeing this, he tried to shake my hand, and said '*Kamerad*'. But I shook him off, and searched him. His terror was pitiable; he turned out his pockets for me, and gave me some papers and ammunition, which I threw away; and an electric torch, which I kept.

When he understood he was not to be killed, his gratitude was extraordinary. As I would not shake hands, he insisted on shaking hands with a Somerset, who, a few minutes before, had been about to bayonet him. He made me understand that there were more within; so I sent him down again, and he returned with six more, most of them wounded by the bombs. They were thin, unshaven and terrified; most had dark hair; a very different type from the Prussians. I had them searched and disarmed, and sent them to the rear. They ran off, holding up their hands. Three more, who were not too badly wounded, were left in the dugout. I saw many other prisoners going back about the same time.

Shortly after this I found that we had got back to our proper position, so I decided to push straight to the front. My party, with many others who had joined me, amongst whom the only officer was Ellenberger, of our battalion, then advanced across the open ground between the German front trenches and the Sunken Road, which runs between Fricourt and Contalmaison. The enemy shell fire was violent, and I remember this rush across the open only as a kind of nightmare.

Second Lieutenant Ellenberger had lived a charmed life that morning, or so it seemed to him when he wrote a long letter to his mother on 7 July. Having prepared (see pages 46–7) an eloquent 'last' letter to be sent to his family in the event of his death, he might well have felt on a number of occasions during the attack that doing so had been a wise precaution. 'When we had advanced about 20 yards into No Man's Land', he recalled, 'we were greeted by a hail of machine-gun and rifle bullets; the Boches had manned the parapet, and when we got near enough they also threw bombs at us: how it was I wasn't hit I don't know.' But then it was the KOYLIs' turn to create mayhem:

As soon as we reached his trench it was all up with the Hun; we had a regular running fight across his first system of trenches, which had been frightfully ploughed up by our artillery, making the going very difficult. The whole thing was so very fast and it was such hot work, that you hadn't time to sit and think over the horrors, but just went on and on, pursued by a decided but unexpressed feeling that you would sooner be anywhere but there.

The Huns ran, and we took a lot of prisoners; he has very unsporting ideas about fighting, has the Hun; he'll poop away his machine-gun at you, and he'll snipe at you, and he'll throw bombs at you, but as soon as you get to close quarters with the bayonet he puts up his hands and shouts 'Mercy, Kamerad!': how can you be expected to consider fighters of that description as 'comrades'?! I saw lots of Huns and lots of Hun rifles, and it's an absolute fact that none of them had a fixed bayonet – when it came to bayonet work they put up their hands; the bayonets we found afterwards down in their dugouts!!

After this running fight we reached, about 8 a.m. or soon after, the Sunken Road about 600 or 800 yards behind the German front line. There we stayed for a few hours, consolidating our position, while some of our troops went on another 200 or 300 yards and occupied Crucifix Trench.

The sunken road provided access to a striking component of the German defence system: an extremely large and well-furnished German dugout from which over forty Germans were extracted and subsequently sent back to the British lines as prisoners. Four wounded Germans were left in the dugout, with an unwounded man to look after them: 'We also used this dugout, which was a most palatial affair, to accommodate our own wounded. In this same dugout (which was about twenty feet below ground) we found quantities of stores – bread, cigars, cigarettes, chocolate, and some form of seltzer or soda water. There must have been a cartload of the latter commodity there, as it was being drunk by our troops, especially the wounded, all Saturday and Sunday night.'

At 1.30 Ellenberger with several others 'rushed forward' to Crucifix Trench, where Lieutenant Gordon was already installed. Having got there they had no option but to remain where they were and eke out the hours of daylight: 'We stayed there till late in the evening; we didn't have a very good time there, as we had nothing but Boches in front of us, and both of our flanks were in the air [i.e.

unsupported by other British troops]. However we held on there till the evening, when we were relieved and went back again to the Sunken Road.'

Gordon's account states that the relieving battalions, Lincolns and Green Howards, 'crossed the open in fine style' to relieve the KOYLIs in Crucifix Trench and that this manoeuvre 'stirred up the enemy into a particularly violent spell of shelling which lasted a long time, while the men took what cover they could.' At last the guns fell silent and at about 9.15 p.m. two officers of the battalion, who had remained behind at the transport lines during the attack, arrived at the Sunken Road, allowing Gordon to relinquish command of his curious little army.

One of the two officers who relieved Gordon was Lieutenant Lancelot Dykes Spicer. Having missed the action of the day through the rule that a core of officers should always be held back at such a time, he was able to gain a wider perspective than that of his heavily involved comrades. The battalion had suffered badly, in that not only its CO had been killed but also eleven other officers had lost their lives, half the number who had gone into action. Subsequently three more would die of wounds, while a further eight would be listed as wounded. Only one – Ellenberger – would be untouched. Profoundly moved by their fate, and by the deaths of so many of their men, Spicer wrote to his mother on 5 July: 'It was the most marvellous show I've ever seen or had anything to do with! If it wasn't for that our losses would be unbearable, for we have suffered, particularly in officers ... But they all died a magnificent death, and if they know, as I am sure they must do, what they have achieved by sacrificing their own lives, they would be perfectly satisfied.'

The fate of this many-talented battalion immortalized a story which has now become part of the folk-lore of the Somme. Its commanding officer, Colonel Lynch, had not been popular. On 28 June all officers had received a summons to Battalion Headquarters, for a final drink before going into action – at a time when everyone's thoughts were on that moment so soon to come when the guns would change targets from the enemy's first line to his second, thus leaving the stage to the advancing infantry. In the absence of the Adjutant and the Second-in-command, the Acting Adjutant approached the senior captain present, Captain G. Haswell, suggesting that he should propose a toast to the CO's health. Haswell refused, but after a moment's hesitation stepped forward and, raising his glass, said: 'Gentlemen, I give you the toast of the King's Own Yorkshire Light Infantry, and in particular the 9th Battalion of the Regiment'; then, after a slight pause: 'Gentlemen, when the barrage lifts ...' Describing the event, Spicer wrote: 'We emptied our glasses and were silent. Dramatically, Haswell had avoided an unpleasant scene, and the toast has never been forgotten.'

Captain Haswell was among those killed on 1 July. His moving words, however, lived after him. From 1921 until the 1980s they were quoted, under the name of the battalion, in the In Memoriam column of *The Times* on every 1 July.

* * *

Opposite Fricourt, not far from where the 9th KOYLIs went into action, Lieutenant-Colonel Fife and his 7th Green Howards of 50th Brigade, 17th (Northern) Division, had a day of troubled fortunes. They were not involved in the first wave but had orders to take part in a supplementary advance provisionally timed for 2.30. 'First phase of attack started punctually at 7.30 and seemed to be successful,' Fife noted in his diary, though watching and waiting also carried its price in that 'we had a good many casualties in trenches.' Sometime later, however, he received a report so startling that his first reaction was one of shocked incredulity: 'Soon after 9 I got a message from B company, in centre, to say that A Company on their right had assaulted at 8.20. I did not believe this but sent the Adjutant to find out. He reported that it was true. I could only account for this by supposing that Kent [Major Kent, commanding A Company] had gone mad. Later a report came from Wilkinson, saying that what was left of A Coy were lying out in front of our wire, waiting for our artillery to lift, that Kent and Tenney were wounded and that they were being heavily fired on by machine-guns and snipers.'

There seems to be no known explanation for the aberration of this premature one-company attack. The officer concerned was so badly wounded that he was immediately evacuated back to England. Some three weeks later Fife would note that he had received a letter from

Kent 'who is still unaware of the terrible mistake that he made in the attack on Fricourt'. Clearly it was not held against him in that he was later promoted Lieutenant-Colonel and was in command of the 4th Green Howards when he was killed in action on 31 May 1918. His mistake, however, left Fife with some hurried improvising to do on 1 July. He recommended to his brigadier-general, Glasgow, that he should substitute his reserve company, D, for the one he had now to all intents and purposes totally lost, and asked for a company from the 7th East Yorkshires to take over the reserve role. This was accepted, but fear of a repeat of what had taken place earlier preyed on Fife's mind as the proper time for the battalion's attack drew near:

At 1.50 p.m. received message from Brigade that zero was fixed for 2.30 provisionally, but that we had to await definite orders. After what had happened this morning I did not dare to tell O.C. Companies the time until definite orders arrived which was not until 2.10. I hustled the Companies as much as possible but B Company did not receive my order till 2.20 and had not got into their position at 2.30. When the moment arrived I climbed on to the railway embankment above my Head Quarters and could see 22nd Brigade advancing on our right apparently with no casualties. A storm of fire met my men as they crossed the parapet and officers and men fell by scores. In about 1 minute all officers of B Company were hit, all of C except Roper so far as I have up to now ascertained and all of D except Bartrum. Seeing the enemy standing on their parapets of the Tambour trench I collected the Battalion bombers and officers' servants of Hd Qrs on the railway embankment and opened rapid fire to keep the enemy's heads down and cover the advance. Seeing that it did not progress I sent Cotton to the front line to report and he returned to say that there were no officers left to lead the men. I then sent three platoons of the reserve company of the E. Yorkshire Regt up into the front line trench, to be ready to advance in a last effort to reach the enemy position. I left 1 platoon at Hd. Qrs. and got a Lewis gun into position on the embankment to cover the advance. I then telephoned the situation to Brigade Hd. Qrs. and went into the front line trench to satisfy myself as to the situation. I could see my men lying half way between our trenches and the enemy's, most of them evidently dead or wounded. I came to the conclusion that any further advance would only sacrifice my last remaining men.

The casualty figures for the 7th Green Howards during this afternoon attack were fifteen officers and 336 other ranks. As for Major Kent's A Company, only 32 remained unwounded out of the 140 who went over. The assigned company of the 7th East Yorkshires – who did make an attempt which came to grief in the first few yards – lost 5 officers and 150 other ranks. The official history concludes its account of the action on this part of the front with the sentence: 'Further operations of the 50th Brigade were therefore stopped'.

One other battalion of 50th Brigade had suffered more than the 7th Green Howards, indeed more than any other battalion that day. In the honours list of casualties it holds the dubious distinction of having topped the 700 mark, losing 22 officers and 688 men, a total of 710.

* * *

So far this account of 1 July has been largely a chronicle of failure, but there were considerable successes, especially at the southern end of the British line, where they attacked in close company with the French.

Private Robert Cude, battalion runner of the 7th East Kents – or the 7th 'Buffs' as they proudly called themselves – in 18th (Eastern) Division, was a witness of the right wing of the attack, where the British made good progress. He was also in the vicinity of a famous exploit of the day: the launching of the attack of the 8th East Surreys, a fellow unit in 55th Brigade, by the kicking of footballs into No Man's Land. This was the idea of Captain W.P. 'Billy' Nevill, a gesture which won much applause in the British press as a prime example of sporting gallantry but which would be contemptuously derided as 'an English absurdity' by the Germans. Cude's diary gives a vivid if impressionistic account of what he saw and heard on 1 July, though he is certainly wrong in one particular, in that Nevill left the kicking of footballs to others, while he, in a manner adopted by many other officers that day, strolled with an air of nonchalant unconcern across No Man's Land, smoking and joking until he was fatally struck down close to the German wire:

At 7.28 two minutes before the line advanced Capt Nevill, 8th East Surreys, kicks off the football that is to take the boys across to Jerry. He is killed as his leg was uplifted after kicking the ball. Now, although the line to right and left have moved, I am too busy to take in the surroundings other than our immediate front. E. Surreys and Queens go over singing and shouting and the ball is punted from one to another. They are followed by the 7th Buffs who are mopping up; in other words they are Pioneers for the time being, their time will come if Jerry is refractory. They have to clear the dugouts etc., West Kents are lying in reserve.

Soon after the lads get going, we can see that contrary to expectation we are not to have things all our own way. Here I may add that I am up forward on a message, and determine to stop and see a bit of the fun. Jerry's machine-guns open a terrific fire on our chaps and the first wave is speedily decimated. Others jump forward and fill the gaps, I am aghast at the accuracy of the fire. He has plenty of machine-guns and is making a frightful carnage. I long to be with Battn so I can do my best to bereave a German family. I hate these swines! At the 3rd line we are held, and the Buffs are called in to play again. They are soon off again and the 3rd line is soon theirs. It is a wonderful sight and one that I shall not forget. War such as this, on such a beautiful day, seems to me to be quite correct and proper. A day such as this, one feels a keen joy in living, even though that living is to say the least of it very precarious. Yet men are racing to certain death, and jesting and smiling, yet wonderfully quiet in a sense, for one feels that one must kill, and as often as one can. My hand strays to my pocket. Have 2 'Mills' bombs in each, and there are some Jerries against me. They are prisoners and had it not been for the fact that they were being closely watched, I would have put one at least of my bombs among them.

10–0 a.m. Boys are still fighting in the trenches and dugouts and I must say that considering the gruelling Jerry has had and the opposition he is met with [sic], he is fighting a battle for life itself. No quarter is asked or given in a good many places, and today I was astounded to think that men could fight so bitter as that which is on view all around me. The reason is not far to seek, for tens of thousands of our men are lying low, never to rise again. They are England's flower, the men that England can ill afford to spare. As far as my eye takes me I can see rows of dead. I am afraid that had it not been for the fact that I was too busy dodging the shells, I should have broken down. Poor Newcombe and Sgt McClusky, Sgt Whipps, Lt Baddely, and almost all my old platoon was there, and most would not rise again. Have lost my old pals today. Still, some will be left, if I am.

Our boys gave no quarter for a long time, but even the wholesale slaughter of a beaten but not disgraced enemy is, or grows, obnoxious and so from 10 o/c prisoners began pouring in. They had even caught a General with members of a big staff. Prisoners were thoroughly fed up.

11 o/c off again to get through to Battn, and now instead of travelling by trench, walk over the top to Jerry's old line. Have plenty of chance to observe the havoc wrought by the guns, ours mostly. Constant streams of wounded are passing backwards and some with terrible gaping wounds. But the stretcher-bearers cannot cope with 1/10th of the wounded, and so if a man can crawl at all, he is asked to do so. Plenty of souvenirs about, watches, purses, rings and brass hats, helmets are kicking around everywhere, but still having just returned from leave, am not going to be littered with carrying too much.

Several of the prisoners I spoke to speak of our Artillery as fiendish, and I saw tears in the eyes of many a German when thinking of it. One point worth mentioning. The burnt faces and hair of some of the Boche bear excellent testimony to the effectiveness of our liquid fire, which was used considerably. The Germans opposite us have come from Verdun for a rest – rather a good rest too I think.

A note on the 8th East Surrey's role in the 1 July attack survives in the papers of Major-General Maxse, sent to him for possible use in a history of 18th Division. It refers to Captain Nevill's footballs, gives details of casualties and comments on the small number of prisoners taken: 'They only took 22 prisoners – they did kill Germans – General Maxse told them to.' Its most choice paragraph, however, is the following: 'Lance Corporal Brain, within ten minutes of the arrival of Headquarters of the Battalion at Montauban, turned up with luncheon for officers, Heidseck 1906 and cold tongue – The East Surreys always did themselves well.'

Maxse was well satisfied with 18th Division's performance. He concluded a summary of fighting on 1 July with this sentence: 'The best thing that can be said about the Division is that it captured all its objectives and held them.'

* * *

Whereas the German accounts of 1 July included so far have shown the British in defeat, that of Leutnant Busl (also quoted in the previous chapter) of the 6th Bavarian Infantry Regiment, in the line near Montauban, offers a different picture, with Busl himself being one of the day's victims:

> From 5 a.m. in the morning there was heavy artillery and mortar fire on our positions and again a dugout collapsed. At about 6 a.m. we also thought we detected gas. However, the gas masks could soon be taken off again. At shortly after 7 a.m. the infantry attack began. While the enemy made some advances on the flanks, he was held up for a long time by our frontal wire. After I was wounded at 8.30 a.m., Dratz took command of the platoon, assisted by one of the few remaining NCOs, Löb, of the Left Section. He in particular was able to keep up lively fire right until 10.15 a.m.
>
> In some positions, where the barrage had torn great gaps in the wire, the enemy managed to penetrate. Our men attacked them with hand grenades and eventually succeeded in holding them at bay. However, the platoon stood at breaking point owing to the superior English forces, since in the meantime of its 6 NCO and 56 men, about two thirds had fallen.

Leutnant Busl's account arguably presents a 'best case' interpretation of what took place on the sector where the British had their finest hour on 1 July. The letter to his parents on 6 July by the Signals Officer of 30th Division's 90th Brigade, Captain George McGowan, offers a more appropriate index of Allied success, at a time when so many other divisions elsewhere were down and out in No Man's Land. Attacking units had been issued with means of identification to wear on their uniforms so that their progress could be monitored. Most of these in most areas had been soon lost to view in the fog of battle, but here things were different. McGowan, who inevitably spent the first hours of the battle in his signals headquarters at Brigade Headquarters, wrote:

> Unfortunately I was not able to get out at first to witness the advance of our troops and you may wonder how the observers in the O.P.s were able to send back news of the advance step by step.
>
> The fact is the ground on which these posts were located overlooks most of the ground between our original front line and the village of Montauban (some 1500 yds away) and every man in the advance carried a sheet of yellow cloth and a bright tin disc on his back which made it comparatively easy for observers to watch and report progress.

And that there had been, on a scale unimaginable along most of the British front, and producing some bizarre consequences. McGowan continued:

> About 10 a.m. just about the time our front line troops reached their objective, I went forward to one of my visual signalling posts. Things outside were far different than I had anticipated. Every man not on duty was perched up on top watching the show. Instead of being obliged to keep to the trench I was able to make good progress over the top and when I got to the point at which the O.P.s were mostly situated I saw groups of artillery observers with their telescopes fixed out in the open instead of the narrow peephole of the observation post dugout.

One possibility that has always concerned those who have studied the first day on the Somme is what might have happened had the British exploited their breakthrough on their extreme right, in the area of Montauban – where men could look beyond the devastated landscape of the trench-lines and see green, virgin country beyond, apparently there for the asking. McGowan's letter described 'the Boche fleeing backwards in hopeless confusion and our men thoroughly enjoying themselves trying to stop their flight'; but, as he saw it, further advance was not an option: 'Montauban was our objective and it would have been no good going further forward without help or co-operation on our flanks.'

*   *   *

Lieutenant Russell-Jones's 1 July diary, begun early that morning, contained two further entries. This at 9.15:

We got our rounds away quite nicely, heaps of stuff all around us but just seemed to miss each time. Our troops going over was a magnificent sight. At the given signal they were all out of their trenches, lined up as if on parade, and set off for Berlin. The front line presented little difficulty having been almost levelled or rather filled in by the artillery fire, but of course their curtain of fire did a heap of damage and many poor fellows only got outside the trench to be knocked in again. We're sitting now in an underground dugout, which if it were only propped decently would be a decent place, but the props we have are none too strong, and as a shell falls within yards of us every few minutes, I don't like it, but there are at the moment thousands of men out in the open without the slightest cover, so we ought to be thankful for what we have got.

There are three poor fellows lying in here with us, one a sergeant has had his left foot blown off, and the other two are pretty badly messed up. It is useless to try and get them away at present, we're waiting to see if things will cool down a little. I can't write any more yet a bit.

His third entry was written at 2 p.m. He was able to report the advance of about a mile in depth along a sector some three and a half miles wide, noting Mametz and Montauban as the chief prizes, and also the effective strike by the French, who gained what has been described as 'a brilliant and complete success' on their sector.

Yet these successes also had been won at a high price:

Am back in Maricourt writing this; after writing my last we endured perfect Hell for a couple of hours, shells landing within a few feet of us every few seconds. Then three men came across from the opposite dugout to say it had been blown in and ten men lying buried in it. Not the slightest use trying to dig them out. It would be a day or more's job and they're already dead. One of the men who came across was Davidson, my old servant in England and sometime servant to Watson. He has caught it very badly. He cannot see and has a piece of shell in his chest which apparently has entered his lungs for he cannot breathe properly poor lad I very much doubt if he will get over it, and I'm afraid two other of my very best boys are dead in that other dugout.

Both my guns were out of action and there was no use in keeping the men up there, so off I went to get medical aid for the many wounded that we'd taken in and to ask the HQRA [Headquarters Royal Artillery] if I might get the men away. Coming down the trenches I was chased by shells all the way, and the wounded passed on the way, too horribly mangled for words. What a ghastly business this whole affair is, but on the other hand what a success it has all been. The Boches are simply giving themselves up in hundreds. We've captured Montauban, on our left they've got Mametz and on our right the French have taken Hardecourt. Let us hope we are in sight of the finish. All the Allies are advancing and behind the dark clouds there is just a little ray of sunshine which we trust will mean peace for ourselves, our children, our children's children, aye and even Peace for ever and a day.

* * *

The worst day in the history of British arms was over. It would be a long time before the casualty figures would be fully assessed. The official statistics would finally read: 57,470 casualties overall, comprising 35,493 wounded and 19,240 killed.

However, the Fourth Army front did not present the whole picture. There was also the Third Army front opposite Gommecourt, which would contribute substantially to those figures and have its own mix of success and disaster.

CHAPTER FIVE

THE FIRST DAY:
THE THIRD ARMY FRONT

The VII Corps attack at Gommecourt was perhaps the most forlorn endeavour of the whole day, for this was purely a diversionary manoeuvre which was not even intended to succeed; 7000 men fell at Gommecourt, and it was not clear that a single German was 'diverted'.

THUS THE VERDICT of the historian long known as Haig's most consistent admirer and apologist. Yet the troops who fought on this Third Army sector believed they were contributing to the hoped-for British success as much as their Fourth Army comrades further south and went into battle with equal commitment and expectation.

The two divisions involved did not, however, meet with equal success. The focus of the attack was Gommecourt Wood, the plan being that the 46th (North Midland) Division would attack to the north and the 56th (London) Division to the south and that they would link up beyond it to the east. However, whereas the London Division made some headway, it was 'left in the air' by the failure of the North Midland Division to match its progress. Through gaps in the smoke during the final barrage German sentries observed the forward North Midland brigades, the 137th and 139th, massing to advance, and, with time enough and to spare, summoned their comrades from their dugouts. Thus at zero hour the Midlanders were met with a devastating retaliation from machine-guns as soon as they went over the top and, with German artillery adding to the carnage, their attack rapidly stalled. In addition, there were insufficient gaps in the forty-metre barrier of barbed wire facing them, with the result that their assault troops had to bunch to try to get through, thus offering the easiest of targets. The first wave was virtually blown away, though some men of the second wave, consisting of Territorial battalions of the Sherwood Foresters – the 'Robin Hoods' – from 139th Brigade, did fight their way into the German trenches; to little advantage, however, in that they were speedily 'mopped up'.

Private Bernard Stevenson was a member of the 1/7th Sherwood Foresters, the northernmost battalion of 46th Division and thus the left-hand unit of the whole 1 July offensive. This is his terse, almost 'stream of consciousness', diary account of the day:

Saturday July 1st we go over the top. Lieut Wilkins leads five platoon. 'Come on the Robins'. Out of the smoke come bullets. Someone falls dead. On we go. Thro' the German wire and into their front line trench. Our artillery has not stopped and is dropping shells near us. A red light is burned to try and stop them. Wilkins wounded in arm. Sgt Buckley slightly wounded, also Berry. Capt. Leman sees Germans emerging from the smoke between their first and second lines. Shoots at them with his revolver. Is shot in arm and face. Germans advance with bombs from right and left. Everyone attends to himself. I tumble out of trench and see small trench just behind their wire, about 6 yards away. Get in this. Germans throw a bomb into it and the dirt half buries me. Lie doggo. Cpl Small (of 6 Platoon) and a C company private with me. Take subdued counsel, and decide to wait till nightfall and then attempt an escape. Wait 15 hours. British bombarding German trench all day with heavies, whizz-bangs, rifle grenades and trench mortars. Earth keeps falling on us. Can hear Germans talking and firing.

At about 11 p.m. when it is really dark wait till a rifle grenade has just exploded and then crawl out one after the other. I go last but join the second chap in the German barbed wire. Lose direction but also have to stop in deep shell hole during lively exchange of artillery fire. Find three men with broken legs in a shell hole and help two out on to side. Finally find our way into trench held by the 8th. Make our way out via Greek and Regent Street trenches. Latter blocked in one place by dead bodies. Find Robin H's have gone to Bienvillers. Follow. Have rum and tea and go for a sleep into billet with wire bedsteads.

Left unsupported on its left flank, and exposed on its right where no attack was being mounted, the 56th (London) Division's advance could not be sustained, with the result that accounts by survivors are no more triumphalist than those of their North Midland comrades. Thus Corporal Arthur Hubbard of the 1/14th Battalion, the London Regiment, better known as the London Scottish, writing to his family on 5 July:

Dear Mother and All

No doubt you have been worrying about me very much, but now you can rest assured I am quite all right, [though] suffering from slight Shell Shock.

Went over and took the Huns 4th line of trenches on Saturday morning at 7.30 a.m. and held same until 3.30 in the afternoon when by that time their artillery had completely wiped our battalion out, and what was left of us had to crawl back to our own trenches, but the bounders mowed us down with machine-gun fire as we were returning. I managed to get back safely after a long and weary struggle over 300 yards of rough ground. I got buried over in their second line by a shell but managed to work my way out. My steel helmet saved my life, a piece of shell knocked it off my head without the slightest injury. I shall be quite myself in a week or two, as you will notice by my writing, only my nerves are shook up, severe headache now and again when my mind is on the affair.

Poor Isaacs must have gone under as I did not see him when we got back to our own trenches.

Major Claud Low of the same battalion wrote his account of the attack on the following day, Sunday 2 July, from the military hospital to which he had been evacuated after being wounded. In a letter in a sprawling hand ('this is written under some difficulty', he noted at the end), he assured his wife ('My darling Joanie') that he was 'going on well', adding, 'I want you to know that the doctors are very satisfied'. He then gave her a description of the course of events:

It happened thus: the Battalion was allotted a certain portion of the German trenches to take and C Company in turn was allotted a portion of the whole. The hour of assault was 7.30 a.m. We had all the trenches by 7.45 a.m. It was a furious piece of work while it lasted. Directly the assault started the Germans opened fire with shrapnel making a barrage of fire along the whole front, this had to be got through quickly. I received a piece of shrapnel in the left shoulder during the scramble, it knocked me head over heels and I fell into a German trench somewhere about their 3rd line. I was not very bad but losing a lot of blood, the sight of C Coy going over those trenches did me good, and I soon began to fuss around, later I found Lamb my Second in Command and told him to take command of the Company because I was not sure if I could stick it. All sorts of funny things happened about which I will not write but I was brought down again by shrapnel and lost the use of my left leg; I thought I was gone. While I think of it I gave your prayer book to one of my men with some writing in it. So if you get it just put it aside for me and consider it non est. One of my men called Wilson carried me on his back a very long distance to the dressing station and then by stages I have arrived here, No 3 General Hospital B.E.F. by the sea and I think it possible I may be sent home soon, so don't come to France. I shall regain the use of my left leg and be quite fit again and there is no necessity to worry at all, an X-ray photo shows that I am not carrying metal and I am free from pain; this is written under some difficulty. Love my sweetheart.

Your devoted husband Claud.

For some hours after the opening of the attack Lance-Corporal Sidney Appleyard of the Queen Victoria's Rifles, whose experience of the Somme had begun almost a year earlier (see Chapters 1 and 2), was little more than a passive observer. His function was that of a Company bomber but his task was to wait in reserve and only to go forward if his help was specifically required. (Originally part of 5th Division, the QVR had been transferred to the 56th (London) Division on its formation in March 1916.) Appleyard shortly afterwards wrote a characteristically vivid account of the events of the day, first as watcher, and then, as matters went awry and the call for help came, as participant, in which role he was to win a commendation for 'distinguished conduct in the Field'.

At 6.30 a.m. our artillery started an intense bombardment – every gun in the sector fired rapid. This was kept up for an hour, at the end of which we sent over our smoke bombs. I witnessed the exhibition from the old original front line and it was the finest spectacle I have ever seen. The smoke varied in colour and as each cloud intermingled with the other, it formed beautiful tints.

By this time the artillery had lifted and carried on with the pounding of the Huns' rear positions and batteries. Mr. Fritz was by no means taking this lying down and we soon realized that he had almost as many guns as we had, but it was chiefly heavy stuff that he sent over and this led us to suspect that he had shifted his field guns back. The Wood and all the enemy's trenches were now obscured from sight and all that could be seen was the front waves of men advancing to their unknown fate. Line after line advanced and disappeared in the clouds of smoke, and on several occasions one could see batches of men disappear as a shell exploded in their midst.

By 8 o'clock all the smoke had cleared and it was risky to look over the parapet, for the Germans had machine-guns fixed on these trenches. I had a good look over on several occasions but failed to see any signs of the fight, so we had to wait patiently until our assistance was required. The first news to reach us was from the London Rifle Brigade who reported that they had successfully carried the first three lines and had taken a large number of prisoners. This sounded good but no news was received from our boys until 9.30 a.m. when B Company sent word back that they had reached their objective in the Huns' second line, but the other Companies with the Queen's Westminsters were held up at the third line, where the Germans were offering a stubborn resistance.

Orders were then issued that the Company bombers would have to go over with a fresh supply of bombs and render assistance. At 10'o clock we started off under Mr. Mackenzie with 24 bombs per man, and as soon as we advanced over No Man's Land the Germans opened a very deadly machine-gun fire, which laid a good number out. On we went and it seemed marvellous how the pieces missed us, for the air appeared to be alive with missiles. At last after advancing about 30 yards I was struck in the thigh by a bullet, the force of which knocked me over. The only thing to do was to crawl back, and this I did and explained things to Captain Renton.

Knowing that a good number had been hit, I decided to crawl out on top again and give any assistance that might be required. My efforts were fruitless for the only man left out had been shot through the head and killed instantly. After this I went down to the dressing station and found my wound was not serious though the flesh had been badly ploughed up.

In reserve, to the rear of the London Scottish, were the 1/5th Cheshires, Pioneer battalion to 56th Division, with Lance-Corporal Sam Chandley among their junior NCOs. This is his diary account of the opening attack, together with his comments added on the following day, from which it is clear that even being behind the front line on 1 July was no picnic:

The first platoon of the Jocks [London Scots] fell as soon as they put their heads over. We stood by in that trench at Cross Street till 10 o/c pm Saturday night under the most deadly fire. I was in a Gun Pit and shells were dropping all around, for 16 hrs we were under shell fire. At 10 pm were relieved and coming through the orchard did put the wind up me. MG fire all over and they were shelling the village [Hébuterne]. An advanced dressing station was shot up and was blazing like hell. We ran across the plain all the way to Sailly till we were clear of shell fire and arrived back at Souastre at 2 o/c Sunday.

Our lads took the German trenches up to the third line part of the village and Gommecourt Wood but were driven back by Bombing parties.

The London Scottish are 250 strong out of a full Batt. The Rangers 100, QV and QWs are about the same. We had enormous casualties but the General says everything went off as desired. Our part was only a drawing on plan, and we took many prisoners.

Chandley was clearly less than fully persuaded by the general's reassurances, however. 'I am absolutely fed up and wish I was out of it all again,' he commented on the 4th. 'But that cannot be.' In the event the casualty figures he quoted would prove to be somewhat exaggerated, but the fact remains that all the battalions involved suffered heavily, while the London Scottish and the Queen's Westminster Rifles – the QWs as Chandley called them – were among the thirty or more battalions whose losses on 1 July 1916 topped the 500 mark.

What then of Percy Jones and his comrades of the Queen's Westminster Rifles? Jones was captured, to spend the rest of the war as a prisoner in Germany. As for his friends, his diary contains one final entry, a note written at some later time, presumably on his return home following the Armistice. 'Of No. 7 Platoon,' he wrote, 'only one wounded man, Jack Newnham, answered the roll call late in the evening.' Some had been wounded, one had gone missing, two, including himself, had become prisoners; seven had been killed, among them Jack Newnham's brother, Howard, and Billy Green. The buoyant eighteen-year-old who had so impressed and delighted his fellows had not been spared. Above the list of the dead Jones wrote in capitals the single word: FINIS.

There is a sad postscript to this story. Jones resumed his career as a journalist in 1919; however, in August that year he was drowned while on holiday in Wales. He was twenty-three.

* * *

If there were one consolation in respect of the diversionary attack, particularly that of the Londoners, it is that it certainly impressed the enemy. The War Diary of one of the German regiments involved, the 55th Reserve Infantry Regiment of the 2nd Guard Reserve Division, covering the eight days from 24 June to 1 July, somehow fell into British hands. Circulated as item SS 536 in an important series of documents translated from enemy sources, it offered an exhaustive analysis of the situation before and during the opening attack and included the following accolade:

> It must be acknowledged that the equipment and preparation of the English attack were magnificent. The assaulting troops were amply provided with numerous machine-guns, Lewis guns, trench mortars and storming-ladders. The officers were provided with excellent maps which showed every German trench systematically named and gave every detail of our positions. The sketches had been brought up to date with all our latest work, and the sectors of the attack were shown on a very large scale. Special sketches

showing the objectives of the different units and also aeroplane photographs were found among the captured documents.

The diary makes clear that the German defenders, while inflicting heavy casualties, also suffered themselves. Under the heading 'OUR OWN LOSSES' it listed:

> KILLED: 3 officers, 182 men.
> WOUNDED: 10 officers, 372 men.
> MISSING: 24 men.
> TOTAL: 13 officers, 578 men.

Commenting on these figures (assumed by the British translator to refer to the 2nd Guards Division as a whole), the diary stated:

Though our losses are regrettable, they must be regarded as small when one considers the severity of the fighting. Many casualties were avoided by holding the front trenches, exposed to the most intense bombardment, with the minimum strength required for defence, and in nearly every case the garrison succeeded in leaving the dugouts and manning the parapet at the right moment.

Understandably, in view of the outcome of the opening day, the writer of the diary could not resist a triumphalist conclusion:

The 1st July terminated in a complete victory for the 2nd Guard Reserve Division. Every man in the Division is proud of this result and of the success won. The most westerly point of the German line on the Western Front remains intact in our hands. Full of confidence, the brave troops maintain their watch with the same strength and endurance in order to annihilate every fresh attempt on the part of the enemy whenever it may come.

*   *   *

How can one sum up the first day on the Somme?

One thing that is certain about 1 July 1916 is that it is destined to be a subject of continuing controversy. It has stimulated a debate to which there can never be a decisive conclusion. Deplored by one historian, it will be explained and apologized for by another. It was the worst day in British military history; it was just another day in British military history – the arguments ply back and fore. One particular misunderstanding should be set to rest: it did not set a pattern for the Somme Battle nor for any other later similar encounter. As already stated, there were over 57,000 casualties, about a third of them fatalities: figures rounded up in general usage to 60,000 and 20,000 respectively. However, no such figures applied to any other day on the Somme, or at Passchendaele, or during the hard-fought campaigns of 1918. The toll was appalling, but it was unique.

Yet the cost was such that it is too facile to dismiss the first day on the Somme as an unfortunate blip in what was undoubtedly, taking the war years as a whole, a remarkable progress for an Army which in 1914 had been a mere task-force for a small-scale emergency and which by 1918 was prime mover in the defeat and humiliation of the military arm of Imperial Germany. In the popular imagination, indeed in popular mythology, it remains an awesome disaster with ripples of sorrow that still eddy today. Nor, whenever the story is told, has it lost its power to shock.

To inject a personal word: when I first approached this subject twenty years ago I came to know a number of veterans, most of them former members of locally recruited 'Pals' battalions, for whom the events of 1 July 1916 were still extraordinarily close, so close that they were still a matter for actual grief. As well as grief, however, there was a deep disappointment and frustration, together with a still unresolved bewilderment as to why there had been so catastrophic a failure. (I recall a former corporal of the Sheffield City Battalion, D.E. Cattell, repeating the anguished cry of a fellow solider on 1 July: 'Cattell, Cattell, *what went wrong?*') They had responded to the nation's call to arms, trained enthusiastically over many months for the great day, and they had achieved – nothing. The dream had all ended in ten minutes of shattering disillusion.

This book has avoided hindsight, deliberately, but on a subject of this magnitude and resonance the backward glance of a former soldier is surely permissible. The following is from a conversation I recorded in 1976 with George Morgan, who served in the 16th Battalion, West Yorkshire Regiment, otherwise known as the 1st Bradford Pals. Morgan went over the top opposite Serre on 1 July in the attack by 31st Division and lost most of the comrades with whom he had marched since the heady days of 1914. The memories and

attitudes of men like Morgan – almost all of them now dead – are an
essential part of the equation of the Somme:

> When I go back there I feel I'm on consecrated ground. That
> ground has been trod by all those lovely friends of mine, who
> never came back ... You imagine them as they were – young, and
> in their prime, and never grown old. The companionship was
> marvellous. Everyone seemed to help one another and agree with
> one another. We were all pals, very happy together; and they were
> such good people. They were fine young men, the cream of the
> country. That spirit lasted until 1 July 1916. We had so many
> casualties that we were all strangers after that. The new men who
> came were fed up, they were conscripts and they didn't want to
> come, they didn't want to fight. Things were never the same any
> more ... After July 1st I hated the generals and the people who
> were running the country and the war. I felt we'd been sacrificed
> ... We didn't do anything. We didn't win a thing.

*   *   *

Yet there was no question of calling off the campaign thus unhappily
launched. As has been well said, if the first day on the Somme was
remarkable, the second was equally so, in that the offensive was
maintained. The Battle of the Somme had begun and in earnest. The
process of gripping the public imagination would have many weeks
in which to establish itself before it was finally closed down; it would
then become an icon, a standard of comparison, a permanent
metaphor for one kind of war, which explains why it has been ever
since, and will doubtless remain, a subject of intense interest and
concern.

CHAPTER SIX

THE SECOND DAY
– AND AFTER

AFTER THE TUMULTUOUS events of the first day of the battle, the second provided a striking contrast. At Maricourt Captain Harry Bursey, Royal Horse Artillery, 30th Division, noted in his diary:

> *2nd July 1916.* I have just discovered it is Sunday. The firing has died down and except for a gun now and then everything is quiet and peaceful. Over the fields comes the sound of church bells.
>
> It is from Corbie, which is many miles behind us. I wonder when I will see Sundays in England.
>
> What a long way off they seem now.

Some men who had lain out in No Man's Land since the launch of the opening attack did not come in until the morning of the 2nd. Private Cyril José of the 2nd Devons, in 8th Division, was one of these.

A seventeen-year-old who should not have really been there at all but had either lied, or been allowed to lie, about his age when volunteering, he had attacked with the first wave on the previous morning. Among things he would always remember (José's is a later account, valuable for its frankness and quality of clear recall) was that just before they 'bounced' (his expression) one of his comrades, Dai Watkins, was hit in the head by enemy shell fire, and that as they went over their platoon officer, Second Lieutenant E.M. Gould, had led them yelling 'Remember Belgium, Remember the Lusitania'. 'We yelled back "— Belgium and — the Lusitania." The Belgians had not shown us much friendliness in Flanders and we hadn't much sympathy for over-rich, pleasure-seeking Americans who had died a comparatively quick death.'

Out in No Man's Land there had been the familiar pattern of execution: 'Men went down like corn before a scythe.' Among those who fell was Second Lieutenant Gould and his batman: 'Both were killed instantly. I jumped to clear them. A bullet thumped through my left shoulder and chest knocking me down. I panicked and yelled "I'm hit".' In spite of the directive that a soldier must never stop to help a wounded comrade, two of his friends ran over to him, tore open his tunic, got out his field dressing and drenched his wound with iodine. 'This only 15 to 20 yards from the German trenches.' He rolled behind Gould and his batman and tried to hide behind their bodies and his own steel helmet. He remained where he was all day. 'Occasionally I lapsed into consciousness. After a while fear almost left me and I became calm – I began to think that I might yet survive.'

As the hours went by, however, with the sun beating down from a clear sky, he had suffered dreadfully from thirst, even though, without any obvious movement, he had contrived to drink from his own water bottle and from the bottles of his dead comrades. The night had also had its hazards, as German patrols came out, looking, or so he thought, for wounded men to take prisoner. 'I lay doggo clutching a Mills bomb ready to pull the pin with my teeth. Rather than be taken prisoner I would take the patrol with me. They passed me by.'

It was not until 7 a.m. on the Sunday morning that, stiff and in pain, his uniform purple with blood, he felt it safe to move. His return was not, however, to be without its difficulties:

Slowly I began the long crawl back – the grass was fortunately long. It seemed that I was alone in a field of dead men. The wounded had either made their way back or had been killed in their tracks. Then, about half way, I encountered Private Lamacraft – a hardened regular soldier 35 years old. He was wounded in the back and legs. We struggled along together with my right arm under his body whilst he tried to walk on his hands wheelbarrow-race style.

In an hour we had made very little progress. We were both too weak from loss of blood and we had made ourselves conspicuous – Jerry had started firing at us. Luckily, his shooting was very erratic – he too was beginning to feel the strain.

I dragged Lammy into a large shell crater and we rested while we took stock. We decided that it was impossible to reach our lines. Lammy had to be carried. There was still a faint chance that I could make it alone. I gathered some water bottles from nearby corpses and stacked them around Lamacraft. Then I set off again snaking my way through the grass.

An eternity later, I spotted a gap in our '*cheveux de frise*' [barbed wire] and a sentry's periscope above the parapet. When I drew near enough, I got to my feet and hurled myself into the trench.

When I came to two officers of the Royal Berks. Regiment were trying to make me swallow some rum. I told them where Lamacraft was and asked them to send out a stretcher party to bring him in. They said it was impossible to send anyone out there.

I was taken to a field dressing station, then by lorry ambulance to Bushvillers. Next day I was on a hospital train to Le Tréport. All that I remember of the train journey is that it was packed with wounded soldiers. As I could stand, I was in the corridor. In the adjoining carriage, a young Scottish soldier who had lost a leg was singing a song I had never heard before nor since of which the last lines were:

> And, oh, the thought you'll not be mine
> 'Twill break my heart, Margarite, Margarite.

José was to spend six months in hospital. On returning to barracks in Devonport in January 1917 he met Private Lamacraft, who was on regimental police duty on the gate, being only able to walk with a stick. He told José that he had spent a further three days between the trenches before being rescued.

* * *

Lieutenant-Colonel Ronald Fife's 2 July was a much better day than its unhappy predecessor. To all intents and purposes he took the village of Fricourt single-handed.

His 7th Green Howards had been relieved at about 9 p.m. the previous night, by which time the enemy's fire had slackened and it

had been possible to bring in some of the wounded. While this work
was proceeding he went to Brigade Headquarters to report, leaving
Major Cotton in temporary command. He had previously telephoned
Brigadier-General Glasgow to say that in his opinion the only way
to carry the German positions which they had so far failed to take
was to withdraw all British troops from the front line, and then turn
the heavy artillery on to the German trenches until they were
smashed to pieces. He had found a ready response to his proposal,
which it was agreed would be implemented in the morning. It had
already been decided that his own 50th Brigade was to be pulled out
and that its place was to be taken by 51st Brigade. In view of this
new development and since he knew the ground well, the divisional
commander, Major-General Pilcher, attached him to 51st Brigade
Headquarters to assist in these operations. He subsequently
described in his diary the course of events, which did not fall out
quite as he had anticipated:

2 July. It was now 3.30 a.m. and getting light. General Fell,
commanding 51st Bde. kindly let me sleep in his dugout for 2½
hours and after an early breakfast I went with him down to the
front trenches and explained the ground to him and to Colonel
Forrest, commanding Lincoln Regt, who were now holding our
trenches. There was no fire coming from enemy trenches and I
formed the opinion that they had gone back. General Fell and I
returned to his Hd Qrs and he telegraphed a request that artillery
fire on Fricourt should cease in order that patrols might go forward
to reconnoitre. This was arranged. I then walked down the road to
Fricourt. Where the road crosses our front trenches I saw a man in
the trench belonging to the South Wales Borderers, 22nd Brigade,
who had been sent to get in touch with 51st Brigade. I told him
that I was going to see if any of my men were lying wounded in
front and asked him to come with me, which he did. We followed
line of advance of A and D Companies and found the dead lying
very thick on the ground, but no wounded. I felt that what I
needed was to see some dead Germans, so sent the man back with
a message to Colonel Forrest, Lincoln Regt, saying that I was going
into Fricourt, which I believed to be unoccupied, and should be
glad of a small escort. The man did not return and after waiting a
quarter of an hour I walked into the German trenches. They were

much battered and a good many dead were lying in them but no living. Coming to a very deep dugout I shouted down 'Komm heraus' ['Come out'], but there was no reply. I then climbed onto the parapet again and saw my messenger returning. He brought a message from Colonel Forrest to say that the Lincolns were going to 'attack' Fricourt. I sat down and waited and soon after saw the Lincolns coming out of their trenches in attack formation. After they had passed me I returned to 51st Brigade Head Quarters and watched the Lincolns, with S. Staffords on their left, advancing in attack formation through Fricourt and all the German front line trenches to the high ground beyond. Not a shot was fired at them but as they advanced batches of the enemy emerged from dugouts and surrendered. I saw 5 or 6 of these parties numbering from 8 or 10 to 25 or 30, all unwounded.

His duty completed, without the need of the concentrated artillery barrage which he had earlier advocated, he returned to his battalion, which was just leaving its billets at Ville to begin recuperation at Heilly, several miles to the rear. 'Arrived there at 5.30 pm. The A.S.C. [Army Service Corps] kindly invited me and half a dozen of my officers to dinner.

'Slept heavily last night in a comfortable bed in a cottage,' he noted at the beginning of his entry for 3 July, 'and awoke much refreshed.' He continued in more sombre mood, however, listing the names of the officers of his battalion who had been killed or wounded, and assessing the casualties of its four companies by comparing the number who had taken part in the attack with those who had come through unscathed. These were not cheerful statistics:

Went into Action	Not killed or wounded
A Coy. 140	32
B Coy. 160	90
C Coy. 177	80
D Coy. 171	110

1 Platoon of Company were not put into the assault.

Went in	Killed & Wounded
648	336
	51.8 per cent

That day he received two messages of congratulation. One was from Major-General Pilcher, the Divisional commander: 'Owing to the gallantry and self-sacrifice of the 50th Bde. the Fricourt position was occupied this morning without casualties.' A similar message came from 50th Brigade's commander, General Glasgow. Fife decided to emulate them: 'I published an order of my own, saying how proud I felt to command such gallant men. Spent the evening making out recommendations for immediate reward of officers and men. Sent in 18 names, most of whom would formerly have got the V.C.'

He recorded the special bravery and determination of two of his men: 'On hearing that Lieut Coates, the Battalion Bombing Officer, had been killed, two bombers in different parts of the line got up and walked on alone, each saying that he was going to kill a German. One was shot dead before he had gone 10 yards but the other got to within 20 yards of the German parapet before he was killed.'

For Lieutenant-Colonel Fife, this was not the end of the matter, however. He would later return to the scene of his battalion's attack and – more as a matter of analysis than of anger, for he was not one for easy criticism of the staff or the generals – wrote the following comment in his diary:

> *2nd August.* Marched at 6.15 to a field S.E. of Albert, leaving our tents behind by Divisional orders. Walked with Cotton to the German trenches, now in our hands beyond Bécourt Wood. In the evening rode with Cotton to Lozenge Wood and from there walked all round the old Boche trenches north of Fricourt. It is very evident that the task set for the West Yorkshire Regt on 1st July was as hopeless as ours and that not less than three Battalions should have attacked that part of the position, which even then would have been practically impregnable against assault until nearly all enemy machine-guns were out of action. Also the W. Yorkshire should have been ordered to seize enemy's front line as their first objective and not to press on quickly, as they were ordered to do.

* * *

If for Fife 2 July had brought some satisfaction after the misfortunes of the 1st, for Brigadier-General Rees, by contrast, it was a day of great disappointment:

> On the 2nd July, I was informed that General Carter Campbell had returned from sick leave and would resume command of his brigade. This was a bitter blow to me. I hoped to have retained command although I was only acting for General Campbell. I said goodbye to Piggot and Stirling and walked back to Colincamps, where I picked up a car and so to the division. I went on later to HQ 8th Corps and gave General Hunter-Weston an account of the battle. He put my remarks into his own language and I think that particular report of mine is somewhat more ornate that anything else I have put my name to.

He was not to be deprived of command for long, however. He was posted to the 11th Brigade in 4th Division, whose commander, Brigadier-General Bertie Prowse, had been killed on 1 July, the most senior officer to die that day. Of the four battalion commanders of 11th Brigade three had been killed and the fourth wounded. There was clearly a major task of reconstruction to be done.

*   *   *

Many units had been so completely shattered on the first day that they had to be withdrawn from the Somme to re-form. Captain Bundy's diary described the movements of the 2nd Middlesex over the next two days:

> *2nd July.* Remnants relieved by new battalion. Our Battalion moved out and marched about 4 miles. Then on by lorries to Albert. Gather my few remnants into billets and got two hours sleep in a gunner's bed.
> *3rd July.* In Albert all day. Our Division has been so cut up it is being moved somewhere else. Thank God for a change from this Hell. Stacks of dead. Wounded in all directions. Hear attack has been successful in some places but a failure on our Brigade front.

Early on the 5th the remnants of 8th Division entrained at Albert, arriving at Béthune after a 'terribly dreary journey' – Bundy's second railway journey in a week – at 12 midnight. They would spend the next three and a half months rebuilding their fighting capacity in comparative quiet of the Loos sector, not returning to the Somme until the final phase of the battle.

*   *   *

Over the days following the beginning of the offensive survivors hastened to send messages of reassurance to their families, in many cases adding accounts of their experiences or commenting on what had taken place; some have already been used as evidence in this book. Frequently a standard field postcard would be despatched first, with a letter following as soon as circumstances allowed. Such letters were not always welcome to the eye of the censor, as the mother of Private Bernard Stevenson, who had gone over with the 'Robin Hoods' at Gommecourt, discovered when she received his of 3 July:

> Dear Mother,
>   Knowing that you would probably hear of the fighting on this front I sent you a field postcard as soon as I was able to do so to tell you of my safety. The battle was certainly a trying experience and I'm sorry to say that Nottingham will be plunged into mourning when the casualty lists are published . . .

At this point the page was ripped across; a note at the top of the page reads 'Torn by censor'; part of the following page, by definition, was also removed.

Such excisions, however, seem to have been rare. There appears to have been no concerted attempt to delete expressions of distress or disarray following the events of 1 July. Witness Second Lieutenant Lipscomb's outcry – 'Somebody ought to be hung for this show' – already quoted (page 70), or the following comment by Captain Ronald Wilson of the 4th Yorks and Lancs, written on 9 July: 'We have been disappointed. Every man in the battn has. Our dreams of glorious fighting and pushing the Germans back and back to the Rhine are all gone. But we all had them and were confident that we should get through in our part of the line. Bad luck and the Staff have spoiled it all. Perhaps I ought not to say the latter, but it is true and our Corps Commdr has already been sent back to England.'

Many letters inevitably included depressing lists of friends who had fared badly in the battle. Captain Norman Adams of the 1/6th South Staffordshire Regiment, like Stevenson, had been in the unsuccessful 46th Division attack at Gommecourt; himself among the casualties, he wrote to his sister in early July from No. 3 General Hospital, Le Tréport:

> I am afraid we have lost heaps and heaps killed and wounded. Dickenson I heard a rumour of but I pray it isn't true, and little Page, engaged to Jessie Smith, Wilmot Evans, wounded in leg like me, [name unclear] broken rib, Evans lost part of his nose and one ear, Robinson blown in the air by shell not wounded but deaf and dumb, Dennis Lewis wounded, Dickens wounded in leg, his third time, Sutcliffe wounded, Hailey wounded in two or three places. Oh I don't know who else, these I heard of at the various dressing stations on the way here. I expect Ainsworth is in the bosom of his family by now and really glad to get back if the truth was known.

*　*　*

The story of the Somme is one with little feminine presence apart from the mothers, sisters, wives and girlfriends in Britain and elsewhere to whom men wrote their letters. But there was always another category on the edge who became an important, indeed an invaluable, part of the action in the wake of a major attack. Dorothy Field was one of this group, a Voluntary Aid Detachment (VAD) nurse working in the summer of 1916 at No.10 General Hospital, Rouen. Throughout her war service, which had included a spell at a hospital at Versailles and would later take her to Italy, she chronicled her experiences in a series of tiny 'soldier's diaries', scribbling in barely decipherable pencil the gist of the events of the day. Often the entries were minimal, there being little except routine to report, but her pencil was especially busy – and more than usually illegible – over the first phase of the Somme battle. Understated, with only an occasional hint of emotion, limited by space, her annotations nevertheless convey something of the pressures of this stressful period and of the massive scale of the work involved. She had her own shorthand: 'g.g.' was the condition of tissue deterioration known as 'gas gangrene', while 'g.g.w.' was a gas gangrene wound; the reference to the 'dying' in tents and a YMCA hut indicated that these had been set aside as 'moribund' wards; 'biscuits' were easily portable mattresses made up of several sections; 'evacuation' was the assignment of patients to other hospitals or, if they were Blighty cases, by train to Le Havre, whence hospital ships sailed regularly across the Channel to England.

Convoys of lorries and ambulances with about 120 or 130 patients per convoy had been coming in regularly during the last days of June; meanwhile the sound of the pre-battle artillery barrage had risen steadily in intensity – 'heard guns more and more clearly each night', she had noted on the 26th. But it was in the early morning of the second day of the battle – during the night-time of Saturday-Sunday 1–2 July – that the spate began:

1 July Sat. Night – convoy in at 4 a.m. – 170. First lots from the bombardment – the 'going over the top' results. Practically all surgicals. Another in about 8 a.m. about same size. Heard guns more distinctly than ever and faster than ever during the night. The Infantry 'went over the top' about 7 a.m. according to the men.

2 Sun. Convoy came in at 4 a.m. – about 170 and another as we were coming off duty. Two evacuations during day and another convoy in about 8 p.m. Ambulances and trains full of sitting cases running all night. Another convoy in about 4 a.m.

3 Mon. Waked up about 5 p.m. by band heading endless column of drafts marching we imagine to station en route for the Front. Convoys coming in almost all night. They say we had 11,000 in 24 hours – dying on floor on biscuits in 4 tents and YMCA hut.

4 Tues. Went to station to see Ambulance train – saw them de-training. An Australian took us down in his Ambulance, very jolly. Train loads of sitting cases still coming up.

5 Wed. Spent most of night specialling in D.1. with two awful head cases or in A.1. with 7 amputations – 5 done yesterday. A perfect nightmare and my feet hardly bearable. Convoy in after we left – about 9 a.m.

6 Thurs. Not quite such a ghastly night. Specialled in A.1. not much in D.1.

7 Fri. Hospital fairly empty again, tho' mostly bad cases left. Helped to special a poor man who died from g.g., the third during the week I have had to do with. The other two – boys of 21 – both g.g.w. in chest.

8 Sat. Specialled a poor little kiddie until 5 a.m. – he died about

5.45, awfully wounded in thigh and probably gas gangrene. Another rush expected any time. Have been evacuating hard the whole time, very few will be left for tonight.

By 11 July it seemed that there was at last an opportunity to relax. She noted: 'Came off night duty and slept – stayed in bed all day and was told to have the next day off.' But this was not to be: '12 Wed. Waked at 7.10 and told to get up and go on duty in Medical Hut!!! Poor Sgt Bromey there – very bad – g.g.w. in chest, he died about 5.30 p.m.'

She managed a whole day off on the 13th, going for a long walk with a fellow nurse in the morning and sleeping in the afternoon. But then there was a new challenge: 'Crowd of German wounded came in', she noted later that day. There was a further upsurge about 21 July, producing the comment: 'We had a lot of deaths which are always so depressing.'

The work would continue indefinitely.

* * *

There had been many roll-calls at the end of 1 July, but more often than not these could only produce provisional figures. Over the following days units began the often complex process of assessing more precisely the numbers of dead and wounded, and also of attempting to establish what had happened to those who were unaccounted for, and who therefore had to be listed as 'missing'. Some would shortly be traced to hospitals in France or Britain. Information from Germany and elsewhere would eventually move many other names, to the great relief of relatives, into the category of 'prisoner of war'. In countless cases, however, families would have to endure the ordeal of a long period of uncertainty, marked by a strengthening assumption, as the weeks passed, that 'missing' in effect meant 'killed'. More, all too frequently they would have come to terms with the fact that they might never discover the circumstances of a soldier's death, and also that he would never have a known resting-place.

This was to be the outcome in the case of Second Lieutenant Jocelyn Buxton of the 2nd Rifle Brigade, attached Machine-Gun Corps, who had set out his thoughts so eloquently in his letters home in the last days before the attack. First reports suggested that he had been wounded, but not severely. 'We looked forward to having him back at some hospital in London,' his parents wrote in a printed tribute to his memory produced one year later, 'but days went by and still no further news.' Then followed letters from various sources; and interviews with soldiers who had been wounded in the same attack and might have some light to throw upon his fate. An early correspondent was his Chaplain, Revd T.A. Lee of 25th Infantry Brigade, who wrote that he had heard that Buxton had been wounded and had 'tried to find him and hear how he was, but he did not come through either of the Divisional Ambulances as far as I can make out ... I am told that he did extraordinarily well in the battle, acting well on his own initiative.' Next, his company commander, Captain M.E. Gray, wrote in the first place to say that Buxton had been wounded and then later, on 16 July, to state that, while he had no firm news to report, he had been told by several men of Buxton's section that he had been brought in from No Man's Land by his servant, Private Rycroft, who had also been wounded. He added, by way of consolation, 'Your son behaved with great gallantry in the action of July 1st, and led his guns forward under very heavy Machine-Gun and Shell fire.' On 22 July, however, a letter arrived from Private Rycroft, sent from a hospital near Birmingham, denying Captain Gray's story, but offering a last sighting which would be the only information his parents would ever have about the fate of their son:

By some means unknown to me, a report has circulated that I brought Lieut Buxton in. It is my deep regret and sorrow that I could not do so, for owing to several hindrances I was about 30 or 40 yards behind him when I was hit, and so was unable to know *definitely* if he had been hit, for I fell into a hole ... As you are no doubt aware I was his servant all the time he was in France, and was the recipient of innumerable acts of kindness, and had more than the ordinary feeling of a servant for his officer. He was always regardless of danger in his duties, and on the 1st of July I had to restrain him several times, and when we left our trench to advance it was to lead a Battalion who had lost all their officers. The last words he said to me were, 'Are you ready, Rycroft?', and then we jumped up on our parapet, and standing up at his full height, he shouted, 'Come on, the —, follow me.' We then started to run across 'No Man's Land' in a hail of machine-gun bullets, and just as I got through our wire I was hit in the hand, then in the leg, and dropped ... Whatever may have happened to your son, I shall never forget him or cease to admire him as a soldier in the best sense of the word, but above all as my ideal Englishman and a Christian gentleman.

'By this time,' his parents wrote in their tribute, 'we were feeling that the hope of seeing our boy again in this life had burnt very low; and it was no shock therefore to get another letter from his kind Chaplain, Mr Lee':

I suppose there is no doubt now that Jocelyn Buxton was killed in the trenches after having been wounded first, and so I should like to send you just a short note to tell you how extraordinarily grieved I am about it ... From a Chaplain's point of view, his loss is a very great one. He was one of the few officers who used to come to voluntary Services and who was not ashamed or falsely shy about witnessing to Christ. I shall never read the 15th Psalm now without thinking of him. I venture to regard his death as a great loss to the nation. In the reformation that is bound to come in England after the war, I always felt that he would understand the right line to take and I knew he would have the courage of his convictions and would try to do all that he thought was right.

The final letter quoted in his parents' tribute was by another chaplain, Revd Edward Talbot, whose friendship the young officer had greatly valued while he was at the front. Talbot was writing, not to the Buxtons, but to his own younger brother at Harrow; they included it not because it added to the knowledge of their son's death, but because of the light it shed on his state of mind before the battle and the high seriousness with which he faced his ordeal. Looked at from generations later, his attitudes might perhaps seem naively idealistic, even sentimental, but there is no doubt that he was not alone in holding them. Talbot wrote:

I am this moment quite near a certain wood, which, when I pass it, always brings Jocelyn to my mind; for we walked up and down in it last June and talked of many things; and I remember feeling how costly an offering he was making, precisely because his mind and spirit were so sensitive to the moral atrocity of war – and how, therefore, he was bringing redemptive power out of its very horror. For I feel sure that it is only so far as we unite a certain profound repudiation of war (not of its pain and discomfort, but of its hate) with a readiness to share its sacrifices that we shall be able to draw out of it the insight and power which may renew this groaning old earth. It was because Jocelyn both in his soul repudiated war as something radically devilish, and also was ready to endure its stripes, that he was so rare a person and combined what so many others can only keep in separation. It is all, I should suppose, an echo of that agony of our Lord which combined at once a heart-broken abhorrence of the sin which was closing upon Him, and a deep resignation to the bearing of its burden. At least I think so.

One much-used means of attempting to clarify the fate of a missing soldier was the request for help printed in a local newspaper, in the hope that some surviving comrade might come forward to provide definite information. The father of Private George Pickup of the 11th Battalion East Lancashire Regiment published such a request in a Liverpool newspaper in late July. It was seen, and immediately answered, by a friend of his son's who was recuperating in a military hospital in the city:

Dear Sir

Just a few lines in answer to your inquiry which first came to my notice this Sunday Morning July 30th in our Local Paper the Observer and Times. Regarding your Dear Son Pte George Pickup who belonged to the Machine-Gun team. I am very sorry to inform you that he was killed by Shrapnell at about 8.30 Pm on July 1st. He also had a bad wound upon his Leg. He was along with me and two other comrades in a shell Hole about 95 yards off our own Lines when a shell bursted behind us a piece of it caught your Son in the Chest. I also got a piece off same in my Back. He died a peacefull Death a few moments afterwards.

I remain your Sincerely
Pte J. Baron

* * *

Concern for the dead was not, however, a luxury that could be afforded by the commanders at the front, who still had an enemy to fight and a battle to win. As the survivors of the units which had fought on 1 July withdrew, it was the turn of others to take their place and carry the offensive forward.

Captain Lionel Ferguson, who had begun his war as a volunteer in the Liverpool Scottish, was now a company commander in the 13th Battalion of the Cheshire Regiment, 25th Division, Reserve Army. For him and his battalion the days after the opening of the battle were a time of anxiety and tension as they prepared to join the action. In particular 1 July – while furious fighting on a massive scale was going on just over the hill – had been a doldrum. Awakened, as he noted in his diary, by 'the crash of artillery at zero-hour', he had got up early, eager to 'get out and see the sights'. But from the little village of Warloy, some miles west of Albert, there had been little to see if much to hear, so he and his his fellow officers had settled for a peaceful breakfast in the garden ('full of roses and other beautiful flowers') of the house where they were billeted. It had been clearly seen as a special occasion: 'The servants are trying to make a show for our comfort, and we found the table had a linen cloth on, which I discovered was a sheet robbed from our bed; as this must have been in use for months, we would rather have had the bare table: but what matter, the effect was beautiful.'

The rest of the day had been spent at BHQ – Battalion Head-quarters – on the main Albert–Amiens road, the sight of which, wrote Ferguson that night, 'made me stand in wonderment for ages', watching thousands of troops of all kinds and endless lines of lorries going up to the front, the latter then returning empty or filled with wounded. 'It makes one think,' he commented, 'what may happen when our turn comes; but it can't be long now.'

Sunday the 2nd also passed quietly, literally, in spite of their closeness to the front: 'A beautiful day, and in our garden we cannot believe we are so near this big battle: perfect peace except for the hum of planes.' The main road, however, was still as busy as on the previous day: 'What numbers of wounded; our losses must be appalling. Most of the cases I see are light ones, but a number of them are bound for Blighty so are as pleased as Punch.'

Uppermost in his and his comrades' minds was the question: when would they be thrown into the battle and what would be their allotted task? 'Awaiting orders is most trying, as we have to be packed up, dressed in battle order – i.e. haversack on back in place of pack, with only urgent wants in it; we are not even to take washing or shaving kit with us. During the afternoon we went to BHQ, Colonel Finch having just had orders (official) of the show. It appears the situation is "rather obscure", a word used by the Staff which means failure.'

The third of July began with a similar uncertainty: 'I hate this waiting, wanting to get into the show, and get it over. Officers are to go over the "top" carrying rifles and 150 round of SAA [small arms ammunition], also to hide glasses, etc. under the tunic, as the Huns have been picking off our leaders.'

Later, however:

We are to move tonight down to Bouzincourt, just behind Albert. We left Warloy at dusk, meeting a very tired Highland Division coming out of the show. It was a sight new to me to see really tired men, they were just walking along in twos and threes, holding each other up for support, unshaved, covered with mud, and war worn, in fact never have I seen troops in worse condition. I met with them Major Popham, whom I had known in Bebington days, he had now a staff job with that division. He was pleased to see me, but told me they had had an awful time, and that they were a smashed division. We arrived at Bouzincourt about midnight.

It was in such unpropitious circumstances, and with such examples of hardship and failure to sober them, that many of the battalions who were to launch the second phase of the battle readied themselves for war. If there had been scales on the eyes of those involved in the fighting of 1 July, a similar innocence was not always possible for those who took over the torch in the days that followed.

CHAPTER SEVEN

TO PRESS THE ENEMY HARD

On 3 July General Sir Douglas Haig noted in his diary: 'Fight fluctuated this afternoon about La Boisselle and S. of Thiepval, the advantage remaining with us.' This was in line with his philosophy for the furtherance of the offensive as expressed the previous day: 'The enemy has undoubtedly been severely shaken.... Our correct course, therefore, is to press him hard with the least possible delay.'

Thus was the tone set for the weeks that followed. The enemy was to be harried at all times. There was to be no pause. There had been many casualties but there were also many replacements trained and to hand. Informed on the 2nd of the latest casualty estimate for the first day – 40,000, at that stage – Haig had noted, 'This cannot be considered severe in view of the numbers engaged, and the length of front attacked.' Even when the higher, actual figure became known, this was not seen as any deterrent. Nor indeed did the troops on the ground think for one moment that they would be called back and the campaign abandoned. They had started their offensive; it would be maintained.

* * *

So far the story is one that has become very familiar not only to *aficionados* but to anyone with even a vague interest in the First World War. A great attack launched with great hopes that ended in a great disaster – the Somme's first day is now more or less assimilated into the general culture, accepted, packaged, understood. But after that? The story, of course continued; this was, after all, a serial battle, not a one-day encounter. But in what way? To what effect? Even to the knowledgeable or the would-be expert the scene can appear oddly confused, out of focus; grey shadow-play on a grey stage. It is almost as though a five-act opera were memorable only for its tragic overture.

Yet the 'true texture of the Somme', as John Terraine has argued, consists also of the 141 other days which came after. This is undoubtedly correct, but how to make sense of those four and a half months of almost constant fighting, how to find a clear, graspable pattern, is a major problem. As compared with 1 July, the 'plot' of the period 2 July to 19 November might seem to require a great deal of unravelling.

One way of arriving at some kind of overview is to amplify the concept established in the opening chapter of the 'vast linear fortress' constructed by the Germans during the long period of relative quiescence before the battle; a fortress of miles of barbed wire, superbly constructed trenches, elaborate dugouts, linked to similar fortresses behind, so that the breaking of the first line of defence resulted in an equally daunting confrontation with a second, while beyond that lurked a third.

The attack of 1 July – despite its failings – had broken the first position in a number of places, particularly to the right of the Albert–Bapaume road. To the north, initial targets such as Thiepval, Beaumont Hamel and Serre would be left for future attention, but over the next fortnight a series of small but significant advances were made in the south, resulting in the seizure of La Boisselle, Bernafay Wood, Mametz Wood and Contalmaison, while fighting in Trônes Wood went on over several days. In this way, the second layer of the linear fortress became exposed to attack, and Rawlinson's Fourth Army lost no time in assaulting it. The offensive on 14 July, officially known as the Battle of Bazentin Ridge and lasting until the 17th, caught the enemy by surprise, took a 6000-yard bite of ground from the enemy, and in terms of landmarks taken or threatened, completed the seizure of Trônes Wood, and opened the door to the ultimate capture of the village of Longueval and of Delville Wood. Meanwhile the Reserve Army, taking over the ground to the north from the axis of the Albert–Bapaume road, took Ovillers on the 17th. The Australians were now part of the Reserve Army, and a major saga of the Somme, which would continue until well into September, began on 23 July with the attack by them which would become known as the

Battle of Pozières Ridge. Pozières village – actually on the Albert–Bapaume road – stood just in front of another part of the German second line. Some idea of the formidable nature of that barrier can be gathered from the description of it by the Australian Official Historian, Dr C.E.W. Bean, as 'an immensely strong system comprising two parallel trenches (and many long approaches), which ran along the actual crest [of the Pozières ridge] 500 yards behind the village.' In the truly terrible fighting at this point, Pozières was not just destroyed, it was erased from the surface of the earth.

Thus was the second layer of defence of the German fortress broken – if again only in part.

Slowly, doggedly, the British continued to edge forward. Other names would come into focus as the weeks went by: Delville Wood, High Wood, Guillemont, Ginchy to the right of the road, Mouquet Farm ('Mucky Farm') to the left. Ahead lay the German third position along the line of such villages as Flers and Courcelette – far-distant places to those who began their confrontation with the Germans along the line from Montauban to Serre. There in mid-September a major set-piece offensive, a second big push, would be attempted.

However, through the long weeks of July, August and early September the battle took on a new, different complexion. The Germans were put under constant strain by local attacks intended to provide the best possible 'jumping-off positions' for the big offensive to come. Yet the strain was not one-sided. There might well be ultimate advantage in such small-scale attacks, but, as the Imperial War Museum's senior historian, Peter Simkins, has written, 'the broader tactical benefits were not always instantly apparent to the officers and men who saw the strength of their battalions progressively eroded by minor yet costly "line straightening" operations.' In the period from 15 July to 14 September – sixty-two days – Fourth Army advanced 1,000 yards on a five-mile front incurring approximately 82,000 casualties. It was in these summer weeks that the Somme became what General Haig would call 'the wearing-out struggle'; in other words, it became a battle of attrition.

What fed the casualty figures, massively, on both sides was the German response to the Allied attacks, as mandated by its high command. General Erich von Falkenhayn, the Chief of the German

General Staff, the author of the Verdun offensive – founded from the first on the principle of attrition – decreed from the start of the Somme offensive that any ground lost should be retaken 'by immediate counter-attack, even to the use of the last man.' 'The enemy', stated the commander of the German Second Army, General Fritz von Below, 'should have to carve his way over heaps of corpses.' Thus it came about that while the British, in Haig's phrase, pressed the enemy hard, the enemy pressed hard in return. It is therefore not surprising that the personal accounts that follow – by officers and men unaware of the overarching framework into which they can now be more or less neatly fitted – have one particular message in common, that this was a time of awesomely severe fighting.

* * *

Adding to the severity of their ordeal was the fact that, as the British tried to pull themselves together and move forward to the next stage, attacks were frequently launched without the careful planning and organization which had characterized the first phase of the battle. Those who went over the top then had been fully briefed as to what they were expected to do and had spent valuable time in rehearsal. Now there was a feeling in some quarters at least that attacks were being made piecemeal, without clearly declared targets or sufficient preparation. Certainly there were gains in the first days of July: but there was much accompanying chaos and confusion.

Friday 7 July saw the launching of a substantial number of attacks by units of seven separate divisions. On 17th Division's front a two-battalion advance, undertaken by the 12th Manchesters and 9th Duke of Wellingtons of 52nd Brigade, was mounted against a strongly defended German trench known as Quadrangle Support to the north east of Fricourt. In the light of the experience of 1 July it might seem surprising that the Official History in describing this attack should state that 'in broad daylight the two battalions had no chance of reaching [their target] over bare and open ground.' It was as though no lesson had been learned. Immediately afterwards one of the officers of the Manchester Battalion, Captain O.P. Eckhard, wrote in his diary an angry account of the day's events, of which these are the keynote paragraphs:

July 7th, 8 a.m. The Battalion attacked the Quadrangle support trench, (between Contalmaison and Mametz Wood) advancing over the open in 4 lines for a distance of 700 yards. The Battalion went into the trenches 840 strong with 22 Officers, and came out with 250 men and six officers.

Casualties were N.C.O.s and men 590, Officers 16.

Out of 16 Officers who actually charged only 3 came back.

Causes of failure. The attack was planned for 8 a.m. and was part of a general attack by several divisions. The artillery were to bombard the German first line from 7.30–8.0 and then 'lift' on to their support lines. Our Battalion should have crept up to within 150 yards of the German front line under cover of our bombardment. The attack on this part of the German line was to have been carried out by another battalion, our battalion H.Q. received orders to attack at 7.26 a.m., i.e. the C.O. had a 10 minute walk to get to the battalion from the H.Q. dugout, the battalion had then to be organised for the advance and had 800 yards to cover to the German line. Naturally all this could not be done in 35 minutes, so that instead of being within assaulting distance at 8 a.m. the battalion had over a quarter of a mile to cover when our bombardment 'lifted', and the Germans could calmly *stand on their parapet* and shoot us down as we advanced.

We were told that our flanks would be secured by battalions on our right and left. But the assault of these flanking battalions seems to have miscarried. Anyway there was a deadly machine-gun fire from the flanks, which it was impossible to get through.

The battalion advanced in straight lines as if on parade with rifles at the high port, whereas I think they should have advanced in short rushes by sections, i.e. the advancing lines lie flat and then in succession, first from one point of the line and then another, a small group of men join up together, dash forward 30 yards and then fall flat again. The machine-gun teams went over the open with their companies and were shot down with the rest. They should have taken up positions on the flanks when they could have kept down the enemy's fire. Or if this was impossible, they should not have gone forward at all until the trench had been captured.

The Official History gives the conclusion to the episode: 'The survivors were brought back, Lieut Colonel E.G. Harrison of the Manchesters being wounded while superintending the withdrawal.

Only a few posts remained out, and these were engaged all day with the enemy's bombing parties.'

Eckhard himself later added by way of footnote: 'The 17th Division had about 6000 casualties in operations extending from July 5th to 11th.'

Captain Lionel Ferguson's 13th Cheshire battalion, 25th Division, finally went into action as part of this offensive of 7 July. They were to the north west of Eckhard's Manchesters, on the other, northern side of the Albert–Bapaume road. As already indicated, this was now the virtual dividing line between the Fourth and Reserve Armies. The Cheshires' starting-off point was the head of Mash Valley, their initial task to be an advance in the direction of the heavily defended village of Ovillers. Except that La Boisselle was now in British hands they, in company with the 9th Loyal North Lancashires, were attempting a virtual re-run of the 2nd Middlesex's effort of 1 July – though this time the plan was to push on for a further 500 yards beyond Ovillers. This would allow their Division to link up with Fourth Army's 19th Division further east.

The Cheshires had moved up to the front on the 5th. Passing through Albert, they met a battalion coming out, and a stretcher-bearer called to his fellow SBs in the Cheshires that 'they would find lots of work to do'. This in a somewhat different form was also the message given them by their CO, who had told them that they were to carry on the fight within forty-eight hours and that they must expect 'a hard fight with much bayonet work'. Yet, having made their way with many delays to the captured defences of La Boisselle, they were put to digging defences against the possibility of a counter-attack from the Germans instead of preparing to attack themselves. From Ferguson's diary, written up sometime later for reasons that will become evident, it would seem that they were given no information about the attack they were to make early on the 7th until the late evening of the 6th:

About 10 p.m. that night we got orders we were to go 'over the top' at 8 a.m. next morning; no definite details were given till 3 a.m. when we were informed the 1st objective would be a trench 250 yards in front, to be followed to the 2nd objective at Ovillers

–La Boisselle road junction, known afterwards as 'Ovillers-Post'. We were badly handicapped by having no maps and little time, and during the remaining hours of the night we spent in fixing the men with bombs, SAA, flares etc.; also getting a good position for the assembly.

Our first objective was an old communication trench, now held for defence by the Boche. Our Staff work on this occasion I consider was very bad; as the attack was merely formed on our sketch maps that we had sent back. No staff officer had visited our front line during our occupation. We were ordered to go over the top on a square held on three sides by the enemy. Secondly we had to change direction between objectives, always a fatal plan. Those who had better ideas of 'stunting' than myself were very pessimistic about the show.

Pessimism was not confined to Ferguson's circle; there were others who had no relish for what was clearly going to be a high-risk affair:

The 11th Lancs. Fusiliers had come up into the position also, in order to support and follow afterwards. Some of them got 'windy' and called out to get back, what might have turned nasty nearly occurred. I held up one of them with my revolver, refusing to let any past, till I found out who gave the order, but at that moment the order came for them to return, when at once they took up their positions again. I was very pleased with No. 3 Coy, for not a man moved out of his position, lying up against the parapet.

Ferguson, nervous as to how he would perform in action, duly went over the top and found his personal battle resolved – 'my blood was up now, my fear was gone and I wanted to kill' – but the enemy machine-guns soon made havoc and he was among those almost immediately hit, falling headlong into a shell hole with the impact. Losing much blood and feeling increasingly weak, he decided his only course was to withdraw. He ended his first Somme experience in a motor ambulance heading for Corbie, from where he was sent back to England. Looking back in some anger, he summed up the results of the attack: 'I afterwards found out that the Battalion had lost heavily, the first objective was only won at 6 p.m. Two officers and 60 O.R. being all that was left out of 600. It was a bad show, also a very sad one, for the battalion. But once again the Staff thought they knew better, and we were asked to do the impossible. I was lucky, my wound being slight, a bullet through my left shoulder, but no damage to any bones.'

He would return to the Somme, and would fight there again, in 1918.

* * *

Friday 7 July also saw the blooding of the 38th (Welsh) Division. This was composed of the Welsh equivalent of the 'Pals' battalions of the north and elsewhere and was to a large extent the product of a personal initiative by the future Prime Minister, David Lloyd George. Their task was to take Mametz Wood, which they eventually cleared but at a very heavy cost. A first unsuccessful attack on the 7th was followed by a further more productive effort from the 10th to the 12th, though there was much desperate fighting.

Lieutenant Henry Apps of the 11th South Wales Borderers chronicled the progress of events in a pocket 1916 diary; though terse and restricted for reasons of space, his entries nevertheless convey the atmosphere of a stressful and challenging time:

Thursday 6. Arose at 4.30 a.m. Lovely morning. The guns still hard at it. Had a rifle inspection and dumped packs ready for battle.

Moved off at 8.0 p.m. I was in charge of Signallers. Very slow going. Shells dropping just over the battalion. The Guns are awful.

Friday 7. Arrival at our destination at 2.0 a.m. I got the men into shell holes. The enemy started shelling us with gas shells. The General addressed the officers at 5 a.m. We attacked at 8.0. All went well till we reached the ridge and then machine-guns opened on us and snipers picked off officers. Hamer the Adjutant killed. I took over his job. B Coy lost all their officers. I paraded the Coy after the battle. 16 men, 3 Sergeants. Battalion withdrew at 9.0. The road out was awful.

Saturday 8. (My birthday) Arrived at bivouac at 5.0 a.m. Absolutely dead beat wet through and muddied up. Fell down to sleep just where I arrived. But could not. Somebody covered me up. Held a roll call of my platoon. 8 Killed, 12 Wounded, 2 Missing.

Sunday 9. Called up at 5.30 a.m. to go into action again. My nerves are all over the place for want of sleep. I reported sick to the Doctor and tried to sleep. It is useless.

Monday 10. The bombardment is awful. The General called round at 8.45 a.m. to see the Colonel and I had to go and find him. Mametz Wood was attacked at 4.30. The wood was gained and a large number of prisoners taken. A counter attack was launched by the Hun and our two remaining Companies went up under the Colonel in support. I wanted to go but was refused by the Colonel and was put in charge of the camp.

Tuesday 11. Very busy all day with Adjutant's work. Took over 20 Prisoners of War and sent them to the Provost Marshal except the last six which I placed under a strong guard in the bivouac. Things are going badly in the battle for the wood. We hear that Brigade Staff has been knocked out. Lt Fletcher killed and Heppel wounded.

Wednesday 12. The battalion began to straggle in about 2 p.m. I had some hot tea ready for the men. They have had a very rough time. The Colonel is absolutely done and had to be led to bed.

Thursday 13. Moved off at 5 a.m. Arrived at Warloy-Baizieux at 12.0. Everybody dead beat. Can't get anything to eat. Moved off in Motor Buses to Couin. Arrived at 11 o'clock.

Thus ended the 38th Division's involvement in the Somme campaign. It had suffered nearly 4000 casualties, among them seven battalion commanders. As its battle-worn remnants withdrew its mood was a world away from that of 'the sturdy column that' – in the words of one of its young officers – 'swung its way down the hedge-bound lanes in the early mornings of the end of June, a bare fortnight past, singing and laughing in the happiness of relief from the fetters of the trenches in Flanders.'

※ ※ ※

Private Roland Mountfort, 10th Royal Fusiliers, 37th Division, recorded his experiences in this phase of the battle in a letter written on 23 July from the Mile End Military Hospital in London, to which he had been sent after receiving a Blighty wound on the 15th. This is the account of a Kitchener volunteer of high intelligence – he had been head boy of King Henry VIII School, Coventry – who had preferred to remain in the ranks rather than bid for a commission, and who was no great enthusiast for military attitudes and practice.

But though sceptical and fastidious, he was not aloof; sent to a School of Instruction for NCOs in May he had written: 'I feel that I should like to be with my pals if they have to go through it.' Freed from the censor by his being away from the front in England, his letter describes in vivid and at times acerbic terms how they went 'through it' on the Somme.

Their first involvement was on 10 July. They, like Ferguson's Cheshires, had been ordered to La Boisselle, but they were with Fourth Army, and their valley was Sausage, not Mash. They had begun the day improving trenches and burying dead of both sides while under shell fire from Contalmaison, which was still German-held. But not for long: 'In the afternoon we saw a fine sight on our right, the second and successful attack on Contalmaison. It was thrilling to see the lines of infantry advancing in extended order despite the shrapnel bursting all around them. They disappeared into the trees and presently we heard the attack had been very successful. Later appeared strings of German prisoners being taken back.'

Their spectator role ceased abruptly, however, when Mountfort's C Company found itself thrown into an attack without warning or, indeed, orders of any kind:

In the evening we got our first taste of fire in the open. The R.B. [i.e. 13th Rifle Brigade] were holding our front line and we were under the impression we were to relieve them. The way up was over ground for a little way, then along some trenches, and then up a light railway line for nearly half a mile from which the trenches turned off to the right and left. We moved off without knowing definitely what we were going to do (our invariable custom) and with many maddening halts and crawls we got up near the train line. Suddenly we saw that in front they were starting to run. Our Captain stood at the corner where we came out on to the line yelling 'Buck up, they've gone over' and off we went at the double. What was meant to happen I don't know now. What did happen is that the R.B. went over the top to the German trenches opposite them, and we came running up the line past the trenches the R.B. had vacated and on towards the German lines. The attack ought never to have been made and an order was sent up cancelling it. But the R.B. were already in the German trenches and we were nearly there. We came out, not knowing where we were, where we were going, or what we were going to do when we got there. The Germans of course had got the train line taped. Shrapnel was flying all over the place and a machine-gun on the left caught us with the protection of a bank about 3 feet high. We seemed to go on for a year. Men were going down every minute, and since there had previously been bodies lying all the way the place began to look a bit rotten. Here and there the lines had been torn up by shells and the holes had filled up with water, so that often we were nearly knee deep and one or two who preferred not to pick their way under the circumstances I saw struggling up to their waists. Then just as I became aware that there was nobody leading us and we should just go running on till nobody was left, there was a check in front, and the order came down to retire. The advance had been steady enough, but I am afraid at first the retirement was a bit of a scramble. It was not for far though, and then we turned some right and some left into what had been the front line trenches. Our orders were to spread out and man the parapet, which we did. The trenches were being heavily shelled; we didn't know what was happening and consequently when we saw men advancing towards us fire was opened for a few moments until we saw that some were English. They proved to be R.B.s bringing back wounded and prisoners. Of the latter over 200 came or were brought in, and some of them are supposed to have said that if we hadn't fired there was a whole Battn. ready to come over and surrender.

This was merely an overture, however, to what was to happen on the 15th.

* * *

Before that, however, the British Fourth Army produced an undoubted, indeed a spectacular, success. In contrast to attacks in full daylight over open ground, on 14 July an attack was launched at 3.25 a.m., after a minimal preliminary barrage, which caught the Germans entirely off-guard. The Battle of the Bazentin Ridge, as this initiative would be called (its official dates are 14–17 July), showed what could be achieved by playing the card of surprise. Lieutenant-Colonel E. Craig-Brown, serving in a brigade not involved in the action, was an admiring spectator. He wrote to his wife that morning:

It is now 5.35 a.m. and we have been up since about 3.

A big assault, on our right, came off at 3.25 with an intense bombardment which lasted five minutes and which was a sight to be seen. The whole horizon seemed to be bursting shells in front of us, and behind us flashing guns. No news of the assault has yet reached us, but we think the Boche must have had rather a disturbed morning.

Our part in the show is passive so far, merely forming a defensive flank, and the 79th are in Brigade reserve today.

Later: The Battle goes on apace; I hear the casualties on our side are not heavy.

The attack of 14 July has become justly famous in the annals of the Somme, a riposte to 1 July which delighted the French as much as it shook the Germans, and as it also gratified the British, especially the commanders of Fourth Army. 22,000 infantry, plus supporting troops, went over without alerting the look-outs in the enemy trenches. John Terraine has rightly described this as 'an amazing feat', explaining: 'Most of the troops belonged to the New Armies; their Staffs were the same men whose inexperience had weighed so heavily in the first planning of the Somme battle. Both now revealed those hidden qualities of adaptability and military instinct which had been stifled in the débâcle only thirteen days before. There was no mistake about this assault.' However, as he went on to admit, 'the problem of momentum, in the conditions of 1916, remained' – a problem compounded by the German policy of fighting as a matter of doctrine to regain every yard of ground the Allies had gained, irrespective of cost. Nor was the setting conducive to easy success. In this notorious centre stage of the Somme campaign, where those woods of evil reputation, the Bazentins, High Wood, Delville, themselves fearsome killing grounds, pressed in to shape the battle to the defenders' advantage, the attack lost pace and came to a halt. The casualty list was long – Craig-Brown's initial optimism on this aspect was premature, for the Germans were too professional not to respond immediately and with full vigour – but it was smaller in proportion than that of 1 July. One notable result was that there was more pride than distress in the accounts which participants sent home.

Units from several divisions, the 9th, 3rd, 7th and 21st, spearheaded the attack, among them, opposite the village of Longueval, the 8th Black Watch of the 9th (Scottish) Division. Lieutenant John Bates was the newly appointed Medical Officer of that battalion; he was to win the Military Cross for his outstanding work in this action.

Educated at Highgate School and Pembroke College, Cambridge, Bates had already launched his career as a medical practitioner in north London when war intervened. He was not among the first in uniform but by the summer of 1915 he had taken a commission in the RAMC and also become engaged to the young lady, Alice Dickens (usually addressed in his letters as Girl or Girlie), who would eventually become his wife, and to whom he wrote almost 600 letters during his period of service. His letter of 19 July 1916 shows both aspects of the ordeal from which he had just emerged, with a fine balance between awareness of loss on the one hand and, on the other, pleasure, even a sense of elation, in achievement. It is also a fascinating example of a letter which purports not to tell and yet tells, a device possibly adopted to ensure its safe passage through the censorship machine but which also gives it an extra dash of drama:

My darling old Girl.

Ever since Friday last we have been in a perfect hell of fighting. We were relieved this morning and thank God I have got out of it safe and sound. We have suffered so many casualties that we are going right away back to refit and reorganize. So you need not be anxious any more. I've been through it and come out safe and sound – how – I don't know. The regiment did simply splendidly and what we have done has been worth the cost.

Our battalion led the attack at dawn on Longueval on Friday last July 14th and we have hung on there ever since in spite of incessant artillery bombardment and 2 strong counter attacks. I went up with the Colonel in the attack and we were heavily shelled on the way up. Got through the Germans' barbed wire all right and found the village practically flattened by our artillery and several fires raging. I can't tell you the whole story now, Girlie, it would take pages and pages, but one day I'll tell you how the house next to my dressing station was blown up by one shell and the barn opposite set on fire simultaneously – how we had to hurry the patients out – how yesterday we were bombarded for 7 hours continuously and the concussion in the dugout we were in blew out the candle every minute or so – 7 hours of it – from 10.0 a.m. till 5 p.m. we sat in the dugout with shells bursting all around at the rate of about 24 per minute, continuously all the time – how the entrance was half blown in – how the enemy came over right past my dugout but never discovered yours truly and 3 patients who were inside – how our fellows drove the Hun right back again so that I was able to escape – I will tell you about it all one day and thank God I am safe and sound, out of it, never a scratch.

I am going to try and get some leave as soon as possible as it may be easier to get now we are going back to refit than later on. I am absolutely all right and my nerve has not been broken, thank heaven.

So I'll see you for certain soon, Girlie – how soon I can't say. I've got two Boche bayonets and a Boche hat as a remembrance of the most exciting, tiring and ghastly 5 days I have ever spent – at Longueval. In spite of our losses we are all happy and confident.

How cheery I feel now! It has been a most wonderful experience and I wouldn't have missed it for worlds. But I never want to see anything like it again. Once is enough!

Heaps and heaps of love

   Your old boy   John

Three Leicestershire battalions, the 6th, 7th and 8th, were also among the units that contributed to the dawn attack; they were on the front of 21st Division, opposite Bazentin-le-Petit. Of the 8th battalion, one company only, D, took part, the rest being in support. Some time later, in August, it was suggested to the Company Sergeant-Major of D Company, Ben Stafford, that he should write to his Company Commander, Captain Ward, who was recovering in England from wounds received in the action, to give him a detailed account of what had happened during the four-day battle. Stafford's letter is a remarkable document of the time, for the simple clarity of its description, for the light it casts on officer/other-rank relation-ships, also perhaps for the powerful impact of its litany of names, but above all for the attitude of stoic determination and willingness to continue on despite adversity which was a widespread character-istic of those fighting on the Somme, certainly at this early hopeful stage. Disenchantment undoubtedly existed and would grow, but there were countless officers and men, arguably the large majority, for whom their only thought was that the struggle had to be carried forward and pressed home. Stafford's deposition expresses such a view, without overtly saying so or indeed suggesting at any time that such things needed to be said:

> 'D' Company 8th Leicestershire Regiment   21. 8. 16.
> Captain F. Ward.

Sir

Mr Goodliffe has today shown me parts of a letter you have written to him. He suggested that I should write to you and give you as many details of the Battle as I possibly can. First of all, Sir, I remember you lying there wounded with a man holding you up. You were shouting to the Company to go on, and I took up the cry also. They who were not hit 'carried on', but how anyone reached the German trench I do not know. I am pleased to say, sir, what remained of the Company got into the right Trench. One party about a dozen lost their direction a little and were making for the Bazentin Wood, they, however, were redirected and recovered the proper direction.

We did not catch it from our front but from the left flank. The enemy seemed to have collected on the left of that communication trench and treated us severely with liquid fire, bombs and their devilish machine-guns. When we eventually reached their lines most of 'em retired to the left (our left, their right). I sent as many men as I could spare to clear that trench which they did remarkably well. We had no trouble from that quarter the whole of the 4 days we were in. Their dugouts were packed and no man escaped from them whilst we were in. They were all well bombed and the only retaliation they made in the trench from a dugout was one bomb which did not reach the top of the Steps, but made myself and L/ Sgt Hills A.E. jump. We had no more trouble from that Quarter.

'D' Company took one prisoner which we had to as he had both legs broken and was absolutely helpless. We blocked the junction of their fire trench and the communication trench in no time and every man set to work and we soon had some fire steps made and the trench deepened. On the right of the Company the enemy attempted to force their way into the trench luckily after we had had a breather and it was there that the Colonel was killed. We had a job to keep up with them in bombs, but we had all the bombs collected from the casualties in front and the German bombs came in handy too. L/Cpl Mason fought well in this defensive action but was unfortunately killed. We were shelled fairly heavily too, on occasions and suffered a few more casualties. We were in the trenches 4 days and every man breathed a sigh of relief when we marched through Mametz Wood for the last time.

The Company suffered heavily, Sir, 4 Officers (2 killed, Messrs Greenaway and Bowells) 2 wounded, you and Lt. Ewen, and 130 other ranks. There were no Sergts killed, Sgt. Kirk was very badly wounded but is in England now. Sgts Buxton, Croker, Hills were wounded badly before we reached our objective. Sgt. Reed of the Lewis Gunners was killed on the last day in the trench. L/Sgt. Hills was wounded by shrapnel a day or two after the attack. Cpl Rayson, L/Cpls Rogers, Wheeler, Morley G., Holyoak, Mason, E., Dunn, West, Chesham and Clarke were all killed, Sir.

Unfortunately, Sir, the boys had no opportunity of showing the ability with the Bayonet. The Bayonet work was done in Bazentin Wood which we missed. L/Cpl Clarke, A.A., showed great pluck, Sir, I believe he was the first man over, but was killed by a rifle bullet. Our Lewis Gunners suffered heavily, Sir, only about 3 or 4 getting through. In one sense, Sir, the Company was lucky to have had one left.

Personally, Sir, I was extremely lucky, bullets pierced my clothing and equipment in six places and a bomb dropped at my feet but I jumped out of the way and caught a tiny bit in the cheek, the force knocked me over though.

I think, Sir, you have every reason to be a proud man (I hope you will pardon me saying so). Only well trained and well disciplined troops could have faced the Hell we faced. It was *your* training, Sir, and I'm a proud man to have served under such an Officer. The 'Boys' did wonderfully well, Sir, and I'm proud to be Com Sgt Major over the 'Remnants'. We have *always* prided ourselves on being the BEST Company in the Battalion and I think Bazentin-le-Petit proved it.

My ambition is, Sir, to bring the Company up to its old efficiency. It is our Duty in remembrance of our late C.O. and you, Sir, who made the Company what it was.

I hope, Sir, you will soon be in good fettle again, I hope your wounds will heal quickly and with as little pain as possible. I'm not going to wish you a Speedy Return to the Front, Sir, as I should be wishing you no good. With every wish for a speedy recovery from *everyone* in 'D' Company. I know the boys would want me to include their good wishes.

I remain, Sir,
  Your sincere Sergeant,
    Ben. W. Stafford
    Coy. Sgt. Major
    'D' Company.

* * *

In contrast to the attack of the 14th, that of Mountfort's 10th Royal Fusiliers, 37th Division, on the following day was a more conventional affair, conceding to the enemy the advantage of an attack made in broad daylight. The target was the village of Pozières on the Albert–Bapaume road. His account covers only the first part of the action, since he became an early victim:

In the morning of the 15th we got 'stand by ready to move off at an hour's notice'. As we had been in the habit of standing by ready to move off at 5 minutes' notice this looked well. Then at 8.30 we had orders to be ready at 9.30, and then suddenly at 9 o'clock 'get dressed'. (That means equipment, of course.) Nobody was half ready, and from that moment everything was a scramble. We moved off in platoons, overland, towards the front line, jumped over the support lines, and lay down just behind the front line. Then came the order to advance, and before we knew where we were we were 'going over the top'. In the distance – a fearful way it seemed – was Pozières; and we knew by now we were attacking it. Then the crumps began, and, what proved our undoing, machine-guns crackled from the village. We advanced at the walk. There was a good deal of shouting – 'Keep up' – 'don't bunch' – 'half left' – and so on, but only necessary orders. We didn't dribble footballs, neither did we say 'This way to Berlin, boys', nor any of the phrases employed weekly in the *News of the World*.

We crossed over another trench with troops in it, and about 200 yards further on, as I was running forward a little with my head well down I felt a punch on my shoulder, and lay down in a shell hole to think things over. It didn't hurt much, and I could hold my rifle and it seemed to me I ought to go on. On the other hand I could see the hole just behind my shoulder strap where the bullet had gone in, and I could tell it hadn't merely gone through clothing because my shoulder felt funny. So I lay for some time feeling a good deal of self-contempt, because I knew that if I had the real V.C. instinct I should have got hold of my rifle in my left hand and gone forward with set teeth and a look of grim determination, or else with a strained smile and a joking remark suitable for headlines.

A man with a bullet through his leg shared the hole, and after a while he went off back. Then a man with a bad wound in the back came in. After a while stretcher-bearers, who behaved magnificently, I never admired anything more in my life, came along, dodging from man to man, patching them up with field dressings, helping them into shell holes and carrying on as though it was Hampstead Heath on manoeuvre days; while the whole time heavy lyddite shrapnel was bursting overhead and the machine-guns were playing as freely as ever. They patched up the other fellow's back and wanted to do mine but I sent them to look for somebody worse. After a while some more came along and as they didn't seem so busy I let them look at my shoulder, and when I saw the back of my shirt and cardigan jacket well soaked with blood I reconciled myself to the idea of getting out of the scrap.

On 15 July the 10th Royal Fusiliers lost in killed, wounded and missing eleven officers and 245 men. Mountfort, hearing the first news of casualties, commented: 'I'm afraid the 10th will be practically non-existent.' Still shocked by the impact of what had happened, he would write on 28 August: 'The end of the war seems to be the only thing worth looking forward to.' He never returned to the Western Front, being despatched on recovery to East Africa, where he joined the Regiment's 25th Battalion. Commissioned in 1918, he survived to return with relief to civilian life, only to die of cancer at the age of forty.

*   *   *

The day of the 10th Royal Fusiliers' attack, 15 July, also saw the beginning of the process of linking South Africa emotionally with the territory of the Somme. The South African Brigade, like the 8th Black Watch part of the 9th Division, was ordered to take Delville Wood. 'It clearly shows the opinion those in authority have of the S.A.I. [South African Infantry] that they should have been given the task of cleaning the wood,' wrote one eighteen-year-old soldier who took part in the operation, from his sick bed in a Military Hospital in Lewisham, London, where he had been sent after being wounded in the attack. He was Private Percy Robins, the younger of two brothers – he was junior to his brother Willie by just under a year – who had volunteered, travelled, trained and now gone over the top side by side. This was most fortunate for him, as he had explained in an earlier letter to his family posted from the Canadian Hospital at Boulogne. 'We weren't at it more than 10 minutes or maybe 15 when I got a bullet through the calf of my left leg. Luckily, old Will was with me and he put a field dressing on it. I tell you Willie was a perfect Angel of Mercy and a little Hero.'

Willie Robins, writing from France on 21 July, reassured the family back in South Africa about his brother's state of health. 'Percy was lucky and was hit through the calf of the leg the first day we were there and I don't mind telling you I envy him very much.'

He felt unable, however, to give the background which might explain why he took that view. 'I'm afraid the censor will not allow me to give you a description of the affair so I will leave that to another time.' But he felt free enough to sum up his feelings overall. 'We've been through a terrible experience and I'm perfectly convinced it was only through God's good grace that we were both spared to come through alive.'

In fact the orders to the South Africans had been that Delville Wood was to be taken 'at all costs'. These three chilling words were to become a keynote phrase, almost a keynote slogan, of the Somme battle from this time forwards. In a potent and by no means uncritical passage from his book on the Somme, a soldier of a later generation, General Sir Anthony Farrar-Hockley, would write:

'At all costs' – the phrase came too readily to the lips of the higher commanders. Foch used it to invigorate Sixth Army in the rebuffs it suffered as the corps closed up painfully towards Péronne on either side of the river. Sixt von Arnim used it at Longueval where he believed he had the strength to push the foe back across Caterpillar Valley. And Congreve used it as Delville Wood became truly an inferno, the trees burning fiercely after days of bombardment, despite a drenching rainstorm. The South Africans earned the ungrudging praise of their comrades and their enemies in holding and counter-attacking this awful corner of the ridge, in the crumbling Longueval streets, in the ravaged orchards and wood whose defences drew in six divisions before acknowledging defeat. Horne decided that High Wood must be taken 'at all costs' but the cost was too great for the numbers of men he had to expend. At Pozières Gough ordered the capture of the village by 1st Australian Division without waiting for the remainder of the Anzac Corps, but he mercifully used the fatal phrase only for the capture of a stretch of trench.

Private Percy Robins put the ordinary South African's viewpoint in these words, in his letter from the hospital in Boulogne: 'What price the S.A.I. now, eh? They've made a name for themselves but at a sad cost.'

* * *

Sunday 16 July was a remarkable day in the life of Second Lieutenant Charles Carrington. He found himself in a situation which would turn him into something of a hero; it might so easily have ended quite differently. He would later describe his adventure in his book *A Subaltern's War*, and, though he did so without self-glorification, he would subsequently be acclaimed as a thrusting officer of the highest class. This is his first account of the episode, in a letter to his mother written five days later, only three days after he came out of the battle.

A good deal has happened to us lately. I have been through a big show and took half a company on my own to the wrong German trench and held it for 48 hours. It was the wrong trench but it was luckily a useful one, and I got congratulated when I would have certainly been court-martialled if it had not been wanted. Whether the Censor will pass all this I don't know. We are in reserve just now again and I am acting in command of a company. My Second pip has been struggling through the War Office for some weeks and came through yesterday, so I am now a full Lieut.

I got quite a good German helmet out of one of their dugouts, which I hope I shall be able to get home. Fritz has got plenty of kick in him, yet, but is beaten if you go for him hard.

I never met a Boche face to face, though we bombed them at 20 or 30 yds down a trench. Some of my men met them closer. We were cut off in our trench almost surrounded, isolated by day, and with very little water. It was most romantic but we should have been wiped out if they had attacked us heavily. I don't think they knew quite what to make of us. I was in charge there for a few hours until the Colonel came up. On the second day they attacked the positions behind us, and we were relieved. We were very lucky. It might have been much worse.

Carrington later referred briefly to the event in his 1965 memoir *Soldier from the Wars Returning*, giving the necessary context to the story thus first described:

Without preliminary bombardment we crossed a thousand yards of open ground and occupied a knot of trenches in rear of the defenders of Ovillers. It fell to me to lead the assault, and to hold the farthest point we reached against a German bombing attack, which might have been pressed more resolutely if they had known our strength – or rather our weakness – and how we had got there. By such tactics the Division contained the garrison of Ovillers and compelled its surrender on the afternoon of the 16th, for what we thought a moderate cost in casualties.

He added that this attack by his 1/5th Royal Warwickshires was 'thought worthy of one line in the official history'.

* * *

The Somme produced its individual heroes. It also produced its individual tragedies. The diary of the RHA officer, Captain Harry Bursey, records this story under the date 18 July:

Standing in my Camp this morning I saw a figure ride in smothered with mud and wet through. He came towards me and saluted. I saw it was an officer and he asked me if the Colonel was about. 'Is

No.4 Section far from here?' he asked, passing his hand wearily across his eyes. 'It's half an hour's ride', I said, 'won't you dismount?'. 'No thanks', he said, 'I've got to report'. 'I've been in Hell the last twelve hours.' Again he held his head in his hand. 'Get down old man', I said, 'and rest'. A sergeant took his horse. 'I've been gassed', he said. 'I was up with the wagons last night and the Huns started shelling us with gas shells and I can remember no more. I've been wandering about with this horse since 3 this morning.' He swayed towards me and I caught him just in time.

We laid him down and opened his shirt and removed his equipment. I managed to get a drop of whisky from the O.C. No.2 Section and gave him a drink. It revived him for a moment, then he fell back again in an utter collapse. I have just sent him to a field ambulance in a wagon on a stretcher. I covered him with my waterproof sheet, my one and only, which I shall probably never see again. He hasn't been out of England a week yet. I fear he is done.

Two of my drivers, suffering from shell shock, have gone with him. He was in charge of 20 wagons last night with 2 other officers, all 2nd Lieutenants.

I hear all wagons are back but that one driver is missing. '*C'est la guerre.*'

We move tomorrow. It is in the right direction, towards Germany. The French on our right must be pushing for there is a tremendous cannonade going on just now in their lines.

One gets weary sometimes of the awful sights one sees. It's all so sad that men should be flying at each other's throats – aye and far worse than that in this war. I hear that the Colonel of the Seaforth Highlanders was shot by a Hun prisoner after a lot of them had surrendered. The men were so enraged that they – well I will leave that out.

* * *

Despite the mixed fortunes of the events of these first weeks of July, there was undoubtedly a widespread feeling that progress was being made, that the enemy was being pressed hard, or, in more front-line trench terms, being given a bloody nose and a run for his money. A gunner, Lieutenant C.J. (Joe) Rice of 84th Brigade, Royal Field Artillery, wrote to his parents from the Somme on 17 July: 'I don't know what people at home think about it but considering the Germans have tried for 5 months to break the French front and failed while we are dealing with the Germans' third line system in 18 days I think it is great. The fact that we have been able to use cavalry is a good sign. The battery has advanced twice, a total distance of 2¾ miles. The horses and guns are getting a bit tired as you can imagine, but they have certainly stood it well.'

By this time, however, as the arrival on the scene of the concept of 'at all costs' clearly shows, there was also no doubt that this was going to be a hard, attritional struggle, in which ground would be dearly gained and in which substantial casualty figures could not, indeed would not, be avoided. Lieutenant-General Sir Thomas D'Oyly Snow had been much involved in the first stage of the battle as commander of VII Corps of Third Army, to which belonged those two divisions, the 46th North Midland and the 56th London, which had been involved in the diversionary attack at Gommecourt. From 2 July VII Corps had returned to normal trench warfare but Snow had followed the campaign in close detail and had strong views about its conduct and progress. Striking a note in tune with the views of many of his fellow commanders and which would be heard increasingly throughout the weeks ahead, he wrote in a personal letter on 16 July: 'Of course the advance is a tremendous success, not a bit a false one. The enemy has got to be fought everywhere and hard. It's not a bit of good sitting down and saying you are wearing him out. The gain in land matters little as long as you inflict damage on him. Everything is going very well indeed and no one minds the losses as long as we are moving.'

At the level of the ordinary soldier carrying out often sacrificial attacks, however, the pattern of slowly developing success was somewhat less obvious. The diary covering this period of Corporal Norman Edwards, a member of the maxim gun section of the 1/6th Gloucesters, 48th (South Midland) Division, tells a story of confusion, of attacks announced and then aborted, of men psyching themselves up for battle and then being abruptly instructed to stand down. (As early as 2 July, an order to mount an attack on Beaumont Hamel was countermanded by a a last-minute command to about-turn and go back; no doubt wisely – a 'hard-bitten Regular NCO' had said to him as they had made their way forward: 'God help thee. We tried yesterday and I'm one of 28 left in our battalion!') When finally he and his comrades went into action, in the Ovillers-Pozières sector, on the 21st (to the sound of their officer spurring them on, 'rather shakily', with a cry of 'No shirking, lads, no shirking!'), there was the now standard response from the enemy side. Alerted by the explosion of a bomb store hit by a chance missile from a Stokes mortar, the Germans had flares and a red Very light up even as the Gloucesters crossed the parapet:

> I took a bearing of the North Star and knew my direction but we had hardly gone ten yards when their machine-guns started. From then onwards it was pure and undiluted HELL. The fire became so hot that it was almost impossible to move, but we made another 10 yards and found a lovely deep shell hole and we hung on there. Vic came tumbling in with the gun and said cheerily: 'Wot ho, knocker, if you knows of a better 'ole. . .', and we all laughed.
>
> Then somebody made the appropriate remark that 'This is a bloody game', and I pulled out a fag, lit up and agreed.

For Edwards the 'game' ended shortly after with his being wounded – 'a sledge hammer seemed to hit me in the arm' – and he had to make his way back as best he could through bullets and bursting shrapnel. 'I gave my name in at Coy HQ and went on out towards the dressing station. As I went down the road I met "Haggis", who had been shot through the shoulder, and we toddled down together.' At one point he and his fellow casualty paused to rest, and Edwards was able to apprehend something of the awesomeness of the scene behind them:

> We sat for a while and looked back at it all and shuddered. Two boys almost, miraculously pulled out of a cauldron of death.
>
> A few piles of smashed brick and broken trees was all that was left of La Boisselle and Ovillers. The huge white mass in front was the debris of chalk thrown up by a mine, while away on the right I could see Contalmaison and Mametz Wood. The Germans were still shelling heavily in front of Pozières and every minute an 8-inch shell would come lazily over and burst down in the valley. Yes, we have made some ground, but my God, the price has been

awful. We got up and I turned my back on it all and devoutly hoped I should never see it again.

Despite all this, his Tommy's basic thirst for souvenirs had not been entirely extinguished: 'I scrounged an old helmet on the way down and we staggered into "Crucifix Corner".'

CHAPTER 8

SOMME SUMMER

CAPTAIN REGINALD GILL, 28th Battalion, 7th Brigade, 2nd Australian Division, went into the lines at Pozières on 27 July. The 1st Division had opened the battle on the 23rd, and the 3rd Division would take over from the 2nd on 5 August. Writing from Belgium after his division's withdrawal, to a friend with whom he had shared a much enjoyed pre-war trip to Darjeeling, Gill commented, wistfully: 'If only those days could come once more, life is a very uncertain factor here old man, we have been having some terrible fighting since I last wrote you, on the Somme, the Australians made their name at Pozières, which we took, also the "Heights of Pozières", where desperate fighting took place, it doesn't matter much telling you all this now as it is all over and is public property.'

In one charge Gill's battalion lost nineteen officers (fourteen killed and five wounded) and 670 men in about one hour. Pozières would indeed make a name for the Australians – and make public property of their extraordinary tenacity and courage – so that by the time Gill wrote his letter he would be able to add: 'They are working the Australians for all they are worth just now.'

Pozières would be both a proud and a bitter memory for the 'Aussies' of the Somme. '22,826 Australians fell to win a few yards of ground,' a later Australian historian would write, 'and only a minority, by great fortune, survived. It was a monstrous sacrifice, which tumbled the romances and grand illusions of the past into the dust, whence they rarely rose again. After Pozières many soldiers looked back to their boyhood, and saw an unfamiliar world. . . . The Australians never forgot Pozières, nor the English staff which sent them there, nor the mates killed, nor the New Army Divisions which had failed so often on their flanks, nor a thousand scenes of horror and heroism, nor, most terrible of all, the ceaseless, merciless, murdering guns.' Dr Bean's account confirms the awfulness of the sustained shelling of the battlefield around that doomed Picardy village. Though 'typical of the Verdun and First Somme battles,' he wrote, 'on no part of the front in France were such bombardments more severe than at Pozières.'

* * *

The battle would shortly leave behind the places associated with its first phase, moving on to the broad plateau which would be the principal theatre for the greater part of the Somme campaign. Today the pocket-sized woods and the little villages with their squat, assertive churches are back there as though they had never been away, giving shape and feature to a pleasing if undistinguished landscape. But in 1916 the woods became abstract sculptures of distorted trees intermixed with shell holes, while the villages mutated into heaps of grotesque ruins or, as in the case of Pozières, a wilderness of dead ground. 'The country around looked fearfully ominous,' wrote one new arrival on the Somme in August, 'in fact all this district is the picture of the most dreary ruination and desolation that has ever been, and one worse would almost be impossible to think of.'

For the ordinary soldier plodding to and from the front the most ominous places of all were those dangerous avenues of approach he would have to traverse to get to the trench lines. Of these one of the most exposed was the appropriately nicknamed 'Death Valley', which ran northwards past Mametz Wood on one side, Flatiron Copse on the other and then on between the two woods of Bazentin-le-Petit and Bazentin-le-Grand. This was rarely the healthiest of places to be.

Private Arthur Wrench came to the Somme in late July to join the 4th Battalion Seaforth Highlanders in the 51st (Highland) Division. With several other new arrivals he tried to find battalion headquarters in Death Valley by night. 'Old Fritz is shelling fearfully with tear-gas shells,' his diary account reads. 'The air is stinking with it and it is terrible. We put on our gas goggles at first, but could not see with them and it was too dangerous getting in the way of excited and restless horses and mules of gun and wagon teams that more than once some of us were nearly down beneath the wheels. So it was safer to have to put up with watery eyes, painful as it was, for they nipped like fury.'

His duty was that of runner and he had barely joined the battalion before he was sent to 'find the Colonel "somewhere in the old German second line trenches" and ask him for any information for the general's orders':

It was a terrible journey, especially when I did not know where I was going and it was pitch dark, except for the flashing of the guns which seemed to be everywhere, barking out all around me so that it is impossible to hear the German shells coming. This bombardment was Hellish, to tell the truth about it, and it was almost maddening as I groped my way, hopelessly lost among battery after battery of artillery in action, and further forward among old trenches into which I stumbled. After a while I spotted a gleam of light away down in an old mine crater or something. In this shelter were some Seaforth signallers so they gave me fuller instructions how to get to their H.Q. So I continued on as it began to get daylight, and soon I began to be chased backwards and forwards along some old shallow trenches, obviously German ones at one time.

Every time I stood upright or got out, I was shot at by some damned German, and I couldn't find a soul about anywhere. At last I came upon the first man in the line here, and he told me that the colonel had passed along this way just ten minutes earlier. So I went on while the awful uproar of the battle was now quietened, and soon I overtook the colonel. It was now long after sunrise. In fact it was exactly 6 o'clock by my watch as I asked him the question I had set out to do to which he replied with a shake of his head, and said, 'No, I have no information for the General's orders.'

That journeys up or down 'Death Valley' were high risk affairs was of course due to the frequent and severe 'strafes' from the German guns, which had all the likely targets precisely registered. On one occasion Wrench found what he described as 'timely and, as it proved, sufficient shelter' under a water cart from which on his treks to and fro he regularly filled his water bottle. After a while, judging it safe to move, he emerged, but he had ventured too soon:

A few yards further on I threw myself into a little shelter by the roadside, cut into the bank. It was an officer of the artillery who heard this shell coming and called to me, 'In here, quick,' and I avoided the shell just in time, for it landed where I had stood. Made my hair stand on end. Lay with this officer in his cubbie hole with no room to move and our heads touching the roof, as the bombardment swept the valley, and watched the bursts as every minute we expected to be blown to pieces. Then right across the road from here, a heap of sticks and all went flying in the air and soon a party of men seemed to issue from nowhere and set to feverishly to dig out two or three men who had been buried there. One was found in very bad shape, and the other was dead. Our own artillery goes just as hard at it and at night was so terrible that it was impossible to hear anyone talking, only the shells that burst close by.

Relieved and sent back to a field near Méaulte, which they reached at midnight, the Seaforths found that the cooks 'had some hot stew ready for us and it tasted the most wonderful stuff in the world. Then we "got down to it" in our greatcoats just as we were, all huddled together in the open field, and soon fell sound asleep. The most blessed rest we have ever known.'

* * *

Wednesday 4 August brought the second anniversary of the outbreak of war. The date brought sombre thoughts to Private Wrench, who wrote in his diary: 'Today commences the third year of this ghastly war. How much longer, I wonder, is it to go on? If only the people at home could realize what it is like, they would surely demand that it be finished.'

The war was indeed finished that day for Lieutenant Alan Lloyd, of C Battery, 78th Brigade, Royal Field Artillery. Exuberant, optimistic, and showing every sign of actually enjoying the hard fighting on the Somme, he had come there in the wake of the opening attack and had seen hope and signs of success in every action in which he had been involved. Aged twenty-seven, he was married and a father, with a young and much doted-on son, David. He and his wife Dorothy Margaret, née Hewetson, had advanced their marriage because of the outbreak of war, though they had had all the trimmings of a peacetime wedding: invitation cards, handsomely printed orders of service, photographs, even an announcement in *The Times*. Both his and her letters have been preserved and to read them is almost like an intrusion into private happiness, a happiness which was to mutate all too rapidly to its grim opposite. He was 'Hubkins' or 'Hub', she was 'small wife', or sometimes 'My own little Margot', and there was much love and longing, and dreams and plans, in their correspondence. His letters from the Somme exude the confidence of someone who had no doubt that the Germans were coming second in the campaign. Thus on 6 July: 'We've been very busy lately and you can well guess why because you were quite right in your little surmise, what a smart little wife for a dull Hub! We are very flourishing and are *not* having a bad time at all. It's great sport advancing over the Hun trenches and I hope it will continue. It's also much more comfortable because the Hun has to take back his heavy guns and has only small stuff against us. And we go for him with heavies!'

He wrote in similarly breezy terms on the 10th, at a time when there was good news from the Eastern Front, with reports of a successful Russian offensive: 'We're all very cheery and bright so don't fret your little self, beloved. The Hun is having a rocky time with the French and us and the Russians all together. He shoved in the Prussian Guard when we'd burst thro' his first line the other day to try and stop us going further. But we got on to them with machine-guns and nearly annihilated them. They had to go out to re-form and did no good at all.'

On the 13th: 'Is small wife happy please because Hub is and there's no reason why small wife should be anxious because we're quite all right and enjoying ourselves, tho' we have plenty of fighting and work at present. We are doing quite well and so are the French and we are gradually pushing the Hun back. I don't think he likes it very much, he's bombarded all day and all night and he gets blue Hell.'

This admission of serious fighting, even though wrapped in his usual cheerfulness, led him to add a reassuring postscript: 'Don't worry, belovedest little angel, all is going quite well and Hub takes ever such care.'

A letter of 21 July not to his wife – presumably to an officer friend in England – stated that he was now serving as a Forward Observation Officer, a position of some risk as compared to the relative safety of the gun lines, especially during a period of hard and continuous fighting:

> We have had a strenuous and to some extent dangerous time during the operations of his Majesty's junior service for the last 3 weeks. But these operations have been attended with marked success and we have the Hun pretty well hammered.
>
> So far I have a whole skin and sleep like a top despite the terrifying and never ending noise. I have been FOO several times, once in the big attack on his 2nd line which was very successful. On this occasion I was right up with the Infantry and got a machine-gun bullet thro' my tunic on the right elbow, it tore the shirt and vest and never scratched the skin! This was a very exciting day and I enjoyed myself. I was signalling back by flag. Yes, the Warwicks got it hot and it's a great pity so many were wiped out. Guy Field and Esmond Roger were very good chaps. Topping weather now and I'm in great form.

By the 25th he was describing some of his dangerous adventures to his wife, though softening the admission with the news that they were temporarily out of the line:

> Beloved little Margot
>
> We are resting! Aren't you pleased now? I don't know for how long but it's very pleasant. 2 days ago we saw a Hun bty. from the OP. Marshall sent me up to shoot at it and I think I knocked 3 guns out. At any rate it didn't fire any more! Best bit of fun I've had out here. Got fairly in to it and simply plugged shells into it as hard as I could. I don't think the Huns in it can have enjoyed themselves much. 2 Ammunition pits went up with a big blaze. Fine weather still and we push on.
>
> Bye-bye dearest
> Am very well
> Yr Hub

On 1 August, by which time his wife was on holiday in Devon, he wrote:

> Just a scrawl to say all well and flourishing and still comfortably in rest. Awful hot and dusty but much better than rain.
>
> You'll be in Devon now I expect, I wish your Hub was there too. What a time we'd have and we'd bathe together in the briney and do all sorts of funny things. Bye-bye, beloved.
>
> I hear my name was sent in as recommended for a Bty Commander the other day.

He wrote three letters of the 3rd, including what would be his last to his wife. Again, his thoughts were with her in Devon, and there were his usual assurances of progress at the front: 'Please, would you like Hubbins with you at Salterton, 'cause he'd like to be there. Here, we go steadily on bit by bit, smashing the Huns with guns of all sorts and the Heavies accounted for 31 batteries yesterday which is awful good.' This letter was almost especially tender, showing a deep concern for his family – 'Please, is small wife very well and David too?' – and following his usual sign-off with the expression 'Loads of love!' and the fond postscript: 'Hub has had some lovely parcels from his little spouse; she is a darling.'

In the early hours of 4 August Lloyd was killed. He was up near his forward Observation Point with a signaller and another officer when they came under severe shell-fire and was badly hurt. He died of his wounds shortly afterwards.

The standard War Office telegram was sent to Mrs Lloyd on the 6th. On the 5th, eager to put detail to the bare fact of her husband's death as conveyed by the arid formula of an official telegram, Lloyd's fellow officer, Lieutenant Arthur Impey, wrote her a remarkable letter of consolation. This was quite different in tone from the often perfunctory if well meant letters sent to relatives following a fatality, in which praise for gallantry and assurances of esteem among the victim's peers were included virtually as a matter of routine. Impey was clearly well aware of this tradition, and wished to make a distinction: 'I have read letters written at times like this that didn't sound quite true, and I don't want to convey the impression that I am writing in that spirit; it would be an insult to his memory and to you, but it is the simple truth that he was personally the bravest man I ever knew ... You and he have a son who will want to become as fine a man as his father was, and will be proud to know what his father's pals thought of him, and in saying this I am saying what I know is felt by every one in the brigade.'

About the circumstances of Lloyd's death Impey wrote with great care. It was more or less standard in consolatory letters to inform the bereaved that their loved ones had suffered no distress; Impey did this in such a way as to suggest that this was no conventional reassurance, and indeed there is no reason to suspect that his account was anything other than genuine: 'Poor old Alan was very badly hit, he never had a dog's chance, and died in about 20 minutes, he was quite conscious and asked if he was badly hit; they told him no, and he seemed quite happy and in no pain, and said he would be all right soon, he never knew what was really the matter and died without knowing what was happening.'

The officer with Lloyd on his last mission was a young second lieutenant from another battery in the same brigade, R.J. Yeatman, who was himself severely wounded, and who did all he could to save his superior officer's life by dressing his wounds and then making his way through the barrage to obtain medical aid. Later in the year, Yeatman wrote to Lloyd's father giving an account of the event, pleading for forgiveness should any inaccuracy be found if his description were compared with that of the signaller who had been with them, 'as the shock of high explosive at 2 yards is very great and my recollections [are] mercifully vague.' He added: 'Much more worthy of telling, I think, is the gallant disregard of the most obvious danger by your son on this and all other occasions of this kind. Your son was a very good soldier, and a most valuable trained artilleryman. It is the prospect of meeting again his sort that makes one contemplate calmly one's own future in this War.'

Both Lloyd and Yeatman were awarded the Military Cross for their conduct at this time, Yeatman specifically for his efforts on behalf of his companion. A further footnote to this story perhaps worth recording is that Yeatman went on to win considerable fame as the author, with W.C. Sellar, of the spoof history of England *1066 and All That*, which, following its publication in 1930, would become favourite reading for numerous generations of school-children.

Captain Lloyd was one of many officers, like Jocelyn Buxton, who inspired a strong affection and admiration in his servant. Gunner Manning was deeply distressed at his master's death and made his own rough wooden cross to put on the grave, scratching in it the tribute:

HE DIED AS HE
LIVED
BRAVE AND FEARLESS
A TRUE BRITISH
HERO

Later a more substantial wooden cross was erected and then after the war the usual War Graves Commission headstone. In recognition of Manning's devotion, when devising an inscription for the head-stone the family retained the first part of his tribute, stopping short of the 'hero' claim, and also kept the wooden cross, which is still a most treasured possession.

* * *

Second Lieutenant Geoffrey Lillywhite, 9th Battalion East Surrey Regiment, 24th Division, arrived in the Somme area on 2 August. His first impression, as they reached the village of Méaulte, south east of Albert, was *not* that this was a benign English-style country-side; on the contrary – but then this was high summer and the land had been home for months to thousands of men, horses and guns. 'We are now in a kind of desert,' he told his mother, writing that same day. 'It is chalky rolling downs and very dusty with no water. Kind of South African place. The heat is terrific.' On the 3rd he wrote again, having had time to observe the visual effects of the sustained attentions of the Allied artillery: 'You cannot imagine how completely our gunners wipe out every feature of the landscape. It looks as though a giant with an enormous shovel had dug up all the ground for miles around uprooting whole woods and little hills.'

Nor had the giant completed his work. This from a letter to one of his sisters, sent on the 4th: 'As I am writing this there is the most terrific bombardment going on all round. There must be hundreds of big guns pounding away for all they are worth. It is like a dozen people playing drums as hard as they can rattle them, only each beat is a huge explosion. The banging is so continuous that it is utterly impossible to distinguish even the tiniest fraction of a second during which there is not some gun going off. They all just merge into a continuous roar. Poor old Fritz, he must be fed up.'

He noted the inevitable consequence of all this hard pounding: 'All over the place are huge piles of empty cartridge cases where the guns have fired and and have now pushed on.' Another equally obvious sign of the Allied momentum came from the view skywards: 'What I like to see is how every day our sausages [observation balloons] creep nearer and nearer to Hunland. We have crowds up, but if the Hun puts one up our airmen immediately go for it to bust it.'

As in the case of many ground-based soldiers, especially at a time of constant activity, the air war was a constant source of fascination for the young second lieutenant. On the 16th, by which time his battalion had moved to the fighting zone, he wrote to his mother:

You would like to see our aeroplanes out here. They are like flocks of birds, always coming and going. They are of all sizes. Some very fast little scouts that fairly dart about, others a little larger, until you come to the great big 'Dreadnought' of the aeroplanes with two engines, two propellers, four rudders and a gun. They have enormously long wings. Then there are an enormous number of sausages all along our new lines. We have made such a big bite into the Hun lines that they seem all round us.

What this letter did not mention was that the battalion was about to take part in an attack. This was a thrust in the direction of Guillemont, which resulted in the gaining of some 300 yards though at considerable cost. When he did refer to the fighting, in his letter of the 17th – by which time the battalion had moved back towards Montauban – he did so at first obliquely and in some temper, though the focus of his anger was not the enemy, nor the Staff, nor the British high command, but the civilian world back home, with its callow, unthinking ignorance about the realities of the conflict being fought in their name. Above all, it would seem, he was targeting those Western Front watchers who shook their heads and tut-tutted over the apparently slow progress of the Allied push in spite of the weeks of hard and sacrificial effort:

> I should just hope the people *are* satisfied with what is being done out here! I would give anything for the wretched shysters to see a fine battalion go into action, and then see it crawl out a few days later a shattered wreck, nothing but a handful of men. But those little handfuls are very proud, because they say the same as the Gurkha said, 'If only a few come back they will know we have been fighting'. The Hun realises that in spite of his terrific efforts we are every day snatching back a fresh little piece of his ground. The result is so insignificant on the map, but the cost is heavy. It makes one realise what a hopelessly impossible task it would be to storm the whole line and drive them bodily back.

It was almost as an afterthought that he added, at the end of the letter: 'Last night we had a hell of a scrap. Eight officers killed and one wounded and a great number of men also. Many of those killed came from the 11th with me. Still the job on hand was a big one.'

* * *

Private Edgar (Ted) Gale, 8th East Yorkshire Regiment, came to the Somme in mid August. Writing to his parents on the 17th, he informed them by a secretly agreed code (i.e. by giving a series of key letters an exaggeratedly backward slope, thus spelling out the appropriate names) that he was on the Somme, and then gave them a detailed description of his adventures:

> One day we went as a working party to make a dugout, at about 5.0 p.m. and we got lost and kept getting in the road of the shells. It became dark and still we were stumbling and slipping along the muddy tracks. The place we were in has been nicknamed the 'Valley of Death' I think, and truly the looks thereof spoke vehemently of the dreaded death so many had gone through.
>
> We in advancing had to break up into two parties. I was in the second and it wasn't long before the two got separated by shell fire and lost to each other.
>
> We had to retire to some old disused trenches for cover, and

stayed there until a guide was called, for the betterment of our progress towards where the dugout was to be fixed. We set off again and the great 'Johnsons' and 'Coal Boxes' were casting volumes of blackness up into the air, around and on every side of us. At last we were told to make for a certain light which was dimly seen in front of us. It was a good two hundred yards away and what with our weight of pack, or rather equipment, the heavy and slippery trudging along and the constant job of looking for shell holes, lumber and ruin in general, we couldn't make decent headway.

But I leave it to you to imagine what it would be like when we had to keep ducking to avoid the shells we were moving straight towards; in fact it was more than just 'ducking', it was a case of getting as low as possible to avoid the 'bits'.

We filed along until we were within a few yards of the light, and then there was a fearful scream, the scream of a shell in flight. I guessed it was falling near me, so down I dropped in the thick mud and paused. There was a deafening, metallic-sounding bang and a cloud of blackest darkness covered one side of the sky from view. Then on my back and steel helmet came a heavy shower of mud and other things; and I found myself still unharmed, though if some of the oddments lying about in that part had been thrown at me by the explosion, I should probably be in Blighty now.

We all remained in the trenches for some time, then went out and dug, and filled sandbags and did all sorts of jobs until the necessary dugout was completed.

Day dawned, and still we were there, and with day, other truths dawned, more telling than the large waste of dreary desolation that the daylight unfolded. One by one in the valley beneath us little parties of the Red Cross were doing their doleful tramp back from the trench on the ridge. Great shells began to fall again and I was one of many told off to fetch something up from the stores down the hill. It was not long after my return, and whilst I was standing on a high open part, that a shell came whizzing down the valley. It exploded, causing many poor chaps to drop down and hide or run away. They all seemed to have cleared it at first, but as the smoke rolled aside it was obvious someone had suffered. There on the road, one of our own company, lay a sergeant with great wounds to the head. I don't know for sure but I think he died; and out of

the working party we supplied that night for different trenches, he
was *not* the only one.

Gale did not long survive himself; he was killed on the day after
he wrote this letter, not in another working party but in an attack on
Delville Wood. His body was not found and he has no known grave.
For reasons never established, his name was not included among
those inscribed on the Thiepval Memorial at the time of its construction; it was not added until 1978, in the wake of a family enquiry.
His service on the Somme had been only a matter of days.

*   *   *

Second Lieutenant Lillywhite of the 9th East Surreys was also
destined to serve only briefly on the Somme; his exit, however, was
the result not of death in action but of serious wounds. Although
this was not clear from his letter telling his family about his
battalion's 'show' on the 16th, he had not taken part in the attack
himself – doubtless this was why he had felt able to write about it so
proudly and with such emotion. Now, however, as he informed them
on the 20th, he was 'second in command of the company, or should
I say what is left of it', and when the battalion attacked again on the
21st, Lillywhite went over the top into battle. The first indication of
any trouble was a standard War Office telegram to the family –
'Regret to inform you that 2nd Lt G Lillywhite East Surrey Regt
was wounded 21st August will report any further news.' This was
followed by a range of messages of which the most alarming was
from the Matron of the 2nd Stationary Hospital, Abbeville, stating
that 'owing to the poisoned nature of his wounds he is seriously ill'.
At least one of his wounds had developed gas gangrene, while other
superficial ones had become septic. Reassurance eventually came in a
letter from Lillywhite himself, though written by another's hand:
'There is nothing to worry about, my arm is broken which is why I
cannot write myself, and I have one or two other small cuts. I will
let you know where I am directly I get to England.'

Lillywhite eventually found himself convalescing in a hotel in
Worthing, his wounds being sufficiently severe to keep him out of any
further fighting for the duration of the war. He would later return to

uniform, however, as an Assistant and Deputy Director of Ordnance Services with various units in the UK during the war of 1939–45.

* * *

Battery Sergeant-Major Douglas Pegler, B Battery, 106th Brigade Royal Field Artillery, came to the Somme, like Second Lieutenant Lillywhite, with 24th Division in early August. He had served in a number of other sectors further north, including Ploegsteert, which he had found a relatively peaceful area, and Loos, which had been far from peaceful, in that he had taken part in the battle fought there in September–October 1915. One of the first sights to catch his attention on reaching the Somme was the hanging Virgin of Albert – 'a greater wonder than the leaning tower of Pisa', he called it in his diary on 11 August, 'suspended by a miracle of balance'. He was soon apprised of the widespread belief that the statue's fate was inextricably linked with the ending of the war: 'A local wise woman has prophesied that on the day on which the statue falls to the ground, so on that day will fall the Hohenzollern dynasty and Prussian militarism. As the good lady in question has commonly been supposed for some years past to have had a bat in her belfry, one must not place too much reliance on her soothsaying.' Nevertheless a fortnight or so later, having heard a strong rumour to the effect that the predicted moment of *dénouement* was imminent, indeed that an actual date for it had been named, he could not resist a backward glance from the battlefield: 'Today is the day on which the Virgin of Albert was prophesied to fall, but now (at 8 p.m.) I can just make it out through my glasses, and it still hangs from the top of the tower.'

By this time, like the rest of his division, Pegler was involved in more serious business than the monitoring of local superstitions. It was not long before he concluded that whatever had been his experience at Loos, it was as nothing compared with what was taking place on the Somme. At the end of his first period of active fighting, he summed up the Division's performance, noting also the losses and the gains:

> *6th September.* We withdrew our guns today for a short rest and a general overhaul. In the month that the 24th Divisional Artillery has been in action on the Somme, my Battery has fired 17,342

rounds and the Divisional Artillery has had 25 officer casualties with a proportionate number of fallen NCOs and men. We had one officer, Lieut. Westerberg (a Dane not a Bosche) killed this morning just before we came out. Last night we got possession of the whole of Leuze Wood, fighting still continues in Ginchy. The British right and French left are closing in on Combles and the Boche are in a precarious position.

7th September. This morning General Philpotts, Comdg the Artillery of the 24th Division, conveyed to us the congratulations of the Guards Division and the 20th Division. The General Officer Commanding the Guards Division said that 'The Artillery of the 24th Division have these last few days put up the most magnificent shooting I have ever seen, and their barrages were walls of fire which nothing could penetrate and live, and the Officers and men of the Guards Division want nothing better than to be covered by the gunners of the 24th Division.' Some reference that.

Within a very short time, they were back: '*10th September*. We are in action again. Yesterday afternoon and evening was the biggest "Matinée" strafe I've ever been in and the casualties on both sides were appalling, *but* we took Ginchy – the crown of the ridge and the key to the German positions in this part of the line – Cheery oh!'

Guillemont had also fallen by this time, being taken in a fierce sub-battle dated 3 to 6 September. Lieutenant P.F. Story, of 96th Field Company Royal Engineers, 20th Division, wrote a moving description of this episode on the same day, 10 September, on which Pegler recorded the seizure of Ginchy. Sappers feature too rarely in this history, but the following account shows that they also made their contribution, and paid their price:

At last a chance of writing. I hope the Censor will not be unkind and cross [out] the name, but I don't really think I am giving anything away in telling you, especially as it is now about a week old, that we, as a division, took Guillemont. My brigade was on the right. We have all been very much congratulated on the result, as we sappers played no small part in the affair; both Brigadier and Divisional General have been most laudatory in their congratulations and thanks. Casualties, alas, pretty high, two officers wounded, and some forty-one men in the Company. We fairly pasted the Boche – some six hundred prisoners and a large number of killed and wounded. My orderly, alas, was badly wounded at my side by a whizz-bang, which sent me head over heels, but I am thankful to say I came through unscathed, but dead beat to a turn. Three nights without a wink of sleep would in the ordinary way seem an impossibility, but I've done it.

The Company did very well, and with few exceptions worked itself to an absolute standstill; you can't do much more than that. The Boches were good specimens, mainly of the 73rd Fusilier Regiment (Prussians). They had Gibraltar embroidered on their cuffs – a prisoner told me they had at one time helped to defend the rock. One of our hireling regiments, I expect. The prisoners fraternized fairly well with our men, and carried back many a wounded man; they were very good stretcher-bearers. Guillemont was blotted right out, not one brick standing on another – nothing but a sea of crump holes of all sorts and sizes; it was very difficult moving about in the dark. The fight itself went through without a hitch, the real bad time comes when you are consolidating and have to face the counter-attack with its heavy shelling, but we managed to get consolidated early, and were able to defy the Boche.

We are resting at the moment, and feel we deserve it. Our General came today, and inspected us, pouring out many kind words.

* * *

The attacks mounted in August and early September were undoubtedly vigorous and produced many casualties, but they were about to be outclassed in scale and ambition by a major new offensive – a second 'big push' – that was being planned for mid-September. As ever, the cavalry was being made ready to make its, by tradition, spectacularly decisive gesture: to 'go through the gap', to deliver, once those more mundane military arms, the artillery and the infantry, had swung the door on the hinge, the ultimate *coup de grâce*. It was the military dream of centuries, compared with which the plod of the PBI – the 'Poor Bloody Infantry' – or the mechanistic technology of the gunners, lacked drama, historical resonance and, above all, style.

In fact the cavalry had spent most of the summer inactively watching from the sidelines, though desperately eager to join in.

They had been used in July, but sparsely and to modest effect. In the attack on the 14th one squadron each of the 7th Dragoon Guards and the 20th Deccan Horse had moved to the high ground between Delville Wood and High Wood, and the Dragoons had made an advance – it could hardly be called a charge – towards some German infantry and machine-guns hidden in the crops. But at 3.40 next morning they had withdrawn from their overnight position, having made little more than a token contribution to the course of the action. The frustrations aroused by this dearth of cavalry involvement were admitted by a young Territorial cavalry officer, Lieutenant A.B.S. Tennyson of the 1/1st Leicestershire Yeomanry, in a letter he wrote to his distinguished stepfather, the Right Honourable Augustine Birrell, Secretary of State for Ireland, on 17 July – the same day on which the artillery officer Lieutenant C.J. Rice had written so proudly to his parents about the gunners' gratifying contribution to the campaign. In contrast with Rice, Tennyson was clearly dispirited, even bored:

> Since the great battle has begun we have been dodging about in the vicinity of the firing line, sometimes fairly near and sometimes afar off, waiting for an occasion to do a little cavalry work. So far only one Bde has had an opportunity of sending mounted troops thro'. We spend our time in woods to elude the enemy aeroplanes which are all right when it is fine but damnable in wet weather. At present the weather is absolutely filthy – torrents of rain and the whole place is a quagmire. We spend our time under a tarpaulin, eating, sleeping, chattering, playing cards, telling stories and generally frittering away the time as agreeably as possible, under the circs.

He was optimistic about the general progress of the campaign – 'We have really done wonderfully well considering the Boche held all the high ground round Mametz, Contalmaison, etc., and had spent two years in fortifying it' – but was clearly deeply unhappy at the cavalry's virtual demotion from active participant to docile spectator.

This was also a matter of much concern to Captain Frank Ash of the 10th Reserve Regiment of Cavalry, 4th Hussars (2nd Cavalry Division). Aged twenty-three and educated at Uppingham and

Cambridge, he had come to France in January 1916. He was fully aware of the cavalry's intended role on the Somme but even before he arrived there he was highly sceptical as to whether there would ever be an opportunity to fulfil it. Somewhat more swiftly, it would seem, than some of his superiors, he concluded that there was little or no chance of realizing the cavalry dream, not at any rate in this swamped and cratered terrain. The diary he kept at this time is arguably an important document in the history of this legendary military arm. In a tiny pocket-sized notebook headed 'Somme 1916', he related his adventures, such as they were, during the later stages of the battle, lacing his account with his views on the problems facing the cavalry in this kind of war.

His most forthright statement on the subject occurs in his entry for 11 September, by which time, having moved from Hazebrouck near the Franco-Belgian border, he and the party of dismounted men of which he was in command had joined the rest of their regiment at a camp near Fricourt – a camp he described as consisting of 'a bare bit of well sodden ground, no tents or cover of any kind', requiring both officers and men to sleep in the open. They had got there at midnight on the 10th after a four-hour march from the railway station at Albert. Next day a pattern was set which would continue throughout their time on the Somme, offering the prospect not so much of splendid martial glory as of dreary hard labour: 'Marched off at 2 p.m. on a working party. Our job was to prepare a track for the cavalry to come up when they go through the gap but I don't suppose it will ever be used as I am quite sure there will never be any gap.'

This was a nutshell summing-up of a position half expounded, half implied, in his diary's opening pages, which read almost like an introduction to a cynic's, almost a dissident's, ABC of First World War cavalry practice on the Western Front:

During the winter, cavalry are rendered even more useless than they are at any other time of the year. The reason is not far to seek; it rains or snows, sometimes both, every day and usually all night. The water thus accumulated when mixed with the earth forms what is known as mud, which varies in depth from six inches to six feet. On the roads it is usually about eighteen inches deep in the bad weather.

It is impossible for a horse to go faster than a walk, and if a cross-country journey is attempted, the horse is almost certain to drown in the first shell hole it comes to. As this is the case cavalry, during the winter, are sent back to what is called winter billets, usually forty to fifty miles behind the line. Here they do various jobs such as going up dismounted and holding a bit of the line or going up as a pioneer battalion to make roads, wire the front line or bury the numerous and very smelly corpses which litter the ground.

Then the spring comes round and we get orders to move out of billets and come up nearer the line. Now when a cavalry regiment moves out of winter billets, it does not merely get its horses saddled up and go off. Take the case of a Squadron, of which there are three in a Regiment. There are at least thirty more men than horses. Consequently, when the Regiment moves there are at least ninety men left dismounted. These men form what is known as a Dismounted party. One officer or sometimes two are left to look after them. This party follows the Regiment either by train or else in lorries.

When we got orders to move this spring or rather summer we were at Pradelles near Hazebrouck. The Dismounted party went to a camp just outside Hazebrouck and waited there four or five days until the Regiment was in Camp on the Somme. I was in charge of the IVth Hussars Dismounted party with 2/Lt Arkwright to help me.

It appears that the Regt. was moved up to the Somme so as to be ready at any time to rush through our own Infantry and attack the Huns. It will be seen later that the job of the Dismounted party was to prepare a road as near to the front line as possible. It simply meant filling in shell holes and old trenches on a track 15 yards wide and having a few shells popped at us in return for our trouble.

Away from the line did not mean, however, away from danger. Ash's first working party on 11 September soon found itself under serious fire. This caused a change in the tone of his diary from gentle theory to harsh fact, and, in terms of his own attitude, from one of mild amusement to outright anger:

We marched about 3½ miles. They took us onto the forward slope of a hill within view of the German OPs and also well under observation from some dozen Hun balloons. The whole Division was marched up in columns of sections and told to work there. I said to myself at the time, 'In about seven and a half minutes the first shell will arrive'. As a matter of fact it was ten minutes before the first one came. It landed at the head of the party. (I was working about ⅓ the way down.) Only one was wounded and he passed me on a stretcher with his napper cut about a bit. The next half hour was fairly lively. I had three shells land about thirty to fifty yards from my party. No casualties. By this time there were about a dozen casualties in the other Regiments. One man in the 12th Lancers was killed. As things were getting a bit too warm we retired about ½ a mile. The other Brigades rushed home in a disorganised mob and the 3rd Brigade was the only one who seemed to have any discipline in them. I formed them up in a valley and waited for orders. I at last found the Major who was in command and we got leave to go off home. This afternoon's exhibition was a criminal mistake on the part of Major — of the Lancers [Ash's omission]. He actually sent us up in full view of the Germans, in full daylight and only about 1800 yards from our front line. In future this work is going to be done at night. It was a needless sacrifice of life and I have no confidence in him.

He added an equally angry postscript to this episode on the 13th: 'I hear today that where we were working on the first day of the digging when we had all those casualties, was only 1500 yards from the Boche front line and in full view of it.'

He also noted under the same date: 'The Guards marched up to take over a section of the trenches preparatory to their attack.' Significantly, when the attack thus foreshadowed took place, on the 15th, he would write: 'This was the great day ordered for the cavalry push. We got no orders till 10 a.m.; we were then ordered to proceed up the 2nd Cav. Div. track and work on that.' His doubts about the prospect of 'going through the gap' had been justified at the first strike; while their horses stood idle, the cavalrymen made roads.

In a sense Ash's diary can now be seen, not so much as an analysis, more, almost, as a kind of obituary. For about to appear on the battlefield of the Somme was a new military arm, conceived behind closed doors and developed in the utmost secrecy, which would ultimately be the principal means of dismissing the cavalry dream to the history books.

Before moving to this next major stage of the campaign, however, it is perhaps timely to focus on the experience of the enemy in this great attritional struggle on the Somme.

CHAPTER NINE

THE GERMAN EXPERIENCE

How did the Germans fare during the Battle of the Somme? Were they seriously discomfited by the sustained Allied attack? What was the state of their morale?

These were questions that, inevitably, deeply interested the British at the time, at the level both of the high direction of the campaign and of the soldiers engaged in the actual fighting.

In spite of the disastrous opening to the offensive, it soon came to be assumed among the British commanders that the Germans were making heavy weather of their resistance and that their will to continue was suspect. Thus Lieutenant A.S.B. Tennyson could write in his letter of 17 July (quoted in the previous chapter): 'Our generals seem very confident that the Germans have come to the end of their reserves and that we shall get thro' their line very soon. Yesterday there was a rumour emanating from a distinguished British statesman who has been in this neighbourhood that Peace was only a question of days. I find it hard to believe myself but I hope it is true.'

Several weeks later, on 6 September, a young officer in the Coldstream Guards, Lieutenant Alex Wilkinson, broached the same subject in a letter to his father:

The news lately has been splendid. The Hun appears to be genuinely pressed, and a considerable advance may be made almost any day. Judging by letters and diaries found on prisoners he is having an awfully poor time. He no longer has beautifully constructed trenches with comfortable deep dugouts, but his main defences appear to be nothing more than a line of shell holes connected up, and such defences as these do not afford much protection against the terrific bombardment which he has to put up with. Our supremacy in the air is a very real thing and the aeroplanes not only supply invaluable information, but actually fire on the Huns with their machine-guns.

One Hun said that they almost expected the aeroplanes to descend and pull them out of their trenches by the scruff of the neck!

One officer complains in his diary not only of the morale of his men, but also of his brother officers, of whom one had apparently gone sick with a slightly bruised foot.

It is not clear from Wilkinson's statement whether he was referring to letters and diaries he had actually seen, or whether he was reporting at second hand. From his excitement and enthusiasm one would tend to assume the former to be the case. Be that as it may, there is no reason to doubt that such material, suggesting that the Germans were finding the Somme an extremely hard and torrid experience, was by now falling in some quantity into Allied hands. What is more, it was being given serious attention. In fact – and this had been going on for quite some time – the collection, translation and sifting of evidence of this kind had now become a small industry, as the Army's intelligence staff strove to break into and report on what would now be called the 'mind-set' of the enemy. Printed to high professional standards by the Army stationery service, compilations of letters, diaries and other useful documents which the British had acquired were circulated from time to time during the Somme battle and beyond. They constitute a valuable source of contemporary evidence about German morale and attitudes.

It has to be said that to the fighting troops, and not just to the 'other ranks', reports and bulletins from Army Intelligence were not always regarded with the highest respect. Hence the following definition in the classic work on soldiers' songs and slang, *The Long Trail*: 'Comic Cuts. An Intelligence summary or report. Officers' slang.' Yet in other quarters they, or at least the burden of the message they conveyed, were certainly given some credence. Extracts from captured enemy diaries are included in the war diary of Sir Douglas Haig held in the Public Record Office, as are also reports on the interrogation of captured prisoners. What, therefore, gives them an especial interest is the assumption that, to some extent at least, it was on the basis of this and similar material that plans were constructed and strategic decisions made.

Clearly such evidence needed then, and needs now, to be treated with caution. At a period, despite continuing heavy losses, of officially cultivated optimism, the compilers of such digests might well have been tempted to favour accounts expressing disaffection and distress, as opposed to those indicating high confidence and an eagerness to fight on. The climate of the time was such that most commanders up to and including the highest in rank wanted to hear, so that they would be able to pass on to their superiors, good news rather than bad. (Most famously of all Haig's senior intelligence adviser, Brigadier-General Charteris, was always prone to offer best-case interpretations to his chief.) By contrast, the fate of the purveyor of pessimistic assessments or gloomy forebodings was all too frequently that of being 'stellenbosched', 'ungummed' (the English equivalent of the well-known French term for dismissal, *dégommé*), or, to put it in simpler terms, presented with an immediate one-way boat-ticket home. The intelligence authorities would be fully aware of, and by no means immune to, such pressures.

Despite such caveats, however, there seems to be no reason to doubt the authenticity of the material used in the official circulars; to have had recourse to invention in such circumstances would have been as culpable as it would have been absurd. One arguable weakness is that the evidence quoted hardly ever has the virtue of being assigned to a named soldier; it is, however, in almost all cases assigned to a specific unit. How representative it was overall is difficult to judge – particularly since by definition it was collected at random, and was therefore, in modern opinion-testing terms, a singularly unscientific poll. Nevertheless, it is impossible to read this material and not conclude that for the Germans this was not a campaign they relished or enjoyed.

The War Diary of the 55th Reserve Infantry Regiment of the 2nd Guard reserve Division, already quoted in Chapter 5, was a document in this 'Stationery Service' series. (It is perhaps worth emphasizing, in the light of the above discussion, that, while paying handsome tribute to the British effort, the main thrust of that particular document was that the Germans had won the contest at Gommecourt almost with ease and were fully confident of maintaining their battlefield superiority; there is certainly no hint here of evidence doctored to provide an upbeat interpretation.) Those which dealt with questions of enemy attitudes and morale were members of an occasional series entitled 'EXTRACTS FROM GERMAN DOCUMENTS AND CORRESPONDENCE'. The first four in this series had as their lead subject 'Conditions on the Somme Battle Front'. Here is a collage of quotations from them, given in date order:

Written by a man of the 5th Guard F.A. Regiment,
3rd Guard Division

10-7-16. On the 1st July I was still in Valenciennes, and then on the 2nd the business started and we went straight into a bad position, for the Englishman is a damnable enemy. At any rate, the Frenchman and the Russian are not so cunning as these.... Down with England!

From a man of the 110th R.I.R. [Reserve Infantry Regiment]
in hospital

15.7.16. There are also many wounded of the 110th here with me. I had extraordinary luck, for I was wounded in the head by a hand grenade in the first assault of the English on the 1st July. The wound is now beginning to heal, and I like being here so much. But I have had enough of war; I am fed up. What we went through from the 24th June to the 1st July your comrades can tell you.

Extracts from the Diary of a man of the 28th Regiment
(16th Division)

10th August, 1916. For me a day of despair. At 6 p.m. we march off with attacking equipment to release our poor comrades of the 22nd Regiment from hell. The march is very fatiguing; with great trouble we drag ourselves along; now and again I have a sip out of the bottle of brandy that I have bought with the pay just received.

We pass through a village – the church is the only whole building in it ...

From the Diary of a man of the 8th Company,
28th Infantry Regiment

13/14-8-16. On the 13th, only the 6th Company was relieved and left the trench. Heavy artillery fire continued throughout the night and the list of the wounded grows ever bigger. Every evening a long procession of wounded goes back along the top of the trenches, headed by a medical orderly with a large Red Cross which is not fired on. Bad drinking water, dirty looking and chalky. I have got stomach pains and diarrhoea. We suffer much from thirst. It is torture. Yesterday a Battalion of the 68th made an attack and suffered very heavy losses from the English counter attack. In isolated places the English penetrated the positions of the 29th and killed the Germans who were sheltering from the artillery fire in the dugouts. All the Regiments have suffered very heavy losses here. Everybody is asking when we are to be relieved. *16-8-16.* Everybody is wishing for rain or at least bad weather so that one may have some degree of safety from the English aviators. One daren't leave one's hole all day or else one immediately gets artillery fire on the trench for half an hour.

Letter from a man of the 119th Regiment, XIII Corps
22-8-16. Since the beginning of July, I have been in the infantry. I was in the trenches before Ypres several times, then I was moved to the Somme and we are now having a pretty hot time of it. Every day we have dead and wounded. We get very heavy gun and trench mortar fire, almost enough to drive us mad. Only the hope that we shall be soon relieved gives the necessary strength to hold out and stand firm. I should never have believed that men could endure so much. . . . You can imagine how heartily sick men get of this sort of life, especially seeing that many have been already at it for $1\frac{1}{2}$ to 2 years. The great desire for the ardently-expected peace can be understood.

From a man of the 17th Bavarian Infantry Regiment,
3rd Bavarian Division
1-9-16. We are actually fighting on the Somme against the English. You can no longer call it war, it is mere murder. All my previous experiences in this war, the slaughter at Ypres and the battle in the gravel pit at Hulluch, are the purest child's play compared with this massacre, and this is much too mild a description. I hardly think they will bring us into the fight again now, for we are in a very bad way.

Letter from a Landsturm man of the 211th R.I. Regiment,
dated France, 10-9-16
When you read these lines, I shall no longer be among the living. I shall have breathed my last before the enemy on the Somme. I could not prevent Prussian militarism from driving me to death. Oh, from

the very beginning, I had the sad feeling that I should not see my dear ones in this world again. You can form no idea what the poor soldiers have to go through here in this place and how cruelly and uselessly men are sacrificed: it is awful.

From a man on the Somme Front
September, 1916. We are here on the Somme in such an artillery fire as I have never experienced – indeed no one has in the whole war. Cover there is none, we lie in a shell hole and defend ourselves to the last man. He who comes out of this fire can thank God. It's frightful; such murder here. Day and night the earth quakes with the bombardment of the heaviest guns.

In addition to letters and diaries, captured documents were included in these intelligence digests. The following items are from No. 1 in the series, under the headings 'Company Reports' and 'Divisional Orders':

2nd Company, 5th Guard Grenadier Regiment (4th Guard Division) to 1st Battalion, 5th Guard Grenadier Regiment
27-8-16 (evening). I *urgently* request that I may be relieved *tomorrow night* (28/29) in case no relief takes place today. The men have to lie in holes (there are no longer any dugouts in my sector). In addition, there is continuous very brisk and well-aimed artillery and trench mortar fire. They have necessarily to be extremely watchful at all times. They are, therefore, so exhausted physically and mentally that with the will (and that is not lacking) they are no longer in that physical state of readiness that is absolutely necessary.

Report to the 3rd Battn., 62nd Regt., or to the 27th Infantry Regiment in Courcelette
The 9th and 12th Companies of the 62nd are, in view of their great losses, the hardships of the preceding days and inexperienced drafts, hardly in a position to resist further attacks during the night. They therefore urgently request relief in the early hours of the evening.

Extract from a Divisional Order of the 53rd Reserve Division, dated 28-8-16
The Enemy's Artillery carries out a methodical bombardment, with short pauses and of considerable intensity, of all portions of ground which are of any importance to us, as well as all artillery and infantry positions, all natural cover, rear slopes, hollow roads

and villages behind the battle front. Numerous aeroplanes flying very low assist in registration and the direction of fire. Bombs are frequently dropped by day and night.

The Enemy's Infantry attacks with great energy, usually full of confidence in the enormous mass of artillery engaged. The ground captured is stubbornly defended. Portions of woods and groups of houses are immediately occupied by machine-guns and selected machine-gunners.

What adds to the value of such material is the fact that postwar evidence would seem to confirm that feelings of disillusion and war-weariness were widespread, if by no means universal, among the German units fighting on the Somme. German regimental histories rarely print personal testimony, but occasionally a first-hand account is included, not always only to the greater glory of the unit concerned. The following is from the history of the 66th Infantry Regiment (referred to in the diary of a soldier of the 28th Infantry quoted above), a Bavarian unit which in early September 1916 was in trenches in the Ancre Valley in front the little village of St. Pierre Divion. The writer is Leutnant Meyer, platoon leader of No. 3 Machine-Gun Company, and the context is that of an attack, presumably a large-scale raid, by the British (or rather the English, as the Germans invariably described their British enemy at that time, whether English, Scottish, Welsh or Irish). The attack was repelled, but at high cost:

As soon as I had reached the dugout in the front trench, one could hear the call 'They're coming, they're already here.' The enemy batters at the door of our defences. The machine-gun of 2 Machine-Gun Company, 99 Reserve Regiment, which I was due to relieve, had begun firing since it was already in position. However, it jammed after 100 rounds, so it was so much the better that my gun, under Sergeant [*Unteroffizier*] Horn and Corporal [*Gefreiter*] Müller could come into action. As we had correctly anticipated, the enemy followed on foot directly after the last burst of shrapnel. We [later] found orders on the English stating that the nearer you stayed to your own [creeping] barrage, the lower the number of casualties. The dead, who lay fifteen paces from the trench, showed how near the enemy had got with his attack. Right in front of my dugout lay a dead English officer. My gun-team leader, Sergeant Horn, my aimer and the other privates were wounded. Of course, in a defensive battle you are busy defending; above all you are concerned about the enemy so you can't even help a wounded comrade. Corporal Müller had lost a leg through a shell splinter and a doctor could probably have saved him had he been there. As it was he had to die in the dugout. My machine-gun was concentrating more to the left, where the enemy had already got into the front-line trenches, trying to prevent a mass advance by them. In the meantime the 9/66 [9th Company, 66 Regiment] was engaged in a brutal close-quarters fight with hand-grenades in the trench about 50 metres from me. At this time the 9/66 lost two thirds of its men, among them a lot of people I knew. Many of its N.C.O.s lay there, ripped to pieces and with smashed skulls. It is simply impossible to get rid of the corpses, among them many English, as the rear areas are under extremely heavy fire. Even our own wounded had to lie out a long time until a doctor could get to them. Their groans and whimpers did not have a particularly cheering effect on us. Some 30 English had got into the 9 Company trench and attacked the occupants of the dugout by throwing grenades. Lieutenant Kusel had barricaded himself in one half and he was freed, as the English were driven out by a counter-attack during which Lt Bötticher and Lt Hädrich were killed. The trenches have completely caved in, and only the dugout entrances are free, the rest is simply a field of craters.

Other sources, too, suggest that the Somme was a major trial of the enemy's martial will. A famous repository of German soldiers' experience is the anthology of students' war letters, edited by Dr Philip Witkop and published in Munich in 1928, and subsequently issued in an English translation. Allowing for a certain floreate quality in the translation – or possibly the originals – the tone of the letters quoted coincides remarkably with that of the letters in the 1916 summaries.

For example, the following, by Friedrich Oehme, a sergeant, formerly a law student from Leipzig, killed on the Somme on 25 October 1916; the extract is from a letter written on 21 August:

Life here is absolutely ghastly! I have been three days and four nights in the front line. It is horrible. On the evening of the 17th we had orders to occupy the 4th line. Soon we were moved up into the 3rd, and finally into the 2nd. The way up even so far is indescribable. It runs uphill past a shell-shattered convent. The whole sky is lit up with flashes and flares. The air is full of the thunder of guns, the crash of bursting shells, the howling and whistling of projectiles flying in both directions. The roads have been torn up by shells, but the holes have been filled up so that the motor-ambulances can be driven along them. Only one, a yard deep, is still gaping. An ambulance, loaded with wounded, has fallen into it.

The Company proceeds in open order, one behind the other, to reduce the number of casualties. Motors flash noiselessly by, to fetch wounded. One by one they return, crammed full. Ammunition-columns bring fodder for the insatiable jaws of the guns. Troops who have been relieved are hurrying back. We meet parties of wounded – walking-cases – each with a white label attached to his second button-hole. They are out of it now. They won't have to go up the line again. And so, in spite of their sufferings, they jog along quite merrily.

Gradually we enter the zone of continuous fire. Our march becomes a trot, or rather a gallop. Here and there a man who can't keep up falls out. Panting and sweating, we at last reach a village. Yes, it was once a village. Six weeks ago Martinpuich was a pretty place, inhabited and secure. Now it is a region of horror and despair. '*Lasciate ogni speranza*' – abandon hope – are the words over the portals of hell in Dante's *Divine Comedy*. I kept thinking of them as we tore through the village.

At last somebody arrives with instructions and guides us forward. It is well for you that you are not obliged to look on such horrible sights! Quite apart from the bombardment, the mere appearance of utter devastation everywhere is enough to make one shudder. Not a house is left standing. Everything is completely destroyed – beams, bricks, and blocks of stone lie in the street. One shell hole has filled up another. The chalky mud is splashed far and wide over everything. Trees, wagons, corpses, knapsacks, horses, rifles, tins, wire, bits of equipment, lie all about on the trampled paths between the craters.

Under the fiercest shrapnel and shell fire the Company dashes forward – leaping over obstacles, tumbling into shell holes, stumbling over bodies, or falling, wounded and unable to continue.

We reach the end of the village. There, close by, is the beginning of the front line. The opening is on the left of the road. We plunge in and find a shallow trough which was once a trench. A few men are already lying in the holes which are all that is left of the dug-outs. They look dully at us with cowed and desperate faces.

Now the men are divided up, one here and one there. At last all the necessary dispositions are made and I can sit down for a moment. I meet a comrade of the 5th Company which has just been attacking with five other Companies. Owing to the fog the attack was frustrated by our own barrage. Now they were cowering despairingly here, these poor comrades, and were supposed to attack again, but they hadn't gone, they didn't know which direction to take.

Day now begins to dawn. Suddenly, just as the sun rose behind us, came the order: 'The 10th Company will advance 350 yards and dig itself in!'

We were lying in the second line, the first having been captured by the English, and now we had to dig a new front line close to the English one. I collect my men, so as to lead them forward all together under cover. When I look back not one, not a single one, has followed me. I go back, reason with them and order them to go with me. This time it has to be over open ground, as some parts of the trench have meanwhile been blown in.

At last we are far enough and we start digging. We work sideways, from shell hole to shell hole, so that a continuous trench is made. Another sergeant drives the rest of the men forward with his revolver, until we have about 40, out of the 90 we brought with us, to occupy our 200-yard sector.

Work on the new trench now proceeded feverishly. The few men who have advanced did splendidly. We had scarcely finished when drum-fire started, and for two hours the new trench was heavily shelled, but no attack followed.

In rain and cold; without overcoats or blankets; without any-thing warm to drink (all we had was seltzer-water), we spent three days in the line. Spare me from giving any description of the condition of that company of men – frozen, dead-tired, and broken down by shell fire. I conducted the relief myself; therefore I had to go through all that fire and horror twice more. Now, tonight, we are at last back in billets.

This second example is by Friedrich Georg Steinbrecher, a Leipzig Theology student, who was killed in April 1917 in Champagne. (His letter is assigned in Witkop's anthology to 'April 12th 1916', but this is clearly incorrect, as this date preceded the battle; a more likely date might be August.) It is noteworthy that he was fighting on the French front, proof that there too the campaign was pressed hard:

Somme. The whole history of the world cannot contain a more ghastly word! All the things I am now once more enjoying – bed, coffee, rest at night, water – seem unnatural and as if I had no right to them. And yet I was only there a week.

At the beginning of the month we left our old position. During the lorry and train journey we were still quite cheery. We knew what we were wanted for. Then came bivouacs, an 'alarm', and we were rushed up through shell-shattered villages and barrage into the turmoil of war. The enemy was firing with 12-inch guns. There was a perfect torrent of shells. Sooner than we expected we were in the thick of it. First in the artillery position. Columns were tearing hither and thither as if possessed. The gunners could no longer see or hear. Very lights were going up along the whole Front, and there was a deafening noise: the cries of wounded, orders, reports.

At noon the gun-fire became even more intense, and then came the order: 'The French have broken through. Counter-attack!'

We advanced through the shattered wood in a hail of shells. I don't know how I found the right way. Then across an expanse of shell craters, on and on. Falling down and getting up again. Machine-guns were firing. I had to cut across our own barrage and the enemy's. I am untouched.

At last we reach the front line. Frenchmen are forcing their way in. The tide of battle ebbs and flows. Then things get quieter. We have not fallen back a foot. Now one's eyes begin to see things. I want to keep running on – to stand still and look is horrible. 'A wall of dead and wounded!' How often have I read that phrase! Now I know what it means.

I have witnessed scenes of heroism and of weakness. Men who can endure every privation. Being brave is not only a matter of will, it also requires strong nerves, though the will can do a great deal. A Divisional Commander dubbed us the 'Iron Brigade' and said he had never seen anything like it. I wish it had all been only a

dream, a bad dream. And yet it was a joy to see such heroes stand
and fall. The bloody work cost us 177 men. We shall never forget
Chaulmes and Vermandovillers.

There is confirmatory evidence too in the account by perhaps the
Somme's best-known participant on the German side, Ernst Jünger,
in his classic war-book *Storm of Steel*, first published in Germany in
1920 and in English in 1929. That he could find the Somme battle
hard going is especially significant in that he enjoyed the war as a
kind of spiritualized gladiatorial combat, and not just with hindsight;
therefore his description of the rigours of the Somme arguably carry
more weight than that of some unhappy conscript – or a student
plunged into fierce warfare far from his peacetime university. The
following passage, from the chapter entitled 'Guillemont', covers
Jünger's introduction to the Somme battle; like Friedrich Oehme
quoted above, he resorts to quoting Dante's famous cry *'Lasciate
ogni speranza!* – 'Abandon hope' – in his description:

On the 23rd August we were transported in lorries to Le Mesnil.
Our spirits were excellent, though we knew we were going to be
put in where the battle of the Somme was at its worst. Chaff and
laughter went from lorry to lorry. We marched from Le Mesnil at
dusk to Sailly-Saillisel, and here the battalion dumped packs in a
large meadow and paraded in battle order.

Artillery fire of a hitherto unimagined intensity rolled and
thundered on our front. Thousands of twitching flashes turned the
western horizon into a sea of flowers. All the while the wounded
came trailing back with white dejected faces, huddled into the
ditches by the gun and ammunition columns that rattled past.

A man in a steel helmet reported to me as guide to conduct my
platoon to the renowned Combles, where for the time we were to
be in reserve. Sitting with him at the side of the road, I asked him,
naturally enough, what it was like in the line. In reply I heard a
monotonous tale of crouching all day in shell holes with no one on
either flank and no trenches communicating with the rear, of
unceasing attacks, of dead bodies littering the ground, of maddening thirst, of wounded and dying, and of a lot besides. The face
half-framed by the steel rim of the helmet was unmoved; the voice
accompanied by the sound of battle droned on, and the impression

they made on me was one of unearthly solemnity. One could see that the man had been through horror to the limit of despair and there had learnt to despise it. Nothing was left but supreme and superhuman indifference.

'Where you fall, there you lie. No one can help you. No one knows whether he will come back alive. They attack every day, but they can't get through. Everybody knows it is life and death.'

One can fight with such fellows. We marched on along a broad paved road that showed up in the moonlight as a white band on the dark fields. In front of us the artillery fire rose to a higher and higher pitch. *Lasciate ogni speranza!*

Soon we had the first shells on one side of the road and the other. Talk died down and at last ceased. Everyone listened – with that peculiar intentness that concentrates all thought and sensation in the ear – for the long-drawn howl of the approaching shell. Our nerves had a particularly severe test passing Frégicourt, a little hamlet near Combles cemetery, under continuous fire.

As far as we could see in the darkness, Combles was utterly shot to bits. The damage seemed to be recent, judging from the amount of timber among the ruins and the contents of the houses slung over the road. We climbed over numerous heaps of debris – rather hurriedly owing to a few shrapnel shells – and reached our quarters.

It is perhaps worth adding, in the light of a view held in some quarters that the British effort on the Somme was both incompetent and ineffective, that in introducing the English edition of his book in 1929, Jünger stated: 'Of all the troops who were opposed to the Germans on the great battlefields the English were not only the most formidable but the manliest and the most chivalrous.'

*   *   *

One other small but telling fragment of evidence in respect of German morale occurs in a letter written sometime in early October by an officer newly arrived from England, Captain G.N. Rawlence of the 6th Duke of Cornwall's Light Infantry. His battalion was serving not on the Somme, but at Arras, at this period a peaceful sector, certainly in comparison with the battle zone 'down south'. 'You must not worry yourself at all about me;' he had assured his wife on going into the line, 'except for the beastly separation from you and the little girl I am enjoying myself immensely. The danger is very slight, in fact negligible.' Some days later his battalion was moved, though it still remained on the Arras front. Rawlence hastened to tell his wife that this meant no increase of risk: 'In the new sector of trench we are going to, things are also very quiet. A few days ago the Boche put up a notice "We are resting after the Somme. If you do not shoot we will not".'

Evidently some Germans were only too happy to suspend hostilities – to play the 'live and let live' card – when away from a sector where the fighting was so demanding that such behaviour would have been unthinkable. The implication is clear: the Somme battle was so severe that after it the enemy felt he needed a holiday.

* * *

Against all this is the undoubted fact that the Germans continued to fight hard and vigorously not only on the Somme but also elsewhere for two more years. Nor was it by any means universal for Germans involved in the Somme fighting to take a downbeat or defeatist view. Admittedly writing many years afterwards, the medical officer Stephen Westman, quoted in earlier chapters, saw the Allied effort as a virtual defeat, not even a Pyrrhic victory. Describing the final stages of the battle, he wrote:

> After several months the mighty Franco-British offensive on the River Somme was petering out. The deepest penetration of the German lines was less than ten miles of useless, devastated scorched earth, like a moonscape, and this was achieved at the cost of over six hundred thousand Anglo-French casualties. The generals, however, who ordered, planned and conducted this criminal mass murder, were promoted, decorated and later became peers of the realm – instead of being court-martialled and severely punished, together with the politicians who had spurred them on.

Yet unquestionably the Germans had suffered heavily in this hard-fought campaign, so much so that when the new German supremos, Hindenburg and Ludendorff, took over the direction of affairs on the Western Front at the end of August 1916 they decided to carry out, in due course and in their own time, a strategic withdrawal from the Somme front, to a new defence line yet to be established. This, the British Official History would claim, was 'an admission that they could not stand up to this terrible milling at close quarters when the next campaigning season came round.'

Nevertheless, the Germans were not yet defeated, and, in respect of the intelligence digests here quoted, it is possible that the consistently optimistic nature of their, and similar, evidence might have combined with other factors to exercise an unfortunate effect on certain command decisions on the Somme. For there is a case for arguing that the next big push there, that of 15 September, was launched with almost impossibly high hopes and to an over-ambitious strategic plan built to a considerable extent on the assumption that the Germans were, if not quite at breaking-point, in a state of some disarray. Thus when in late August General Rawlinson submitted his proposals for the September attack, the Commander-in-Chief commented: 'In my opinion, he is not making enough of the situation with the deterioration and all-round loss of moral[e] of the enemy troops. I think we should make an attack as strong and violent as possible, and plan to go as far as possible.'

A similar optimism is evident in the GHQ Instructions for the forthcoming offensive – already named as the 'Battle of Flers Courcelette' – issued on 31 August to General Sir Henry Rawlinson, Commanding Fourth Army, and General Sir Hubert Gough, Commanding Reserve Army, by Haig's Chief of Staff, Lieutenant-General Launcelot Kiggell. Its keynote paragraph 2 reads: 'During the two months that the Battle of the Somme has lasted the enemy has suffered repeated defeats and heavy losses and has undergone many hardships. All this has undoubtedly told on his discipline and moral, and signs of deterioration in his troops are not wanting.'

There were, however, other elements that contributed to the sense of optimism emanating from the High Command at this time. As Kiggell's document went on to state, several fresh divisions would be available to be thrown into the scale, while on the German side such limited reserves as they were thought to have available would consist 'mainly of tired troops which had already suffered severely'. Additionally, the British would have a special trick up the sleeve, in the shape of 'a new weapon of offence' which it was hoped, 'coming as a surprise to the enemy', would be 'of considerable moral and material assistance' to the Allied cause.

The new weapon thus referred to would surprise the British as well as the enemy, and convince not a few of the latter that the very Devil had come to the battlefields of France.

CHAPTER TEN

TANKS – AND THE
SEPTEMBER OFFENSIVES

ON SUNDAY 10 SEPTEMBER, Captain Sir Iain Colquhoun, 1st Scots Guards, noted in his diary: 'Church parade 11 a.m. Walked with Miles and Lionel to see the Land Creepers. They look wonderful things but rather vulnerable.'

That the curious newcomers to the battlefield thus described by Colquhoun were already known at the front by their permanent name is clear from a diary entry made that same Sunday by Captain H.C. Meysey-Thompson, 21st King's Royal Rifle Corps: 'Church parade in the morning. In the afternoon we are told that we can see a demonstration of "Tanks" which by a brilliant guess I suggest are the new heavy armoured cars of which we have heard rumours. I cannot go as I am doing a "contact" stunt with an aeroplane, but those who do come back absolutely thrilled.'

In fact 'tanks' – referred to throughout in inverted commas – had been the subject of a GHQ Instruction as far back as 16 August, but this had been for restricted consumption only. By now, however, awareness of the existence of the new vehicles of the 'Heavy Section, Machine-Gun Corps' – their official cover-name at this time – was beginning to spread, and to generate a considerable amount of excitement.

On the 13th Meysey-Thompson saw the new phenomenon for himself: 'Parade about 2.30 and march up over the old line and past Fricourt to Pommiers Redoubt near Montauban, where we spend a thoroughly uncomfortable night in some dilapidated old trenches. At a halt on the way up some Tanks that are to go over with us pass us on the road, to the intense delight of the men.'

'A new form of frightfulness – armoured cars, on caterpillar wheels, which go over or through everything,' was the first description of Captain Arthur Gibbs of the 1st Welsh Guards, writing on 18 September. In a letter on the 23rd, however, mingled with his satisfaction at their arrival on the scene was a certain amazed surprise: 'I saw a whole herd of them the night before they started off, and the whole thing seemed too good to be true. It seemed extraordinary that we should be first in the field with anything, and that the slow-minded authorities at home should have ever taken them up.'

When later the same month, after their blooding in action, Major R.E. Cotton of the 7th Green Howards had his first sight of the new machines, he was not only greatly impressed, but also agreeably relieved: 'Demonstration of tanks practising over trenches etc. The first impression of these engines of war makes one pleased that they are on our side and not on the enemy's. Most awe-inspiring monsters.'

That they had been 'taken up' by the British authorities and first used in action on the Allied side was due to the vision and energy of a handful of activists, initially working independently rather than in collaboration, who saw the need of some revolutionary device to counter the devastating effect of the machine-gun and to tackle the problem of mounting attacks over trenched and cratered ground. Credit for originating the concept has long been a subject of controversy – in 1919 a tribunal was set up to adjudicate between no fewer than nineteen claimants – with a range of figures in the frame including Winston Churchill, Colonel Ernest Swinton, the engineers Walter Wilson and William Tritton, and behind them I.S. Bloch, a Polish banker who wrote a six-volume treatise on future warfare in the 1880s, even H.G. Wells who wrote a story called 'The Land Ironclads' in 1903. Under the stimulus of war, and after much lobbying to overcome a reluctance in some quarters even to consider the concept, the weapon which would in due course revolutionize the nature of land warfare lumbered slowly into existence. Early names assigned to it, while prototypes were being secretly developed in England, included 'caterpillar', 'machine-gun destroyer', 'landship', and 'land cruiser'. Challenged at a conference on the subject at Christmas 1915 to find a better, less tell-tale name, Swinton and a fellow officer, Lieutenant-Colonel W. Dally Jones, suggested the simple monosyllable 'tank' as being 'likely to catch on and be remembered'. Their hunch would be justified. 'And thus, on Christmas Eve, 1915,' Swinton later wrote, 'was given a new significance to a simple little English word, which, nine months later was to echo round the world and eventually to become incorporated in the language of every nation possessing a military vocabulary.'

Once the first tanks were produced, there was serious disagreement as to whether they should be immediately committed in combat or held back until they had got over their numerous teething troubles and more of them were available. Swinton, who was appointed to train the necessary personnel in England but was not allowed to command in the field, was all for delay, as was so distinguished an authority as Colonel Sir Maurice Hankey, Secretary to the War Committee. Haig, however, who had expressed interest in the idea at a very early stage and whose belief in them had been bolstered after seeing the tanks in trials, was eager to make use of them as soon as possible. They were introduced in the major Somme offensive of 15 September 1916.

That their advent created a considerable sensation is clear from the reactions already quoted. Another witness who was deeply impressed was Battery Sergeant-Major Douglas Pegler of the Royal Field Artillery. 'Last night everyone went barmy on the advent of the landships', he noted in his diary on 14 September. He then wrote a detailed description from which it is clear that his response had gone beyond mere admiration and that he had instantly done some serious homework:

These are huge armoured cars built on the caterpillar system with a prow-like front which enables them to take obstacles, they go over trenches, trees, walls (up to 4ft 6 inches) with ease. They are armoured all over with ⅜ inch steel, weigh 27–30 tons and are fitted with 105 HP engines. They are to advance in line in front of the infantry. Their armament is of two kinds, some are fitted with light machine-guns, and some with two quick-firing six pounders and five machine-guns. If they don't put the wind up Fritz he's absolutely hopeless. Their crew is one officer, one non com and 6 gunners.

* * *

The arrival of this shining new example of military technology would not, however, change the nature of the experience facing the great majority of those preparing to take part in the offensive of 15 September. For them, this would be in essence a repeat of 1 July, with the difference that now everybody knew of the huge cost in casualties such large-scale initiatives could entail. In comparison with the scatter of minor 'shows' which had taken place through the summer months, this was to be a major Franco-British effort, in which the British were to attack over a ten-mile front from beyond Thiepval on the left to Combles on the right. Both Rawlinson's Fourth Army and Gough's Reserve Army would be heavily involved. The Canadian Corps would be engaged for the first time in this action, as also would be the New Zealand Division. They would be faced by six and a half German divisions. Despite the air of confidence emanating from high places, it was clear that this was going to be a very hard fight, in which the challenge facing the men of the assault battalions would be the standard one of going 'over the top' against well-armed enemy positions. The tanks would take part in the action at only a handful of selected points.

Everywhere men steeled themselves for battle. As before 1 July, some resorted to the ritual of writing letters to be sent to parents or wife only in the event of the writer's death. Eric Lever Townsend, aged twenty, was a second lieutenant in the 1/15th London Regiment, also known as the Civil Service Rifles. On 8 September he wrote a letter for his parents, of which the following are the principal paragraphs:

Dearest Mother and Father,
    You are reading this letter because I have gone under.
    Of course I know that you will be terribly cut up, and that it will be a long time before you get over it, but get over it you must. You must be imbued with the spirit of the Navy and the Army to 'carry on'.

You must console yourselves with the thought that I am happy, whereas if I had lived – who knows?

Remember the saying attributed to Solon, 'Call no man happy till he is dead'. Thanks to your self-sacrificing love and devotion I have had a happy time all my life. Death will have delivered me from experiencing unhappiness.

It has always seemed to me a very pitiful thing what little difference the disappearance of a man makes to any institution, even though he may have played a very important role. A moment's regret, a moment's pause for readjustment, and another man steps forward to carry on, and the machine clanks on with scarce a check. The death of a leader of the nation is less even than seven days' wonder. To a very small number is it given to live in history; their number is scarcely one in ten millions. To the rest it is only granted to live in their united achievements.

But for this war I and all the others would have passed into oblivion like the countless myriads before us. We should have gone about our trifling business, eating, drinking, sleeping, hoping, marrying, giving in marriage, and finally dying with no more achieved than when we were born, with the world no different for our lives. Even the cattle in the field fare no worse than this. They, too, eat, drink, sleep, bring forth young, and die leaving the world no different from what they have found it.

But we shall live for ever in the results of our efforts.

We shall live as those who by their sacrifice won the Great War. Our spirits and our memories shall endure in the proud position Britain shall hold in the future. The measure of life is not its span but the use made of it. I did not make much use of my life before the war, but I think I have done so now.

To me has been given the easier task; to you is given the more difficult – that of living in sorrow. Be of good courage, that at the end you may give a good account.

Adieu, best of parents
  Your ever loving son
  Eric

By contrast, Alec Reader, a young private soldier of the same battalion, who, being under age, should not have been there at all, but who when offered the option of returning home or continuing to serve, had reluctantly taken the latter course, approached the coming battle with an almost angry cynicism. On 10 September he wrote to his father: 'We have been told for the last month or so that we are going into the "real thing" at last and other news calculated to produce "wind up". While on church parade we have such hymns as "Nearer my God to Thee", "Forever with the Lord", etc. They are trying to make us "resigned to our fate". Of course the beauty of the game is that although they are always trying to kill us they can only succeed once. It would be painful if we had as many lives as a cat.'

* * *

Fourth Army Instructions for the already named Battle of Flers-Courcelette issued on 9 September over the name of Rawlinson's Chief of Staff, Major-General A.A. Montgomery, contained these sentences, echoing the tone of the official documents already quoted: 'The attack will be pushed home with the utmost vigour all along the line till the most distant objectives have been reached. For the last two and a half months we have been gradually wearing the enemy down, his moral is shaken, he has few, if any, fresh reserves available, and there is every probability that a combined effort will result in a decisive victory.'

For the élite Guards' Division, this offensive was their introduction to the Battle of the Somme. It was to mount its attack towards the right of the Fourth Army front. Its direction of advance was north-east from Ginchy and its prime target was the village of Lesboeufs. Captain Sir Iain Colquhoun, whose thoughts about the vulnerability of the new 'land creepers' are quoted at the head of the chapter, took part as a company commander of the 1st Scots Guards. He was a soldier of high reputation whose Western Front career dated back to the Mons Retreat and the First Battle of Ypres. It was because of this that he had been able to walk away with impunity from what in the case of a less successful officer might well have left a considerable stain on his record. Together with a fellow officer of his battalion, Captain Miles Barne, he had been court-martialled earlier that year for allowing his men to participate in the fraternization initiated by the Germans in the Laventie sector at Christmas 1915. Barne had been acquitted, but Colquhoun had been found guilty, despite an eloquent defence by his 'prisoner's friend', Captain Raymond Asquith of the Grenadier Guards, the eldest son of the Prime Minister. His sentence had been a mild one – in effect little more than a slap on the wrist; he was to be 'reprimanded'. Nevertheless it had been instantly quashed by no less an authority than the Commander-in-Chief himself, who, while formally confirming the court martial's findings, remitted the sentence 'because of Sir Iain's distinguished conduct in the field'. Captain Asquith equalled Haig in admiration, describing Colquhoun, in a letter to his wife (13 January 1916), as 'rather a sweet man of his type – arrogant, independent and brave'. Both Colquhoun and Asquith were now to be tested in the Guards' advance on the Somme.

The long experience which had so impressed his C.-in-C. had also given Colquhoun a sharp and critical eye with which to view the prospects of any action in which he might be involved. Far from reflecting the breezy optimism of Fourth Army Headquarters and GHQ, his diary account of the preparations for and implementation of the 15 September attack focuses largely on the disarray and muddle with which it was planned and carried out:

Sept. 14th. At 10.30 the Colonel gave out orders for attack. We attack at dawn tomorrow, and lie out all previous night. Very busy day explaining everything to Coys issuing rations and the hundred and one things we carry. It is still showery and wet. Rather a horrible day as everyone is a little on edge, and the waiting gets on one's nerves. The Cavalry are all behind waiting and this is the biggest show there has been on the Western Front, but it appears to me there is very little stuffing behind it. However, I hope for the best.

Paraded 11 p.m. and marched up behind Coldstream and Grenadiers to our position just N.E. of Ginchy. The whole road is crowded with transport and troops of all sorts. A few tear shells troubled us near Guillemont. Through Guillemont and Ginchy the whole countryside is devastated in a way it is almost impossible to believe. Dead lie everywhere in Ginchy, and the smell is horrible. Halted at Irish Guards HQ where Roche told us what to do. The Company was then led up at about half a mile per hour to a position N.E. of Ginchy. It is a flat piece of ground behind our

present Front Line and one maze of shell holes. We are supposed
to attack in 16 waves of which my Coy is the 5th.

Sept. 15th. Started digging 2.30 a.m., finished 3.15 a.m. Went round
all my Company to see they were all in their right places, etc.
Anyone can see that there must be hopeless confusion when we
start. Lay down in a shell hole at 4 a.m. About 4.30 a.m the Tanks
began to arrive behind us. The Germans heard them and sent up
many rockets and shelled slightly. At 5.40 a.m. the Tanks started
and went through our front line. At 6.30 a.m. the entire British
Line advanced, the 1st Guards Brigade on our left, the 6th Division
on our right. As we anticipated the entire wave formation had
disappeared before we had crossed our own front line, and we
advanced in a great mass, Grenadiers, Coldstream, Irish and Scots
Guards all inextricably mixed up. Within 30 yds I found myself in
front of the Grenadiers with a few of my men. Our barrage was
about 50 yds in front of us, and the whole landscape was obscured
by smoke, and it was impossible to see anything or keep direction.
About 100 yds on we found a few Germans lying in shell holes. I
shot one and clubbed one. We then came under heavy machine-
gun fire, and the Lines disappeared into shell holes.

The Lines again [moved – word unclear] on, passed over a
German Line which no-one knew existed, and came under heavy
fire from German 1st Line. Many men began to fall, and the
Coldstream lost almost their whole Batt. by walking into our own
barrage. The lines began to move in parts, some swinging to the
right, and others to the left, and eventually everyone got into shell
holes. In 10 minutes, we were off again, and the officers took
charge of any men they could see, and began to try and get some
order and direction.

Somewhere in this mêlée Captain Raymond Asquith was hit in the
chest while leading the first half of 4 Company of the 3rd Grenadier
Guards in the attack. Sensing the wound was fatal, he lit a cigarette
to prevent his men from realizing how badly he had been hurt. He
died while being carried by stretcher to the dressing station. Meanwhile Colquhoun briefly became part of the history of Asquith's
regiment, in that, with the 3rd Grenadiers' Adjutant, Captain Oliver
Lyttleton (the future Lord Chandos), two officers of the Irish
Guards, and a mixed bag of men mainly from the 3rd Grenadier

Guards, he carried out a major foray towards enemy lines. As he put it in his understated account: 'Between us we got up a composite company of every regiment and advancing out of the trench took up a position on high ground overlooking Lesboeufs. I went down along the trench to try and get reinforcements and take Lesboeufs.'

In the event Colquhoun and his company of like-minded warriors held out in their advanced position for most of the day, taking every precaution against surprise and placing Lewis guns on each flank. When it became evident that no reinforcements were forthcoming and that they would simply be overwhelmed by the enemy if they stayed where they were, they effected a swift and dramatic withdrawal. The Grenadiers official history's map of the Guards attack of 15 September records as its furthest point of advance: 'Position of Captain Sir Iain Colquhoun's party' – a rare honour for a member of another regiment, but given with acclaim in the case of an officer whom the Grenadiers' historian described as 'the bravest of the brave'.

* * *

To the left of the Guards' attack, the target was the village of Flers, and whereas Lesboeufs still remained in German hands by the end of 15 September, Flers, famously, did not.

Battery Sergeant-Major Pegler was a witness, if at an artilleryman's distance, of this success, albeit one gained with an inevitable high toll. 'Today has been some day,' he noted that evening, adding with perhaps understandable exaggeration: 'Tens of thousands of Tommies and Officers lie dead in heaps. We of the Artillery who have come through are to be particularly congratulated on our good fortune.'

Advancing in the wake of the infantry attack had allowed a perspective of the battlefield denied to the foot soldiers in the forefront of the action:

Once in the open we could see the infantry struggle up the hill towards Flers, our fellows advancing shell hole by shell hole and the Boche retiring just as slowly and steadily. Whatever Fritz's faults he is a great fighter.

Here there is not a yard of ground unbroken by shell fire and there are half a dozen bodies to each shell hole. When we were through the defile the Colonel gave the order 'Brigade will form line', and then away at the trot, canter and finally mad gallop up the ridge to Flers. The air was thick with shrapnel, and drivers, gunners and horses were going down in all directions, and by the time we got the order 'halt action front' we in my battery had lost fifteen drivers, twenty horses and several gunners. By good fortune all the gun teams came through and we were able to get into action.

What he could not see was that at Flers the *coup de grâce* was delivered by the 'landships' about which he and his comrades had gone 'barmy' less than twenty-four hours earlier. Thirty-six tanks went into action on 15 September and whereas those in support of the Guards' attack made little impact, at Flers they were dramatically successful. When the advance faltered on the edge of the village, four tanks seized the initiative by driving into it with an accompanying surge of Tommies and the new weapon wrote its signature firmly into the history of modern war. 41st Division provided the infantry who walked cheering down the main street of Flers and their striking memorial – of a tin-hatted infantryman with pack, rifle and bayonet – now stands permanently on his plinth gazing up the street along which they came. The tanks' contribution was acknowledged by another of those quoted at the head of this chapter, Captain Meysey-Thompson of 21st King's Royal Rifles. He noted in his diary: 'The attack is helped by Tanks, used on this day for the first time and proving most valuable.'

*   *   *

Elsewhere, however, others commented far less favourably on the effect of the new machines on the progress of the action. One such was Captain Frank Deverell, Transport Officer of the Post Office Rifles (1/8th London Regiment), a battalion of the 47th Division, whose starting-off point was further to the left of the Fourth Army front, opposite that by-now infamous German strong point, High Wood. Long seen as a place of menace – 'like a dark cloud on the horizon' was one description of it, before it was taken – it was to fall that day after many hours of bitter and sacrificial fighting. Writing to a fellow-officer of the battalion at that time at the regimental base in England, Captain Deverell stated: 'As you know High Wood was our objective, and our Trench Mortar Batteries under jolly old Goodes really saved the situation, as the Tanks were not worth a d—n there, and never did anything except spoil the show.'

This forceful criticism stemmed in part from a decision to the effect that, where the tanks were to go in, there were to be deliberate gaps in the barrage to allow corridors clear of shell fire along which the new machines could proceed. This might provide easy avenues for the tanks but it would also create artillery-free zones which the Germans could exploit. From the diary account of an Artillery officer on the 47th Division front involved in the High Wood attack, it is evident that this whole concept, not to mention the tanks themselves, came as a last-minute surprise. Major P.H. Pilditch of 7th London Brigade, Royal Field Artillery, noted in his diary on the night of 14–15 September: 'Operation orders came in very late and and I have been issuing orders to the Batteries all the evening. Quite late, orders to change the barrage came in, and to keep away from fixed lanes where "Tanks" are going to attack! *Lord knows what tanks are; some sort of armoured cars, I hear.* [Author's italics] Worked on till about 2 a.m. and went to lie down for an hour or two, feeling stone cold with anxiety.'

All this might have been satisfactory had the tanks been fully effective, but at High Wood a near worst-case situation was created by the decision of the local corps commander to order the tanks to advance through the wood itself. Captain Deverell continued: 'The Boche was not touched there when the attack took place, and it was hung up until Goodes had done wonderful work with his guns. Then, things went all right.'

Four tanks had been involved. Two had turned away to more open ground, and had ended up ditched, one with its crew so confused they had fired on their own men; a third had entered the wood, crossing the German front line and enfilading the support line until put out of action; a fourth had ditched ineffectively in No Man's Land. Yet despite this repeated attacks by the infantry had pressed home the attack and High Wood was taken.

But at very high cost, as Captain Deverell also told his
correspondent:

> We have had a very stiff time, as you know, and there is no good
> my giving you the names of those we have lost, because you have
> as good, or better, means of knowing in your own Office. A lot of
> good men have gone, and we shall miss Mitchell, Webb and
> Chichester very much, to say nothing of a crowd of our old stager
> NCOs and men. The new Regimental Sergeant Major was badly
> hit too, which will be a loss, as he was very good in training men.
> As you know, the Division did remarkably well from the Bat-
> talion's side of things, and our own better than any, if that were
> possible.

The Post Office Rifles had gone into the attack behind the 1/15th
Battalion – the Civil Service Rifles – of which Second Lieutenant
Eric Townsend and Private Reader were members; indeed Townsend,
and almost certainly Reader, went over with the first wave. Some
sense of the hard fighting experienced by these two battalions in the
High Wood action can be gained from a narrative of the operations
of the P.O. Rifles subsequently compiled on the basis of contemporary letters, diaries and reports by one of its company commanders,
Captain George Clark, later Sir George Clark, Professor of History
at Cambridge and Editor of the Oxford History of England. (It
should be noted that Clark differs from the official account of events
in that he refers to only three tanks, not four; also that, writing as
historian rather than participant, he uses the third person throughout
his description.)

> Dawn broke and showed the ragged and ghastly remnants of the
> wood, stripped and fallen trunks and a tangle of obstacles below
> them. At 5.45 three tanks were seen coming up the hill behind, but
> appeared to have lost their way. One of them fired several rounds
> from its six-pounder gun and stopped close to battalion head-
> quarters. The officer asked the way to the crater or gravel-pit on
> the eastern side of High Wood. This was just before Zero, and the
> tanks then vanished. Afterwards they were found to have stuck
> just inside the Wood, one over Glasgow Trench, the other between
> High Alley and the south corner of the wood. This was the first
> hitch, and a grave one, and needless. The artillery had been mainly

attending to the more advanced positions, since the tanks and the 15th Battalion had been expected to deal with the front line trenches. At 6.20 a.m. the 15th assaulted and the Post Office Rifles took their places in the British front and support lines.

At no moment in the war had they a finer battalion than that which waited there for the next lift of the barrage, better men in physique or in courage, better trained or more closely knit by mutual trust or understanding. The senior officers, who had made them, felt a deep confidence and pride. Major Vince, whose allotted place was behind with the transport, had come up of his own accord to see how well they would do. At seven o'clock they got out of their trenches, and ten minutes later they were smashed and lacerated by bullets. The 15th had been held up by rifle and machine-gun fire and were lying in shell holes in no man's land. The Post Office tried to push through, but for the most part were held up. Captain Chichester, Captain Mitchell, Captain Webb – three of the four company commanders – were killed, along with Lieutenant Kennedy and many men. A line of corpses [lay] shoulder to shoulder along the crater-bank.

On the right, indeed, No. 3 Company and some of No. 2 who had to make a right incline to reach their objective, got clear of the wood on its eastern side, found that the right company of the 15th had gone ahead, and themselves pushed on right up to their objective in the Starfish Line. Out on the left of the wood the same thing had been done by other battalions; but, although both the right and left had gone past it, in the hideous wood itself the 15th and 8th were still pinned in their shell holes. At 9.0 a.m. it was decided to try the effect of a rapid bombardment for 15 minutes by Stokes Mortars. From 9.30 to 9.45 the 140th Trench Mortar Battery led by Lieutenant Goodes, one of the bravest of the brave, poured out a heavy fire. Soon after reports began to come in that batches of Germans in the front line were surrendering. The turning point had come. By about 11.0 a.m. the enemy front and support lines in the wood were taken, with about 200 prisoners, and in conjunction with the remnants of the 15th and of the 141st Brigade from the left, the Post Office dug in on the far edge of the wood and beyond it.

This was far from the end of the battle, nor did it mean the end of fighting for these two hard-pressed battalions. On the 18th their remnants, some 220 of the P.O. Rifles, a mere 100 of the C.S. Rifles, attacked again, achieving their allotted targets with complete success. The 8th battalion's CO, Colonel Whitehead, expressed his satisfaction at the successful completion of what he described as 'the devil of a job': 'Everybody – Brigadier, Barter, Corps Commander – was delighted with it all, but all the nice things they said were not half good enough for the men, who were simply grand.'

The seizure of so notorious a strong point was to become a badge of pride for the numerous battalions who had contributed to it, each of which might be forgiven for believing their own part to have been vital. Thus on 20 September a Corporal of the 1/20th London, Reg Davy, wrote in confident mood to his mother:

> On our way back, Major-General Barter met the battalion and as our company passed him, he said 'Well done, 20th, you have done splendid work, I am proud of you.' He might with reason be proud of us, for the battalion of which I am more than proud to be a member, had done that day what 2 other battalions on the same occasion and many other battalions on previous occasions had failed to do – namely, had driven the Germans out of the wood and kept them out. We have had to pay the price, however, although our casualties were not nearly so severe as one would expect.

Casualties, of course, covered everything from a fatality to an injured finger, and men could join the casualty list in the oddest of ways. Lance-Corporal C.H. Morden, for example, of the 1/7th London Regiment (popularly known as the 'Shiny Seventh'), fought through the worst of the High Wood battle, going over the top with the first wave. He had conquered his pre-battle fears, which he compared to 'the kind of feeling you get just before a tooth extraction – a sort of "I'm not afraid but hope it won't hurt" sensation. We got the word to go over at 6.20 a.m., and then from that moment I felt all right.' His description of the attack is low-key and practical – 'my platoon reached there about a dozen strong out of 30 who started and we quickly got to work to clear up a bit' – and the main hazard he recalled was the threat from 'an enormous machine gunner [who] stood by his gun and even had the cool audacity to put his gun on the opposite parapet and commence firing at the remainder of our boys who had crossed us and were forcing the Germans still further back. Four of us tackled this chap and made short work of him, the only really brave German I saw.'

Once the platoon had gained its objectives, Morden was ordered to report to Company Headquarters, which he found further forward in the German third line, except that there was hardly a line at all, there being no recognizable trenches – 'they had all been battered by our own artillery before the attack'. His company commander had had to take up position in a shell hole.

'Now followed the most awful part of the whole thing. For two days and two nights we were shelled to "Blazes".' Morden found himself praying as he had never prayed before while this 'hellish pantomime' went on; and then 'as if by Divine Command Sunday morning dawned in comparative peace and I was ordered to go and see about some rations.' Attempts had been made during the previous night to 'connect up the various shell holes and make some sort of a trench, but in places the work had not been finished and anyone requiring to get across had only one way – over the top.' His account continues:

I was on my way to one of these isolated posts, with – of all things – a bottle of whisky for an Officer. It was about 7.0 a.m. and broad daylight, I lost direction and stopped to look round. That stop nearly cost me my Life. I heard a noise like the lash of a whip and then a sting in my arm and I saw my right arm flap down to my side. Simultaneously I dropped down, I let the whisky stop where it was. All I troubled about now was putting the largest possible distance between myself and the German shells in the shortest possible time. I had to crawl about 400 yards before I got my wound roughly bandaged by some fellow in a machine-gun section. From there I stumbled on to our support dressing station and then from one station to another until I reached the Field Ambulance. Here I was inoculated and then redressed and put in the Ambulance for a further clearing station. From there by train to Etaples on the French Coast. At Etaples three days and then by train to Calais. Thence by boat across Channel to Dover and dear OLD ENGLAND at last and here I am. TRUTH IS STRONGER THAN FICTION. THIS IS PROOF!!!!!!!!

Morden's story is told not in a letter or a diary but in a brief personal account pointedly entitled not, say, 'My Adventures in the Recent Somme Offensive', but 'How L/Cpl C.H. Morden was wounded'.

* * *

There was a notable codicil to 47th Division's brave but costly performance in the battle for High Wood. Its General Officer Commanding, Major-General C. St.L. Barter – the same who had delighted Corporal Davy and his comrades by his praise for their 'splendid work' during the action – was shortly afterwards abruptly dismissed and sent home. He was deemed to have defaulted on two counts, which, on the surface at least, would appear to be somewhat contradictory: 'lack of push' and 'wanton waste of life'. An alternative explanation is that he had objected somewhat too forcibly to the decision of his Corps Commander, Lieutenant-General Sir William Pulteney, to direct the four tanks assigned to his division's attack – against the advice of the specialists in the new form of warfare – through High Wood itself, with the result that they failed to play the key role assigned to them. This failure undoubtedly contributed to the very high casualty toll suffered by the division, for which someone's head was required. Barter, the junior officer in the argument, was the chosen scapegoat. He was to fight for the rest of his life to clear his name. At a dinner in honour of the 47th Division in 1919, he defended himself with the utmost vigour: 'I was charged with wanton waste of the men entrusted to my command at the battle of the Somme. I repudiate that charge with indignation. The measures taken which led to this loss were either in opposition to my representations, or I was not responsible for them.' His demand for an official inquiry to establish the facts of the case was never answered. He died, his reputation still clouded, in Madrid in 1931, a late casualty of the September push on the Somme of fifteen years earlier.

* * *

At the farthest end of the Third Army offensive, 11th Division of II Corps were opposite the still untaken target of the battle's first day,

Thiepval − 'as nearly impregnable as nature, art and the unstinted labour of nearly two years could make', according to Sir Douglas Haig in his post-battle despatch. A prime jewel in its defences was the so-called 'Wonder Work'. On 13 September, Sergeant Edward Miles of the 8th Duke of Wellington's West Riding Regiment, a veteran of Suvla Bay, Gallipoli, explained in his diary:

> Tomorrow we go into the line and the following evening (the 15th) we are going to take, or try to, Thiepval Wood. We have had the encouraging news imparted to us that seven divisions have previously tried to take it. The sector we are responsible for is called 'Wunder Works' [sic] by the Germans. So called, because it consists of a revolving platform containing innumerable machine-guns, which disappear when our artillery starts to bombard, but which quickly 'pop' up again as our infantry commence to advance.
>
> Cheering news, eh?

In the event, Thiepval remained intact, though the official history states that the 11th Division 'made progress between Mouquet Farm and the Leipzig Salient, south-west of Thiepval'. Miles, claiming their achievements as a success, summed up his experiences thus:

> *September 17th*. Phew! Those three days seemed like an hour's nightmare. We went up on the night of the 14th with three days rations in our haversacks, and on our way up we passed field guns wheel to wheel from Crucifix Corner to Railway Alley (a trench leading up to the front line).
>
> There must have been thousands of guns there, and I think it was that that gave us the victory. We lost about two hundred (out of 500) killed and wounded and unfortunately my chum was amongst the wounded, being hit in the elbow soon after we went over. There was a tremendous amount of old iron thrown about but I was lucky enough to be missed. The chief praise is due, I think, to one of our Companies and a Company of the W. Yorks who as we went forward, came behind and dug a communication trench from 'Jerry' front line to our own.
>
> How those poor devils worked while we held on was marvellous. The Brigadier General, as we came out of the line, shook hands with each of us, (those that were left). Of course it was a

feather in his cap, but we didn't get anything. Still, who cares, we get a shilling a day.

* * *

The September attack had scored some notable successes and made some notable gains: both the villages after which the battle was named were taken, Flers as described, Courcelette in a vigorous assault by the Canadians, while 15th Division, with minimal help from tanks, had captured Martinpuich. Overall the tanks had had mixed fortunes on their first run, but for those not involved in their use, the fact that the British had the new mysterious weapon at their disposal and had, by most accounts, given the enemy a considerable scare, was good and encouraging news. On the 16th Sergeant John Poucher of the 51st Overseas Battalion, Canadian Expeditionary Force, had noted in his diary: 'At last old Fritz has got the wind up him and I guess he wondered what the dickens was on the way. Our men are giving a good account of themselves, and I hope now that we get Fritz properly on the run. If we could only get this war over by Xmas it would be great. I wonder if the people at home know what the surprise is. Some pick-me-up for the lads in the trenches.'

Equally impressed by the shock-waves the tanks produced was a young Second Lieutenant of the Cheshire Regiment newly out from England, Brian Hickey, who wrote enthusiastically to his parents on 2 October: 'I saw a Tank last night for the first time, and they looked A1 things. Solid as a wall. We are not allowed to say anything about the mechanism thereof as I believe the Boche hasn't yet got the secret of them.'

Searching for a suitable description, a Canadian corporal, Garnet Durham, who saw them about the same time as Hickey, called them 'a cross between a turtle and a submarine', adding that a German prisoner he had talked to, whose company had tried to tackle one with the bayonet, had said it was *'ganz gut'*. *'Ganz gut'* in this context represented a measure of approval way beyond its straightforward translation as 'quite good'; 'something else' in today's phraseology; 'not half bad' in the jargon of the Tommy – the phrase 'not half', according to Brophy and Partridge, being regularly used 'in all kinds of connections to express emphasis'.

There were, however, two sides to this. Battery Sergeant-Major Douglas Pegler had ended the battle in hospital, though he was not so severely wounded that he could not write up his ever thoughtful and eloquent diary. Under the date 18 September, after describing his wounding on the morning of the 16th – 'Fritz got my battery with salvoes of 5.9s and I made my undignified exit on a stretcher' – and his subsequent journey by motor-ambulance and train to Le Havre, he reflected on the positive and negative aspects of the new phenomenon:

I have forgotten the 'land crabs', the great armoured cars that took part in the battle of the 15th – some are lying on their backs mangled masses of twisted and broken iron, others are back in their repairing yards, all are more or less crocked but Gad the execution they did was awful. It struck me as I saw them from the corner of Leuze Wood, how symbolic of all war they were. Then one saw them creeping along at about four miles an hour, taking all obstacles as they came, sputtering death with all their guns, enfilading each trench as it came to it – and crushing beneath them our own dead and dying as they passed. I saw one body on a concrete parapet over which one had passed. This body was just a splash of blood and clothing about two feet wide and perhaps an inch thick, an hour before this thing had been a thinking, breathing man, with life before him and loved ones awaiting him at home, probably somewhere in Scotland, for he was a kiltie.

Nothing stops these cars, trees bend and break, boulders are pressed into the earth. One had been hit by a large shell and the petrol tanks pierced, she lay on her side in flames, a picture of hopelessness but every gun on the uppermost side still working with dogged determination. The firing gradually slackened and she lay silent, the gallant little crew burned to death each man at his gun.

* * *

The Battle of Flers-Courcelette officially lasted from 15 to 22 September. Now once again there was a major surge in the tide of telegrams or official forms of notification announcing a death or a wounding, and of letters from battalion officers, chaplains or fellow-soldiers expressing regret and offering consolation. At some point the family of Alec Reader of the Post Office Rifles would have been informed that he had been killed in action on the 15th. His body would never be found so that his name would eventually be recorded on the Thiepval Memorial to the Missing of the Somme. Among the letters sent on by some fellow officer's hand was that written by Second Lieutenant Eric Townsend, which he had thoughtfully enclosed with his will. He had been wounded in the first wave of the attack on the 15th and had died of his wounds two days later. He was buried in the Dartmoor Cemetery at Bécordel near Albert where Lieutenant Alan Lloyd had been interred six weeks earlier. His letter was subsequently published, first in the *Daily Mail* on 25 October that year under the heading 'The Boy Who Died', and then in a finely printed pocket-sized booklet entitled 'The Happy Hero', price one shilling, complete with a drawing of the writer and an eloquent appreciation by a family friend, which ended with a quotation from Milton's 'Samson Agonistes':

> Nothing is here for tears, nothing to wail
> Or knock the breast, no weakness, no contempt,
> Dispraise, or blame, nothing but well and fair,
> And what may quiet us in a death so noble.

For Raymond Asquith, Shakespeare would provide the epitaph, when later his headstone was carved for his grave in the cemetery on the Guillemont Road. At thirty-seven much older than most who fell in the September battle, he was nevertheless widely seen as a symbol of lost youth, of brilliant but unfulfilled promise. The words are from the speech by the Chorus at the end of *Henry V*, a comment on another warrior who fought in France and died young:

> Small time, but in that small most greatly lived
> This star of England.

* * *

We came out of battle at 5 a.m. this morning and are about a mile from the firing line. Well we are all absolutely filthy and awfully tired but everybody is as happy and proud as they can be as we have had a magnificent victory again. I suppose now it is over and we don't know from Adam where we go next, there is no harm in saying our job was to storm Lesboeufs. I suppose if there *is* any harm in mentioning the name the Censor can cut it out.

The writer was Major Harry Dillon, acting commander of 1st East Yorkshires, 6th Division; he had assumed command because the C.O. had been evacuated to hospital. The censor did not delete the name (no more than he did in the case of Lieutenant Story's account of the seizure of Guillemont, quoted on pages 158–9) so that the recipient of the letter would have no doubt that Dillon had been involved in the offensive opened towards the eastern end of the Somme battlefield on 25 September with Lesboeufs and Morval as target villages; a French attack had also taken place to the right of the British one. In effect, this action, which would become known as the Battle of Morval, took over where the Flers-Courcelette battle had left off, but with much greater success. It would last until the 28th and would claim not only Morval and Lesboeufs but also such other desirable prizes as Combles and Gueudecourt.

Dillon was delighted with the competent way the attack had been managed, and with his own and his battalion's contribution to it. This was a highly professional performance, without the tanks (which had had their turn on the stage and departed), but with the comparatively new technique of the 'creeping barrage' meticulously and effectively applied. Moreover, planning and briefing had been detailed and thorough. Officer bravado, however, soon to be seriously discouraged because it drew enemy attention and added unnecessarily to the subalterns' casualty lists, was clearly still part of the accepted code. Dillon continued:

I had besides the Battn two companies of another Regt, 2 Sections machine-guns and two Sections R.E. Quite an imposing force. We did not move into our battle positions until the morning 25th, and this time I had lots of time to think it out and get out proper written orders. There is a big sunken road between our first line and the village and this was the first objective of two other regiments. Having taken that there was to be a barrage for 1 hour to clear up and my lads had to be timed to get to this point at the moment the barrage was due to lift.

After giving them all their orders I shifted with my Adjutant up to the front line and got there about half an hour before the infantry went over. About 6 minutes before this the barrage started. It was really a wonderful thing – so precise that one might have thought someone had pressed a button. Thousands of screaming shrapnel shells just over our heads and bursting 100 yds in front. At the same time the heavies increased and the whole Hun line about 300 yds off went up in a cloud of dust and debris. Two minutes later our trench, a harmless looking ditch, came to life and as far as I could see (some miles) out came thousands of British soldiers and far away the other side of Combles one could catch the occasional gleam of the French bayonets. It really was a most uncanny sight. They crept out in no man's land, the officers smoking cigarettes and pipes and getting the men into line. Then this line got up and quietly and very slowly marched in perfect line on to the Hun trench, the barrage creeping along in front lifting 50 yards every minute. 50 yards behind a third and then a fourth and almost before one realised it, our front line was in the Germans trench and streams of Germans were coming back, some wounded but mostly all right. They then put up red flares all along the German trench to show we had got it.

I watched them disappearing into the village and then could see no more. You can't imagine how anxious it is waiting for news, and how relieved when an hour later a panting runner came with a message that they had taken the whole village and were consolidating on the other side.

The Guards Division also went over on the 25th, and this time gained all their objectives; they were side by side with Dillon's 6th Division, and jointly took part in the clearing of Lesboeufs. 'We are attacking at the same place that we left off the other day,' wrote Captain Arthur Gibbs of the 1st Welsh Guards, 'and I think we ought to go through well. As I write this, there is a tremendous battle going on. We are advancing again on a big front. At 12.35 we went over to our first objective. I have just been outside and seen the Boche prisoners simply streaming in.'

Gibbs had taken part in the earlier attack – and would also join the battle briefly on the 25th – but for Lieutenant Geoffrey Fildes of the 2nd Coldstream Guards this would be his first action on the Somme. Ordered, to his intense disappointment, to stay behind on the 15th, he had spent an anxious day waiting for news while hearing 'wild rumours' from the dressing station near by. 'The Guards were being exterminated; the "Tanks" were clearing all before them; the right flank had been held up and the Division was left in the air. We could only resolve to disbelieve all news good or bad.' The outcome had been a mixture of both, but the battalion had suffered heavily, and many of his friends had been killed. He and the other officers in reserve waited in vain for the summons to go forward. 'News at last reached us from Brigade HQ that no officers were being sent for as there were not enough men left to command.' Next day the remnants had returned:

> Never shall I forget the homecoming of the poor old battalion. In front, with the early morning sun flashing upon the side-drums, marched the 'drums'. They were a fine sight and played with tremendous style. Behind, marching alone, unshaven, and rather haggard, came the Colonel followed by a pitiful two hundred and fifty of the magnificent body of men I had known. Their efforts to smarten up into a march were one of the most pathetic things I've seen.

Now, on the 25th, it was his turn. From 5 a.m. he and his right-hand company were in position, with seven and a half hours to go to zero hour, in a muddy communication trench with nothing to eat except biscuits and chocolate. Rain would have added misery to their other hazards, but 'fortunately it grew to a gloriously fine day. The blood-red sun climbed upwards into a cloudless sky, while we were left to our own solemn thoughts. Strangely enough the time did not drag so much as I had feared.'

Fildes' description of 25 September is a classic account of a young man's experience of battle which reads so well that it might suggest a leisurely reminiscence in postwar tranquillity, but in fact it was written in his diary just one week later when at last he had time to draw breath. Son of the artist Sir Luke Fildes, himself an architect who had been educated at Eton and Trinity College, Cambridge, he had enlisted in the Artists' Rifles on the outbreak of war and had been commissioned into the Coldstream Guards in 1915. No stranger to style in other forms, he could write with style as well. The story

told is simple yet remarkable – a real-life 'Red Badge of Courage',
with pre-battle fears giving way to elation, combined with a sense of
marvellous competence, when the challenge actually came. His
battalion was to go over in the second wave, with the 2nd Grenadiers
going first – which fact extended the period of waiting, and therefore
the period of anxiety. The following is a much abbreviated version:

At 7.30 a furious fire of all calibres was opened upon the enemy
positions, but very little reply was made. Hour after hour the air
shrieked to the sound of shells. I found what distraction I could in
watching the wanderings of the beetles and insects that crawled
about the bottom of the trench. A feeling of intense tension held
me, and my thoughts seemed to travel with lightning rapidity over
the events of my past life. I was not really afraid, but extremely
nervous as to what sort of figure I should cut as soon as above
ground. I found much support in the reflection that the eyes of the
batt^n would be on my company, and that one could only be killed
once. I was exceedingly anxious that that solitary event should be
done as befitting a gentleman.

Slowly the hands of my watch crawled round to 11 then 12
o'clock. In another hour, I reflected, we should have commenced
our great adventure with Fate.

I cannot describe the emotion with which I watched the last five
minutes go. They seemed hours.

Sharp on Zero to the minute, the din overhead swelled to an
unparalleled volume. The air howled like a storm and presently the
ground beneath and beside one commenced to beat and tremble. A
new note joined into this tempest of war: the dirge I remembered
so well at Festubert – machine-gun bullets! I wanted to get up and
cheer for England. I was trembling with excitement.

Presently, I suppose it was only a minute or so, the heaving of
the earth seemed to have grown to an earthquake. Terrible crashes
and concussions smote all round us. We huddled down onto our
heels, straining our necks upward to watch the grass on the sides
of our trench. I realised that the Germans were replying at last.
Their barrage was being poured down upon us.

The crashes seemed to follow at every second until they grew
into one continuous roar of tumult. I could only speak to my
neighbour by shouting. Presently, the shocks seeming just over our

heads, and the narrow trench drumming deafeningly to the sound of shells, I commenced to pray as I have never prayed before. I was horribly afraid at last, I thought in a daze of souls in hell. I wondered if *this* would resemble it. It was awful. I felt like one of the insignificant insects that now staggered frantically about the bottom of the trench, shaken down by the concussions and alarmed at the inexplicable convulsion that had suddenly engulfed their world.

With what relief did I receive the order to move along the trench!

With a sort of gasp I became a man again. As soon as I began to move I felt my horrible mid-day nightmare slipping from my mind. I began to think and marvellously clearly and collectedly. Mortal men had gone through this before me, I reflected, so where they had gone would I follow with all my resolution.

Eventually, the order came to attack:

I remember giving two tremendous blasts on the siren and then turning toward my front I slowly gave the signal 'advance!'. Those who had got out [from the trench] rose to their feet. There was no cheering. I began to run forward over the long grass, looking back to see if the remaining platoons were following. A line of moving flashes over the parapet showed me that they were climbing out, the sun gleaming upon their bayonets. At last! The Coldstream [sic] were entering the battle. I have no very clear recollection of the next few minutes. I was alone, running steadily towards the line of German wire. I could hear the clatter of equipment behind me, that was all I wanted. The company was at the charge! I do not remember any more shells, only the whistle overhead of bullets. They never seemed very near. I saw nothing of the Grenadiers, only huddled khaki figures, through which I picked my way. Some moved, but I could not attend to them, my eyes were glued on the enemy front line. Presently the bodies grew thicker. It flashed across my mind that there might be lurking Germans near, so I pulled out my revolver and crouched as I ran. A ghostlike figure seemed to drift past me. It was a Hun in a round service field cap. I believe his hands were up; at any rate I did not shoot, but went for the wire, wondering why I was still alive.

A feeling of tremendous exultation filled me. I felt like a beast of prey. No man of mine should enter the Green line ahead of me.

It seemed very easy. Numbers of dead Grenadiers lay around everywhere. I only felt the more invigorated. I remember glancing down into the trench and noting there was no one there. I was in it the next moment. Then panting figures with flashing bayonets loomed up behind me and my men tumbled into the German front line alongside me. I had outrun the lot.

For Fildes the supreme moment of the day was what became a kind of hectic charge into the heart of the doomed village:

In a scattered irregular line we marched onwards, still keeping a vigilant look out for stragglers or any who should still desire a fight. The line of trees on the further edge of the village came into view, their tops wreathed by our shrapnel bursts. Over gardens and orchards we strode, a tumult of exultation throbbing in our hearts and lending vigour to our step. It was too great a moment for even a cheer. If only our drums were with us, I thought! They alone would sound the glory in our minds as our line stumbled over the remains of our enemy's positions, pressing onward to victory. Those were sublime moments, for we were England upon the field of battle; conquerors offering to her yet further renown; so, with our bodies throbbing our *pas de charge*, we burst through fences, ditches and ruins to our goal.

*   *   *

Late September also saw the Battle of the Thiepval Ridge, in which Thiepval and the Schwaben Redoubt were finally taken. Another first day target, Mouquet Farm, fell on the same day. Playing a key role in what was a striking achievement by the Reserve Army was Major-General Maxse's 18th Division. Thiepval, on its bluff dominating the Ancre Valley, had defied the British attack on 1 July and subsequently. With its château, its church, its attractive, red-tiled houses, and its fine views, in peacetime it had been a popular place for Sunday afternoon visits by the citizens of Albert. Now, with its buildings devastated, its pleasant aspect destroyed, it was a warren of winding trenches, tunnels and dugouts occupied by an élite German regiment who had held it since 1914. Maxse's doctrine was clear: 'Without preparation the bravest troops fail and their heroism is wasted. With sufficient time to prepare an assault on a definite and limited objective I believe a well-trained division can capture almost any "impregnable" stronghold.' This he intended to prove. On the evening before the attack, 25 September, he sent this message to all his troops: 'The 180th Regiment of Württemburgers have withstood attacks on Thiepval for two years, but the 18th Division will take it tomorrow.'

This was not bluster and the target set by Maxse was duly achieved, thanks in very large part to the scrupulous build-up before battle on which he always insisted, with rehearsals over specially prepared ground and a sharing of information down to the level of the ordinary soldier had a crucial part. 'The system in the Division,' he stated in his report on the battle after its successful conclusion, 'is to tell subordinates as much as possible of impending operations long before they occur.... It is better to risk information leaking out through captured prisoners than to run the greater risk of ordering infantry over the parapet unacquainted with what they are expected to do or where they are to go.' 'In fine fettle', is the Official History's description of 18th Division as it prepared for action, adding that it had 'received three weeks' battle training on its way back to the Somme from Flanders'.

The British were learning their trade. There would be many errors and disasters to come, but this was a far cry from the simplicities with which for so many the Somme campaign had begun.

The campaign had not, however, ended. In fact, it was about to enter its most dour and, from the point of view of the men engaged in the fighting, most disheartening phase.

CHAPTER ELEVEN

'THE PITILESS SOMME'

> Our last relief from the pitiless Somme, where 200 of us have been
> buried or left unburied.

THUS THE COMMENT of the medical officer of the 2nd Royal
Welsh Fusiliers in his diary in March 1917, when his battalion finally
withdrew from a territory with which it had become all too familiar
over many months. This was the now-celebrated Captain J.C. Dunn,
whose superb battalion history, *The War the Infantry Knew*, originally published anonymously, has justly been hailed as a classic of
the Western Front war.

Dunn's adjective 'pitiless' was never more deserved than in the
final weeks of the 1916 campaign. This was warfare at its most grim
and unrewarding, with negligible gains on maps accompanied by
huge casualties and a major decline in morale. Why, therefore, was
the offensive maintained? The French example at Verdun and the
ever-present pressure from the French commanders to keep on
fighting were powerful arguments for continuance, though very
likely another part of the equation was the belief, beguilingly
supported at GHQ by Brigadier-General Charteris and fuelled by
more intelligence summaries quoting defeatist Germans, that the
enemy's will to continue was about to collapse. There was a moment
of hesitation in early November, when the commander of XIV
Corps, Lieutenant-General the Earl of Cavan, an officer of high
reputation, forcibly argued that further attempts to advance would
only end in failure and pointless sacrifice; he underlined his case by
stating that 'no one who has not visited the front trenches can really
know the state of exhaustion to which the men are reduced'. At first
it seemed his plea might be heeded, but after an interview between

the British Commander-in-Chief and General Foch, a cancelled plan of attack was reinstated. There was the predictable result: no ground gained and 2,000 names added to the casualty roll.

Doubts about Haig's strategy in continuing the campaign through October and into November have not been confined to his critics. Even so stalwart a supporter as Charles Carrington was moved to write: '[H]e was too stubborn to remain content with a partial success. Up to this point, the Somme Battle, which the French generalissimo conceived as a battle of attrition, could be justified. It was the attempt to push on in the vain hope of forcing a break-through, so late in the season, that may be condemned. The last stage of the battle took us down the hill into a new valley of humiliation where the enemy again had the command. Why did we go on?'

Carrington's 'valley of humiliation' was not merely a metaphor, it was also a fact. Answering his own question, he continued: 'However, we did go on and the line had been pushed down the forward slope, in full view of the enemy guns to the village of Le Sars, a little salient astride the Bapaume Road.' Here the men of the Fourth Army found themselves opposite a curious feature of the Somme landscape that few who faced it would ever forget. 'Not only was [that salient] commanded from the Bapaume ridge; it was dominated by a monstrosity. Beside the road, which rose up the slope beyond Le Sars, and only 500 yards away, was a round barrow, a prehistoric tumulus, standing up like Silbury Hill beside the Bath Road. What Gallic chieftain slain by Caesar in the land of Ambiani lay buried here we neither knew nor cared, but this outgrowth, which we called the Butte of Warlencourt . . . terrified us. A dome of gleaming white chalk from which all the vegetation had been blown away by shell fire, it was the most conspicuous object in the landscape by daylight or moonlight.'

The Official History describes the Butte de Warlencourt thus: 'A chalk mound some sixty feet high, on the slope of the spur overlooking the Bapaume road where the Grid lines crossed it. The Butte afforded excellent observation of the low ground to the south-west and also in the opposite direction towards Bapaume in which area were many battery positions; its importance was fully appreciated by both British and Germans.'

Geographically and militarily correct, this gives no hint of the impact it had on men faced with the task of attempting to seize it, or when they failed to do so, of coexisting with it under its apparently hostile glare. George Harbottle, a former Company Quarter Master Sergeant of 6th Northumberland Fusiliers, 50th Division, writing in a later memoir, offered this more acerbic, soldier's description:

> This butte was just like a pit heap and doubtless had been a prehistoric burial place all grown over with grass. With constant shelling it had now lost all its vegetation and appeared as just a great heap of chalk. It was however still a useful observation place for the enemy. There were heavy rains which made life a misery for both friend and foe plus, as ever, mud, mud and more mud. With the weight of equipment, extra ammunition and Mills bombs, any attacking force could hardly stagger forward and one felt that any general must have known the folly of driving troops forward in these impossible conditions.

*   *   *

On 7 October, the Civil Service and Post Office Rifles were in action for the second major battle within a month, as part of the first of numerous attempts to take the Butte de Warlencourt. They had not had time properly to rebuild. As the P.O. Rifles historian Captain George Clark noted in his narration (see previous chapter): 'Only a week was allowed for the partial restoration of the battalion. Drafts of over four hundred "other ranks" came up from the base; the men forming the new drafts were keen, but untrained in the very special methods the Somme fighting entailed. Only two officers came.'

The attack in which they were to take part along with other units of 47th Division would officially become one of a long series of actions eventually lumped together as the Battle of the Transloy Ridges, but for those at the western end of the sector Le Transloy was a distant name on the map, and they had quite enough to concentrate on with their eyeline dominated by the Butte. The plan was that at zero hour the Post Office Rifles (the 1/6th London) were to advance under cover of a creeping barrage and seize a point called Diagonal Trench. Eighteen minutes later the 1/15th and 1/7th were to pass through them and seize the final objective, with its left-hand troops resting on the Butte.

In comparison with their September effort at High Wood this one was a total failure. The Official History states: 'The 1/8th London was checked by terrific machine-gun fire, and the 1/15th London and the 1/7th London ... suffered a similar fate.' For once Clark's precise, understated narrative becomes almost emotional:

> Not very much will ever be known about the history of this attack. The men had little rest and heavy showers during the night had wet them through. The creeping barrage was far feebler than had been expected. It is said that in parts of the line there was a tendency to bunch, but the men went steadily on, and crossed the sunken road. As they were topping a slight rise, Lieutenant Davis noticed cleft sticks bearing white rags (this was confirmed by others) and as the attacking wave passed through them heavy machine-gun fire broke out from flank and front. When about eighty yards from the German line and when the heads of the garrison were distinctly visible, Lieutenant Davis turned to call on his men. But hardly a dozen were left. With these he dug in and got into touch with the remnants of the Seventh Battalion. Lieutenant Watson, who was wounded in the arms, wrote from hospital: 'They went steadily ahead under that awful fire. They did not even look back.' That is the only epitaph of two hundred men.

The 7 October attack here had one positive result; it was on that day that the village of Le Sars was taken, by 23rd Division. The Butte – which seems to be only yards from Le Sars to the visitor driving today along that historic road towards Bapaume – remained inviolate, an untouched citadel, as it would throughout the rest of the 1916 fighting.

For 47th Division, this marked the end of its involvement in the Somme battle. In the early morning of the 10th, when it was relieved by 9th Division, the survivors of the Post Office Rifles collected at Mametz Wood and marched to Albert, where the battalion remained for four days before being ordered elsewhere. In the words of Captain Clark: 'Here it was reviewed by an officer of exalted rank, of whose speech it had been indignantly noted that it did not allude to the two terrible battles of the last month, and that the gist of it was: "Keep yourselves clean, my lads and always fill in your latrines before you leave your billets".'

The battalion marched away from the battle. 'Their last impression of the Somme', Clark recorded, 'was a peaceful one, of crops gathered into neat ricks and cattle contentedly cropping the autumn grass in the pale October sunshine.'

* * *

The 56th (London) Division, of Gommecourt fame, was also in action on 7 October, in an attack next to the French at the eastern end of Fourth Army front. The 1/12th London Regiment, known as the 'Rangers', was one of the assault battalions, with, among its new members freshly arrived from Britain, a young rifleman, Private Arthur Dornam. Ten days later, writing from a hospital in Bath, Dornam related his adventures in France in a letter to his 'dearest mother and dad', enclosing with it a piece of the shrapnel which had sent him there. He was one of many soldiers whose part in the Somme campaign was not so much a long hard slog as a brief, high-risk encounter, being hardly in the battle before he was heading back home with a Blighty wound.

His first spell in the trenches had been less than exciting as the Rangers had been merely in support to a successful attack by the London Scottish – 'they simply walked over', was Dornam's comment. Subsequently they had had 'rather a ticklish time' going through 'Death Valley' – 'we caught a bit of a strafing' – and had spent a day or so at Trônes Wood – 'where once upon a time there were some trees – there are only shell holes there now'. From there they had gone forward through Guillemont to the trenches, to make ready for their attack:

> Our first job was to hold an advanced trench, 50 yards from the Huns for two days, during which time we had no casualties. On the night of the 6th we moved into a new position and had to dig ourselves in just at dawn – we were under shell fire 20 minutes after we started so you bet we worked jolly hard.
>
> Later on in the morning word was passed along that we were to go over the top at about 1 o'clock. The bombardment by our guns on the German trenches started. I've never heard anything like it, and never want to again – the air seemed full of shells and the Huns replied furiously. They must have had news of the attack for

when we went over we were met by a hail of shrapnel and machine-gun bullets. I know that these were spitting up dirt all round me and although I had several narrow squeaks, I wasn't hurt.

From what I can learn nearly all my pals were either killed or wounded.

One narrow squeak was that I had the brass snake on my belt smashed, I think a bullet struck it, then tore my cardigan, tunic and shirt, and just touched the skin on my side and off again. It was just the merest scratch, and now the scab has gone.

I landed eventually in a shell hole with a German sniper potting at me every time I moved, so I waited till dark and then crept farther to my left until I found some of our boys in a trench. I acted as stretcher-bearer all night and all that were left of us were relieved early on Sunday morning. 'C' Coy went in 138 strong and came out 25 strong.

In the official history's account of the 7 October attack, the 'Rangers' are accorded this reference: 'Advancing four minutes after zero hour, the 1/12th London failed before Dewdrop Trench, northeast of Lesboeufs, which had been shelled by Stokes mortars as it was too close for artillery bombardment.'

Dornam had survived this first baptism; however, the battalion's part in the action was not yet finished:

We went about a mile back to have a roll call, etc., and rest, but at 12 o'clock on Sunday night we were called up again, this time just to hold a trench for a day, then unfortunately we got shelled very heavily, and it was one of these shrapnel shells which burst just close to me and one bit went through my right forearm and the enclosed lodged in my right thigh. I had the wound roughly dressed, but had to wait till dark to get to the dressing station. After some trouble I had a 30-hour journey to Rouen where I was in hospital for about 4 days. On Sunday morning I was put on a train from Havre, and put from there on HMHS *Asturias*, which sailed at about 11 o'clock. We reached Southampton at 7.30 and at 1 o'clock embarked on a train which brought me to Bath. I am quite comfortable but I shall be glad to get some of *My Ma's cakes.* . . .

* * *

Major Harry Dillon commanding the 1st West Yorkshires in 6th Division had been elated by his battalion's performance in September, but after taking part on 12 October in another of the surges of the Battle of the Transloy Ridges, he was in a much less triumphalist mood. He wrote home on the 15th:

> We have been brought back about 3 miles. This last battle was so horrible and so terrific that I shall not try to describe it to you. We did part of what we were asked to do but could do no more for the simple reason that there was nobody left to do it, and the few survivors were too shaken and dazed to do any more attacking, our trenches were just heaps of bloody earth. My General just sent me a line and says 'Your battalion had a most exasperating time up in the line. Great credit is due to you all for carrying on so well under such disadvantageous circumstances'. We are in reserve now and I have had a big reinforcement last night, so perhaps they will send us in again. They are at it hammer and tongs and we are just waiting in case we are wanted.
>
> This battle seems to go on with ever increasing fury. An endless procession of more and more men and guns. The men are absolutely splendid and nobody seems to take any account of life whatever.
>
> Well if I live through this battle I think I shall have seen war at its worst. Hell must have some bottom.

*   *   *

The failed offensive which so dismayed Major Dillon produced, in the case of one young officer, what would undoubtedly be the most memorable experience of his life.

Nineteen-year-old Second Lieutenant Alistair Crerar – 'Tim' to his family and friends – had joined the 2nd Battalion Royal Scots Fusiliers on the Somme in early September. On 12 October, together with the 17th Manchesters, the battalion went over the top as part of 30th Division's contribution to that day's attack. They had barely begun their advance before intense enemy fire forced them to withdraw. During their advance, however, Crerar was badly wounded. As his comrades retired and the Germans established their control over the battlefield by their machine-guns and artillery fire, he found himself stranded in No Man's Land waiting for rescue.

He was to stay there for thirty-six hours. Sometime on the 13th – a Friday – frustrated by the failure of all his efforts to catch attention, he took out his Army Book 153 and his pencil and wrote a report on his predicament:

A.H. Crerar 2nd Lt. 2nd R.S.F. About 2.8 on Thursday I was hit on the leg somewhere round the thigh after advancing about 100 yards, tumbled into a shell hole where I lay till dark and attempted to dig myself in a little with my hands. After dusk someone appeared and I called, he approached and said he was taking a message from Mr King (my Coy Comm) and would tell him I was here, and would come back. He never came. Two other people I think approached and heard me whistling but seemed to take away someone else. No one else came, though I waited all night and at 4.30 I thought of trying to crawl back, but could hardly move, and our men were sniping.

This morning I tried to bandage my leg with two bandages and it felt much better and I saw two men in the distance and whistled, they also went away. I spent a long dreary day, how I wish someone would come. They must come tonight otherwise I will try to crawl in again. My ideas as to the right line are rather hazy, but I know which way safety lies. It is wretched to feel fairly well and no way of getting to safety.

Clearly Crerar's instinct was to provide an explanation of what had happened in case he was later found dead or too confused to describe his situation, but he was in no way reconciled to either of these possibilities. Although it might seem when he wrote his report that there was 'no way of getting to safety', as time wore on he became increasingly determined to find one.

The factual, low-key account Crerar produced later describing his escape from No Man's Land tells a remarkable story of fortitude and determination; in a conflict in which so often the focus is on the mass attack, the fate of a battalion, the success or failure of a division, this is a striking individual adventure, almost a one-man saga of the Somme. What gives it an extra dimension is that he was in what was widely perceived as a worst-case predicament on the Western Front. As Sidney Rogerson wrote in his classic of the late Somme, *Twelve Days*, 'to be alone, and lost and in danger' was 'my worst nightmare' throughout the war. 'Worse than all the anticipation of battle, all the fear of mine, raid or capture, was this dread of being struck down somewhere where there was no one to find me, and where I should lie till I rotted back slowly in the mud. I had seen those to whom it had happened.' Crerar's plight was a precise realization of that nightmare:

I was leading my company in the first wave, and as we went over the top at 2 p.m. we were greeted with a very heavy fire, the air being filled with the staccato crack of thousands of machine-gun bullets, and the explosion of numerous shells all round us.

After covering about 100 yards there seemed to be very few of us still advancing, as the murderous machine-gun fire had taken a heavy toll, and a few minutes later, having advanced with a handful of men about another 150 yards, I felt a sledgehammer blow on my left thigh, and fortunately for me, tumbled into a shallow shell hole where I lay partially stunned, and feeling rather like a shot rabbit in the mouth of its burrow wondering what had happened.

I listened to the din of battle overhead and wondered how long it would be before I got picked up by stretcher-bearers. I raised myself to look out of my shell hole, but soon a spate of machine-gun fire directed at me made me realize that our attack had failed and that I was uncomfortably nearer the German lines than our own, so I decided to wait a bit and hope for the best.

After dusk a khaki-clad figure appeared and I called out. He approached and said he was taking a message from my Company Commander and would tell him I was lying out there and would come back. This quite cheered me up but the man must have been killed because I heard some weeks later that no message was received, and in fact, that one of my own men who must have been near me when I was hit, got back after dark and told my Company Commander that I had been killed.

Two other people approached later in the evening and heard me whistling to them, but seemed to take away someone else. By this time I had attempted to bandage my leg with my field dressing and a face towel, which at least stopped the bleeding, though I don't think a Hospital would have approved of the mixture of earth and gauze which was well mixed. At 4.30 in the morning I thought of trying to crawl back, but could hardly move and a lot of sniping was going on, so I had to give up that idea until later.

The moonlight made objects look weird and fanciful and I remember wondering what on earth a tar boiler was doing on the edge of my shell hole and then later finding it was a dead man with a large spade standing upright beside him. I was glad to get his water bottle as mine had been shot off.

Next day I tried to work out in which direction I would have to go, which was very difficult as there were no landmarks in this battle area, everything having disappeared during the months of shell fire. It was impossible to look round to any extent in daylight and even the shells whining overhead gave little clue.

As night fell it got very quiet, the stars shone out and there was a full moon, and now it was a question of saving my own life if I could.

Crawling in was very exciting. I could only move very slowly, dragging one leg after me, and every few yards got so exhausted that I fell asleep, and of course lost my bearings. Both sides must have seen me moving in the moonlight as I was shot at both from in front and behind.

Several times flares went up and floated silently down, flooding the landscape and, of course, anything moving. On these occasions as soon as the flares went up I turned over on my back and tried to look as much like one of the many corpses all around, but on one occasion one came down within about four feet from my head, and remaining quiet was very difficult.

With all these diversions it was no wonder that my course towards the British lines, as I hoped, was somewhat erratic. After some hours, about three in the morning the worst moment came when I nearly fell into a deep pit, which had been dug probably for a machine-gun emplacement. My legs were both in the hole and I was too weak to lift them clear, however I hung on and after what seemed several minutes I managed to pull myself out, and again I must have been heard or seen, because several bullets from somewhere in front whistled over me as I lay still.

Then the moon went behind a cloud and I decided that I would have to lie out another day and discover for certain which way I should go. I got into a shell hole and began to dig a little with my hands, but decided that it was not safe enough, and I would make one more effort, so I crawled out and was looking round when I saw two helmeted heads a short distance off and also the glint of a machine-gun. This was the supreme thrill. If it was a German trench I had stumbled on I had no chance of getting away, and as it was three days since our attack, it was unlikely that a British post would take me for anything but a German.

I called out 'Don't shoot, I'm British, I'm coming in' and crawled the last few yards staring at dimly seen helmets and the barrel of the machine-gun, which was pointing straight at me. As I was lifted over the parapet into the trench and explained who I was, one of the gunners said, 'Were you crawling out there some time ago?' 'Yes, I was,' I said 'and for a good long time before that too.'

'Well,' said he, 'that was us who were shooting at you.' I said, 'Thanks very much, now could you give me something to eat and a drink of water in return.'

I found that I had rejoined our lines about 400 yards east of where I had gone over the top, and that my Battalion had left the line two days ago. The trenches here were too narrow and twisty for stretcher work and so presently with my arms round the neck of an RAMC man and one leg trailing, I set off on a long journey by stretcher, horse ambulance, and hospital train which got me to Hospital in Le Touquet about forty-eight hours later.

In hospital Crerar received a delighted if apologetic letter from his Company Commander, Captain King, who, however, had evidently not heard the whole tale. 'By Gad,' he told him, 'I could have kicked myself a thousand times over when I heard you had been brought in or did you come in yourself and that I had left you out there all that time.' He had taken no action because he had received what seemed to be reliable reports that Crerar had been killed; 'if I had known you were wounded only somebody would have gone out'. King's letter also confirmed that the attack had been a failure, with the battalion suffering many casualties: 'We lost 250 from the four Companies out of 400, [and] we have just received drafts amounting to over 500 with 12 new officers.' There had subsequently been a second attack with a similar lack of success: 'They had another go at that front the other day but nothing was done. On our left they gained a little ground but I believe further up the South Africans lost heavily and only got over 50 yards. The 17th on our left lost heavily and on the right the gains were very light. I could tell you a lot if I saw you which I can't put on paper.'

King wished the young officer a speedy recovery: 'Cheer up and get well quickly, and let us see you again, or wouldn't you rather say goodbye to the Somme?'

Crerar did not return to the Somme. Sent from Le Touquet to 'Blighty', to an officers' hospital in London's Park Lane, he eventually made a good recovery, following which he transferred to the Royal Air Force (as the Royal Flying Corps became from 1 April 1918). At the time of the Armistice he had just completed his training as a pilot.

* * *

Pity there was on the Somme in the last weeks of the battle, but not always for the humans in this inhuman situation. Garnet W. Durham, a corporal in the 3rd Divisional Cyclist Company of the Canadian Corps, came to the Somme from Ypres in September to carry out salvage work in the vicinity of Pozières – of which there was so little left that, he wrote to a friend, 'I wandered around Pozières salvaging ammunition for two days before I realised it had been a village.' His 'home' was an old German trench with a funkhole for a bedroom in 'Death Valley', which place prompted the wry comment 'it is not ill named'. In mid-October he was witness to an episode which he described as 'one of the most extraordinary things I have seen out here':

Near our dugout, or rather hole, there is a battery of French 150mm Creusot guns, a revenge battery to replace a 75mm battery blown to pieces by the Huns; near them is a Howitzer battery of ours (6"). One of our planes went over and spotted a new trench packed with Germans, and the two batteries started in to destroy the trench and its garrison, with the plane doing the observation work. They got on to the target quickly and were blazing away, getting direct hits. The French were firing salvoes under the direction of the battery Commander, who stood on a barrel, I never saw a man so pleased. Every salvo a flare from the plane said 'Direct Hit' and they were getting a sweet revenge for the 75 Battery's crew, still lying dead near by, when over came a huge covey of partridges, about 30, and dazed by the firing settled about

50 feet in front of the guns. The French officer who was directing his battery like a cheer leader with shouts and arm waving, held up his hands. '*Tenez. Tenez.*' ['Hold it. Hold it.'] and sent a sergeant to drive the birds to the left, lest the concussion of the guns should destroy them, believe it or not. I shall never forget his rolling tongue as he shouted what seemed to me like '*le bruit des canons les écraserait*' [literally, 'the noise of the guns would crush them']. They then continued the slaughter of mere men.

Now increasingly during fighting the philosophy was one of 'no quarter', even – and virtually by order – 'no prisoners'. When on 21 October Lieutenant-Colonel Frank Maxwell VC DSO left his 18th Division battalion, the 12th Middlesex, also known as the 'Die-Hards', a farewell message was included by his successor in battalion orders. Maxwell expressed his deep regret at leaving 'this happy family' after six months which had been 'amongst the happiest, saddest and proudest of my life', then stated:

> No failure has spoiled our record since real business began nearly four months ago, and none is going to. In that period we have begun to learn that the only way to treat the German is to kill him, but that lesson is only half learned, for we either do not want to kill him enough, or we forget to use that best of weapons, our rifles, to down him, we shout for bombs, instead of shooting with our guns.
>
> Discipline has a knack in this Battalion of looking after itself, and as CO, I hardly know what a prisoner looks like and one of the reasons for this is that the Battalion knows how to look after its thirsty souls. Its turn-out is gradually approaching the stage when we shall look like what we are, first class, but we can still achieve something in this respect.
>
> Finally remember that the 12th 'Die-Hards' DO KILL, DON'T TAKE PRISONERS UNLESS WOUNDED, and DON'T retire ... and with this one 'DO' and two 'DON'TS', I wish all ranks 'Goodbye' and 'God speed'.

* * *

Meanwhile for the cavalry officer Captain Ash the dreary round of desultory inaction had continued. Following the 15 September attack his Regiment had spent ten days at Bray, during which period, daily, one squadron from the Division had been moved up 'mounted' to Carnoy 'in case of a sudden gap being made in the enemies' lines, when it would be at once pushed through. We had to start at 4.45 a.m. and got to the valley at 7 a.m. Nothing occurred all day and we had a very quiet time.'

By mid-October he was back superintending road construction work, which if nothing else offered a privileged insight into the scale of the destruction left behind as the battle lines moved slowly eastwards. This is his diary entry for the 15th:

Got up at 5.45 a.m. Parade at 7 a.m. Marched up to Longueval which is about 2000 yards south of Flers. The whole village of Longueval is flattened. There is only a piece of a shed left standing at the northern end of it. Nothing is left of the church or any of the houses. The whole place is a mass of wreckage, bricks, beams, bedsteads, old clothes, etc.

Our job was to fill sandbags with bricks, these were going to be used to improve the roads somewhere near Flers. We filled carts up with these bricks. The men turned up lots of souvenirs, old silver spoons and images of the Virgin Mary. I got an old edition of Don Quixote in French with prints. As it may be of some value I shall keep it. I also got a book of comic pictures in German.

They were dropping some shells about 200 yards north of us but none came any nearer and no-one was hit by the pieces. We got back at 1 p.m.

Nothing exciting happened in the afternoon. The last two days have been fine. I hope the rain will keep off as I have had my mackintosh stolen and have only a British warm [overcoat] left. Fine clear night but blowing up for rain.

* * *

On 17 October Lieutenant Charles Carrington undertook a difficult task, to write a letter to his mother following the death of his elder brother, Christopher, a Captain in the New Zealand Field Artillery, who had died of wounds at Flers on the 8th. He associated his younger brother, Hugh, also serving in France, with a message which, typically of the time, mixed consolation with encouragement:

I hardly know how to write to you today. Of course, by the time this letter arrives, the news will be old and perhaps I would be wiser to leave the subject alone. We all agree that the blow is harder on you than on any one. Poor old Chris is well out of a bad business and we are too hardened to it, to think of it any other way. We are a large family, and if it must be, perhaps he was the worthiest of us.

But we don't want you to think that we are miserable. Hugh and I will carry on as cheerily as ever with just one more reason to finish the show.

We have had too many friends killed to fret about it, and I hope you will try and keep cheerful too. Keep smiling and you can depend on us to do the same. The War can't last much longer.

The men are more wonderful than ever. The worse time they get, the more they smile.

So let's do likewise.

*   *   *

On that same day, 17 October, Captain Alfred Bundy's 2nd Middlesex, which had suffered so badly on 1 July at La Boisselle, came back to the Somme. Their three months in the Loos sector had been no rest cure, with bouts of gas warfare and numerous casualties lost in raids and to the much-feared German trench mortar, the *Minenwerfer*, but conditions were in no way comparable to those 'down south'. Even their arrival in that ominous region was unpropitious. After a march of ten miles from the railhead, the Middlesex with the rest of 8th Division were brought by motor transport to Méaulte, near Albert, reaching their destination at 6 p.m. 'Billets uncomfortable and completely unfurnished,' Bundy noted in his diary. 'Servants got fire going with wood scrounged from somewhere. Stewed bully for dinner and bed on the floor.' They had barely settled when, at half past midnight, orders came instructing them that they were to proceed to a camp near Trônes Wood. So that morning they again clambered into lorries which took them on a long, tortuous journey via Fricourt, Mametz, Montauban and Bernafay across the Somme battlefield. The next day, Thursday 19 October, produced the following terse but eloquent description in Bundy's diary:

Visited trenches to be taken over and we are to do a 'show'. I have never seen such desolation. Mud thin, deep and black, shell holes full of water, corpses all around in every stage of decomposition, some partially devoid of flesh, some swollen and black, some fresh, lying as if in slumber. One bolt upright, a landmark and guide, another bowed as if trying to touch his toes. Our trenches are little more than joined-up shell holes, mostly with 12 inches of water above 12 inches of mud. A sunken road provides the only access under cover and this is almost constantly under shell fire. The casualties on this road are terrible. I had a very narrow escape myself. A 5.9 shell plunged into the mud just in front of me and *didn't explode* – 1,000 to 1 chance. I was smothered with slime and had to scrape it out of my eyes to see. Passed several derelict tanks on our way back to Trônes Wood Camp where we have nothing but bivouacs. Weather cold and wet. Sat in deep shell holes for shelter completely and utterly miserable.

His diary entries over the next few days are a countdown to an attack the purpose of which he does not mention and for which there would seem to have been no great enthusiasm or expectation. 'Rain all day. Religious services that are portentous of big events,' he wrote on Friday 20 October, while the 21st produced only: 'Resting and trying to get comfortable.' On Sunday the 22nd: 'Quiet morning except for crashing of 15-inch howitzer just outside my bivvy. Every 15 minutes this gun sends its 1,600 lb projectile, costing £90, hurtling through the air.' Later that day he went exploring: 'Had a stroll through Trônes Wood – (or what is left of it). Quantities of equipment, bombs, rifles etc. lying about as well as many dead bodies of Boche and Briton.' On the 23rd he noted that the intended attack was to commence at 11.30 a.m. on the following day, adding that he had written to his wife, mother and sister, leaving the letters with the Quartermaster.

On the 24th he was sufficiently advanced in his preparations to devote some time to his diary ahead of the attack, uppermost in his mind being the wretched state of the 'so-called trenches' from which the 'show' was to be launched, and the curious, somewhat unexpected, effect on morale of the dismal circumstances in which he and his comrades found themselves:

Liquid mud lies at the bottom in some places 2 feet deep. Several times this filthy slime has been well above my field boots and my legs and feet are, and have been for hours, completely wet and numbed with cold. In my own misery I feel intensely for the men who, with puttees only, are worse off than the officers. They are marvellous in their uncomplaining fortitude but I think I understand the secret. Contrary to what one might believe to be the case, I have found that the desire to live is strongest when the conditions of existence are most dangerous and depressing. It is hope for an escape to the normal and safe that keeps the spirits up. I do not, and will not now, believe that it is natural to long for death in conditions of the most abject temporary misery – the more the misery the greater the desire to live.

The purpose of the attack in question, to be made in collaboration with the French, was to take German front-line defences, and establish a new line on the crest of a spur, in front of the strongly defended village of Le Transloy. Zero hour had been fixed for 11.30 a.m., but mist caused a three-hour postponement. Meanwhile the preliminary bombardment ground on. Bundy's account described the course of events:

Our guns which are axle to axle have been literally pouring H.E. on the Boche trenches since about 6 a.m. The effect is exactly that which would be produced by a giant hose – the ground in front as far as one can see is leaping and splashing up like water under a downpour, only on an enormous scale. We go over at 2.30 p.m.

My company has reached its objective 2.45 p.m. About one-third of my Company casualties. Lieut. Hall shot clean through head by my side. He fell on me and I cursed him at first but then I saw he was dead. Boche trenches worse than ours. Mud over knees everywhere.

The reference to 'Boche trenches' shows that, to a point, the attack was a success; together with the 2nd Scottish Rifles the battalion stormed and took part of an important defence line known as Zenith Trench. But attempts by the Rifles to seize a further trench, Orion, 200 yards further on, failed when their forward troops were shelled out on the edge of nightfall, and there was a similar rebuff to efforts by the Middlesex to bomb their way northwards. Bundy's diary entry for 24 October concludes: 'Warned to be prepared for counter attack. Several of my men hit from shell hole somewhere to our front. Snatched one hour's sleep, sitting in the driest spot I can find – never expected to wake.'

Next morning at 5 a.m. he sent out two men to find the shell hole from which the Germans had been firing with such deadly effect. The result was a brutal little incident typical of this stage of the war, which, although dictated by the hard-line policy adopted and encouraged by all sides, clearly left a sour taste in the mouth:

Location reported about 70 yards centre front. Go out myself with Sergeant and two men. Creep up to within about 6 yards. Can see three Boche. They see us also and drop rifles and put up hands. I fire and hit one. We rush and our men despatch the other two. We rapidly search bodies and I take from my man pocket-book and rifle. All return safely. Examine pocket-book and find only photograph, presumably of the poor devil's wife and family (seven children) and a number of letters. Send in to Battalion Headquarters and hear afterwards letters are from wife, son and daughter!

Bundy ended the day severely depressed: 'Very wet, very miserable and very nervy, and longing for food, water and the relief it is rumoured is to come tonight.'

In fact, the rumour was premature; the battalion had to survive a further twenty-four hours in the front line. They faced it as philosophically as they could: 'Interminable night – wet, windy and cold. Lot of shelling but no casualties. Astonished that flesh and blood can stand this sort of thing and yet we are all quite cheery in an apathetic sort of way. The general feeling seems that, what is to be will be, but we are tremendously bucked by news that we are to be relieved tonight.'

Relief took place at 11 p.m. on the 26th. 'What a sheer delight – merely the prospect of getting away from that ghastly place,' Bundy noted. Yet even the battalion's departure was to claim its victims, though not in this case through enemy action:

All 'dog' tired and the 'going' most wearisome with mud up to the shins. Men have to help one another and yet some fall and cannot recover their feet. RAMC men comparatively fresh give what assistance they can but some of the poor fellows drown. The biggest man in my Company walked into a shell hole and wasn't seen again.

At Trônes Wood got my Company into formation and had roll-call. 62 missing out of 146 (18 are afterwards reported wounded, leaving 48 undoubtedly dead). Bivouac at Trônes Wood and sleep.

Bundy was not to see the Somme again. Following a period of home leave ('Thank God from whom all blessings flow' he noted in his diary), a bout of illness on returning to France which resulted in his being swiftly repatriated, and some months of light duties and training in England, he spent the rest of the war in Salonika.

*   *   *

Late October saw 18th Division again in the vicinity of Thiepval, scene of its outstanding recent victory. The 7th Buffs had their battalion headquarters at Mouquet Farm – by now a farm in name only, so that in practice their headquarters added up merely to 'a couple of small dugouts'. The description is from the diary of Private Robert Cude, in an eloquent entry in which he bemoaned the lot of a battalion runner in the prevailing conditions:

> Day succeeds day and the rain continues to fall, and everything around is a veritable quagmire. This place is simply awful, and our work is extremely difficult, even in daylight one can easily lose oneself, but at night it is ten thousand times worse. The ground is one sticky mass of shell holes and mud, just sheer barren waste, without a landmark of any description to act as a guide, and what trenches are left are impassable owing to their caving in. At night we are in a sorry predicament, but our proud boast is 'We have never brought a message back undelivered', and so we plod on until we do deliver it. Altogether this place is an unholy place, so if we have to attack here I hope it will be soon and enable us to clear out.

Withdrawal from the line might mean respite for the majority of the battalion, but not for Cude and his fellow runners – though they soon found a way of lightening the burden: 'Today Oct 26th the "heads that be" decide that the men forward require a change and so

Buffs and Queens are relieved by E. Surreys and W. Kents. This means a walk to Albert every message as Brigade HQs are staying in line, still there are 5 men per unit now so the 14 mile journey only comes once daily, and as we can get a lorry each way usually, we do not worry about that mileage.'

The end of the month provided a break for everybody in the battalion. Cude arrived in Albert eager above all for a bath and a clean change. Of these, the Tommies' view was that it was no use having the one without the other: 'Next day we start off with a pay-out – very acceptable too, this is followed by parade for bath. No clean clothes being available bath is refused by practically everyone, it is the only thing to do under the circs.'

Their '48 hrs respite' over, the battalion set off in buses to return to the line – 'Jerry strafes us pretty badly on the way up' – and Cude was back once more at Mouquet Farm. Fortunately the next few days were very quiet, though, he noted, 'it was exceptionally wet'. 'Mucky Farm' was its nickname to the troops – surely never more apt than in these late weeks of the Somme campaign.

* * *

On 27 October Captain Ash's 10th Reserve Regiment of Cavalry began the process of withdrawing from the Somme. They had taken no part in the fighting. On the 25th, while Bundy was engaged with his German snipers in their shell hole, Ash's concern had been for his horses and their sufferings in the continuing wretched weather. 'Still raining hard. Spent a quiet day fighting through three feet of ooze round the horse lines. The poor brutes are all in the open and well over the hocks in it. How they don't die is a marvel. Not one of them has lain down for 6 weeks. If they did they'd drown.'

Then at 1 p.m. on the 27th they were off, heading west; their departure, however, was no picnic. 'Rained solid all the time,' he noted wearily. 'Found ourselves in the open for the night and everything wet through, no tents or cover of any kind. Could not sleep as the cold was awful.' It was the worst night he had spent since arriving in France.

On the 28th they moved off at 8 a.m., marching along the left bank of the Somme, passing through the edge of Amiens and then continuing another fourteen miles along the river. At last there was opportunity to think of other things than the war. 'Very interesting passing through all the villages, some very nice looking girls in some of them.' They finally encamped on the 30th, four miles west of Hesdin. Nearby was a battlefield famous centuries before, where fighting men on horseback had also found themselves outmoded, this time by the 'new' technology of the longbow. 'Went through the *Forêt de Crécy* and through Crécy village, very interesting.' It was perhaps as fitting a place as any in which to end their less than satisfactory involvement in the Battle of the Somme.

* * *

And so into November, and to the attack which went ahead despite the protestations of the Earl of Cavan.

The Australians took part in this ill-fated show, among their number Corporal Oswald Blows, a signaller of the 28th (Western Australia) Battalion of the Australian Imperial Force. His account – another one written in hospital – pays high tribute to the success of the creeping barrage as the advance began, and there was the familiar thrill in the drama of a mass attack. 'It was marvellous seeing the shells hitting the ground just in front of our men, and the range getting longer and longer. A line of men also went over on our left (English) as far as we could see.' There was also the familiar response from the enemy. 'Fritz opened fire with machine-guns, and scores of shells (mostly H.E.) hit all around us, and the Lord only knows how Lt Curran and self escaped – we had to stick to our duty in the open – no cover but shell holes around absolutely filled with water.' The soft ground prevented the shells from being as effective as they might have been, but also made heavy going for the attacking troops. 'Yet still they went on, dragging one foot after another in the slush, and as steady as if on a Parade ground.' However, it could not last. 'Men very quickly began to fall to the heavy machine-gun fire, and before our fellows reached the enemies' line, there were very few who were not wounded or killed, so few that nothing could be done.'

Blows later learned that three out of the five signallers who had gone over were killed or wounded, he being in the second category: 'Fritz got a bullet through my right calf – something like a burning horse-kick.' Out of the action, he felt angry and frustrated by his inability to help: 'Let me say the feeling one has, when a man is helpless and the firing still continues, is unspeakable – like kicking a dog when he is down.' A slow and painful exit from the battlefield followed, culminating in an agonizing ride in a motor-ambulance: 'The road was awful, and tho' the driver was careful, it was torture.' After that it was a hospital train and a hospital ship for the young Australian, then, once in England, a hospital near Birmingham, where at last he could comment: 'The leg is very stiff, but things here are comfortable.' As for the attack: 'I have heard that no objective was gained, part of the trench was won, but our boys were bombed out again.' And there was more to come: 'On the night of the 5th, when the wounded men were trying to crawl in, the Hun put a creeping barrage over no man's land, and that added to our killed list.'

His diary also records a small propaganda battle which followed this particular action: 'The Huns put out a wireless [report], pertaining to that fight, saying most sanguinary losses were inflicted on the British, and especially the Australians. This was denied next day by the British (in all newspapers) but the Bns which took part in it suffered very severely.'

* * *

Mud was now claiming its victims in all sorts of ways. On 5 November, after a spell in the line in appalling conditions, Major R.E. Cotton of the 7th Green Howards wrote in his diary: 'The trenches are from 3 to 4 feet deep in mud and water and there was absolutely no shelter from the rain. Every officer and man was done up when they eventually got out of the trenches and many were sick from cold and exposure and a number had contracted "trench feet" (feet, ankles and legs very swollen and very painful).'

A severe outbreak of this particular affliction in a unit could get its commander sent home. Cotton's own CO, Lieutenant-Colonel Ronald Fife, noted at this time the departure of a colleague 'stellenbosched, on account of number of trench feet in his Battn'. His diary also recorded the pathetic situation of a horse immovably mired in Somme mud: '10 November. Walked to Brigade HQs to see Brigadier. Near there I found a horse which was said to have been stuck in the mud 5 days. Gave him whisky and got him some hay and oats which he ate, but he was too weak to stand. Had him covered up to keep him warm and then started for Mansel Camp near Mametz. Mud very bad all the way and didn't arrive till 6.30.'

* * *

The best form of relief from the 'pitiless Somme' was being sent on leave. The next best was being moved to a 'cushy' sector elsewhere. There was, however, a nearer means of escape, if the opportunity arose, and that was to pay a visit to Amiens, the capital of Picardy, barely twenty miles in distance from the battlefield but a world away in mood and atmosphere. Major P.H. Pilditch went there in September:

> A great day. It is extraordinary how one's power of enjoyment is increased by the increased discomfort of life. I got up early and joined Morgan and Ballantyne of the 19th, and rode ten miles or so from here to a village on the way to Amiens, picking up Leslie Lloyd on the way. At Méricourt we sent our horses back and took the train, arriving at our destination about ten.
>
> Amiens was full of colour and movement. Crowds of French and English soldiers and officers thronged the pavements and shops, military and civilian cars jostled each other in the crowded streets. Everywhere there seemed an air of briskness, partly from Staff Activity (4th Army H.Q. are stationed quite near) and also the presence of hundreds of fellows from the fighting front, bent on enjoying to the full a few hours in a real town.
>
> We did much the same as the rest; shopped and lunched heartily at the Rhin Hotel, shopped again and laid in stores for our messes. After tea I saw the Cathedral, quite warlike in its coating of sandbags and pit-props. It reminded me of our wanderings amongst the Normandy churches and cathedrals in those Easter tours before the war. How infinitely peaceful they now seemed!
>
> I missed the last train but managed to get a car back to Albert and then a lift in an ambulance from there to Bottom Wood, getting back to our dugout in time for dinner. At once Amiens became a far away, unreal place, as remote as England almost. Only the absence of my 100-franc note and the mackerel for dinner served to remind me that such a place existed.

Captain Alfred Bundy went there in November, not long after his departure from the battle. For him, however, the contrast between the two adjacent worlds of war and peace was not a source of easy relaxation; rather it raised questions made more disturbing by the nature of the experiences from which he had only recently emerged:

> Amiens for week-end. Fine town as French towns go. Shops are large, well fitted and stocked. Magnificent Cathedral but all the finest windows removed and walls protected 10 feet from ground by sandbags. Service in progress with the usual pomp and ceremony which always creates in my mind a mixed sensation of sublime solemnity and absurd pantomime. Worshippers are constantly entering, crossing themselves and kneeling in apparent devotion. The organ whines plaintive notes and priests (I suppose they are) chant monotonously. Meanwhile sightseers clatter round, some with guides who pause in their descriptive talks only when their voices are smothered by the music and chanting. This sort of thing makes me sceptical. Is it possible to believe that God Almighty can be permitting the ghastly carnage of this war and can, at the same time, require to be worshipped with the most ornate and brilliantly coloured ritual? And it's happening in Germany also.
>
> There is little doing in the way of amusement. All theatres are closed and the only three cinemas are open on Sunday only. There are several quite passable hotels but the charges are high though only to our people I understand! Slept at Hotel Belfort.

It is perhaps worthy of comment that, though Pilditch writes of seeing 'officers and soldiers' in Amiens, such high-quality escapes to civilization were largely the privilege of the former; for the latter, particularly the shilling-a-day Tommy, the standard bolt-hole was more likely to be much nearer to hand and less of a threat to his meagre finances. Hence the popularity of the 'estaminet' (a French word happily adopted by the British), an institution to which there was no precise Anglo-Saxon equivalent, being not quite a public house, a café or a restaurant but having some of the qualities of all three. These abounded in the hinterland of the trenches and were virtual lifelines to men condemned to spend so much of their time in drafty billets or muddy holes in the ground. Their value was never higher than during major battles such as the Somme. Fifty years on John Brophy and Eric Partridge, both of whom had served in the ranks, celebrated the typical estaminet with this affectionate portrait:

It was never large and was found only in villages and very minor towns. It had low ceilings, an open iron stove; it was warm and fuggy; it had wooden benches and tables. It sold wine, cognac and thin beer, as well as coffee, soup, eggs and chips and omelettes. The proprietress (a proprietor was unthinkable) had a daughter or two, or nieces, or younger sisters who served at table and made no objection to tobacco smoke and ribald choruses in English and pidgin French. No doubt some estaminets overcharged but in general they provided for the soldier off duty behind the line many and many a happy hour. The name had a magical quality in 1914–18 – and still has for those who survive.

CHAPTER TWELVE

THE ANCRE – AND CLOSEDOWN

THERE WAS TO be one more major offensive before the end of the Battle of the Somme. This would be undertaken by the former Reserve Army, which from late October had been officially styled the Fifth Army, remaining under the command of General Sir Hubert Gough. The setting would not be the plateau over which the main action had been fought for most of four and a half months, but the sidestage of the Ancre Valley. Indeed, the Ancre would provide the name for this last phase of the campaign. It would gain ground, salve some pride, add one or two notable names to the list of British trophies – including places which had been targets of the attack on the first day four months earlier. But it would be at least in part a political battle, fought to create a better impression than might otherwise have been the case at the forthcoming inter-Allied conference at Chantilly.

* * *

Lieutenant-Colonel Henry Hugh Gordon Hyslop commanded the 1/7th Argyll and Sutherland Highlanders in this action; the battalion was part of the 51st (Highland) Division, Territorial Force, which was to win a distinguished name in the history of the Somme – and to be honoured by one of the Somme's more striking memorials – for its achievement at this time. Born in 1873, Hyslop had joined the 2nd Argylls in 1894, had been promoted Lieutenant in 1897, and had fought in the South African War both as a Station Staff Officer and, with the regiment's 1st Battalion, in the field. He had later served for four years in India. He had crossed to France in August 1914 as a

Captain, had become a Major in November, and had been awarded a DSO in February 1915. He had been involved in virtually every major action on the Western Front from the Mons Retreat onwards and in November 1915 had been promoted Lieutenant-Colonel and given battalion command. The 1/7th Argylls had fought on the Somme in the summer, being engaged in the early attempts to take High Wood, but had then been moved north to the relative quiet of Franco-Belgian border country. Early October saw them back 'down south', beginning a period of intensive pre-battle training. Their return also afforded them their first sight of tanks. 'They are weird objects and move very slowly and deliberately,' Hyslop noted in his diary. 'I cannot help thinking they will make excellent targets for the German light guns, and they look as if they would get bogged in the mud very easily.'

Mud there was in plenty. 'Very wet and ground in a dreadful state,' he noted on 18 October, on which date they marched from Raincheville to Lealvillers to go into bivouac. 'The roads were just crowded with troops and transport, it took us nearly 4 hours to march 3½ miles.' The prospects of success in such circumstances seemed to him less than even. 'There are great numbers of "Tanks" ready to take part and the number of guns is very large. The weather is dead against operations, however, as little movement could be made across country.' Weather was, in fact, to cause a number of postponements of the date of the offensive.

Four days later they took their turn in the line: '22nd October. Relieved the 5th Seaforth Highlanders in the trenches opposite Beaumont Hamel. A great deal of work to be done in getting things ready for an attack. Patrols are constantly out observing the wire and reporting the result of wire cutting, and the bombardment of trenches by our guns and trench mortars.'

Reaction was muted from the Germans at first, but he was soon reporting a more vigorous response:

> *23rd October.* The enemy have suddenly woken up and are now shelling a great deal themselves. Up to now our guns have had it much their own way and I have never experienced such tremendous fire. The whole air has been one whistle of heavy shells and the

German trenches and Beaumont Hamel seem to have been completely wiped out, yet immediately the fire slackens up pops a machine-gun or a light showing that they are existing through it all in their enormous underground shelters. Still it must tell on their moral[e] if it does no other damage. They seem to have a pretty accurate knowledge of the trenches we use and are making them most unpleasant with both heavy and light stuff as some return for what we are giving them.

As if the hazards posed by the enemy and the conditions were not enough, there was the perennial problem stemming from the volume of manual work mandated on all infantry battalions. Hyslop commented with some asperity: 'The trenches are very wet and in bad order, there are so many carrying parties and so on that it is difficult to do much work on them.'

Nor did being withdrawn from the line offer any improvement: '*26th October*. Relieved by the 9th Royal Scots and came back to shelters in Mailly Wood. A miserable place and very wet. Fatigue parties of three or four hundred employed every day in the Trenches. *30th October*. Marched to Raincheval 2 p.m. in pouring rain and everyone got soaked to the skin.'

There was a pleasing interlude on 2 November, thanks to Hyslop's personal friendship with General Gough's senior staff officer, Neill Malcolm, officially titled Major-General, General Staff, Fifth Army: 'Malcolm came to see me and sent a car for me to come and dine with General Gough and the Staff of the 5th Army. It was a nice change, and very interesting to meet all these Generals. I had not seen General Gough before.' Unfortunately, his diary contains no table talk, nor comments on his host or fellow guests.

Several indecisive days followed, with orders to move being twice issued and twice cancelled. Then the battalion was despatched for another turn at the front:

5th November. Marched 9 a.m. for the trenches. We halted on the way and had dinners near Mailly and then went on and relieved 6th Gordons.

Heavy bombardment by both sides from 4.30 p.m. to 6 p.m. The Germans put over a great deal of stuff and flattened out many of our trenches.

6th November. Very wet. In the evening the 9th Royal Scots attempted a raid but without success as they found the line strongly held. The Germans afterwards bombarded heavily and attempted to come over but our sentries were alert and drove them out.

The battalion came out of the line on the 8th, in an even worse state. 'The trenches were so bad that men stuck in them,' Hyslop noted, 'and several had to be dug out before they could move. Relief in consequence took a very long time.'

If the movement of the infantry was difficult in such circumstances, there were also huge problems facing the men manning the guns, as they prepared for the coming offensive. A subaltern of the Royal Garrison Artillery, Lieutenant R.J. Blackadder, whose 151 Siege Battery was acting in support of the 51st (Highland) Division, kept a diary throughout this period which records a mixture of tribulations, in which technical setbacks and the afflictions caused by the elements formed an almost equal part. 'Nothing done in the rain' was his comment on 25 October, while on the 26th he wrote: 'Rain again. Spent the day in cleaning up and improving men's shelters and the gun pits generally. On duty at Battery till 9 p.m. Very muddy and conditions remind me of the early days of the war in November 1914.'

On the 27th his battery was engaged in its basic task of forcefully reminding the enemy of the British presence when one of its four guns failed: 'Intense bombardment this morning during which No.3 gun stripped its rifling, and now out of action. Various parties called to examine the gun and it appears it will have to be sent back. Rain again and very windy and cold.'

This breakdown of one of the battery's prime weapons was to cause constant problems over the following days. A caterpillar tractor arrived at 9 p.m. on the 29th and after an hour's hard labour the gun was taken out and despatched en route for Louvencourt, where a decision would be taken as to whether it should be repaired or replaced. 'Difficult work getting gun up the steep banks to the road,' Blackadder noted. Next day with twelve of his men he went by lorry to Louvencourt, to resolve the situation with the 'IOM' – the all-powerful Inspector of Ordnance Machinery. No ready solution being forthcoming, they returned empty-handed in the afternoon through atrocious weather – 'very heavy rainstorm and roads flooded' – to find worse news awaiting them. 'Our billets leaking badly and my gun positions and dugouts flooded out. No. 4 gun out of action owing to water in pit and men returned to billets.'

On 2 November, number 3 gun having been pronounced beyond immediate repair, he set off to welcome the replacement: 'Went by lorry to Belle Eglise to fetch new gun. Long journey and great crowds of lorries at the railhead. The gun, weighing 3 tons, lying in truck and no crane etc., to lift it. After 4½ hours we got it off the truck and raised into the lorry and proceeded at a walking pace to the IOM at Louvencourt. Very glad to get there as the gun was very unstable on the lorry, the roads being so rough.' Their herculean efforts did not solve the problem, however, it being decided that a new carriage was required for the replacement gun; this did not arrive at Belle Eglise until six days later, the 8th: 'Very heavy traffic on roads and we blocked the road at railhead with the caterpillar and gun for some time thereby causing much bad language and amusement. 9 November. New gun mounted on carriage at Louvencourt and all ready to bring back to battery, but road traffic suspended owing to surface being repaired.'

At last the task was completed:

10 November. Fine morning. New gun got into position at night and properly placed on planks with the aid of the caterpillar.
11 November. Firing a lot all day. No. 3 doing well.'

However, on the 12th: 'On duty all night and had great trouble keeping No.3 in action owing to wet soil.'

The offensive was now imminent, though, thanks to the vagaries of the weather, it was touch and go almost to the last as to whether it would go ahead. As the historian of one of the divisions involved, the 63rd (Royal Naval) Division, himself the adjutant of one of its constituent battalions, would later write – not without a touch of old front-line cynicism: 'The rain turned into snow and then into a frozen mud and mist. It was only on 9 November that the sun shone for one fitful morning, and all the staffs from all the headquarters in echelon, stretching back to St Omer, came out to inspect the wicket and decided that it would be fit for play in four days time ... [I]t was a perfect morning. It was obviously far too good for regimental officers to be alive.'

The author of a history of the 51st Division, writing in 1918, made the same point in a somewhat different way: '"Haig's Weather" seemed to have set in: days of continuous rain, followed by treacherous intervals of sunshine.' In fact, whatever Haig's reputation for optimistic interpretations of weather conditions, the decision to attack was, ultimately, not his but that of the Fifth Army commander, General Gough. Haig had deputed to Gough the task in hand and the freedom to implement it; his concern was that Gough should be fully confident that it could be carried out. As late as the morning of 12 November Haig's Chief of Staff, Lieutenant-General Sir Launcelot Kiggell, visited Gough in his Headquarters to emphasize that the C-in-C had no wish to see a battle fought unless there were fair prospects of success. Haig himself rode to meet Gough that afternoon to make the same point. He was eager for the profit that a victory would bring, but he was also fully aware that 'nothing is so costly as failure'.

The attack was to take place next day, Monday the 13th, nevertheless Lieutenant-Colonel Hyslop's 1/7th Argylls spent the 10th, 11th and 12th of November not in preparing for action but in 'heavy fatigue parties'. This would presumably mean the carrying of ammunition of all kinds, plus rations, petrol, water, etc., to the forward dumps from which the hoped-for advance would be supplied and maintained – work which all too frequently, in the eyes of those involved in it, fell to the lot of the battalions assigned to take part in the actual assault. Hyslop's diary for these days, however, is more concerned with the departure of an uncongenial staff officer from the Brigade than with the prospect of battle. Then: '13th November. 5th Army attacked. 3rd and 2nd Divisions opposite Serre; 51st Division opposite Beaumont Hamel, and 63rd Division opposite St. Pierre Divion.'

Hyslop's list understates the number of divisions to be involved by a considerable margin. In all twelve divisions would take part; the 2nd, 3rd, 18th, 19th, 31st, 32nd, 37th, 39th, 48th, 51st, 63rd (RN) and 4th Canadian; he had also misplaced the 63rd, in that its point of attack would not be St. Pierre Divion on the south side of the River Ancre, but Beaucourt on the north.

* * *

A 'push' on such a scale inevitably produced its crop of pre-battle letters, as before the previous high-tide offensives of the Somme battle. Among those who would go into action on the 2nd Division front was a family man of over forty named Walter Medlicott, who, after serving for many months in the ranks, was now a sub-altern in the 24th Royal Fusiliers. On 12 November he wrote a brief, thoughtful letter to his wife – herself apparently in some kind of uniformed service – with none of the high sentiment which had been the hallmark of so many earlier members of this genre. (This may well have been, of course, simply a matter of difference of character and background; it would be presuming too much to attribute it to the grey, unromantic conditions in which the battle was now being fought – military ardour would be possible even among the young conscripts of 1918. Nevertheless it is surely a fair assumption that 'death or glory' attitudes were no longer so much in fashion among the generality of soldiers as they had been back in the spring. Medlicott's approach, doubtless widely shared, is summed up in the simple emphatic phrase: 'we must get forward'.)

> Well, darling at 4 we go back and tomorrow we advance on a large front. This letter won't go off till 6 a.m., so by that time we shall D.V. be over the Boche and sitting in a new line. This attack has been hanging fire for a long time but weather has postponed it. I don't call it perfect yet, but we must get forward. I shall be all right, but whatever happens – it is right. Others are writing to solicitors to forward – I prefer to write to you Darling – you are a soldier yourself, and can bear a command to carry on whatever happens. I had a great sleep last night and feel as fit as ever. I meant to write to [name unclear], but can't – as we move at once – and Dad and all – but give them my love – and all to you and Bet – yr husband, Wat.

Medlicott's 2nd division was to the north of the 51st, their point of attack being the well-defended area known as the Redan Ridge,

while further north still the 3rd and 31st Divisions were to attack
opposite one of the most infamous untaken targets of 1 July, the
village of Serre – against which so many 'Pals' battalions had wasted
themselves on that historic day.

Archie Surfleet was a nineteen-year-old private of the 13th Battalion, East Yorkshire Regiment, in 31st Division. No seeker after
heroics, in fact admitting frequently, in his always honest and
thoughtful diary, to being nervous and afraid, he was nevertheless a
conscientious soldier, always willing to do his best to help his
comrades and the cause. On the eve of the Ancre battle he was
assigned to stay behind with the 'details' – that portion of a battalion
kept out of the battle as a nucleus for rebuilding if a disaster should
occur – having won the toss of a coin with a friend who, as it turned
out, then went into battle and was killed. This is his moving
description of the moment when the main part of the battalion began
moving off to the line:

> There was an artificial air of jollity about; a joke here, a coarse
> remark there, a wave of the hand to a pal... 'lucky devil staying
> behind'... 'all the best, old man'... 'get those bloody rations up
> early'... 'we're going back for a rest after this'... 'who the hell
> says we aren't a scrapping division'... 'send you a postcard'... all
> these, and many more remarks, but it was the thinnest of veneers,
> a very feeble covering over the sense of grim reality which I felt
> the whole battalion was feeling. We stood there whilst the boys, in
> column of route, marched forward, slid down the hill, turned right
> and were gradually swallowed up in the mist and the mud and the
> confusion. Their sounds died out; only a rumble of guns and the
> creaking of heavily laden limbers remained in a scene so desolate
> and miserable that one could not help feeling depressed and sad,
> even with the respite of at least one night which we, the 'details',
> had been granted.

*   *   *

Lieutenant Blackadder's account of the Ancre battle is the brief, low-
key description of a man almost exhausted by the sheer slog of
keeping a heavy battery in action during a major offensive, though
he was able at times also to register a touch of emotion:

Bombardment started at 5.45 a.m. and continued throughout the day with varying intensity. The work of getting the ammunition to the guns is very hard. Fire ceased at 7 p.m. and during the day we fired some 800 rounds. I finished at 5 p.m. having been on for 32 hours. Saw many prisoners pass the battery.

14 November. Up at 5 a.m. off to the Observation Post – could see little till afternoon. Spent morning tapping in on the line to the battery. Germans shelling heavily all day on the ground captured yesterday. Rather sad at sights of the dead and wounded being brought in. In afternoon saw the men go over and take further ground. Heavy fire and intense bombardment. Left Observation Post at dusk.

15/17 November. At battery busy keeping guns going and generally on work to enable us to take new lines of fire owing to advance of our line. All guns out of action from time to time mainly owing to lack of packing for buffers and recuperators. These heat with the rapid firing and the leathers perish. My new gun condemned by the IOM but we keep it going as there is no risk.

In the 51st Division attack the 152nd and 153rd Brigades went over first at 5.45 a.m., with Hyslop's brigade, the 154th, in support. His 7th Argylls would be heavily involved, however, before the end of the day. This is his cool, commanding-officer's account of the progress of events:

The men followed close behind the artillery Barrage and completely surprised the Germans. Prisoners began to come back at once. The morning was very misty and the ground in a dreadfully muddy state. By 12 noon the 3rd German line had been reached and our men were into the village. At 11.30 a.m. two of my companies, A and D, went up to reinforce the 152nd Brigade, at 6 p.m. the remainder of the Bn. went into the fight and at 8.30 p.m. the whole village was in our hands.

The greater number of Germans gave themselves up very easily, but the place is a net-work of underground caves, dugouts and passages, and in many of these pockets of Germans held out for some time and gave considerable trouble.

The Division took about 1,600 prisoners the first day and an immense amount of stores and weapons, including 3 enormous 'Minenwerfers'.

This was just the beginning of several days of hard fighting, but in this sector there was no question that a great prize had been won: the place aptly described by Edmund Blunden in his elegant and distinguished memoir *Undertones of War* as 'the terrible Beaumont Hamel, one of the German masterpieces of concealed strength'.

*   *   *

At the level of a battalion orderly in the 1/4th Seaforth Highlanders – a fellow-battalion of the 1/7th Argylls in 154th Brigade – Private Arthur Wrench's diary of the battle was somewhat more emotional, more impressionistic, than the inevitably factual account, more report than description, of Lieutenant-Colonel Hyslop:

> *Monday 13.* Gosh, what a day. The bombardment raged all night tho' with some abatement when at 5.45 in the morning, every gun burst out with a tremendous crash. That was Zero, and nothing has ever been like it before. Then a moment's hesitation while the guns reloaded and after that, Hell! It was terrible. The attack began at six. Shortly after, the 5th Seaforths took the third line and with the 8th Argylls got 120 prisoners. They are poor, miserable, dejected-looking creatures and appeared to be either older men or boys and not the usual sort of German soldier. It is really pitiful to see them, they are as scared looking as can be, and ragged. The 51st took over a thousand prisoners, the fog covering the attack in which the Huns were absolutely surprised, many of them still being in bed at the time. I suppose they must have been following their usual custom of getting well down to it every morning when our bombardment started, and so did not expect this attack this morning. Good job for us, for this fact alone has decided the fate of Beaumont Hamel. So the capture was comparatively easy with few casualties, until Fritz realised what was happening, and then the struggle began. They opened fire on all the roads through here to the front so that reinforcements would be cut off. Were severely strafed all day in Mailly when the place was a veritable Hell.
>
> *Tuesday 14.* Advance continued well with a fierce barrage again in the morning and stubborn resistance now from the enemy, for he has his guns trained on Beaumont Hamel and his reserves up in action. The battle is terrible and we orderlies have been under orders to stand to for reinforcements if required. Fritz is certainly

making a desperate effort to recover the Y Ravine and if he does so then God help us for he will be in a position to hold it at all costs. It has been a most trying time and a wretched fatiguing day with an extra journey up to Auchonvillers grenade dump at night. Getting up along that road is an ordeal one is not likely to forget in a hurry, and the whole way is congested with guns, transports and ammunition limbers moving forward to new positions. The fog is still thick too, so that the whole column is like a phantom procession emerging into distinct forms and then disappearing again ahead. What a queer unholy feeling it gives you.

Thursday 16. Fritz has made it one of the most awful days imaginable for us, and up that valley is a terror of a place. The Seaforth Headquarters are situated on sloping ground directly facing the line, being German dugouts, and also overlook a German cemetery. A verandah runs around the dugouts too and it was smashed now when one of the dugouts was blown in today during a strafe when 500 5.9 shells were hurled about the place. This was just in one strafe too, and in the cemetery not one single cross is left standing over a German soldier's grave, but some of the bodies there are torn up again and lie scattered all over the place. It is horrible to see. Perhaps the Germans are not even human to violate the last resting place of their own men who have given their lives for their country, and it strikes me there is not much glory these days in dying for your country. A whole platoon of the Seaforths was wiped out there too.

* * *

The figures show that the 51st Division captured over 2,000 prisoners in the Ancre battle, and seized a huge amount of stores and ammunition; they also show that there were many casualties. The division lost, in killed, wounded and missing, some 2,500 men, about 45 per cent of those who took part in the attack.

One nineteen-year-old officer of the division who found himself especially concerned with the matter of casualties once the battle was over was Second Lieutenant Norman Collins of the 1/6th Seaforth Highlanders. His battalion was in 152nd Brigade, which had formed part of the first wave of the attack on 13 November. He had 'gone over' himself and had found it a torrid and shattering experience. He had subsequently been made battalion burial officer, with the depressing task of identifying and burying fallen comrades and writing the necessary letters of sympathy to bereaved families. There were also many bodies still littered about the battlefield following the attack of 1 July to which at last decent attention could be paid.

A Field Service card written on the 19th – the day on which the Ancre action, and indeed the whole Somme campaign, officially ended – assured his family that he was quite well. He followed this by a long letter, all the more eloquent for its almost breathless, staccato style, written on the 25th:

Dear All

It is with great thankfulness that I have so far come through the Battle of the Ancre without a scratch.

The last fortnight has been absolute Hell.

On the 13th at dawn the Battalion went over the 'bags' and after a few hours hard fighting captured four lines of trench and *the* village en route, that the Boche has held for over 2 years.

It was a magnificent success and our division has made a name for itself.

On July 1st the Regulars attempted the feat and failed. I suppose you will know all about it from the papers.

We were relieved on the Wednesday following and after two days rest to be reorganised went in the trenches again in support.

This morning we came out again much to my relief.

I have had my first wash and shave for a week!

I needed it badly.

There are only 2 officers of my company left now and I am one of them.

For 3 days I have been O.C. party collecting the dead and it was the most loathsome job I've ever had.

We were shelled heavily all the time as of course we were working in the open in full view of the Boche. He used to spot us from his observation balloons and aeroplanes and send over 'crumps' and shrapnel.

I had a few of my party knocked out and had some miraculous escapes.

A 6″ [shell] on one occasion burst 10 yards away but I was only covered with mud.

We are back a few miles for a short rest.

Yesterday I had tea with the Brig. General as he was so pleased with the work done.

His dugout was a splendid place.

My word, you should have seen and heard the barrage. Every minute four shells burst on every *yard* of the ground.

The trenches were just wiped out and it was only by the mouth of the dugouts that one could tell that there had been a trench.

Of the village all that is left is a few heaps of bricks.

I expect that we will get a rest soon, for a month, at any rate we will not be going over the 'bags' again for some time so don't worry.

Well, there is no more news, so ta! ta!

    Best Love

    Norman

P.S. My poor servant was 'nah-poohed' and I haven't found the body.

In a second letter on the 28th he continued in similar vein:

You will have received a letter written after the big battle, I should think.

I've had enough of 'pushes' for a long time.

Been busy writing to the different homes in Elgin and Glasgow etc of the 'B' Coy men, knocked out.

I found my old servant. I'm very sorry about him as he did look after me well.

I wrote home to his mother.

He has a brother in this battalion also.

I was reading a paper on the 'push' and it gave the Naval Division a lot of credit for work we did.

Well, cheero.

*   *   *

The Naval Division referred to in Collins' letter was the 63rd (Royal Naval) Division which had already served at Antwerp and at Gallipoli and was now part of the Fifth Army on the Somme. Removed from their natural element to fight as infantry, they nevertheless retained their original ranks and named their battalions after distinguished naval heroes such as Anson, Drake, Hawke,

Hood, Howe, Nelson. In the Ancre battle they played a key role in the attack on Beaucourt, a village and railway station in the Ancre Valley itself. A detailed account of the part played in this action by the Hood battalion survives in a letter by Sub-Lieutenant Trevor Jacobs RNVR, written to his brother, Daryl, a subaltern in the 2/4th Battalion Lancashire Regiment. The letter is dated 19 November; one key figure referred to in it is the battalion's New Zealander CO, Lieutenant-Colonel Bernard Freyberg, later Lord Freyberg, who would win the Victoria Cross in this action. The first day produced hard fighting – with Jacobs going over 'very nonchalantly to show how cool I felt (I don't think)' – but their success came on the second:

> The next morning at dawn we took Beaucourt. I fired about 40 rounds with a rifle. It was an extraordinary thing to see the Boches rushing up to surrender, with hands up, any number of them. I commandeered some to attend to the wounded, and was pleased to see one of their own machine-guns drop one of them. The Boches gave us a period of rest for about 2 hours during which I bandaged a few wounded men, not a very nice job, especially when you are a novice, but they were very plucky. Then the Boche artillery started, and they turned on an enormous amount of their Heavies over us, it was absolute hell. Luckily I had insisted just previously upon my men digging hard which gave us a little more depth cover, though we had to continue with entrenching tools. I saw one man blown up 50 to 70 ft high, and come down without any clothing on, and saw the lower half of another man blown up quite near me. I had put my ground sheet and field glasses down, in order to dig better, and a few minutes after they were both blown up.
>
> I had received news that all my Coy. Officers were wounded and had to be ready to take command of my Coy. which was also mixed up with other men I had commandeered. Our C.O. was badly wounded in the neck but I hear that he is getting on well. He is being recommended for the V.C. When night fell the bombardment grew less though of course we kept on digging. Then we were told the relief would arrive shortly, but it did not do so until 2 a.m. following morning, so we carried on digging. During one moment at night I momentarily lost my bearing, it

being a very dark night, and nearly got to the German line, luckily I found out in time, and about turned.

We were eventually relieved and marched back for about 1 hour's rest to the German strong point that had been taken that morning by a tank, and which surrendered with 300 prisoners. Had I seen that strong point and the surroundings earlier in the day I would have shot at least 10 Germans even if they did rush to surrender to us. I never saw anything so tragic. It was a shambles, any amount of our brave fellows being all round in shell holes and with terrible wounds, some of them with half a head blown off, others without legs and arms, and others with numerous bullet wounds. I bound up some pretty horrible wounds myself. I rested from 7 to 8 a.m. in a German dugout sitting up. The smell was appalling, and after inspection I found that my head had been resting practically against a dead German Officer, who was in a fearful state. The tunic I wore has a great deal of blood on it.

When we got back to Englebelmer we were cinematographed. I am marching alone as the second in command of my Coy, but I suppose my steel helmet and unshaven appearance will make me hard to recognise. All the Commanding Officers of the Brigade have been killed, a fine set of men they were. When the GOC General Shute met us at Englebelmer he said, 'You Hoods are wonderful, the men are magnificent, and the officers are marvellous. 2 Army Corps had already tried to take the position and failed. You have accomplished it.' My Coy. went in 150 strong and came out 85. They were very lucky. I am at present acting as 2nd in command of the Coy., also Paymaster and of course Mess President, consequently have an enormous amount to do.

The losses of the 63rd Division totalled nearly 3,500. A sad postscript is that both the Jacobs brothers would lose their lives in the fighting of the following year.

Second Lieutenant Medlicott was among the 3,000 casualties of 2nd Division, which made limited progress in its attempt to seize Redan Ridge. He was not a fatality, however, being seriously wounded, though not so badly that he would not in time make a full recovery; he would, however, take no further part in the war.

If Beaumont Hamel and Beaucourt, and also, south of the river, St Pierre Divion, became prizes of the Ancre Battle, Serre, by contrast, did not. In fact the 'sinister ruins of Serre' would not fall into British hands until three months later, in February 1917, and then not through force of arms.

What of Private Surfleet's 13th East Yorkshires in 31st Division? How did that column of men which he had watched marching away towards the front with a crackle of jokes and a flurry of cheerful waves fare in the subsequent action? They attacked together with their sister battalion, the 12th, and to begin with their assault went to plan and they occupied the German front line; to occupy the support line was much more difficult and they were soon under severe pressure from bombing counter-attacks. No further progress was made and by 5.25 p.m. it was conceded that the 31st Division's attack was a total failure.

The following paragraphs are from Surfleet's diary account of the day:

Woke early on the morning of November 13th and heard the boys went over at 5.45. Breakfast was a rotten meal; news of losses, of wounded, of killed, kept coming through. Each time a man or an officer came up to the dressing station, the news of all he could tell spread like wildfire. Everything seemed jumbled up; no one had a clear idea of what was going on, but it seemed certain that there had been a big counter-attack and that our losses have been terrible. So, too, have those of the other battalions who went over with our lads.

It was five o'clock in the evening when Lt John, who was in charge of us, dashed in and told us to get our fighting equipment on; we were to go up the line to help, though no one seemed to know what the job was to be. My fingers trembled as I buckled my belt: a mixture of excitement and nervousness, but we were pretty well resigned to anything by this time.

The roads were packed with traffic; a stream of living going forward while the wounded and dying or dead came back. We were a very silent party, leaving the road at the Dell and taking to an overland track which led us right through dozens of our guns, every one firing like hell let loose. How Lt John picked his way through that maze of batteries was nothing short of wonderful. We came in for some very heavy retaliation as the German batteries tried to cut off our reinforcements and three of our party were killed and several others wounded by shrapnel and pieces of high explosive which fell around us. It was particularly bad just as we reached the Communication Trench. We halted at the start of the trench and Lt John went along to get instructions. It was a very nerve-racking wait and one or two of our party ... thank God there were not many ... took advantage of the noise and disturbance and slipped quietly down a side trench and stayed there until, all the work done, we were returning. Then the miserable devils slipped back into the file, no one of any importance being any the wiser. There are some things one can understand: I must never sneer at a man who is afraid, for I have been more frightened out here than it is necessary to record. That is one thing; scrounging to the detriment of your pals is another and we who saw those rotters have not forgotten; I don't suppose we ever shall.

When their orders came through they were instructed to report to the Battalion Aid Post 'for duty as required; we had expected much worse instructions'. The next few hours were, however, almost as horrific as if they had been sent into the fighting, as they struggled to evacuate wounded through trenches of which one on their route was 'knee-deep in the thickest and most glutinous mud I have ever seen'. Near to exhaustion, they took shelter on the steps of an unfinished dugout 'until Lt John came along and said he wanted a party for over the top'.

I am afraid the enthusiasm was not very praiseworthy; we felt we had done a lot more than some we knew, but when he spoke to me and a few others, we got out into the trench, quite expecting it was a raiding job. We soon found it was to go over the top to collect the more badly wounded and I know that made us feel rather sorry we had been a bit reluctant and I am sure each one of us went about that job with real enthusiasm. Anyway, we have come to think (as I feel my account will show) that night we more than did our whack (I am thinking of some of those who dodged the whole job).

We climbed on to the parapet and, being shown the direction we were to take, set off into the blackness.

We passed on, the four of us with the stretcher and the cries of the wounded and dying were frightful to hear; it was awful to pass some of these men who shouted for us to take them back, but we

had orders to leave anyone who could possibly get in on his own:
a heart-breaking business ... a nightmare very near to hell. We
went almost to the German front line; they were collecting their
wounded, too, and a sort of mutual tolerance was being observed.
We stumbled over debris and equipment, falling into shell holes
and groping about, almost hopelessly, in the dark until we eventually came to a chap of one of the other battalions in our brigade in
a shell hole. The chap we picked up had both legs broken and his
elbow was shattered ... looked like shrapnel wounds. He had been
roughly bandaged by the Battalion stretcher-bearers and the MO,
who together with that fine gentleman and padre, Capt. Lynn,
worked like slaves through it all. We gradually got the stretcher
beneath him by dint of carefully raising first one part of him and
then the other. This took quite a time; then we raised the stretcher,
one of us at each corner, and set off back to our lines. We set off,
but no sooner had we moved off with the poor fellow than we
realised we were lost on the top. God only knows how we got
back. It took two and a half hours of the most awful, desperate
struggle against dreadful odds in such circumstances as I have never
known before.

He was writing this account on the 16th, having spent the previous
day 'in a trance' of exhausted sleep until past midday, when he and
his fellow 'remnants' were roused by the officers. 'A roll-call was
taken and then the appalling losses we had had became known. The
original attackers had suffered dreadfully; even the "details", we
lucky devils who were, originally, left behind, sustained an almost
proportionate loss of men. Our M.O. was wounded and God knows
how many more of our pals, *we* don't, yet. One thing is certain: we
shall need reinforcing before we go into the line again.'

*   *   *

For Surfleet this was the end of his experience on the Somme. For
Wrench, it came on the 19th, the day on which, formally, the battle
was closed down. His point of exit was White City, where many
months previously Sergeant Robert McKay of the 36th Ulster
Division and his fellow Field Ambulancemen had shared a dugout
with a group of signallers, and where at 7.20 on 1 July Lieutenant
Geoffrey Malins had filmed the explosion of the mine on Hawthorn

Ridge. On this occasion, even as the last hours of the battle ticked by, the violence was the other way:

> White City has been about blown to the Devil today and between 12.45 and 2.30 the strafe was at its worst. Certainly no one could venture out beneath it and it was after that when the brigade got moving. Was one of the rear party to wait behind till the relief was complete. This was at 5 p.m. and it was quiet then for the moment, so we traversed that field back in a double hurry arriving at Café Jourdain in Mailly-Maillet an hour and a half later.
>
> And so, we hope, farewell to Beaumont Hamel. It was the key position to the whole of the Somme where after the disaster we suffered last July, this capture now is sure a feather in the cap of the Fifty-First. We feel proud of it anyhow, even if we don't know whether we are dead or alive, but of this we are sure, which is that unless one has experienced it, it is impossible to realise what the truth of such a battle means, the awful horror and tragedy of it all, and to feel what it is to have come out of it alive.

*   *   *

The last day of the Battle of the Somme was an appropriate day for weather, with a gale following a wet night. Apart from such last-rite 'frightfulness' as that described by Private Wrench, there was only desultory fighting, which simply petered out, thus providing no dramatic or tidy ending. There are therefore few if any references in contemporary writings to the battle's conclusion as compared with the infinity of references to its beginning. In any case, low-level activity of some kind would continue more or less indefinitely, blurring any sense of finality.

As for the campaign's results in terms of territory won, a strip of ground approximately twenty miles wide by six miles deep had been seized by the Allies from the enemy. Bapaume still remained in German hands several miles beyond the farthest advance of the British Fourth Army, while the French had not succeeded in reaching Péronne. The Allies were not in Berlin, but at the very least they were not where they had been four and a half months before. They had moved forward; the Germans had moved back.

Referring to the final phase of the Ancre battle, the British Official

History states that the Commander-in-Chief 'had contemplated a further development of this offensive, but the ensuing period of bad weather had forced him to abandon any such project'. It also records that in persisting as long as he did, he 'was acting in loyal acceptance of General Joffre's policy to harry the sorely battered enemy until offensive action should be no longer possible. Even so,' it continues, 'French opinion blamed the British, as predominant partner in the struggle, for breaking off the battle too soon. Mortified, perhaps, at being denied another chance of encompassing the defeat of Germany, General Joffre has even stated that decisive victory could have been won if the British had persevered.' The French view has won little support on the British side; what it underlines is how much the Somme was a campaign ruled by political as opposed to merely military considerations.

Casualty figures were high on all sides. Britain and Empire forces, 419,654; French, 204,253; German casualties have been variously calculated from 437,000 to 680,000. Whether the higher total of 1,303,907 or the lower one of 1,060,907 is accepted, there is no disagreement that this battle's toll was enough to put the Battle of the Somme among the world's most hard-fought and sacrificial contests.

So ended what the Prime Minister, Herbert Asquith – who had observed the battle both as politician and parent, who had lost one son in September while another had been engaged, if not in the actual fighting, in the Ancre offensive in November – would hauntingly describe as 'the long and sombre procession of cruelty and suffering'.

*　　*　　*

The 'results' of the Battle of the Somme have been a subject of claim and counter-claim almost from the moment it was over. The following are the verdicts of some key players:

For Sir Douglas Haig the outcome of the campaign gave substantial cause for satisfaction. In his despatch of 23 December 1916, first published in *The Times* a few days later, he wrote:

The objective of [the] offensive was threefold:
(1) To relieve the pressure on Verdun.

(2) To assist our Allies in the other theatres of the war by stopping any further transfer of German troops from the Western front.

(3) To wear down the strength of the forces opposed to us.

At the close of the despatch, affirming that all three objects had been achieved, he stated: 'Any one of these results is in itself sufficient to justify the Somme battle. The attainment of all three of them affords ample compensation for the splendid efforts of our troops and for the sacrifices made by ourselves and our Allies. They have brought us a long step forward towards the final victory of the Allied cause.'

The despatch's title makes no reference to the Somme as such, being called 'The Opening of the Wearing-Out Battle', implying that, in the context of strategy (as indicated in his point (3) above), he saw the main purpose of the campaign as attritional rather than that of achieving an outright breakthrough. This does not seem at one with – for example – his comment on Rawlinson's first, cautious September plans: 'I think we should make an attack as strong and violent as possible, and plan to go as far as possible' (quoted on page 179), or his widely acknowledged hope for an outstanding success on 1 July. However, it should be stressed that Haig was fighting an Anglo-French battle on the Somme, and since the French had been playing the attrition card all year, it is understandable that he should do so too. His report also implied that there was still a long road ahead. Yet within his own terms of reference, however, he was clearly claiming a major success.

What of the enemy? A telling comment was made within weeks of the end of the battle by Field Marshal Hindenburg at the conference in January 1917, at which Germany decided to resort to unrestricted U-boat warfare:

We must save the men from a second Somme battle.

General Ludendorff – from late August onwards the effective German commander of the Somme – wrote the following in his war memoirs, published in 1919, conceding much, but, especially in relation to the controversial last phase of the battle, not quite conceding defeat:

The fighting ... made the most extraordinary demands both on commanders and troops. Divisions and other formations had to be thrown in on the Somme front in quicker succession and had to stay in the line longer ... The strain on our nerves ... was terrible; over and over again we had to find and adopt new expedients.

In October the attacks continued in undiminished force, especially in the northern part of the front ... We sustained losses, yet an effective stiffening of our defence began to be perceptible.

Among later comments, the following offer varying, sometimes contrary attitudes.

The respected Australian historian, C.E.W. Bean, made this comment in a book published in 1946, allowing considerable advantage to the British but possibly implying a hint of distaste for the grim arithmetic of attrition:

So the First Somme Battle ended. The armies had taken each other's measure – the British, if not yet fully trained, were at least a growing danger to their opponents and both sides now knew it. But the battle was also the hardest and bloodiest fought by the British in that war ... The British loss of about 415,000 included the flower of the British youth in the New Army. Yet the Allies could afford loss better than their opponents; and, in the terrible determination with which Haig wore his enemy down, the Germans really faced the beginning of the end.

For the expression of a view which would find its first rudimentary expression during the war years and would later be heavily endorsed by a seam of publicly voiced disenchantment running from the writings of the war poets and some of the more high-profile memoirists, such as Robert Graves and Edmund Blunden, to *Oh, What a Lovely War* and beyond, there could be no more forceful spokesman than the controversial Oxford historian, A.J.P. Taylor:

Strategically, the battle of the Somme was an unredeemed defeat. It is supposed to have worn down the spirit of the German army. So no doubt it did, though not to the point of crippling that army as a fighting machine. The German spirit was not the only one to suffer. The British were worn down also. Idealism perished on the Somme. The enthusiastic volunteers were enthusiastic no longer.

They had lost faith in their cause, in their leaders, in everything except loyalty to their fighting comrades. The war ceased to have a purpose. It went on for its own sake, as a contest in endurance.

Two much-quoted verdicts can perhaps be put side by side. First, this by a German participant, Captain von Hentig of the General Staff of the Guard Reserve Division:

The Somme was the muddy grave of the German field army, and of the faith in the infallibility of the German leadership, dug by British industry and its shells ... The German Supreme Command, which entered the war with enormous superiority, was defeated by the superior techniques of its opponents. It had fallen behind in the application of destructive forces, and was compelled to throw division after division without protection against them into the cauldron of the battle of annihilation.

Second, that of Winston Churchill from his book *The World Crisis*, 1916–1918, written in the mid-1920s:

The battlefields of the Somme were the graveyards of Kitchener's Army. The flower of that generous manhood which quitted peaceful civilian life in every kind of workaday occupation, which came at the call of Britain, and as we may still hope, at the call of humanity, and came from the most remote parts of her Empire, were shorn away for ever in 1916. Unconquerable except by death, which they had conquered, they have set up a monument of native virtue which will command the wonder, the reverence and the gratitude of our island people as long as we endure as a nation among men.

For the verdict of a contemporary historian close to the latest findings among military scholars, Peter Simkins' comparison of the tactics of the Somme with the greatly improved tactics employed only a few months later makes a fitting conclusion to this collage of quotations:

The results of these improvements were manifest in the first day of the Battle of Arras in April 1917, when the Canadian Corps stormed Vimy Ridge and the British XVII Corps advanced some 3½ miles at a comparatively light cost in casualties. The true gains of the BEF from the Somme offensive might therefore be best judged by examining the story of 9 April 1917 rather than the bloody assaults of 1916.

* * *

One important part of the equation of the Somme barely touched on so far is the matter of the contribution of the French – junior partners to the British on this front – in the campaign.

In his description of 1 July 1916, Cyril Falls wrote:

> South of the Somme the French gained a brilliant and complete success. Some British historians have ungraciously asserted that this was because the Germans did not expect them to attack at all after their losses at Verdun, but it is clear from German accounts that such was not the case. Their tremendous superiority in heavy artillery, which resulted in the pulverizing of large sections of the German defences, had something to do with it, but they merit the credit due to speed, dash and tactical brains. As on many occasions in this battle, their formations were less rigid than those of the British and proved less easy targets.

A statement such as this from a forthright, indeed, a hard-line, British historian of some rigour, is tribute indeed to the often undervalued contribution by the French to the Somme offensive. It should be stated, however, that there are alternative views. Thus John Terraine has argued, in his essay 'The True Texture of the Somme': 'For the French, as well as for the British, 1 July was a freak. The Germans expected only a demonstration, not an attack, and were taken by surprise. Just as the British never again did so badly, so the French never again did so well.'

Steering a middle course, Trevor Wilson has attributed their success on 1 July partly to the fact of surprise, 'in that the Germans did not think the French capable of making an effort on the Somme given their sufferings at Verdun,' but also to 'the much greater weight of the French bombardment, which in proportion to the area covered was four times as heavy as the British', and to 'the superiority of French infantry tactics, which included the use of lightly loaded bombing parties that rushed into the German trenches in the immediate aftermath of the bombardment'.

On the face of things it would seem extraordinary if the French had not learned some lessons at least from their severe experience at Verdun, where they had been forcibly indoctrinated into the tactics of a Somme-type attack four and a half months earlier. Certainly this is the view of the supreme British chronicler of Verdun, Alistair Horne. In his description of the first phase of the Somme battle, he wrote:

> Whereas, in Joffre's original plan ... Foch was to have attacked with forty divisions and Haig with twenty-five, the needs of Verdun had now whittled down the French contribution to a mere fourteen. But it was Foch's men – in the van, the famous 'Iron Corps', now recovered from its mauling before Verdun in February – who were to mark the only real successes. They worked forward in small groups supported by machine-guns, using the land with pronounced tactical skill, in the way they had learned at Verdun, and emulating where possible the German's own infiltration techniques there.

Yet it must also be admitted that, though the French curtain-raiser on the Somme was impressive, they, like the British, found the task of advancing against a determined and highly accomplished enemy no easy one. Certainly over the following months there was no time when either of the allies notably outstripped the other.

It is perhaps inevitable that in writing about the Somme, British historians should give only cursory reference to the French role, in that this is merely reflecting what was largely the case at the time. Caught up in the strains and pressures of the most arduous fighting they had so far experienced, the British were much more aware of the enemy to their front, than of the French on their flank. This, of course, is one of the unavoidable consequences of a linear war; attacking in parallel, allies are beset by the most obvious characteristic of parallel lines, that they do not meet. References to the French role on the Somme are therefore somewhat sparse in British sources. Yet they do occur. Thus Captain Harry Bursey (in 30th Division, on the extreme right of the British line, next to the French), could write on 1 July 1916: 'A lovely morning. French cannonade, it was some cannonade too.' And later the same day: 'Hear the French on our right have taken 1900 prisoners. They have also reached their objective, like us. The 18th Division (we are supporting them) have done all that was wanted.'

Or there is the warm tribute of Lieutenant Geoffrey Fildes in early September: 'The great battle continues without ceasing. We have over a thousand prisoners and the French six thousand six hundred. They have taken 36 guns of which 24 are heavies. We have had no news today, except a report that an aeroplane has seen French infantry at Bois St Pierre Vaast. If this is true, they have made a great advance.'

In fact, though in most respects his accolade was well deserved, Fildes was premature in claiming the woods of Pierre St Vaast for the French. In September they took Bouchavesnes (a village later to be honoured by a statue of Marshal Foch), Rancourt, Cléry-sur-Somme, Déniécourt, Vermandevillers, and, to the south, Chilly. But October saw them held up at Sailly-Saillesel and at St Pierre Vaast, rather as the British were stopped opposite the Butte de Warlencourt. Indeed, just as the Butte, a potent, and poignant, symbol from 1916 onwards, marks the furthest point of the British advance, so the sombre little chapel of the association 'Souvenir Français' at Rancourt – archetypally French, and the more moving for its vast hinterland of diminutive grey crosses stretching far back from the Bapaume–Péronne road – marks the high-water mark of their progress. French sources allow twelve kilometres of territory gained by the British, while claiming only five to eight kilometres for themselves, though they point out that they were attacking with smaller forces. Whatever the numbers involved, however, both allied armies faced the same appalling conditions of the battlefield in its final weeks, when it had become, in the terse but graphic words of the French novelist Pierre Loti, 'a foul brown mush in which everything sinks'.

For France, however, 1916 was essentially the year of Verdun, just as for Britain it was the year of the Somme. In French eyes defending the border fortress of Verdun, the focus of much heroic endeavour in both the Revolutionary and Franco-Prussian wars, was not just fighting for a town, it was fighting for an icon of national pride, for its own soul. Inevitably, the Somme, by contrast, became a sideshow – though if it were to be left, as it had to be, mainly to the British, the French were determined that they would do everything possible to ensure that their Anglo-Saxon ally should fight there with the same sacrificial determination that they themselves were showing at Verdun.

In the matter of territory seized by the attacker in each of these great battles, comparisons are illuminating. If criticism is made, as it often is, of the small advance achieved by four and a half months of fighting on the Somme, it should also be remembered that all the Germans had to show for their ten months of battle and third of a million casualties at Verdun was, in Alistair Horne's evocative words, 'a piece of raddled land little larger in area than the combined Royal Parks of London'. Similarly, although Field Marshal von Falkenhayn, the German commander who initiated the Verdun offensive, might assert with some justification that Verdun had led to the breaking of France's superbly courageous armies, it can also be claimed that the German Army was never quite the same again after Verdun. As the Crown Prince admitted: 'The Mill on the Meuse ground to powder the hearts as well as the bodies of the troops'. In such reactions one can hear distinct echoes of the comments quoted earlier in this chapter in relation to the fighting on the Somme.

The cemetery count is eloquent in terms of the contribution to the Somme campaign by the two nations: there are far more British ones than French, though there are numerous French ones to account for its many thousands of dead. Thiepval is perhaps a significant memorial in this regard. Its massive imperial arch is very British in concept and content, but facing it are two equal plots, each of 300 graves, one British, one French, like companies of soldiers marshalled on a parade ground. Allies in the waging of the campaign; allies now, and permanently, in their shared place of remembrance.

CHAPTER THIRTEEN

CIVILIANS AND THE SOMME

THE NEWS OF the attack of 1 July reached London later the same day. Raucous voices filled the streets as newspaper boys with huge posters, carrying the legend 'GREAT BRITISH OFFENSIVE BEGINS', ran excitedly along the pavements. Purchasers of evening papers were confronted with striking headlines amplifying that basic message, such as these in *The Star*:

BRITISH OFFENSIVE BEGINS – OFFICIAL
FRONT LINE BROKEN OVER 16 MILES
FRENCH SHARE ADVANCE
THE FIGHTING DEVELOPING IN INTENSITY

These were followed by a report from British Headquarters datelined 'Saturday 9.30 a.m.', stating that at about 7.30 that morning 'a vigorous offensive' had been launched by the British Army on a front extending 'over about 20 miles north of the Somme', and adding: 'It is too early as yet to give anything but the barest particulars ... but the British troops have already occupied the German front lines.'

Officially, this should have been the first intimation to an eager public that a major attack was in progress. However, awareness of the coming battle, and of the precise sector where it would be fought, was already widespread. On Monday 3 July the *Daily Mail*, in an article entitled 'THE BIG PUSH: WHAT IT MEANS', the veteran journalist Lovat Fraser wrote: 'I never remember a secret so widely shared. Not only every man, woman and child in the country, but, as von Bethman-Hollweg would say, every dog and cat has seemed to be murmuring "Albert". The Somme as the scene of a possible "push" has been upon every lip.'

Throughout the months that followed the civilian population in Britain followed developments on the Somme with a huge, indeed almost a proprietorial, interest. That interest was often combined with an equally substantial ignorance as to the reality of what was taking place, and a basic belief that once 'our boys' put their minds to it, the Germans would have no chance and would be soon on their way. This was not always the public's fault; headlines and newspaper leaders tended to be so breezily optimistic that unfounded expectations were easily aroused. Lovat Fraser was clearly aware of such dangers in that, in the article just quoted, he felt it necessary to stress that there was a long road ahead: 'The great British offensive has begun marvellously well, and what we have now to bear in mind is that our troops do not expect to be in Berlin this week.'

*　*　*

Few can have followed the march of events during the Battle of the Somme more intensely from the civilian's vantage point than Mr Frederick Arthur Robinson of Cobham, Surrey, who had started a detailed diary at the commencement of hostilities in 1914 and would keep it faithfully until Armistice Day 1918. Too old to be actively engaged in the war, he was nevertheless deeply absorbed by it, recording its progress by writing out, almost every day, long quotations from newspapers and adding numerous comments or tit-bits of information on his own account. His diary would eventually run to 3,473 pages. 'Time after time,' he would later admit, 'one felt inclined to give it up, but friends said, "You must go on, you cannot leave off now".'

His entries for the period July to December 1916 offer an illuminating commentary on the progress of the campaign as seen from the sidelines: a campaign being fought so close to home that people in southern England could sometimes hear the rumble of the guns, but, in the eyes of many soldiers, so distant in terms of comprehension that they might have been fighting on Mars.

Robinson's reaction to the opening attack on the Somme was one of relief that the nation's armies were finally engaged, combined with a certain impatience that they had taken so long, as he saw it, to take their fair share of the Allied burden. He wrote, tersely, on 1 July:

'We commence the new half year with the following news, that the British have at last got a move on.'

Next day he continued in a similar mode: 'The papers are full of the British advance. The official report states that "so far the day goes well for England and France". God grant that it may continue to go well and that this at last may be the beginning of the end, and not a mere "flash in the pan" such as we have had so many times before. We have certainly waited long enough.'

Yet, though heartily patriotic, Robinson was no mindless jingo; only days later, on 8 July, after quoting reports of further attacks on the Somme, he was moved to comment: 'What fighting, what struggling, what carnage these simple sentences really mean! Such scenes have never been witnessed in the world before and please God may they never happen again. Why they should be permitted to happen now, God alone can tell.'

A great reader between the lines, on 12 July he mused over an official Allied communiqué giving the estimated figures of German losses since the opening of the offensive. 'One thing it does not state and that is how many men *we* have lost. What one feels is that after all, our progress is insignificant, we have thrust back our foes a distance of one or two miles upon a front of 8 miles. What is this compared with the front line which is measured in hundreds of miles? It only shows what a terrific, almost impossible task it is.'

He was also well aware that this task imposed a huge financial strain on the country: 'And so the days pass and each day costs us five million sterling.'

Robinson's standard source of information was *The Times*, but he also cast his net over other newspapers, some of which were capable of allowing their solidarity with the troops to take ridiculous forms. In early July he recorded the launch by the *Surrey Advertiser* of a campaign – clearly a response to the 'push' on the Somme – to persuade all males not in the Army or Navy to forswear shaving, on the grounds that this would result in an immense saving in time, soap, bristles, steel (for razors) and gas (the presumed agent for producing the required hot water). The newspaper's leader claimed: 'A war beard would be an outward and visible sign of a glowing and dauntless patriotism!' Even in the heightened climate of 1916 this idea failed to take root.

More practical was the initiative proposed in mid-July by the Chancellor of the Exchequer. There was to be another 'War Savings Week'. From the terms in which the announcement was made, it seems evident that the perception that the great struggle in France would be no easy one was already being admitted in governmental circles. Robinson quoted its keynote sentences: 'The thoughts of the whole nation are directed across the Channel, where the greatest military effort in the history of our country is being made. This is no battle for a day or two, but is the beginning of a long, patient and arduous offensive, demanding from our soldiers heroic exertions and unimaginable sacrifices.'

Sacrifices were to be demanded of civilians also, Robinson recorded: a notable one that summer was the cancellation of the August Bank Holiday. General Haig was forceful in support of this idea, especially with regard to those engaged in production of munitions. Robinson quoted him: 'The Army in France looks to the munition workers to enable it to complete its task, and I feel sure that this appeal will not be in vain. Let the whole British nation forego the idea of a general holiday until our goal is reached.'

A special conference of Labour representatives was hurriedly convened in London. The result was an eloquent endorsement of the proposal, with the added suggestion that there should be a postponement of *all* holidays, general and local. The core of their message to the Commander-in-Chief read: 'We assure you, and through you the British Army, that we will not relax our efforts to maintain and increase the supply of ammunition, guns, and other war material which is necessary to enable you and the Army to bring to conclusion the great task which you have so gallantly and successfully begun.'

Meanwhile the papers were full of advertisements urging support for the War Savings Week. And not for this cause only. On 19 July Robinson was moved to comment: 'Alongside of these advertisements are appeals to subscribe to the Kitchener Memorial, to the British Ambulance Committee, French Wounded Fund, Serbian Relief Fund, Polish Victims Fund, besides all sorts of other charities and objects. If one gave to all these objects there would be nothing left to pay the 5 shilling income tax.' Clearly there were limits to the ardour of even the most dedicated of patriots.

* * *

By this time, some idea of the scale of the losses incurred in the opening phase of the Somme battle had been conveyed by the newspapers, even though their prevailing editorial message was one of achievement and, if at some considerable cost, overall success.

Signs of anxiety on Robinson's part were evident in his entry for 26 July: '*The Times* correspondent remarks that "the operations on the Somme begin to rival Verdun". Does he mean as regards casualties, or does he mean that it will end in a deadlock?'

It was not, however, until 10 August that he began what would become a regular ritual until the Armistice, the recording day by day of the casualty figures listed in *The Times* – Sundays apart, when the newspaper did not appear. That day's list produced 4,300 names.

Over the following days he noted: 11 August, 4,220 names; 12 August, 4,000; 14 August, 6,229 men and 195 officers; 15 August, 5,661; 16 August, 4,773; 17 August, 4,936; 18 August, 3,831.

On 19 August, noting a figure of 5,674, he commented on the defence by Mr Lloyd George of the Welsh Eisteddfod, which had continued to function in spite of the sombre mood at home. 'Why should the people not sing?', Lloyd George had asked; Robinson answered, 'not much cause for "singing" with a list such as this appearing every day.'

By 27 August, he was moved to reflect on the figures which he had been recording in relation to the encouraging 'war news' put out over recent days from the British front: 'Today's communiqué states that yet another 400 yards of enemy's trenches have been captured, and so it will go on from day to day until perhaps one morning we shall get the news that the enemy is fairly on the run. This day will surely come, but in the meantime we pay dearly for every yard advanced in the heavy casualty lists – numbering as they do some five thousand each day.'

* * *

One of the curiosities about the Battle of the Somme is that a film called *The Battle of the Somme*, compiled from footage shot in France immediately before and after the opening of the push, was being in shown in London and elsewhere – and ultimately even on the Somme front itself – while the actual battle was still in progress. A normal practice today, this kind of instant media coverage was a stunning new phenomenon in 1916.

Inevitably, Frederick Robinson made a point of seeing the film, travelling to London to a showing at the Scala Theatre. Its première had been on 10 August; Robinson did not add to the huge national audience which had been astounded, shocked and moved by it until early September. He then gave it ample space in his diary:

Londoners cannot go to the front to see the war, but the war has been brought to London, for Londoners to see. The official war films which are now being exhibited bring home to one the realities of the war perhaps more than anything else could. One is able to realise the immensity of the operations and the marvellous organisation, and to drink to the full the gruesomeness and cruelty of it all. The films deal with the present 'push' on the Somme. You first see the preparations for the advance, and then, on July 1st, you actually see one of the regiments dash over the parapet of their trench, alas, leaving some of their number shot dead before your eyes. You see the big guns and the Howitzers fired as well as the tiny trench mortars. You see the wounded brought in on stretchers lying in rows; you see the doctors at a dressing station only two hundred yards from the firing line, giving first aid. You actually see one wounded man rescued from 'No Man's Land' and brought in on the back of his rescuer – only, as we are informed, to die of his wounds half an hour later. You see mines exploded, shrapnel and high explosive shells bursting. You see men – British and Germans – lying dead on the battlefield as they fell in all the dreadful huddled up attitudes of their last agony....

In fact, you see in an hour more than you could see at the front in a month, and all this is compressed into sixty strenuously exciting minutes. No wonder after the ordeal you come away both mentally and physically exhausted. You certainly have the realities of the war brought home to you, you feel the sacrifices which are being made by those at the front and you realise how little is your

part. All this is for good and as the King is reported to have said:-
'The public should see these pictures that they may have some idea
of what the Army is doing and what war means' – which is quite
true provided their nerves are strong enough.

Correspondence has been going on in the papers as to the
propriety of shewing the films. There can hardly be any doubt as
to this, but what people properly take exception to is that these
films with all their realism and awfulness should be shewn sand-
wiched in between screaming farces of the Charlie Chaplin type.
At one well known place where I saw the films, they were
immediately followed by a 'screaming farce' called 'Fickle Fatties
Fall', which could certainly not have been in worse taste.

On 16 September, Robinson had an intriguing, new subject to
report. After welcoming as 'very satisfactory' the C-in-C's news of
advances on the 15th by both the British and the French, he noted
that 'a very interesting thing is reported in General Haig's Despatch,
viz: that we employed for the first time a new type of heavy armoured
car, which he says "proved of considerable utility".' He continued:

One can imagine these Juggernauts careering over the ground,
crushing down barbed-wire entanglements and other obstacles, and
belching forth death and destruction to all within reach of their
guns, whilst being themselves impervious to everything except a
point-blank shot from a heavy gun. The Germans have taught us a
thing or two; now we are giving them a lesson, and are shewing
them that inventive skill and manufacturing ability are not mono-
polised by them. We are not told how many of these monsters are
employed. They are known as 'tanks'.

By the 19th, however, he was in more sceptical mood. Recording
that Haig's most recent despatch had claimed an advance to a depth
of about a thousand yards on a front of one mile and had called this
'a highly successful operation', he commented: 'No doubt in any
other war that has ever been, this would be recorded as a great
victory, but on a front of some forty to fifty miles, how little it is
towards that final victory which we are longing for.'

The weather and its effect on the situation in France provided the
theme for his musings on the following day. Reacting to reports of
'heavy and continuous rain' which had resulted in interference with

military operations, he wrote, with perhaps a whiff of sarcastic impatience: 'Someone might suggest that we send out a supply of mackintoshes and umbrellas.'

On the 21st he was back with the tanks – 'these monstrous engines', as a German report had dubbed the new arrivals on the Western Front: 'There is no doubt these so called "Tanks" have caused consternation amongst the Germans. Many stories of their exploits have appeared in the papers during the last few days.' What interested him above all, however, was the bizarre lengths to which the newspapers had gone in their attempts to define them: 'They are compared with the ichthyosaurus, jabberwocks, mastodons, Leviathans, boojums, snarks, and other antediluvian and mythical monsters.' A more humble simile proposed by a correspondent of *The Times*, however, evoked his scorn: '[He] gives a vivid account of them and their doings, but makes rather a faux-pas when he says "a level plain was full of the monsters like cows in a meadow – huge shapeless bulks resembling nothing else that was ever seen on Earth which wandered hither and thither like some vast antediluvian brutes which nature had made and forgotten." A poor description of *what cows are like*.'

On 28 September, a personal note came into his recording of the casualty figures: 'The Casualty list today numbers 286 officers and 2,394 men. We hear of the death of two more young fellows, whose fathers are friends of ours – Capt D.M. Glass and Lieut Vivian Thomas, of Penzance, and so it goes on, day after day.' Yet by 6 October, he was showing a typical civilian's impatience with the lack of the kind of news that produced such high figures: 'Judging by the retrospective reports from General Haig, there seems to be rather a tendency just now to rest on our laurels.'

It is noteworthy that he was making this comment at the start of the battle's last phase, for persisting with which in adverse weather conditions and with little territorial gain Haig would receive much criticism. Informed and intelligent as he was, Robinson shared the desire of most war-watchers from afar, to see major progress combined with low cost – an equation never achieved by any nation in the Western Front war.

His entry for 1 November, after his finding the kind of newspaper item (in the vein of the *Surrey Advertiser*'s war beards) that raised his incredulous eyebrows, had a distinctly lighter touch:

For an act of egregious ineptitude the following is hard to beat.

> The King has accepted and approved a copy of the edition of Shakespeare's works which will be given to every soldier disabled in the war in memory of Lord Kitchener.
>
> The gift is being made through a special committee of the League of the Empire.
>
> The volume has been specially bound, and contains a book-plate on which the name and regiment of the disabled man appears.

One can imagine our disabled Tommies whiling away the weary hours engrossed with the troubles and trials of the Prince of Denmark, or of Romeo and Juliet. I don't think.

On the 3rd he again discussed the matter of casualties, noting that that day's count included the names of fifty-four officers and 3,600 men 'notwithstanding the fact that the essence of the British reports for days past can be summed up in the expression: "Nuffing doin'".' He was therefore much invigorated when he was able to report, on the day after the launch of the Ancre battle: 'Nov. 14. The period of somnolence has suddenly come to an end, even if it existed. Last night we heard that the British had again assumed the offensive.'

As was the case in France, there was no tidy, clear-cut end to the Somme battle as recorded in Frederick Robinson's diary. References became rare, except in relation to the ever-present casualty count. This is from his entry for 30 November: 'Today's Casualty lists include the names of 80 Officers and 1,100 men, which again shews a substantial reduction, only to be explained by inactivity of the Somme.' On 7 December, after quoting Haig's despatch stating 'There is nothing to report during the night', he commented: 'Things have gone to sleep again, but the Casualty lists still go on; today's list comprises 83 officers and 2,210 men.'

Other subjects now monopolized his attention, notably the political crisis which resulted in the departure of Mr Asquith as Prime Minister and the arrival in his place of Mr Lloyd George, though he also discussed more mundane matters such as the request by the Board of Trade to the general public to avoid all travelling by train at Christmas. That season, obviously far less festive than usual, produced an eloquent passage in the diary, with a distinct bias towards pessimism as to the state of the world – a pessimism relieved only by the cheerfulness of some severely wounded soldiers who would almost certainly have been victims of the Somme:

Dec. 25. CHRISTMAS DAY once more! The *third* since the outbreak of war. How quickly it comes round again, what a tremendous lot has happened since last Christmas, and yet how little seems to have been done towards bringing the war to a victorious ending. Peace seems in the air, which is appropriate to the season, but whether recent events are really making for peace, who can tell. At present, the very mention of the word 'peace' seems to arouse greater demand for 'war' to the bitter end. There is certainly no 'peace and good-will' this Christmas. We go to church and listen to the most depressing sermon, nothing but punishment and sacrifice – and worse to come. Later to the hospital in the neighbourhood, where there are some fifty maimed and wounded heroes, leg-less, arm-less, eye-less. Are *they* down-hearted? No! A Christmas tree is provided by kind friends from which each soldier receives a gift of some value. The scene is one of mirth and happiness and acts as an antidote to the morning's infliction.

The publication in *The Times* on 30 December of Sir Douglas Haig's despatch on the recent campaign brought Robinson back to his prime theme of 1916. Noting the scale of the despatch both in terms of the period it covered – from May to December – and the space it took in the newspaper – 'no less than fourteen columns' – he recorded his own summation of the Somme, as 'a battle which was fought incessantly for four and a half months, and which in every respect is the greatest in the history of the world.' He paraphrased with approval Haig's statement (as quoted here in Chapter 12), that the threefold objects of the battle had been achieved: relieving the pressure on Verdun, stopping the transfer of German troops else-where; wearing down the enemy's strength. Reporting Haig's claim that the campaign's successful outcome had been achieved by men unaccustomed to military operations, many of whom had been in training for only a few months, and who were commanded by young officers who had no previous experience, he offered the nation's citizen army his personal endorsement with the words: 'All hail to these heroes!' He quoted at full length the despatch's concluding paragraph:

The enemy's power has not yet been broken, nor is it yet possible to form an estimate of the time the war may last before the objects for which the Allies are fighting have been attained. But the Somme battle has placed beyond doubt the ability of the Allies to gain those objects. The German Army is the mainstay of the Central Powers, and a full half of that Army, despite the advantages of the defensive, supported by the strongest fortifications, suffered defeat on the Somme this year. Neither victors nor vanquished will forget this; and, though bad weather has given the enemy a respite, there will undoubtedly be many thousands in his ranks who will begin the new campaign with little confidence in their ability to resist our assaults or to overcome our defence.

Robinson commented: 'The document taken as a whole is immensely interesting and it describes, in calm prosaic language, events unequalled in this or any other age.'

*   *   *

Robinson's diary is a remarkable document, not only for its colour and detail, but for its thoughtfulness, and – despite its occasional moments of impatience – its attempt to put the battle in a sensible, realistic perspective. He might acclaim the members of Britain's New Army as heroes, but there were no false heroics in his writing. He certainly had no blood lust for casualties. He recorded no encounters with soldiers – apart from the wounded he had seen on Christmas Day – but one suspects that if he were to meet any he would not overwhelm them with prurient questioning as to what life was like in trenches or whether it was exciting going 'over the top'.

The quarrel of the fighting men with the world of 'Civvy Street' was not with such as Robinson, but with those who saw the war as a thrilling struggle in which the participants were deemed to be only too happy to kill or be killed in the nation's cause. For this the soldiers blamed newspapers of the more garish kind which portrayed raids, battles, even routine trench warfare, in glamorous, adventure book terms.

The medical officer of the Hood Battalion, Surgeon Lieutenant-Commander W.J. McCracken, kept in an album of documents and illustrations covering his service career two cuttings from the *Daily Mail* referring to their successful but sacrificial attack in the Ancre battle. One was a notice of the award of the Victoria Cross to his CO, Lieutenant-Colonel Bernard Freyberg, DSO, 'for most conspicuous bravery and brilliant leading as a Battalion Commander'. The other was a report with headlines typical of the style of journalism which made soldiers despair that their true situation would ever be understood: THORNY FIELD OF BEAUCOURT: OUR SPLENDID DEAD: UNFLINCHING BEFORE EVERY PITFALL. Its text was in similar vein, expressing 'an admiration that is indeed reverence for the men who slowly and steadfastly walked that autumn morning one hundred yards after another over fields poisonous with the enemy's devices', or who disentangled themselves from barbed wire 'as coolly as you would dislodge bramble'. The tone grew more florid as the report continued:

> Every man, every little assembly of men, went forward in spite of a hundred barriers that would plausibly hold up platoons or divisions less game than these. They were out to win their spurs . . .
>
> We have had many great fights, but none finer than this. It was heroic in every turn and phase, and the heroism was nowhere vain. Everywhere it won its end – yes, and more than its end. Nor was its cost beyond the measure as figures go. It is only that every fibre of feeling is touched to see one good man fallen before he reached the end.

The writer was William Beach Thomas, who would gain a special notoriety in soldiers' eyes for consistently playing up the glory, while playing down the cost. Hence the comment of a young infantry officer, Second Lieutenant Brian Hickey, who wrote on 20 September after the big offensive of five days earlier (in which he had not been a participant, rather an admiring spectator): 'Not a bad effort getting Courcelette, Flers and Martinpuich in a day, was it? And only a few casualties according to Beach Thomas!!! Those men want hanging if any do.'

For Major R.S. Cockburn, who had volunteered on 4 August 1914

and who had served in the 10th King's Royal Rifle Corps, 20th
Division, both at Ypres and on the Somme, and had won the MC for
his part in a trench raid shortly before the opening of the Somme
offensive, the dramatizations of the press were a matter for anger,
even outrage. He deplored what he saw as the utterly false view
which they imposed on the home population. In May 1918, he wrote
a remarkable polemic expressing his thoughts about many aspects of
his Western Front experience. The past tense which he used throughout most, though not all, of his essay suggests that he might have
intended it for possible publication after the war, when he would be
able to speak his mind released from the constraints of military
discipline. His document remains in its original state, however,
unpolished, with deletions and corrections. He pulled no punches on
the subject of press-induced civilian ignorance:

> How little people at home, hard as they worked, realized what the
> war meant to the men on the battlefield. If they could only
> understand something of that, they would be better able to
> understand the change which they will notice in their soldiers after
> the war. As it is, they have trusted to the newspapers, in which,
> day after day, the obliging war correspondents 'with the British
> Army in the Field' (save the mark!) have supplied stories of men
> laughing and singing as they went 'over the top', and being in the
> state of the most ideal contentment when killing Germans with the
> sword, or counting the enemy dead. Do you really suppose that
> soldiers enjoy a battle? Do you believe that we used to revel in
> shell fire, machine-guns, bombs and bayonets? No, we were not
> such beasts at any time, though we have been at times more animals
> than men. Journalists have made money out of us, and they have
> not hesitated to tell lies about us. Apart from any desirable effect
> which such nonsense may have upon the morale of the people at
> home, this is surely one of the meanest characteristics of war, when
> men can care little for what is either the most foul or the most
> sacred, so be it they can profit themselves by colouring it, or
> distorting it with their pens.

And this was Cockburn's verdict on the Somme battle, a viewpoint
which, especially by virtue of its second paragraph, can also serve as

a justification for a book of this kind, which must necessarily at times make grim reading:

> Ypres was bad, but the Somme was worse. There were far more dead on the Somme. At times you lived with the dead. You could speak to them at night, as I have done, without knowing that they were dead, propped up as they sometimes were at the side of a trench. You stumbled over them, kicked their arms or feet, trod on bits of them, and the air that you breathed was foul with them.
>
> I hesitate to dwell on this sort of thing, but no words about the war would be at all complete without this side being presented somehow. Ask anyone what Trônes Wood was like at the end of August 1916, or if he was not sick (or nearly so) on going over any battlefield on the Somme. Half a head here; battered and black swelling things in the shell holes; torn remnants of bodies scattered by death all over that hellish ground; your best friend blown to pieces by something which (let us hope) he never saw or heard coming; whilst certain men and women in England were having their hands manicured and their faces massaged, that they might 'look their best' at the theatre.

Cockburn doubtless spoke what many, *though by no means all*, fighting soldiers felt, but it must be acknowledged that they were raging at an impossible divide; for in the end only those who were there could understand the reality of the manifold experiences which added up to the Battle of the Somme. In Frederick Robinson's words, they were 'events unequalled'.

CHAPTER FOURTEEN

'SOMMEWHERE' IN FRANCE

HUMOUR AND HUMANITY ON THE SOMME

THE SOMME was no laughing matter, yet, with their usual astonishing perversity and resilience, the men at the front could usually be relied to find things to poke fun at, to crack a joke about, to mock. The war had become desperate but that didn't necessarily mean it should be considered entirely serious. It was Billy Green's laugh, and the fact that there was always 'something to smile at if Billy is about', that so endeared him to his colleagues of the Queen's Westminster Rifles in the run-up to 1 July. The Army had many Billy Greens. One of the most famous quotations from the war poets is Siegfried Sassoon's reference to the Western Front war as 'the hell where youth and laughter go'. There is no denying the sacrifice of the youth, but it is also important to recognize the presence of the laughter.

Soldiers' concerts would hardly seem compatible with the grim first phase of the Somme but Captain Lionel Ferguson's diary records a visit to one in a YMCA hut at Bouzincourt, behind Albert, on 3 July, just before going up to take his place at the front for his division's forthcoming attack. He does not name the artistes, who would probably have been civilian rather than service at such a time – Lena Ashwell's hugely popular concert parties were performing in YMCA huts and open sites in France in 1916 – but these occasions were much welcomed by men happy to enjoy an interlude of mirth and relaxation at a time of stress and challenge. Perhaps the most successful entertainments – given a decent level of presentation – were those where the performers were of the same unit or brigade or division as the audience. Such 'in-house' concert groups could catch a mood that would have a hall-full of Tommies exploding in high good humour. Thus the 'Shrapnels' of 33rd Division (unhappily famous because its GOC sternly forbade the issue of rum to troops in the line) raised enthusiastic applause at a concert in March 1917 with a parody of one of the best known of soldiers' songs, 'Take me back to dear old Blighty'. Their time on the Somme had evidently produced a distinct nostalgia for somewhat less hazardous places elsewhere (even though they hardly fitted the rhythm of the music):

> Take me back to dear old Bethune
> That's far away from here;
> Take me back to dear old Beuvry,
> Where you can get some beer (and your washing done.)
> Put me where there are no High Woods
> And you get your tots of rum,
> I'll stay in the Brickstacks as long as you like
> But take me away from the S-mme!

Lieutenant E.F. Chapman of the 20th Royal Fusiliers, recording the above text in a letter to his parents, described the event as 'a jolly evening', adding that this and 'all the good BEF songs ... come out of the very soul of the Division'.

Trench magazines, of which this war produced an astonishing crop, also provided a way of softening the hard edges of the Somme. Captain F.J. Roberts and Lieutenant J.H. Pearson of the 12th Sherwood Foresters, editor and sub-editor of the most famous of this genre, *The Wipers Times*, moved to Morlancourt with 24th Division in July 1916 and immediately set about producing *The Somme-Times*, which came out on the 31st. Thereafter, serious involvement in the battle brought a pause in production but they were back on 1 December with a new brand-name, *The B.E.F. Times*, under which formula they would continue until they changed it to *The Better Times* in November 1918.

Their two issues produced during and immediately after the 1916 battle represent a clear refusal on their part to allow the undeniable horrors of what everybody recognized as a tough campaign to deprive them of their right to make light of things. The almost mandatory upbeat attitude of the time, requiring cheerful confidence whatever the casualty figures or the relative lack of progress, was a natural target. Thus the *Somme-Times* in an eye-catching half-page mock-advertisement:

ARE YOU A VICTIM OF
OPTIMISM?
—

YOU DON'T KNOW?
THEN ASK YOURSELF THE FOLLOWING QUESTIONS
—

1. DO YOU SUFFER FROM CHEERFULNESS?
2. DO YOU WAKE UP IN THE MORNING FEELING THAT
   ALL IS WELL FOR THE ALLIES?
3. DO YOU SOMETIMES THINK THAT THE WAR WILL END
   WITHIN THE NEXT TWELVE MONTHS?
4. DO YOU BELIEVE GOOD NEWS IN PREFERENCE TO
   BAD?
5. DO YOU CONSIDER OUR LEADERS ARE COMPETENT TO
   CONDUCT THE WAR TO A SUCCESSFUL ISSUE?

IF YOUR ANSWER IS 'YES' TO ANY ONE OF THESE
QUESTIONS THEN YOU ARE IN THE CLUTCHES OF THAT
DREAD DISEASE

WE CAN CURE YOU

TWO DAYS SPENT AT OUR ESTABLISHMENT WILL
EFFECTUALLY ERADICATE ALL TRACES OF IT FROM
YOUR SYSTEM

Limericks, always popular, were standard fare in such publications and the *Somme-Times* had two, the first with a hint of what would now be called sick humour in its pay-off, the second mocking arguably the most frequent German target throughout the war, Kaiser Wilhelm II himself:

> There was a young girl of the Somme,
> Who sat on a number five bomb,
>   She thought 'twas a dud 'un,
>   But it went off sudden –
> Her exit she made with aplomb.

> The Kaiser once said at Peronne
> That the Army we'd got was 'no bon',

> But between you and me
> He didn't 'compris'
> The size of the job he had on.

Localized wit extended even to the sign-off on their last page: 'Printed and Published by/ Sherwood, Forester & Co., Ltd./ "Sommewhere" in France.' *Somme-Times*, Sommewhere: Roberts and Pearson were not the only ones to indulge in such word-play while serving on the Somme.

As was usually the case, however, there was the serious gesture amid the jokiness, such as this poem, entitled 'God-Speed':

> For a year we've taken what came along,
> We've fought or worked and we've held our line,
> Till August finds us 'going strong.'
> The game's afoot and the goal's the Rhine.
>
> Through summer's heat and the winter's gloom
> We've tasted the joys that the Salient holds,
> A filthy dug-out our only room,
> Where our only comfort a jar enfolds . . .
>
> Now we have arrived in pastures new,
> Where the Hun's taking lessons that once he gave.
> Here's the best of luck to all of you
> In the teaching of blackguards how to behave.

The *B.E.F. Times*, publishing in December, had the arrival of the tanks as matter for their wit. Hence this from a half page advertisement on the front page:

GUILLEMONT HIPPODROME
—
THIS WEEK — GREAT REVUE.
HULLO TANKO
FAMOUS 'ALL STAR' CASTE,
BOSCH BEAUTY CHORUS
BOOK EARLY. PRICES AS USUAL.

Trench magazines offered a useful safety valve for pent-up feelings in a number of ways, of which one was that they offered an opportunity for the men in uniform to get back at the press, or rather those members of the press corps who chose to present the war as a glamorous adventure, in which the writer himself seemed to be playing a more heroic role than those doing the actual fighting. 'We all hate the War Correspondents far more than we hate the Germans,' wrote Lieutenant Chapman, already quoted, expressing a widespread view. 'For it is more blessed to be misled than to be misleading.' Among journalists who particularly attracted soldierly anger two names stood out: Horatio Bottomley of *John Bull* – mocked by one Canadian Field Ambulance magazine, the *N.Y.D.*, as 'Ratio Spottom-ley' – and (already mentioned in the previous chapter) William Beach Thomas of the *Daily Mail*. The editors of the *Somme-Times* and *B.E.F. Times* made much mockery of the latter, including in a number of editions a column by 'Our Special Correspondent Mr. Teech Bomas'. This is part of his alleged effort about the tank's contribution to the Somme battle:

> In the grey and purple light of a September morn they went over. Like great prehistoric monsters they leapt and skipped with joy when the signal came. It was my great good fortune to be a passenger on one of them . . . At last we were fairly in among the Huns. They were round us in millions and in millions they died. Every wag of our creature's tail threw a bomb with deadly precision, and then the mad muddled murderers melted. How to describe the joy with which our men joined the procession until we had a train ten miles long. Our creature then became in festive mood and, jumping two villages, came to rest in a crump-hole . . . Then with a wag of our tail (which accounted for 20 Huns) and some flaps with our fins on we went. With a triumphant snort we went through Bapaume pushing over the church in a playful moment and then steering a course for home, feeling that our perspiring, panting proglodomyte had thoroughly enjoyed its run over the disgruntled, discomfited, disembowelled earth. And so to rest in its lair ready for the morrow and what that morrow might hold. I must get back to the battle.
>
>   TEECH BOMAS

Numerous other such magazines functioned at this time, striking similar attitudes and employing the same kind of sharp-eyed wit. One outstanding member of the genre was the *Fifth Gloucester*

Gazette, sub-titled 'A Chronicle, serious and humorous, of the Battalion while serving with the British Expeditionary Force'. Launched soon after the 1/5th Gloucesters went to the Front as part of 48th Division in 1915, and including among its regular contributors the Gloucestershire poet F.W. Harvey, it took the shock of serious involvement in the fighting in its stride. And serious involvement it was. The Official History's account of the dawn attack of 23 July – the first day of what would become known as the Battle of Pozières Ridge – reveals that three Gloucestershire battalions suffered heavy casualties that morning, with the 1/6th being 'literally mown down', while the 1/4th and 1/5th 'fared little better'. The first page of the *Gazette*'s July edition – produced at the end of the month – began solemnly enough, with an editorial under the heading 'The Battle of the Somme' of which these were the key sentences:

> It was on the morning of Saturday July 1st, the memorable day of the great Infantry attack, that the last Number of the Gazette was placed in the hands of our readers . . .
>
> It was not indeed until the Battle of the Somme had entered upon its third week that our Brigade was called upon to attack and consolidate some German trenches. Eventually, after many gallant attempts, the objective was gained. But many of the old hands have shed their blood, many have made the supreme sacrifice, and we mourn the loss of many good comrades.
>
> It is then a Battalion somewhat bent and battered which publishes this Gazette . . .

Yet there was no lack of the usual buoyancy and good humour elsewhere in the edition. The same page printed an item entitled 'Examination Paper' in the best trench-magazine tradition, offered the following 'problems' for discussion:

> Describe briefly the increase in weight of a pack on a route march of 15 miles.
>
> Discuss in as few lines as possible the rise and fall of the bread ration.
>
> A munition worker works 5 hours a day, 5 days a week, and draws £5 pay per week. Compare the scale of pay of those who make shells with those who deliver them.

If parading at 4 a.m. with field operations ensuing until 9 p.m. comes under the heading of 'rest', describe your ideas as to how a *busy* day should be spent.

These questions voiced the standard gripes of the Poor Bloody Infantry – the PBI – at all times on the Western Front; the magazine's last page offered matter more specific to the battalion's current posting and experience, such as these items under the heading 'ADVERTISEMENTS/For Sale':

> Lot No 1. Fine Battalion: going for a Push.
> Lot No 2. Tired Major: going for a Whisky.
> Lot No 3. Big Push: going on for ever.

The edition concluded more seriously, however, with a section entitled 'R.I.P.', of which the final item was the well-known stanza from 'For the Fallen' by Lawrence Binyon, 'They shall grow not old,' – with, curiously, the final line slightly adapted, to the detriment of the poet's original intention and rhyme-scheme, to read: 'We will remember them in Christ.'

A similar mix of serious and comic appeared in the magazine's September issue. Although by then 48th Division had been withdrawn to a quieter sector, the Somme still dominated, even nudging into a light-hearted sequence of poetical definitions which included the following (trenches near Ovillers, it should be noted, had been the starting-off point for their attack):

A Dud. 'Full of sound and fury, signifying nothing' (Shakespeare)
The Leave Train. 'Thou still unravished bride of quietness,
                   Thou foster-child of silence and slow time.'
                   (Keats)
The Rum Ration. 'Rarely, rarely, comest thou,
                   Spirit of delight.' (Shelley)
Ovillers. 'Most loathsome, filthie, fowle and full of vile disdeyne'
            (Spencer)
The Ovillers Hun. 'A Damned, dancing, moist, most villainous
                    body.' (Dickens)

By contrast, a further front-page 'editorial' under the title 'The Battle of the Somme' offered this proud comment on their Division's contribution to the campaign, with a quotation from the speech before Agincourt in Shakespeare's *Henry V* by way of pay-off:

> The part which a single Division is called upon to play in such a Battle is not great, if measured by the actual frontage on which it operates. Nevertheless the 48th Division, our own Brigade, this Battalion, have done their bit in the Big Push. In years to come, their record, in common with that of other Divisions which operated on the La Boisselle, Ovillers and Pozières sectors, will be famous. The men of the 48th helped to make history.

> > 'And gentlemen in England now abed
> > Shall think themselves accurst they were not here.'

More personal to the battalion, a whole page was devoted to a poem in commemoration of one of its young officers, Second Lieutenant R.E. Knight DCM, who had died on 25 July of wounds received in the battalion's attack. Its author was Second Lieutenant F.W. Harvey, a close friend of the fallen officer who had himself by this time been posted missing; he would survive, however, as a prisoner of war. This was the first appearance of a poem which would be published later that same year in a volume of Harvey's work entitled, with distinct echoes of A.E. Housman, *A Gloucestershire Lad at Home and Abroad.* This is a deeply-felt poem of quality, which makes no concessions in terms of thought, style or diction:

IN MEMORIAM (R.E.K.)

> Dear, rash, warm-hearted friend.
> So careless of the end,
> So worldly-foolish, so divinely-wise,
> Who, caring not one jot
> For place, gave all you'd got
> To help your lesser fellow-men to rise.

> Swift-footed, fleeter yet
> Of heart. Swift to forget
> The petty spite that life or men could show you;
> Your last long race is won,
> But beyond the sound of gun
> You laugh and help men onward – if I know you.

> O still you laugh, and walk,
> And sing and frankly talk
> (To angels) of the matters that amused you
> In this bitter-sweet of life,
> And we who keep its strife
> Take comfort in the thought how God has used you.   F.W.H.

If as they clearly did trench magazines offered the opportunity for tilting against the system, on the other hand there is no denying that they also showed overall a feeling of strong support for the cause. *The Outpost*, the magazine of the 17th Highland Light Infantry, carried in its September 1916 edition, among the usual jokes and cartoons, a sturdy leading article celebrating the first anniversary of the Battle of Loos, the 'Somme' of 1915, seeing it one of several milestones in a general upward progress:

> When war broke out we talked glibly of the cause of Freedom, of Honour. We knew not the meaning of the words. But the story of the Dardanelles, of Mesopotamia, of Neuve Chapelle, of Loos, has charged our lives with a new significance and given new meaning to those high ideals. Thrown into the crucible of war, we have been tried, as by fire, and purged and sanctified by the rigours of our own emotions.
>
> All of which makes for good and for the final victory.

A similar message was carried by the Canadian magazine, *The Vics Patrol*, subtitled *The Active Service Journal of the Victoria Rifles of Canada*, in its 'Trench Edition' dated 25 December 1916. It included a poem with the upbeat title 'The New Spirit':

> How different from that long and dreary time
> Of warfare in the trenches, when the slime
> Of Flanders mud clung to our feet, and when
> Defensively we fought – raids now and then!
> But at the Somme the wind of victory blows
> Success our way, confusion to our foes . . .

Less grandly, the same story was implied in the magazine's humorous pages, which printed a number of 'Nursery Rhymes for the Kaiser's Grandchildren', among them this:

3. (Tune: How Doth the Little Busy Bee)
How doth the little busy tank
   Pursue its wobbling way.
It follows Fritzies by the yard –
   A pleasant bit of play.

To Fritz it is an awesome thing;
   He cries out in despair –
'Oh, mercy, Kamerad!' he yells,
   'This sort of thing's not fair.'

But the tank rolls on in chortling glee,
   And gobbles up the Huns;
It loves to enfilade a trench
   With rapid-firing guns.

Nursery rhymes also featured in the *5th Gloucester Gazette* in its February 1917 edition over the initials 'C.S.N'. Names of familiar and, sometimes, hard-fought-for places provided a standard challenge to the would-be versifier. C.S.N. tackled several, one of them being Martinpuich – known inevitably as 'Martinpush' to the Tommies. As in the case of the Canadian magazine, the message was clear: that the Germans had come second in the Somme battle, in that the Allied offensive had forced them back from their previously held positions:

M - R T - N P - S H

   Martin Luther was a Hun
      Many years ago.
Martin was a pushful man
      Many years ago,

   Martin's great great grandsons,
      Tried to do the same.
But the French and English,
      Spoiled his little game.

   Martin pushed, Tommy pushed
      Poilu lent his weight –
Martin's in another street,
      Singing songs of hate.

In the same edition 'W.O.D', (named in an earlier edition as Second Lieutenant W.O. Down), offered some 'Picardy Parodies', one of them a Somme variation of the hugely popular love song 'They wouldn't believe me', from the pre-war show 'Tonight's the Night'. A more sentimental, 'disenchanted' version, presumably of later vintage, was to become a high point of the 1960s stage show and film *Oh What a Lovely War*. In this somewhat caustic variant, the enemy appears not as the Hun, but as the Alleyman, from the French name for Germany, *Allemagne*. Again place names, if in one case adapted for the sake of rhyme, added the required dash of local colour:

> Got the cutest little trench,
> Which we undertook to wrench
> From the Alleyman one day,
> When the dawn was turning grey;
> Ah we gave those Boches hell,
> We were rather rough, I fear,
> From Ovillers to Poseer.

> For when they told us they wanted to give in,
>   They couldn't deceive us, they couldn't deceive us,
> And so with bombs and bayon*its*
> We made an end of poor old Fritz,
>   'Twas the bloodiest day that one could see.
> For when they told us, and they certainly tried to tell us,
> That they'd surrender if we would desist:
>   We wouldn't believe them, they wouldn't believe them,
> But wiped them off the German Army List.

Humour's great virtue was that it cocked a snook at the enemy, at the high-ups on your own side, at the press, at the public, at the war, at the whole situation. It was an assertion of a humanity which in this new industrialized, technological war could often seem hard to find. That point was made with some bitterness by the Australian signaller, Corporal Oswald Blows, writing in his diary at the time of the sacrificial Australian attacks on Pozières: 'The terrors of war are awful, and Britain is paying a terrible price in blood for the deserved peace. We can win, and we will. If it were man to man, we would

RESPONDING TO THE NATION'S CALL

Members of the 1/8th Royal Warwicks marching through Birmingham in the heady days
of the first months of the war. Their losses on the first day of the Somme would total 588;
25 officers and 563 other ranks.

WAITING FOR ZERO HOUR ON THE SOMME

The 16th Middlesex (also known as the Public Schools Battalion) assembling at 'White City' before
the opening attack. Their casualty toll on 1 July would be 522; 22 officers, 500 other ranks.

SOMME SUMMER
Heat and dust; Australian transport passing at speed through Bécourt Wood, near Albert, August 1916.

SOMME DEVASTATION
The site of the village of Guillemont, captured after severe fighting in early September.

SIR MUIRHEAD BONE

Two memorable elements of the Somme campaign, as recorded by the first official war artist, Sir Muirhead Bone.

Above: Amiens, the Picardy capital out of range of enemy guns where soldiers could find relief from the tension and stress of battle.

Below: Tanks, introduced into modern warfare on the Somme by the British in September 1916.

PREPARING FOR BATTLE

Canadian troops being given a final briefing before an attack, October 1916.

COMING OUT OF BATTLE

A still-frame from the film showing the remnants of the Hood Battalion of the 63rd (Royal Naval) Division after the capture of Beaucourt, Battle of the Ancre, November 1916. 'When we got back to Englebelmer we were cinematographed,' wrote Sub-Lieutenant Trevor Jacobs in a letter to his brother. 'I am marching alone as the second in command of my Coy, but I suppose my steel helmet and unshaven appearance will make me hard to recognise.' Jacobs is in the centre of the picture, glancing at the camera.

HUMANITY ON THE SOMME

Above: The YMCA stall at Mailly-Maillet, where Private Wrench saw a wounded Tommy offer coffee to the wounded German whom he had been helping back from the lines: 'Enemies an hour ago, but friends in their common troubles.' (*See Chapter 14.*)

Left: Enemy helping enemy in a scene very like the one witnessed by Private Wrench.

LIGHT RELIEF ON THE SOMME

Above: December 1916.
A signboard in Fonquevillers
advertising the 'Whizz Bangs',
the concert party of 5th Division.
Enjoyed by Private Appleyard (see
Chapter 2) one year earlier, they
were still going strong after the
Somme battle.

Right: Cover design for the Royal
Naval Division's Almanack for 1917.
They might have been fighting on
land, but they had not forgotten the
element on which they had enlisted
to fight. Happily – or otherwise –
the Somme region was not short of
aquatic reminders. From the papers
of Surgeon Lieutenant-Commander
W. J. McCracken.

SOMME 1917

Above: Deep winter; Australian soldiers looking at fresh graves in a cemetery between Albert and Bécordel.

Below: High summer; Wild flowers surround the wreckage of a Mark I Tank.

The Butte de Warlencourt

Above: In a painting by William Orpen in the summer of 1917, when the Butte, a hideous outcrop of white during the battle, 'looked beautiful . . . [and] shone out pale gold against the eastern sky.'

Below: Photographed in September 1917, with the dead ground of the old battlefield beyond, during a VIP visit; the visitor is Cabinet Minister Sir Edward Carson.

absolutely walk over them, but it's their Artillery, which Infantrymen cannot hit back at, and the cruel and apparently inexhaustible supply of shells, H.E.s of all sorts, which breaks up and demoralises a man, and cruelly maims thousands.'

Yet examples of humane treatment, man to man, even enemy to enemy, did take place. Charles Carrington, writing ten years after, added this postscript to an essay on the Gommecourt action:

> It is fair to record that the German troops engaged in this battle, so far from behaving with that brutality which has come to be associated with the name of German, showed an unusual mercy to the English wounded. At 9.45 p.m., 2/Lieut. Petley reported, a German medical officer stopped his men from firing to attend to the English wounded in No Man's Land. Next morning a German officer came out under a flag of truce and arranged a local armistice in order to get in the wounded in front of the Rangers' lines. Further to the south a German came out from his trenches in full daylight and rescued a wounded man of the London Scottish on July 3rd.
>
> The revival of the chivalrous procedure of old wars was misused in none of the three cases.
>
> The historian of the western front rarely has anything so pleasant to record.

On the first day of the Ancre battle, on 13 November, Private Arthur Wrench, 1/4th Seaforth Highlanders, noted another memorable example:

> Coming through Mailly, I saw a wounded kilty of the Argylls walking arm in arm with a wounded German and passing the coffee stall there. One man ran out with a cup of coffee which he handed to the Argyll. He in turn handed it to his stricken companion after which they limped on their way together smiling. Enemies an hour ago, but friends in their common troubles. After all, this war is not a personal affair. Else there would be no war.

CHAPTER FIFTEEN

'GERMANS GONE AWAY'

THE FORMAL END of the battle did not mean the end of the ordeal faced by troops on the Somme. Harassment of the enemy continued, if on a relatively small scale, so that the Germans should not be given the opportunity to assume that the Allies' aggressive aims had been entirely put on hold. There were occasional minor actions, to pinch out a salient or straighten a piece of line – fragments of unfinished business left over from the great battle. Meanwhile, conditions continued to deteriorate. As snow came and subsequently thawed, the battlefield melted to an impossible quagmire, while the state of the trenches reached such a pass that comparisons were being made with the war's first winter, by reputation a nadir period for squalor and misery on the Western Front.

Lieutenant Blackadder, of 151 Battery, Royal Garrison Artillery, had already anticipated this thought from his gun-lines at Beaumont Hamel in the build-up to the recent battle; another who now made the comparison was Captain Arthur Gibbs of the Welsh Guards. Writing on 23 November at the other end of the British line, near Le Transloy, he told his mother that their last spell at the front had given them 'a very good taste' of what the trenches must have been like at that time. He went on:

> We have had the hardest week that I have ever been through, and everything has been done under the worst possible conditions. The time that we spent in the front line was awful. It snowed all the first night, and then turned to rain, which continued until we were relieved. The result was that we were up to our ankles in half frozen slush, in the very best part of the trench! Some parts of the trench, along which we had to pass were up to our waists in the worst places (just wet mud!). We had 8 miles to march back

to camp, and our greatcoats had about 15 or 20 lbs of mud on them.

I managed to get the company out, with only one man falling out, but it was just like driving animals along: I had had very little sleep for 4 days, and I certainly fell asleep at least once on the march. I also went to sleep standing up in the trench at night. It was rather a tricky piece of line, and we didn't know what the Boche were going to do, so we all had to be awake all night.

By early December Lieutenant-Colonel Hyslop's 1/7th Argyll's had left Beaumont Hamel and were now in the extreme north-east of Fifth Army territory in the vicinity of Le Sars – not far from the notorious Butte de Warlencourt. They were occupying ground taken by the Canadians just a few days earlier:

It has not been properly consolidated and as the line is on the slope towards the enemy, it is difficult to work in by day. The weather has been very wet and the mud is unspeakable. There are no communication trenches and as the ground is a mass of shell holes, there is great difficulty in getting stores and material forward. In the dark fatigue parties lose their way and there have been many cases on both sides of men wandering into the opponents' trenches, indeed a whole platoon from the Brigade on our left disappeared in this way.

This was indeed to be a bitter winter, in which the level of hardship was such that at times, in some sectors at least, hostilities virtually ceased as on both sides men struggled merely to survive. Active warfare, indeed, could seem an irrelevance, an absurd excess of unnecessary enthusiasm. Thus Lieutenant A.A. Morris of the 1st Grenadier Guards, Guards Division, in his diary under the date 21 December: 'There is a lot of heavy gunfire up by Flers district. I wonder who are the keen soldiers fighting.'

Sergeant T.D. McCarthy's 2nd Irish Guards, also in Guards Division, spent much of December in trenches at Sailly-Saillesel, a former French area west of Le Transloy on the line of the Bapaume–Péronne road. He wrote in his tiny pocket diary of the 12th: 'The whole area is utterly desolate. West of Sailly rolling ground, the valleys running more or less E and W, a waste of mud with shell

holes touching one another. Here and there the charred stumps of
trees. Equipment, French and German, dotted the ground and rifles,
their muzzles planted in the mud, showed where at some attack
wounded men had lain. The village was just a mound of earth and
mud.'

Compounding all this was the cold and the endless rain. Hence his
comment on the following day, the 13th: 'Throughout, the contest is
far more a question of ourselves v. the weather than English against
Germans.' Out of trenches that night he added: 'The line was in a
very bad condition. The men were forced to move about almost
incessantly to avoid sticking in the mud. Many men were stuck for
hours. A man of the 2 G.G. [Grenadier Guards] whom we relieved
was stuck for 43 hrs and died afterwards.'

Back in the line on the 17th matters were, if anything, even worse
than before. The front trenches, he noted, were 'mere canals of mud
and water with here and there a habitable island. There was no
communication except over the top and that through a swamp of
foul smelling mud. The men worked day and night improving
drainage, etc.'

And there was something else – which McCarthy clearly found
rather discreditable – to record: 'The Grenadiers on going out had
reported to us that the Div on our right had been fraternizing with
the enemy. A Sgt was seen to go and meet a German and drink with
him. The case was reported and orders given to shoot anyone going
out.'

Next day, the 18th, he noted that the battalion they had relieved,
while they had stopped short of fraternization, had hardly been
pressing home the contest with the enemy; this was not a state of
affairs which the 2nd Irish Guards wished to condone: 'The collaps-
ing trenches which left both English and Germans exposed, very
nearly from the waist up should they move about at all by day, had
led to a certain amount of "live and let live" among the opposing
infantry. For a time there was no sniping from either side. We began
sniping, accounted for several Huns and this state of affairs ceased.'

They were back in the line again on the 23rd and were in their
trenches at Sailly on Christmas Day. Given the enemy-friendly
tendencies which had recently shown themselves, the possibility of

some kind of a Christmas truce might have occurred to some on both sides, but if this were so there appears to have been no attempt to arrange one. On the contrary, it was made abundantly clear in this sector at least that such goings-on were no longer to be considered part of the culture. Thus McCarthy's entry for Monday, 25 December: 'The Huns made no attempt to fraternise. All ranks were carefully warned to keep a good lookout. The artillery opened a terrific bombardment of their front line system the first thing in the morning and this evidently discouraged them if they had any desire for Peace and Goodwill. A German officer having apparently selected the top of his own front line parapet as a suitable point from which to sketch our trench was shot.'

Lieutenant A.A. Morris also noted the unmistakable disincentive provided by the Allied artillery: 'An organized bombardment at 8.30 and 11.30 to keep Fritz from fraternising, hope he enjoyed it!'

At the other end of the battlefield, however, near Beaumont Hamel, there was perhaps the faintest echo of the old spirit of Christmas goodwill, though without any suggestion of fraternization. Second Lieutenant Blackadder noted in his diary on Christmas Day: 'Very windy and spent at the Observation Post. It was rather interesting as the Germans could be seen moving about pretty freely and our men did not appear to interfere.'

Classically, during the Christmas truces of earlier years – especially the major fraternization of 1914 – an officer's defence for taking part had been that he had used the comparative calm to military advantage, to increase his knowledge as to the enemy's dispositions. Blackadder instinctively played the same card: 'It enabled me to pick up some doubtful points as to where their front line actually ran.'

* * *

For Lieutenant Charles Carrington, Christmas Day offered what he felt was a well deserved relaxation. He had been buoyant and optimistic through most of the campaign, but by the time it ended he was suffering from both mental and physical exhaustion. 'I think I've seen more of the Battle of the Somme than most,' he had written in a letter earlier that month. 'Major Alabaster MC my old Company Commander is the only officer who has seen more than me. There are only two NCOs and three men of my old platoon left. Now I'm on the look out for a soft job. I've had a year out here and six months on the Somme and my nerves aren't what they were. I can't live up to July 16th now though I've have just commanded a company for a fortnight in front of the Butte de Warlencourt.'

The 25th found him and his friends making the best of things at a seasonal celebration in Albert. He wrote to his mother on the 27th:

Christmas is over and we did well. I'm glad to say we had peace on Xmas Day though yesterday they shelled us with some very big stuff. Perhaps the menu of our Xmas Dinner might interest you:–

Asperges
Consommé Albert
Rissoles au Poisson
Dindon Anglais
Plum Pudding
Fromage
Dessert
Vins. Liqueurs. Café.

That looked very fine on a Xmas Card like the one I sent last week. With a Gramophone accompaniment and a decorated room it was a wonderful dinner.

Despite his six months in the area Carrington had scarcely seen Albert, though like everybody else he knew of the Basilica and its hanging statue. He was less moved by that, however, than by a curious relic of the lost world of peace which had been subjected to the savagery of war: 'There are some pathetic sights in this town. The Church is now famous. But I think what struck me most has been a circus caravan smashed by a shell, wrecked on a patch of grass where three streets meet. I can just picture the day, two years ago, when that circus was scattered.'

* * *

The new year saw no noticeable diminution of activity on the Somme front. If there was little actual fighting, there was plenty of other work to be done. Writing on 29 January 1917, Private Eric Blore (quoted in the Foreword, p. xxiii), recently arrived as a member of

No. 31 Kite Balloon Section, Royal Flying Corps, reported on the beehive world behind the British lines:

Today I took our section out for a march all along the iron roads. How busy everything is! Dumps of ammunition, dumps of food, dumps of wood, coal and coke, dumps of everything that saves life and destroys it. Even men in the dumps. Endless strings of horses who have done nothing to deserve any of it – that's what makes me so furious with war and Germany. Once a glittering batch of generals passed us all dressed up so I gave the 'eyes left!' of my life and fell into a passing shell hole. They flashed past like a savage's idea of god – all angry and omnipotent and expensive – *and* a cloud of dust.

There was no let-up either in the wintry conditions. Blore described some consequences of the extreme cold: 'This morning 16 degrees of frost were discovered by the authorities who take the trouble to issue the results of such research on pink paper each day. Anyway I awoke to find my sponge anchored like a coral reef while my outer blanket simply flew up like a sheet of roofing when I mobilised for ablutions. The balloon also is frozen to the ground thus precluding the possibility of my going up.'

Sergeant Bert Reeve, a regular in the Royal Field Artillery who had landed in France with 2nd Division in August 1914 and who had fought in a number of the early battles though not on the Somme, finally came there in late January 1917. Now with C Battery, 315th Brigade RFA, 63rd Division, he and his comrades found themselves near Aveluy in the Ancre Valley, housed, as he put it in his diary, 'in a lot of funny looking huts and shanties, on top of a hill overlooking the river'. It was a cold arrival. 'Got nearly refrigerated last night,' he stated on the 24th. 'Spent the day making our place a bit waterproof.'

A move to better accommodation provided welcome relief. Summing up his first weeks there he noted: 'We shifted into some dugouts vacated by the Royal Engineers; the one which the S.M. and myself occupied being fitted up quite luxuriously with flooring, matchboarded, beds, shelves and fireplace. We were glad of it as the weather conditions were extremely severe, everything being frozen solid.'

They had received some attention from the enemy – 'by way of excitement we got shelled occasionally and sometimes an aeroplane paid us a visit and left a few bombs' – but conditions were generally peaceable, so that there had been opportunity to do some exploring: 'I had a roam all over the battlefields of Thiepval and saw some gruesome sights. I fell over a skeleton of one of our officers in a dugout, and the ground was littered with half buried dead, both ours and Huns.'

Generally he saw this period of Somme duty as an unexciting time 'without a great deal of variation', but on Sunday 25 February his diary took on a somewhat different tone: 'Everyone seems to be wondering what is doing today. This on account of the Hun dropping back from his hitherto strongly held line at Miraumont and Serre. I went reconnoitring with the CO this afternoon and got through Beaumont Hamel, Grandcourt and Miraumont without a sign of the enemy except that he shelled the roads (what were previously) very heavily.'

A similar excitement was reflected in the diary of Lieutenant Blackadder, who was still in the vicinity of Beaumont Hamel. On the 24th he had noted: 'General Gough was in the area and the Infantry were massing in Ravines etc., preparatory to going up to the line. The Germans were very quiet.' Then:

> *25 February.* Great news came in late last night – the Germans have retired from our immediate front. The infantry were pushing forward and reconnoitring and officers were detailed from some batteries to go forward and reconnoitre for observation posts on the ridges in front of Puisieux. The Germans have carried this movement out under cover of the thick mist of the last week and it explains their silence yesterday and the presence of the General. During the day we had received instructions not to fire in certain areas – no doubt our patrols were pushing out yesterday.

Reeve and Blackadder were describing the first signs of a decision on the part of the Germans which would bring about a remarkable transformation of the situation on the Somme. The enemy was voluntarily giving ground, with a view to establishing themselves in new positions some twenty-five miles to the east of their latest defence line of 1916. The withdrawal would take some time to accomplish, with the abandonment of Serre, Miraumont, Warlencourt, Pys and Irles, on the front occupied by the British Fifth Army, as a first stage.

This new development inevitably produced an irresistible urge for sight-seeing of the newly vacated ground. Thus Lieutenant Blackadder on 26 February:

> It being a fine, clear and warm afternoon I went to Beaumont Hamel and with Dawes went on an expedition to explore the recently acquired territory. The Chaplain met us and accompanied us.
>
> We spent two hours going over the country well known to us on the map and on which we had often fired, and returned to Beaumont Hamel very tired. On the whole it was a depressing expedition, the desolation and sight of the dead lying about – the enemy too kept up a desultory fire of shrapnel but none came very close to us. It looks so hopeless to follow up with the heavy guns – the country is sodden and the roads are non-existent beyond Beaumont Hamel – the field guns, however, are pushing on.
>
> We have no definite news as to the enemy's line but patrols have reached Puisieux, and Serre and Miraumont have been vacated. But the Germans have left snipers behind so progress is slow.

On the 28th Blackadder reported another development, not insignificant in the light of events of the previous summer: 'Gommecourt has been evacuated – how the old Q.W.R. would like to learn of this! Here it was that they were practically wiped out on the 1st July.'

On 2 March he visited one of the most controversial landmarks created on that first day – the site of the Hawthorn Ridge mine, exploded at 7.20 a.m. on that fateful morning: 'I went to Beaumont Hamel to show an Officer the Signal Dugout and on my return journey came past the famous crater under the old German front line. This mine – reckoned to be the largest on our line – was sprung on the 1st July 1916 and did great havoc, the crater is fully 100 yards across. Unfortunately we did not get through this front till the 13th November.'

Having gone from the Fifth Army sector, it was only a matter of time before the Germans abandoned the Fourth Army area further south. Writing on 18 March, the Welsh Guards officer Captain Arthur Gibbs described the elation of a first visit to former enemy-held territory:

> This afternoon I walked out across what was No Man's Land a few days ago, into the Boche front line and beyond. It was one of the most cheering sights I have ever seen. I have never seen ground in such an awful state. Enormous shell holes filled with water, the earth flaked to powder everywhere by our shells. The old German front line is practically non-existent, so wet and battered about is it. I can't think how they lived in it at all. No wonder they have left it. I am convinced that they have gone back because our artillery have made it untenable for them. They are going back every day.

A later letter, from Halle near Péronne on 26 March, added a more sinister twist to the story of the Germans' retreat. It had not been headlong or carried out in disarray, but had been executed carefully, brutally and with much professional cunning:

> The Germans have left any number of booby traps behind, most of them intensely practical. They put a splendid helmet out, for somebody to pick up as a souvenir. Directly you touch it, off it goes, or rather the bomb inside does! You go down into a cellar, put your foot on a step, which sends off a mine. You sit down on a chair, and are blown out of it, sooner than you bargained for. And so on.
>
> There was a very frightening affair, just by one of our posts. There was a big barbed-wire barrier across the road, and several electric wires, running from it, quite inconspicuously, to half a dozen big shells by the road side. There was a dummy gun, too, by the shells. Naturally, we gave this a very wide berth, and scarcely dared breathe when we were near. We got an RE to cut the wires and take the thing to pieces, and the whole thing was a hoax. There was nothing to set off the shells, and the wires led to nowhere. How the Boche would have laughed if he could have seen us! In another place we found three empty coffins, labelled 'For Tommy'!

But at least the enemy had departed. Sergeant Bert Reeve would finally note their withdrawal along the whole of the Somme sector in his diary entry for 19 March with the simple message: 'Germans gone away.'

* * *

This was not quite how the Allies had envisaged a German exit from the Somme but his retreat could certainly be seen as, in its way, an Allied victory. 'The Somme battle is bearing fruit now, and was worth while after all,' wrote Lieutenant E.F. Chapman, 20th Royal Fusiliers, 33rd Division, in a letter home on 20 March, but he added that the situation needed to be put in careful perspective:

> The English newspapers have probably been very misleading. The Boche are not being driven back. They are retiring to a line which they have been preparing for months past, which will already be strongly wired, and will have splendid dugouts in it. We shall have to dig in afresh in front of this line. They will save 15–20 divisions by it. But we shall too, as our line will also be straightened. The thing to remember is that the Boche is retiring deliberately, in accordance with a plan. But nothing can alter the fact that all this advance is the biggest thing that has happened since the Marne. And it is tremendously encouraging.

* * *

Now places where every inch of territory had been fought for could be visited in peace – with the guns a distant echo beyond the horizon or, even, not heard at all. On the same day that Chapman wrote the above letter, 20 March, Captain Sir Iain Colquhoun of the 1st Scots Guards took a brief holiday from trench routine and returned to the scene of the Guards' attacks of six months before:

> Very cold windy day. All the companies are on road fatigue. At 10.15 Miles, Eric and I started for a walk around various interesting places. We first walked to Ginchy to see the old ground we attacked over on 15th September. It is a great gunner camp now, but the trenches still remain, and we were able to follow everything that had happened on that day. We found our old dugout, and the place where Mark was killed, and all the old places. From there we walked to Lesboeufs over the ground the Guards Division attacked on the 25th September. There are many unburied dead lying

beyond Lesboeufs. From there we walked to our own front line
facing Le Transloy. Le Transloy has only been evacuated by the
Germans in the last 3 days. We went all around the German
defences, then went into Transloy, which is a mass of ruins, and
ate our lunch there. The 53rd Australian Battn are holding this part
of the line, and are walking about exploding 'booby traps' etc.
After lunch walked through to the Bapaume Rd, walking along it
for half a mile. It has been blown up by the Germans, but is still a
good road. Branched off the road, and cut across country to our
old front line which we were in at Xmas time.

Got back 3.30 p.m. Very interesting walk. During the whole
time we never heard a gun fire. The whole thing seemed quite
unreal.

Some weeks later, on 1 May, Lieutenant Charles Carrington took
the opportunity to find the grave of his brother. He wrote to his
mother:

I got leave yesterday and rode over to Flers to see Chris's grave. I
can't say how or how far it was but it is a terribly desolate place
right in the centre of the Somme battlefield. It will be two or three
years before even the grass grows there again. He is buried on the
road from Flers to Delville Wood and Longueval in a little valley.
There is a little group of graves by the wayside so there is no fear
of its being forgotten. I found a big white cross with the plain
inscription: 'In Memory of Capt. C. Carrington, RNZA. Died of
Wounds Oct 8th 1916.' And a little painted fernleaf badge. The
cross was dirty and rather unsteady, so I cleaned it and fixed it up
and found some green turf to cover the grave with. I think it's
quite a good piece of work. It's a very lonely spot now that the
tide of war has passed on but might be quite a pleasant little dell
when the grass and the trees grow again.

I thought you would like to know that it is all in order. I tried
to find some flowers but there are none in Delville Wood this spring.

In fact, Carrington was unduly pessimistic about the prospects of
recovery of the former battlefield, which did not long remain a scene
of desolation. As in the case of most areas of deeply disturbed ground,
nature soon took control, cloaking the distortions caused by shell fire,
softening the harsh crusts of broken ground, and turning a mono-

chrome landscape into a blaze of wild colour. The war-artist William Orpen came there some weeks later and was much struck, and moved, by what he saw. He subsequently recorded the amazing transformation of the Somme country not only in his paintings, but also in a classic piece of description, of which this is a keynote paragraph:

> I had left it mud, nothing but water, shell holes and mud – the most gloomy, dreary abomination of desolation the mind could imagine; and now, in the summer of 1917, no words could express the beauty of it. The dreary, dismal mud was baked white and pure – dazzling white. White daisies, red poppies and a blue flower, great masses of them, stretched for miles and miles. The sky a pure dark blue, and the whole air, up to a height of about forty feet, thick with white butterflies: your clothes were covered with butterflies. . . . It was like an enchanted land. . . . Everything shimmered in the heat. Clothes, guns, all that had been left in confusion when the war passed on, had now been baked by the sun into one wonderful combination of colour – white, pale grey and pale gold.

Even that grim icon of the last agonizing weeks, that had glowered menacingly on the Tommies advancing with painful slowness towards it, had been miraculously transformed: 'The Butte de Warlencourt looked very beautiful in the afternoon light that summer. It shone out pale gold against the eastern sky, with the mangled remains of trees and houses, which was once Le Sars, on its left.'

Of course, that radiant transformation mantled a grim reality. On the British side alone 73,000 soldiers had gone missing beneath it, as well as countless relics, from shells to rifles and water-bottles, which would provide an annual 'iron harvest' for decades to come.

* * *

If in 1917 public interest in Britain and elsewhere was focused on other areas of the Western Front – Arras, Messines, Ypres and its Salient, Passchendaele – the Somme nevertheless continued to claim attention. It was not forgotten that 1 July marked the first anniversary of the opening of the great offensive. It was a Sunday that year and therefore provided a suitable occasion for memorial services. At St. Thomas' Church, Upshire, Essex, a service was held at 6.30 p.m. in memory of Second Lieutenant Jocelyn Buxton, 'and other men of

Upshire who have laid down their lives in the service of their King and Country'. Notably, the first page of the specially printed service booklet included, as well as appropriate verses from the Bible, an emotive couplet from A.E. Housman's immensely popular poem sequence *A Shropshire Lad*:

> They carry back bright to the coiner the mintage of man,
> The lads that will die in their glory and never be old.

Housman's poems were much set to music, and one distinguished young composer who had not only written a symphonic rhapsody under the title *A Shropshire Lad* but had also produced a song-cycle which included the poem from which the above couplet was taken, was George Butterworth, old Etonian, graduate of Trinity College, Oxford, Radley schoolmaster, mature student of the Royal College of Music – and, on the outbreak of war, eager volunteer under the influence of Kitchener's call to arms. He had himself fought in the 1916 battle as a Lieutenant of the Durham Light Infantry and had been killed in action near Pozières on 5 August at the age of thirty-one, being awarded a posthumous MC. The rhapsody, first performed at the Leeds Festival in 1913, was given its London première in the 1917 season of Henry Wood Promenade Concerts – this very fact a tribute to the potency of the memory of Battle of the Somme. On the following day *The Times* printed a moving comment by its music critic on the work – at that stage so 'modern' in style that he felt he had to plead for its audience not to come to too hasty a judgement: 'This is not the sort of music to like or dislike immediately at a single hearing, and one hopes that the orchestra will prosecute the acquaintance they have made with it, and give us another opportunity of realizing what it is we have lost in the composer's early death, and of remembering in what cause it was lost.'

Butterworth had been buried by his comrades in a marked grave but this subsequently was not found and so both his name and Buxton's would eventually appear on the Memorial to the Missing of the Somme at Thiepval.

* * *

In August 1917 Private Willie Robins of the South African Infantry Brigade left the Somme to spend ten days of leave in England. He visited relations in the Isle of Wight, where he had 'a splendid time; everybody was so kind to me and I was never a minute idle the whole time I was there'. He then travelled to the West of England to stay with an aunt in Devonport. On the 23rd, two days before returning to the Front, he wrote a long letter to his parents. He gave them a lively account of his leave, then, in an abrupt change of mood, told them what he thought and felt about the conduct and progress of the war. Away from the inhibitions imposed by Army censorship, he pulled no punches.

What might well have given edge to his views was the fact that in April, in the fighting near Arras, his younger brother Percy – back in France after recovering from the wound sustained during the attack on Delville Wood – had been killed. This had been a most grievous blow. A letter to his parents soon afterwards, in which he had described the circumstances of Percy's death and tried to offer some solace and comfort, had ended: 'As I read this through it seems very rough and crude for a letter of sympathy, but [you] will understand as nobody else how much I miss him and how true and deep my feelings are for you.' He had signed off: 'From your loving and sorrowing son.' What had compounded the family's grief at that time was the fact that Percy's body had not been recovered. Fortunately, Willie had been able to write some weeks later to state that it had been found and had been duly and properly interred. Also found had been Percy's personal effects, which he had had with him when he died. Willie had been allowed to look through them. 'They consisted,' he informed his parents, to whom they would eventually be sent, 'of his purse, pocket book, diary, photo album, the big one, and his little Bible. I'm sorry to say his wristlet watch wasn't among them and of course we can only draw our own conclusions as to how that disappeared. I am sorry that has gone as I know you would treasure it greatly. However, I think his wee Bible was dearer to him than anything else he had on him and because they were all he had on him and because they were his own treasures, I know they will be worth more than all the money in the world to you.'

This was, of course, a poor consolation for the death of a much loved brother at the age of nineteen, and that fact, plus, presumably, the growing feeling at that time that the new offensive of 1917, the Third Battle of Ypres, was producing the same mix of slow advance and massive casualties that had been the case on the Somme the previous year, no doubt contributed to his depressed state and helped to energize the remarkable outburst which now followed. But there is more to it than that; there is in this letter of 1917 a sense of anger and protest of a kind thought to be rare during the war itself – indeed generally seen as the stuff of a critical response to the war which would not be articulated until many years afterwards and which would therefore tend to be dismissed as the product of a fashionable revisionism or hindsight.

One important part of the equation, arguably, was Robins' country of origin. Soldiers from the then Empire – South Africans, Canadians, New Zealanders and, above all, Australians – were far more likely to look questioningly at the military practice and performance of the mother country than the native British. Independent rather than conformist, not immediately convinced by outward show, they were prone to view the hierarchical world of the Western Front with a certain scepticism. Robins, brought up to think seriously of the ways of man and God and of the meaning and purpose of life, would certainly expect to make his own judgements, however lowly his rank; and however young his age – when he wrote this letter he was twenty-one. He began by anticipating his parents' inevitable question as to where he had been serving:

I expect you will be wondering what part of France I was in before leaving. Well, I left the Regt. in the trenches on the 11th. We are on the Bapaume front and we are holding the village of Trescault. We do 8 days in and 8 days out and so far have found it a very quiet spot. Of course we are on the scene of this year's retirement and a desolate scene it is; every village is an absolute heap of dust; just wanton and unnecessary destruction wherever you go and I couldn't describe to you the awful desolation and devastation caused by the Huns in France.

It is my firm belief now that this war will never end by fighting. Britain has got to find the man who can equal Hindenburg. Any man can do what Haig is doing now with the amount of material and men at his disposal. The British high command badly wants reorganizing. They are nothing but a lot of mugs with titles, money and whisky, but no brains. Some of them have never been so well off in their lives before. Goodness knows what they are going to do after the war. Just the bulldog pluck and perseverance of the ordinary British Tommy is keeping the British Army where it is and of course the Red Tabs take the credit and the poor old British Tommy is taking his life in his hand and going through hell every day while those rotters sit 20 miles behind the line and sip their whisky and take all the credit and congratulations and CBs and KCMGs etc. It is a mere game of ping pong and the Infantryman of today is nothing but sure cannon fodder. There are thousands of lives being thrown away every day that Britain can ill afford and I am convinced that so surely as Britain has been guilty of so many muddles so surely has she been guilty of many lost opportunities of bringing this war to an end. Myself I wouldn't be surprised if the war were to end next month; and again I wouldn't be surprised if it didn't end for another year or two. Both sides are in a much worse condition than they will admit and I think the end will come as suddenly as the beginning.

Russia has lost the only chance we had of winning the war by fighting, I'm sure. Still, I suppose we must just hope on for the best of it.

There would be worse to come as 1917 went on. Apart from the brief hope inspired by the successful but unexploited tank attack at Cambrai, the year ended gloomily, with Russia out of the war entirely following the Bolshevik revolution, America not yet fully active in it, and, with the exception of the capture of Jerusalem, little apparent achievement to celebrate after three and a half years of effort on the Allied side. More, as 1918 began there was a growing suspicion that the Germans might well be preparing to make one further great effort on the Western Front, where by general consent the most likely target area was – as if it had not had enough hard history already – the region of the Somme.

CHAPTER SIXTEEN

THE SOMME 1918:
THE RETREAT

THE NEW YEAR 1918 found Private Willie Robins back on the Somme, and 'as fit and cheery as a fiddle'. As compared to the situation in 1916 the area was markedly peaceful. 'We are still resting,' he wrote to his parents on 14 February, 'and having a fairly quiet time I am glad to say.' He and his South African comrades took advantage of the lull to visit the scene of their baptism of fire of some eighteen months before:

> We are going to Delville Wood on Sunday to hold a Memorial Service for the boys who fell there. There is nothing left of the wood but a stump here and there and practically the only way it can be recognized is by the numerous little wooden crosses, simple and plain with just the bare inscription 'Unknown South African Soldier', and of several other units who were engaged there. Of course there are a lot of graves of men identified but there are a terrible lot unknown. Taffy has made a nice cross for Joe Ford's grave and I expect will be taking it down himself to the cemetery though of course Joe was buried in a different spot a couple of miles from Delville.
>
> The good weather still continues and you bet we are making the best of it.

Robins was aware that the Germans were thought to be planning a major effort on the Western Front but made light of the prospect: 'The papers seem to be very restless over the much talked of German offensive, but, by gum, when he does come he'll get a rough house and more than he bargained for. Our people know too much of his "stunt" to be caught napping.'

Indeed, expectations of a major push by the Germans had been rife since the beginning of the year. Bombardier Dudley Gyngell, a clerk in 2nd Section of the Light Divisional Artillery Company, Royal Field Artillery, had noted in his diary as early as 21 January: 'We are standing by in expectation of plenty of aerial raiding if the weather breaks at all. I hope it keeps bad! We are also waiting for and marking time on Fritz's big offensive expected on the 27th (Kaiser's birthday).'

The 27th had gone by, however, with no Western Front birthday present to the Kaiser from his generals. Indeed, as the weeks passed, for Gyngell, based at the railhead town of Corbie, life seemed increasingly stable and relaxed. He was certainly busy – 'we get a good many "drafts"' up here and it takes me all my time checking them in, taking particulars and posting them to Sections' – but there were good compensations: '*15th March*. I have found an Estaminet about ½ hrs walk from here, where we can get quite good beer for the French – also quite a decent little girl attends to you. Shall come here again when I find time.'

The 18th found him in an exceptionally cheerful mood:

Awoke this morning to a glorious sunshine and blue sky with fleecy white clouds. Although bearing very many signs of the strife, this place seems pretty peaceful and rather holiday-like. I fancied however that I heard a distant rumbling, but I must have been mistaken.

It is funny how we look forward to finishing our work and 'poshing' ourselves up to go out in the evening – just to wander round the queer little streets, bounded by quaint houses and farms with the fields beyond – or to drop into an Estaminet and meet the boys or try to carry on a flirtation in broken French with the Estaminet wench – strange days – interesting days – heroic days – I trust I may never lose the freshness of their memory.

Gyngell was billeted with an elderly French widower with whom he had struck up a very friendly relationship, and who had even shared close family secrets with him, of a wife dying before her time and a son who had hanged himself over a broken marriage. He noted on the 19th:

I am sitting at my window looking out into the garden. It is a wonderful morning of bright sunshine and golden shadows.

The old Frenchman is tending his flowers.

He came to the window. '*Bonjour, monsieur*, I have picked you some violets to send to your sweetheart', and he handed me a fragrant little bunch.

I wonder what his memories are on this morning and whether he thinks of his wife and his son and the time when he was as young as I.

Suddenly an ominous sound vibrated through the air – the German guns. The villagers gathered in the streets and listened with questioning faces. It is a sound they have not heard for months.

There was a jingle of spurs in the tiled hall and Shirley my orderly hurried in.

'Pack up at once and stand by to move.'

Next day they were 'up and away at daybreak. With the rattle of harness and wagons, the bark of orders and the hundred small sounds connected with a column we moved off.' Their route took them to the north east, towards the old battlefields of the Somme, 'which may perhaps wake again to the bursting of shells, and the rattle of machine-guns.' The journey soon offered a sharp contrast to the pastoral landscapes they had just left: 'Nothing but desolate wastes – villages wiped out and now the ruins all overgrown with grass until it was barely possible to see any trace – roads all churned up – slush and brick dust – old barbed wire – old dugouts – broken wagons – pieces of rifles – shattered tree stumps – wooden crosses with here and there a rifle or a helmet hanging on them – now and again a roadside crucifix marvellously intact.'

This grim territory, however, was not the focus of the present crisis: 'The great excitement has left here and been pushed forward, so on we go and leave this dead land behind. I don't really know how we feel – whether we want to go on into it or stop back here and feel out of it. I think there is "a something" that makes you want to be in the thick of things, where things matter and you know something of what is going on.'

Knowing something of what was going on, however, was a luxury denied to many on the following day when the great German attack of Thursday 21 March – 'Operation Michael' – was launched with a massive bombardment of high explosive and gas shells and under a cloak of fog. Two British Armies faced the Germans, the Third more securely dug in to the north, the Fifth only recently established to the south, less well entrenched and covering a larger area of ground. On a huge frontage from Arras to St Quentin the Germans forced their way through, and within hours the British defenders were either dying, surrendering, or in full retreat. In places whole units ceased to exist. The Third Army was severely pressed and forced to yield some ground, while the Fifth Army was sent back largely in disarray. In the words of the official historian: 'Rendered blind by fog, overwhelmed by one of the most violent bombardments of the war, General Gough's eleven divisions, weak from reduction in infantry and from lack of reinforcements, were driven out of indifferent entrenchments, recently taken over from the French, by the attack of two German Armies, with 22 divisions in the front line and 22 in support.'

Private Maurice Gower was a signaller of the 16th Battalion of the Rifle Brigade in 39th Division, Fifth Army. He wrote to a sister several weeks later, on 4 May:

> Since the 21st March things have been very uncertain out here and we have been moved and shunted about all along the line at a moment's notice. We did the big Somme retirement from start to finish, we were almost surrounded three times and had several awkward moments, but nevertheless I managed to come out with nothing worse than a sore heel and entire loss of my kit; the latter I believe being burnt to prevent it falling into the hands of the enemy.

'The big Somme retirement': in the hurried retreat following the German attack, the ground seized with such tenacity and heroism in 1916 was retaken in a matter of days. Landmarks gained at a cost of many lives were picked up by the advancing Germans virtually on the run. In an earlier, though undated letter to another sister (in which there was no mention of places and scant reference to dates), Gower had conveyed something of the confusion in which what became known as the 'March Retreat' began. He was not in the front line, having therefore a higher chance of surviving to tell his tale:

> On the morning of the 21st we were gassed and shelled out of our billets, one shell landing in the midst of our headquarters, killing our signalling sergeant and several others besides wounding several, also shells were bursting all round our huts. Several men in my hut were wounded, some only a few yards from me. We had been expecting a big German offensive to start any minute and anticipated the shelling of our billets, our orders were to get out as best we could and collect some short distance back. This was carried out in fairly good order, the men keeping remarkably cool under the circumstances. We had to leave everything only taking our fighting order, outside it was dark and thick with mist and gas. I got clear of the village as soon as I could fortunately running into no heavy shelling. I managed to get lost soon after and had to make my way thro' two belts of barbed wire, men were shouting and calling all over the place. I actually met my company commander and CO sitting in a trench and men gradually began to collect.

They spent an oddly inactive day lying about in the fields listening to the guns, though expecting to move at any moment. At nightfall the men were issued with shovels and, moving forward, began digging trenches not far behind their original line. There was much uncertainty as to what exactly was happening: 'There seemed to be some doubt at the time where we were actually facing.' They worked on all night, sustained by tea and hot stew brought from the battalion cookers. 'I had the job of taking back the empty dishes and had to walk about two miles to find the cookers. When I returned it was nearly daylight, but the mist still hung about. I had to squeeze in the trench somehow.'

Later the mist cleared and 'Boche' aeroplanes began to fly over their lines, British planes being 'conspicuous by their absence'. Later still there were signs of activity to their front, which turned out to be a counter-attack by a British brigade; however, 'everything seemed confusion to me and I could not make head or tail of what was going on'. They were soon under heavy shell fire, which kept them well down in the trenches. At last they received some instructions:

A message came down about getting ready to move shortly, which way it did not say. Soon afterwards the order came to move and men started to clear out of the trenches making for the wood at the back. I was the last out of my trench. As soon as I got out I found we were under concentrated machine-gun fire which seemed to come from all directions. Men were falling all round but no help could be rendered as it was a case of every man for himself. How I got away unscathed I cannot say, bullets seemed to strike the very ground under my feet as I ran. I took advantage of every available cover which was very little. I plodded up the hill and over the ridge which meant safety from machine-gun fire, but the shells were following up quickly. No instructions had been given as to where we had to go, but I sighted our 'acting' Sergeant-Major (our old S.M. having been wounded the previous morning) and attached myself to him. We could do nothing at the moment as everyone had scattered and we had only narrowly escaped being cut off as it was, a large number had been captured including the Padre and several officers and headquarters staff.

A group of about twenty got together and, after further delays and confusions, set off about 3 a.m. the next morning to try to find their Brigade headquarters. At one point they came across a deserted camp. 'We managed to find some stray rations and were just trying to boil some water to make tea, when one man came in saying that he had sighted the enemy coming over the ridge.' Tea was abandoned and the retreat went on.

Gower's adventures continued in like manner over several more days. Eventually they found the remains of their battalion, but this was not the end of their wanderings: 'Since then we have been marching about all over Northern France, at the present moment we are near the front again. We are in a very curious predicament, I don't know how exactly I stand, we are all split up and attached to different divisions.'

His later letter revealed something of the casualty toll resulting from the March attack: 'My company has suffered pretty severely and a good many of the old hands will not return.'

* * *

Even on the Fifth Army front, however, the story was far from one of universal defeat. The Germans also suffered heavily in the March Retreat and so high a casualty list was not brought about by soldiers running away. Major C.J. (Joe) Rice, in 1916 a lieutenant in 84th Brigade RFA in 18th Division (see page 140), was now commander of 82nd Brigade in the same division, which as usual was giving a good account of itself – though it was no longer under the command of the redoubtable Maxse. Rice's letters at this time speak of setbacks, but not only to the British. Having been away reconnoitring reserve artillery positions, he was not with his unit when the Germans struck. He wrote on 22 March: 'My captain who was running the battery for me was killed, also another major, who was attached to divisional artillery headquarters, and I and two others are the surviving battery commanders out of 8. But all the batteries did magnificent work, fairly mowing the Boche down, frequently with direct laying, and with rifles as well.'

Private Cude of the 7th Buffs, in the same division, shared Rice's satisfaction at the damage inflicted on the advancing enemy, morale being all the better in his immediate circle for his having despatched three runners (presumably junior to him in experience if not in rank) to loot a canteen which had been hurriedly evacuated, 'leaving a huge stock of eatables and everything that we could need': 'They return loaded with cigarettes, biscuits and a bottle or two of whisky. All for nothing. This is the stuff to give the troops.'

The division also, in Cude's view, had the stuff to give the Germans:

> The whole of the line attacked, and so fierce and unsuspected the attack, that Jerry was taken off his guard. He was lucky to have a few men get away. I have never seen such a glorious attack, and the chaps not only took the village, but 500 yards the other side as well. No quarter was given, and even the wounded were finished off, as it should be too, for we are without food ourselves, and if prisoners are taken, it means that they have to be fed. 1 Prisoner only was taken, and this was a badly wounded man, who was speedily packed off down the line.

※   ※   ※

Among the casualties of the early days of the March attack was the South African Private Willie Robins. He was killed on the 23rd near Péronne, in the former French sector. A letter to his father from one of his friends, David Boyce, explained the circumstances:

He fell fighting a rear guard action with the Regt. A large shell burst near him, four or five were wounded, and Willie and another boy were killed. A piece of shell entered Willie's head causing instant death. Both he and the other boy were buried together in one grave, near where they fell.

A better boy never walked this earth, believe me Mr. Robins. All the time he was with us no ungentlemanly word ever passed his lips and his heart was as clean the day he died as when he left his home. Everyone loved him and he was ever ready to do some service for others. We were in constant touch with each other and often confided our heart thoughts in the quiet of the night when sleep was impossible. Home was ever uppermost in his thoughts and often we would look at his little collection of photos which were constantly arriving in his letters and we would talk of home for hours.

Boyce added a gloomy comment on the fate of the South Africans in the recent fighting: 'We were wiped out as a Brigade, having come through without any officers (only one) and only a handful of men; many will return with wounds healed before long, but the papers will tell you the losses.'

Subsequently the Robins parents had memorial cards printed to commemorate both their sons, including in each case an extract from the famous hymn of the Scottish divine George Matheson, 'O Love that wilt not let me go.' For Willie, described as 'Loving and Loyal; Faithful unto Death', the slightly adapted lines ('We' for Matheson's 'I') read:

> We trace the rainbow through the rain,
> And feel the promise is not vain
> That morn shall tearless be.

For Percy, described as 'Loving, Chivalrous, Noble and Brave', they adapted more boldly; instead of 'My heart restores its borrowed ray,/That in thy sunshine's blaze its day . . .', they wrote:

> Our hearts restore their borrowed ray
> That in Thy sunshine's blaze his day
> May richer, fuller be.

They added their own special message. For Willie: 'Farewell brave heart and true, till death us join.' For Percy: 'In bitter grief we yield him now to meet him with joy in the morning.' The adventure which had begun so buoyantly in far-off South Africa and which had suffered its first tragedy on the outskirts of Arras had come to its unhappy conclusion on a by-road on the Somme.

* * *

Corporal Morris Lee, of the 16th Divisional Signal Company, Royal Engineers, had been working as an Assistant Lecturer at the Divisional Signal School when the German offensive began. At 12.30 a.m. on the morning of the 23rd he was roused in his billet and ordered to report to the Orderly Room. A telegram had been received at the school ordering all personnel, instructors and pupils, to prepare to move at a moment's notice. Shortly after 9 a.m., in a fleet of buses, charabancs and lorries, a motley force of reinforcements was on its way eastwards towards 'an unknown destination'. 'For nine solid hours we bumped along the dusty roads in a never ending procession,' Lee recalled, in an account written for his family in April, 'first of all passing through villages and towns untouched by war, evidently well back from the war zone. As light began to fade, however, we again began to pass huts, dumps, ammunition etc., etc., and the other signs of war. Gradually we entered a flat, desolate area with ruined villages dotted here and there, and finally, as moonlight took the place of twilight, we found ourselves again within sound of the guns while the weird flashes of the Very lights over No Man's Land showed that things were "moving".' The buses – in which they had been confined for so many hours with only a small portion of cold meat and vegetables for each man but with nothing to drink – at last stopped and the men 'fell in' awaiting orders to march.

They soon found themselves part of a solid mass of men and transport 'pressing on and on – not knowing where we were or where we were going.' Exhausted, loaded with equipment, they trudged through one ruined village after another, each of them 'looking ghostly and sinister in the moonlight'. Shells bursting on a ridge to their left showed the close presence of the enemy. 'If a shell had burst anywhere on that road that night it would have exacted a fearful toll.'

It seemed as if there would be no end to their ordeal:

Now men began to fall out, exhausted with their loads, and for want of food and drink. One began to realise that there is a limit to human endurance. I felt a little light-headed. I remember the lines of a hymn kept running in my head 'Death would be to slumber in that fond embrace' – Death would be to slumber! slumber! – Oh blessed word!!! We stumble on till at last a halt is called. On the left of the plain is the battle, intense and vivid artillery fire is visible and audible. We are told that we are stopping in this field for the night, and in this field we lie down just as we are – rifles by our side, overcoats and blankets over us and over all the sky. For sheer fatigue we sleep, to wake in the morning covered with white frost and with feet numb with cold.

Daylight showed that they were on the outskirts of a ruined village – 'we can only conjecture where'. After a breakfast of tea and biscuits they moved on to yet another equally devastated village, where they would remain for the rest of the day.

The one outstanding fact seems to us to be – there is no water! At last the news comes that there *is* a well of fairly pure water about a kilometre away. It is the only supply, apparently, for miles so everybody – cooks included – have to go to this. Standing in the queue to fill my water bottle – from 2.15 p.m. to 4.15 p.m. on that Sunday afternoon – I wonder a little whether it is worse to wait for 'margarine' or sugar, than it is for a drink of water!

And yet some people at home grumble.

Later he and a friend went for a walk around the village to find 'not a house standing, just heaps of bricks and stones, little bits of wall – and so on'. Yet to their surprise the place was not quite empty; a handful of villagers, driven out in 1916, had returned and were living in wooden houses erected in the midst of the ruins of their former homes.

Outside one of these houses a young girl sat reading. We asked whether they sold 'coffee?' Yes ('*oui*') – so we walked in. We found the only inhabitants of the house were the girl and her father, an old man of about 70.

Their story is typical no doubt of thousands of others, so I will briefly describe it.

Their home was ruined and their farm laid waste in 1916. The daughter escaped to friends but the old man was taken prisoner by the Germans. Released (in exchange) by the Germans a short while ago, the old man yearned to get back to their old home, ruined as it was, and had a wooden hut erected in what was the garden of his old house, and lived there with his daughter.

They had only been installed there eight days when we saw them – and they were expecting (on account of the German advance) to have to evacuate again! The daughter was a brave little soul (about 22) and they were evidently quite a good class of people. The remains of their old house showed that it was formerly quite a smart affair – steps up to the door, stone doorways, etc. The girl told me (in French of course) that the village had been quite a large one with many big houses. I asked – Where is the church? She took me to the door of the hut and pointing to a certain quarter she said, '*Regardez l'église!*' ('Behold the church').

Just a heap of stones and mortar remained of what she assured me was formerly a fine church with a high tower.

All the time I was talking to her, and her father, my eyes were misty and I felt a lump in my throat – it was so tragic a tale.

I wonder where they are now – certainly not where I saw them on Palm Sunday evening!

Lee had hoped for a good night's rest after the travails of the previous thirty-six hours, but he returned to camp to find he had been detailed to undertake night duty as NCO in charge of the Signals Office: 'Gradually during the night it was evident that something serious was happening. Urgent messages followed one after another reporting retirement all along the line on our flanks, and we could see by looking at the maps that the enemy was rapidly advancing towards us.'

At 7 a.m. the Signal Office staff was relieved; they were ordered to wait for a lorry that would be sent to collect them and their equipment. They were to be there for many hours, at the side of a main road Lee described as 'one of the main channels of the British retirement'. All day long a constant tide of transport wagons and guns moved one way, while from the other direction came 'a tremendous column of artillery to get into action to protect the rearguard'. The sight of this column of artillerymen, all totally exhausted, having travelled three nights and days without sleep, as well as having been in action, affected Lee profoundly:

> I never took a 'glorified' view of war, and the dead and wounded I have seen, and desolation, have made me hate war more than ever, but nothing I have yet seen has sickened me more with the whole thing than the sight of those artillerymen thick with dust and nearly dead with fatigue. Strong fine-looking men were half doubled in their saddles – at a halt you would see many actually nod with sleep – eyes sunken, lips cracked, suffering, and without that merciful oblivion which comes to the wounded.

The expected lorry did not arrive until nine the following morning. Their departure along the crowded road took place under the scrutiny of the occupants of three German observation balloons, which meant that they would very soon be under enemy shell fire. 'Sure enough presently the shells started coming over, now one side of the road, then the other. It was impossible to move quickly on account of the traffic – so we simply had to "stick it" – not knowing where the next shell would drop.'

* * *

On Monday 25 March, Bombardier Gyngell's artillery column, making its way back from the front, reached Albert. On the Sunday, retreating across the virtual centre of the British part of the 1916 battlefield, they had experienced what seemed at the time a most unfortunate delay. 'At Martinpuich we lost one of the limbers and stopped at Pozières while an NCO went to find it.' Writing up his diary a day or so later, however, Gyngell added: 'This no doubt was our salvation.'

His diary entry for 25 March explains this statement. They had spent the night of the 24th camped uneasily at Pozières and were harnessed and away before daybreak. Then:

> We moved silently along while the pale dawn gradually streaked the sky – past the places of desolation and silence until at about 7 a.m. we arrived on the outskirts of Albert and saw what we had missed. Each side of the road dead Tommies had been piled – it was quite a shambles – I remember noticing a signet ring on the dead white hand of one fellow and wondering who and where his people were, and thinking that if we had not lost our wagon it might have been me.
>
> The streets were littered with dead horses, broken limbers and men lying face down on the pavements just as they had fallen.
>
> Further on past a café that had been wrecked by a bomb we came across some of the remaining civilians – packing up whatever they could lay their hands on – panic stricken.
>
> We are now mixed up in an endless stream of refugees – old barrows, carts etc., packed with the available belongings of the refugees – girls, children, old men, girls wheeling old women in wheelbarrows. We give whatever assistance we can, whenever we can, but are met with abuse and curses on nearly every side for letting the Huns come through.
>
> The whole day we were on the move like this, shells coming over occasionally – food rather difficult, and am getting very dirty.
>
> Towards dusk we arrived at the remains of a village with a good many houses fairly undamaged.

* * *

That same day, in a surge across the whole front, the Germans in the south forced the British out of positions they were holding on the Somme Canal, while in the north German troops reached the Ancre in the vicinity of Beaumont Hamel. On the following day, the 26th, they seized Albert.

For those in positions of command, this onward march of the enemy presented other problems than those associated with the successful management of withdrawal. Their background and training, their whole basic attitude, demanded that they should use every endeavour to stiffen resistance, to block the enemy's progress, to disabuse him of the assumption that this was merely a walk-over. So much is clear from the brief diary, covering the period 21–27 March, of Lieutenant-Colonel M.V.B. Hill, CO of the 9th Battalion Royal Sussex Regiment, in 24th Division, Fifth Army. Written in a London Hospital on 4 April after Hill was wounded, this is not a military report; though displaying throughout the hallmarks of a senior officer describing events in strictly professional terms, it nevertheless admits, engagingly, to normal human frailty. However, its prevailing thrust is unambiguous: that he had done as much as he humanly could to stem the haemorrhage in his sector of the Fifth Army front. The following is from his account of 27 March, when the battalion was at Templeux, just east of Péronne. (Doubtless for security's sake, he did not identify his unit, referring to it as 'A Battn, No. 3 Brigade, Z Division', while other battalions were named simply 'B' and 'C' while the adjacent division became 'V'):

Again tea and rations were successfully brought up during the night. My heels were now so sore and my Achilles tendon so stiff that I could only walk about 1 mile an hour – so I rested nearly the whole night. Although I did not get much sleep, my feet next morning were much better.

9.0 a.m. Heard once more that barking of the enemy machine-guns which now only meant one thing – 'Our men withdrawing' – I rushed out of the gun pit which had been our Headquarters for the night, and saw troops withdrawing in large numbers about ¾ mile on our left, and also small units passed our very door. O.C. 'B' Battalion and myself got to our men in Front Line and told them we were all going to stay whoever went. There appeared to be no infantry attack and the situation was soon restored.

10.15 a.m. Boche got into trench held by details of 'V' Division on L'Estrange's right and started bombing him. They also got a machine-gun into position from which it could enfilade his trench. After spending a great deal of SAA [small arms ammunition] and putting up a very good fight, he was compelled to withdraw to the left, having suffered a large number of casualties from the machine-gun which got bullets right into the trench. They accordingly withdrew across the road which ran through the middle of our line.

Lieut Smith established a block which I saw him guarding with his section. I got Company Sergt-Major Head to make another block further back, and put B Company into the trench running at right L's to Front Line. Then went to see 'C' Battalion and explained position to them and told Captain Stratton – who with another Company was in close support to me – the situation and showed him some landmarks to guide him in case he should have to counter-attack. I then heard once again the machine-guns barking and saw the troops all moving left handed some of them out of the trench. I immediately got the other Company of 'C' battalion to advance at the 'High Port' towards them – with the result that the troops rallied at once. All thanks to this Company of 'C' Battalion. Then I rushed on to First Line and along top of trench to get our men to charge the Boche who had not advanced as far as I thought – when I stopped a bullet from the left. Fell down about 10 yards behind the parapet where Coy. Sergt-Major Head tied up my arm very well so that it did not have to be touched until I got almost to Abbeville. I noticed B Company were still in their trench and am curious to know what happened after.

Hill's papers give no indication of what happened after, but basically what undoubtedly transpired was further retreat. Yet the German attack was beginning to lose its impact. Though Albert had fallen to the enemy, the greater prize of Amiens remained inviolate. 'Operation Michael' – also known as the *Kaiserschlacht*, the Kaiser's Battle; aptly, because this was virtually his last throw – finally came to a halt on 5 April, nine miles short of the Picardy capital. It cost the British 163,493 casualties in sixteen days. The French lost 77,000. The German figure equalled that of the Allies' overall total.

The battle also produced a key development on the Allied side when in a conference on 26 March at Doullens – on the very edge of the territory of the offensive – unity of command was established, with the French General (later Marshal) Foch being appointed, if not quite generalissimo as such a title would be understood in the Second World War, as supreme co-ordinator of Allied efforts on the Western Front. This was done with the full, indeed decisive, support of Field Marshal Haig, for whom clarity and cohesion in the direction of the war in this decisive stage was far more important than the assertion of any national pride.

The offensive could now be seen as offering definite advantages. Major Rice wrote on 12 April: 'It is a good thing that all this fighting has taken place because it is the only way of finishing the war. In spite of the great numbers of the Boche he hasn't got a strategical breakthrough yet and he has certainly used his full force. The ground gained down south means nothing to the Boche provided we are not *routed*.'

Rice's judgement was premature in one respect in that the enemy had not used his full force – indeed, three days before Rice was writing a second major offensive had opened to the north in the area of the Franco-Belgian border. But he was certainly correct in the matter of the lack of breakthrough by the enemy and of the importance of the Allies' not being 'routed'. Ludendorff sub-sequently launched several other offensives, all of which followed the same scenario of shock attack, initial success, ultimate failure. Famously, in the words of Field Marshal Haig, the British had their 'backs to the wall' at one particularly dangerous moment in April, but the line did not break and the enemy's march was halted. At that moment, it could be said, the outcome of the war was assured.

That much fought-over territory, the Somme, had been a crucible once more, if briefly so, with the tide of war moving west. It would be a crucible yet again a few months later, but now the tide would move eastwards, and this would be the final surge.

A notable gesture of defiance, or perhaps of promise of vengeance to come, took place in mid-April. Albert now being in the hands of the Germans, the British were not inclined to allow them the capacity for observation provided by its most notable feature, the tall tower of the basilica of Notre Dame de Brebières. At 3.30 p.m. on 16 April, the 35th Divisional Artillery shelled it with pinpoint accuracy; their third shot brought it crashing down, complete with the statue of the Madonna and Child. Anyone hoping for a miraculous cessation of hostilities, however, would have no cause for rejoicing. Yet, with hindsight, it might be said that the superstition was not entirely misplaced, for if the war was not halted immediately, it would nevertheless reach its dramatic, even sudden, conclusion before the year was out.

CHAPTER SEVENTEEN

THE SOMME 1918:
THE ADVANCE

IF 1 JULY 1916 was a bad day for the British, 8 August 1918 was certainly a bad day for the enemy – and was fully acknowledged as such by General Ludendorff. 'August 8th was the black day of the German Army in the history of the war,' he would write in his memoirs. 'Our war machine was no longer efficient. Our fighting power had suffered, even though the great majority of divisions still fought heroically. The 8th of August put the decline of that fighting power beyond all doubt . . .'

The British Fourth Army and the French First Army launched the offensive which produced this remarkable result. They did so from a starting point some twenty miles behind that from which the 'big push' had been launched two years earlier. In other ways, however, the Allies were far ahead of the situation of 1916. This was not just a matter of German decline; the enemy was outfought by a force which was far more sophisticated in its technical expertise, far better organized, far better led, with a more expert and experienced staff, than that which he had so forcibly repelled two years earlier.

Then the British had been lavish with manpower, but since then manpower had become less easy to come by – it was no self-renewing cruse of oil, not after four years of high-casualty fighting, which had had the typesetters of *The Times* printing so many thousands of names over so many months. They now, however, were rich in fire power, on a scale unimaginable heretofore, and in the means of delivering that fire power with accuracy and skill. A range of technical developments – including sound-ranging, flash spotting, better aerial photography, better maps – meant better use of their better resources. Better tanks were available too, a Mark V, faster, with larger fuel tanks, with increased protection for fuel and crew, and above all far less prone to breakdown than its vulnerable predecessor of Flers-Courcelette, September 1916.

The Allies also had another weapon: surprise. No longer would the prospect of a major push be the worst-kept secret in France. General Sir Henry Rawlinson was now back in command of Fourth Army and his first 'General Instructions' for the coming battle had 'Secrecy' as its first subject, ahead of all others from artillery matters and communications to the role of the Royal Air Force or the mission of the cavalry. Silence was mandated on all troops as a matter of instruction. Fourth Army put this in the simplest terms; its unequivocal message was: 'KEEP YOUR MOUTH SHUT'. A printed notice with this heading was issued to all ranks of all arms and services and ordered to be printed in the 'small book' – in effect a passport of identity – that was carried by every officer and man. Among its key sentences were these:

> The success of any operation we carry out depends chiefly on surprise.
>
> DO NOT TALK. When you know that your unit is making preparations for an attack, don't talk about them to men in other units, or to strangers, and keep your mouth shut, especially in public places.
>
> Don't be inquisitive about what other units are doing; if you hear or see anything, keep it to yourself.
>
> If you hear anyone else talking about operations, stop him at once.
>
> The success of the operations and the lives of your Comrades depends upon your SILENCE.
>
> If you ever should have the misfortune to be taken prisoner, don't give the enemy any information beyond your rank and name. In answer to all other questions, you need only say, 'I cannot answer'.
>
> He cannot compel you to give any other information. He may use threats. He will respect you if your courage, patriotism, and self-control do not fail. Every word you say may cause the death of one of your comrades.

Nor was distribution of this notice confined to the troops in the battle zone; Lieutenant Clifford Carter, newly back from Britain at this time, preserved a copy with his wartime papers, noting that it was issued to all ranks arriving at the training camp at Etaples.

Moreover, there was no question of marching over the top in full daylight on a midsummer morning, presenting perfect targets for the enemy's machine gunners. The hour chosen was 4.20 a.m. and the decision to attack on the 8th was not made until the 6th. (As if in proof of the concept that the gods help those who help themselves, fog would be provided for the start of the attack – as it had been provided for the Germans for theirs on 21 March.)

Field Marshal Haig had been deputed by Foch to command both the armies involved, British and French. 'I am pleased that Foch should have entrusted me with the direction of these operations', was his laconic, if confident, comment. The force assembling on the Somme plateau in the last days before the battle was multi-national in other ways, too. Crucial to the plan was the deployment of the Canadian Corps and the Australian Corps. Their track record was such that they were widely acknowledged as élite troops much unloved by the enemy; they would uphold that reputation in the coming action. This would take its name from the Picardy capital – though its start-line was Villers-Bretonneux, fifteen miles to the east – and the *official* dates of the Battle of Amiens would comprise the four days from 8 to 11 August. In the event, the offensive would continue more or less steadily for the next hundred days.

Private Cecil Penny, formerly a stretcher-bearer but now a Lewis gunner, took part in the battle as a member of the 58th Battalion, 15th Brigade, 5th Australian Division. He had been much involved on the Western Front since the Australians' first blooding at Fromelles in July 1916. In July the following year, in hospital in England recovering from scabies, he had seen a report in a newspaper to the effect that he had been awarded a Distinguished Conduct Medal. He had subsequently received the award from King George V himself at Aldershot, the home town of the British Army.

Shortly before the opening of the Amiens battle, Penny returned to his unit after ten days ('a very enjoyable holiday') at a rest camp at Le Tréport on the Picardy coast. Three days later they marched to

Montières near Amiens: 'We were told we should be here ten days. The first day we practised an attack with tanks, and on the evening of the second day we had orders to pack up our kits and we marched out through Amiens towards Villers Bretonneux. We arrived nr. Brett about 3 a.m. the following night.'

This sudden change in orders was not the result of any official confusion; it was a crucial part of a complicated deception plan, the purpose of which was to move the various elements of the Allied force into position without the enemy's knowledge. Most risky of all was the switch of Canadian divisions from Flanders, a move aided by another trick-card available in 1918: dummy radio-traffic elsewhere combined with radio silence in the Somme battle zone itself.

Penny's diary account continues (his timing differs from that of the official reports by one hour):

On the night of Aug 7th we massed for attack in a trench behind the front line – and at 5.20 the barrage opened and the 2nd Div. went over the top in a thick mist together with many tanks. At 6.30 58th Batt, 15th Bde attacked. We overtook the 2nd Div, near Bayonvillers and started the second stage of the attack, reaching Harbonnières with very few casualties – but a large amount of prisoners, estimated at 8,000 and many guns. The Aust Light Horse took part in this attack. We occupied the old 1916 French Line that evening.

Penny's claim was slightly exaggerated; the Australian historian would state that the point reached was 'the old outer line of the Amiens defence system, very little short of the old Somme battlefield of 1916'. But by any standards the Australians' achievement had been a remarkable one. The Canadians, who had advanced side by side with them in the centre of the attack, made similar progress. The British III Corps on the left, which had had to fight off a German attack two days previously, and the French on the right did not have quite the same success, but they had also contributed in good measure to what Ludendorff would admit was the 'the greatest defeat which the German Army had suffered since the beginning of the war'. Haig noted in his diary that 'the situation had developed more favourably for us than, optimist though I am, I had dared to hope.'

At the humble level of a signaller in the Royal Engineers, David Doe, writing that evening, endorsed these judgements of the high and mighty in his pocket diary: 'Most successful day we have had so far in 4 years. Little opposition. Cavly, tanks and armoured cars going well. Enemy blowing up for miles behind his lines.'

His account of the day includes a minor detail of a kind which rarely finds its way into official reports or histories, and which perhaps only a signaller working a telephone during the battle might be able to confirm: 'One tank comdr on phone said he had surprised a German corps genl staff at dinner.'

* * *

Lieutenant-Colonel C.H. Ommanney commanded 83rd Brigade, Royal Field Artillery, in the Battle of Amiens and the subsequent campaign. His battery was part of 18th Division, which was again to have important business on the Somme. It was now in III Corps, Fourth Army. Its course of advance would take it directly across the old battlefield of 1916. He recorded the opening of the action:

> Thursday August 8. Zero hour 4.20 a.m. Everything very quiet up to then. The whole country quickly covered with dense smoke and mist – can see nothing – just like a thick London fog!
>
> The battle fluctuated a good deal during the day, but finally we ended up just this side of our final objective. We were firing pretty continuously all day, the enemy not replying much.
>
> Haybittel, Hopkins, 4 other officers and about 60 other ranks of A and B Batteries suffering so badly from gas that they had to be evacuated. The DAC [Divisional Ammunition Column] came nobly to the rescue and sent us every officer they could spare.
>
> In the afternoon I walked round the forward area to 55 Inf Bde HQ – Saw the beginning of a Boche counter attack, which I don't think achieved anything, and visited some of the Batteries on the way back.

Next day the Brigade was again in action – feeling its way forward towards the former billet villages of the old Somme battle-front: 'At 5.30 p.m. we attacked Morlancourt and the high ground North of it. The attack was a brilliant success, the Boche hardly fighting at all. The fleeing *soldaten* gave us magnificent targets of which full advantage was taken, and we captured and slew many. Our shells got right amongst them and did some excellent slaughter. By 7 p.m. the whole position was won and we settled down to a protective barrage.'

Ommanney had fought in the 1916 battle and was well acquainted with the territory which they were now approaching. Over the following days well-known names from those now ancient days would appear in his diary with increasing frequency:

Wednesday Aug 14. We hear tales of the Boche going back at all sorts of places. Today it is at Puisieux and Serre. It is a little difficult to understand the situation and what his intentions are. Is he going right back to the Hindenburg Line or merely trying to leave us in the wet valleys and Somme battlefield for the winter? One cannot but think that he will make a very violent reaction somewhere shortly and that perhaps his withdrawals are merely intended to secure good jumping-off places for a great counter-offensive. But time will no doubt show.

Sunday Aug 18. A beautifully clear day with a nice fresh breeze. One could see for miles over Thiepval and Pozières way. I spent some time gazing through a telescope and spotted a German How[itzer] shooting from near Contalmaison. Reported it, but have not so far seen it fired on.

On 25 August he was again expressing his anxiety about the enemy's intentions: 'Expect he hopes to be able to settle down in the Hindenburg Line again for the winter. Let us only push him hard and he should have no chance of settling down anywhere. Meanwhile we have to get across the awful desolation of the Somme battlefield over which we are looking now at the old familiar landmarks – Bécourt, Boisselle, Fricourt, Mametz Wood and the Pozières Windmill.'

* * *

In terms of general awareness, there has only ever been one Battle of the Somme. The devisers of the official Battle Nomenclature would propose the title 'The Second Battles of the Somme' (plural) for the period from 21 August to 3 September 1918, to include by way of subheadings the 'Battle of Albert', from 21 to 23 August, and the 'Second Battle of Bapaume', from 31 August to 3 September.

However, as the Official History would acknowledge, 'the Somme title for 1918 has never come into use, being reserved for 1916'. French usage would appear to differ, in that the famous Michelin Guides give the name of 'The Second Battle of the Somme' (singular) to all the 1918 battles in the Picardy area. For those who fought in the field, however, such official labels, whether attached then or later, were of little interest or consequence. They knew where they were, the more so if they had been there before and had good cause to remember their earlier experiences. Captain Lionel Ferguson was one such returnee. Wounded in July 1916 and despatched home, he was now back in France, participating in the general move eastwards which had begun on 8 August and was currently flowing over the battlefield of 1916.

In practice, Ferguson would not actually set foot on the former battle ground at this time, his division's line of advance being just along its northern perimeter, from Bucquoy on the Albert–Arras road towards Achiet-le-Petit and Bapaume. Nevertheless he would unhesitatingly claim 'Somme 1918' as one of his personal battle honours – together with La Bassée in 1917, Italy 1917–18, and the Nieppe Forest earlier in 1918 – when he wrote up his diary, with certain important letters also included, in a handsome bound volume after the war. In fact, the two Somme campaigns, 1916 and 1918, would begin and end his military career.

He had left the scene two years earlier not only wounded but also dismayed, by an attack which he had seen as badly conceived and ill-prepared. Now, however, writing on 28 August 1918, there was a different tone to his description. In a letter to his parents, he stated enthusiastically: 'We have just had four days of the finest hunting a man could wish for, now thank goodness it is all over for us, till we can get up reinforcements, which may perhaps be some 10 days or more: by then I hope to have worked my Paris leave.'

The attack in which he had fought had been launched on the 21st, the first day of the Battle of Albert. Formerly with the 13th Cheshires, he was now with the 1st Battalion, in 15th Brigade, 5th Division, Third Army. Attacking in fog and guided by six tanks the Brigade had seized Achiet-le-Petit by about 8.30 a.m. after some resistance. 'Though on leaving the village, the fog suddenly lifted and machine-gun fire was received, the 1/Cheshire and 16 R/Warwick-shire pressed on, reached the [Arras–Albert] railway line, and about 9.30 a.m. gained a footing in the third objective on the high ground over a thousand yards beyond, reporting their success by pigeon.' Thus the Official Historian; Ferguson's letter offers a more mixed scenario. It had been far from plain sailing, the Boche had given them 'Merry Hell', there had been very many casualties: 'We could do nothing for them, poor fellows, for it was now neck or nothing and we had no stretchers. I was in a blue funk of being captured, but I killed a number of Huns who got in my way. I can't describe to you the excitement, I felt that I had about 3 tons on each foot, and my strength nearly gave out.' However the tide had turned, they had received 'big praise' from their superiors, and a further assault next day on the 22nd had pushed the Germans firmly back. The gains were consolidated:

We are still on the same ground today, as we fought over, [he was writing a week later] but what a change. Our guns have all passed us. Observation balloons go up from what less than a week ago was a raging battlefield. The Arras–Albert Railway is now in full swing, fresh troops arrive by train. I do think it is the beginning of the end. The first Hun I captured asked me 'if it was our "big push", for in that case the war would finish in a month'. I only hope it may be true.

Today I have been exploring tracks around Bapaume, which town he [the enemy] still holds, but we are not running up against a wall this trip, and are going forward on either side of the town, till we starve him out. I hope I have not tired you with my tale of blood, but it has been interesting to me. I hope to get my Paris leave on 9th Sept. It is now likely to come off, as the B-G [Brigadier-General] will grant me all I want at the moment, the application went forward yesterday. I shall enjoy the rest, as I have had no hot meal for over a week, or a wash, as water is scarce.

* * *

'Got settled down just S.E. of Albert,' wrote Lieutenant-Colonel Ommanney on the 26th. At 1 p.m. he received an order to report to the Bécourt Chateau – whose savaging by enemy artillery Private

Cude had deplored in 1915 and where the Grimsby Chums had had their Headquarters in the countdown to 1 July. He set off at once, arriving there about 2.30:

> Very curious riding over all this country where I was in 16. We have knocked Bécourt and its pretty woods about dreadfully now and it can hardly be recognized as the same place.
>
> Saw Colonel Seymour there and got orders to reconnoitre positions near Mametz, so went off at once through Fricourt, which is almost invisible now, and found positions on the N edge of Mametz and just N of Fricourt Wood. I to work in concert with GOC 5th Inf Bde and to live near his HQ which is on the Fricourt-Contalmaison road.
>
> Went there and introduced myself and then set about looking for a home. Could find nothing except some old trenches and holes near the Willow Copse on top of the hill above Fricourt Farm. Into these we eventually got and spent a rather disturbed night, Hamilton and I sleeping in one hole which was just about big enough for ourselves and our kit and no more. And the dew of heaven dripped through on us.

And so forward. Montauban, Trônes Wood, Caterpillar Valley, Guillemont, Combles; and by 1 September Ommanney was recording the seizure of Morval, Rancourt and Sailly-Saillisel – the furthest point of the 1916 advance. Beyond that lay territory outside the Somme country, including the Hindenburg Line (to be broken with something approaching panache by the Division which had fared so badly at Gommecourt in July 1916, the 46th North Midland); while beyond that again lay the occupied land – *le pays envahi* – held by the Germans since 1914, which would be liberated to scenes of joyous celebration in the weeks leading to the Armistice of 11 November 1918. But before that date there would be much hard fighting.

* * *

'Not running up against a wall this trip'; Ferguson's comment of 28 August had shown the confidence of troops who, after so many setbacks, were at last sensing the possibility of victory. Such confidence was, however, no guarantee of a disaster-free advance. Describing his charmed life under a hail of shell fire in the 21 August attack, Ferguson had claimed that 'the bit with my name on it was "spent".' But on 2 September his battalion was rushed into another attack, on the second day of the Battle for Bapaume, and this time the outcome was less benign. Transcribing into his diary after the war the letter he had written to his wife on 4 September 1916, he headed it: 'Another letter telling why my Paris leave did not come off.' He wrote it from 'No 2. General Hospital, B.E.F.'

On 1 September he had been in high good humour, believing that his company was about to be relieved and that his eagerly anticipated trip to Paris was 'a dead cert', when he had had orders to report to the transport lines. He walked over to Battalion Headquarters 'to find orders for an attack had come in, also that the dump personnel would not be up in time for the exchange. It was a bitter blow, not only for me, but for the many other officers, NCOs and men who were also for a rest.' The fact of the attack was bad enough; worse was the nature of the task – the kind of hurried, under-prepared effort which it was widely assumed, or hoped, was no longer to be thrown into a battalion's lap with next to no notice:

It was then 5 p.m. and we had to take up positions at 8 p.m., everything being a huge rush to get all settled and in order; in fact I was much against the show as we had never seen the ground we had to go over, also everybody expected relief as we are long overdue for rest. Zero hour was 5.15 a.m. next morning (2nd Sept). Up we went into the most awful trench, in some places as flat as the ground outside. The night was pitch dark, and all night long E/As [Enemy Aircraft] flew up and down the line, plugging us with tons of bombs, but luckily these did small damage to us. Our own barrage was due to start at 5.15 a.m., we having to advance at that hour. The Hun showed signs all night of being wide awake and when the 5 a.m. barrage on our right and left opened, he put down everything he could, direct on to our trench, HE, shrapnel, Gas and burning oil were all identified by yours truly. We suffered heavy loss and the only thing to be done was to rush forward and hope not to be caught by our own barrage. I called to my men to follow me, as I was the front company, and those who were left did so, but I had only just got on top, when a shell came and

finished off all my Company HQ, killing my signal man and
runner, wounding my CSM Smith, myself and a number of others.
I dropped back into a hole and hoped for the best, not quite
knowing what part of me was hit, and wondering if I was killed or
not. I knew I was not bad and thought it best to wait till the Hun
barrage stopped.

I must have sat in that alarming position for over an hour,
covered with other people's blood as well as my own, also getting
buried many times by the dirt of the numerous shells. The gas was
also bad. I eventually ventured out, but could see nothing but dead
and wounded, but many Huns were dropping into our trench. I
was getting ready to kill them, when I discovered from them that
they were prisoners, and had been sent back, so I showed them the
way down. I met the CO after walking about a mile and reported
to him the situation. I also thought it was about time he came
forward, but it was as usual. He was very sorry to see me hit and
shook hands and thanked me for my good work in the past. I then
went to the dressing station only to find it empty and the MO
gone (forward I hope). I saw Groves who is acting Adjutant (also
well out of the fight), this Gentleman is working a DSO for himself
and was at least 1½ miles back. So I walked on, seeing many
prisoners and wounded. I called on Brigade HQ and had a cup of
tea with the General who was interested in what I had to tell him.
We also got a report whilst I was there, that the village we had set
out to take, had been captured. This it appears was half true, but
we soon had to fall back, not having enough men to hold it. I
pushed on, finding a car to take me to a dressing station. It
belonged I think to the 62nd Division, but after attention I met a
good Padre who took me to breakfast and I rested for about an
hour, as no ambulances put in an appearance. I started to walk to a
Field Ambulance Station, at last getting a lift on a limber and in
time found a FAS. I met here another officer of the battalion and
we got put on a lorry for the central clearing FA at Gomiécourt. I
got a good fresh dressing here, and again took lorry for a spot
some way back that had a light railway. Cup of tea, bit of bread,
more lorry, more light railway, and about 6 p.m. a CCS [Casualty
Clearing Station] at Frévent. Then a good wash, feed, another
dressing and turned into a stretcher case. The hospital train left
about 10 p.m., so after a good sleep found myself at Abbeville in

the morning. At once saw an MO and was put under the X-ray. I was then operated on to have the wound in my leg cleaned and stitched, knowing nothing more till 3 p.m. when I came round in a nice and very cosy bed, with a ticket marked for England by the first train.

* * *

Lieutenant-Colonel Ommanney's 83rd Brigade came out from the front on 7 September, and on the 9th with three other officers he set off for a 'joy-ride in the RA car':

We had a very pleasant run to Doullens and had lunch there, bought a few things, and then went on to Abbeville, where I had never been before. It is a beautiful town, rather badly knocked about by bombing but not so much as one has been led to expect.

We had a very cheery time, had dinner at the Hotel de France and drove home afterwards, arriving at 12.15 a.m.

A very pleasant day and quite delightful to get back to civilization and unshelled country again.

On the following morning, there was a visit by the Corps Commander, General Godley – 'he was very pleased and congratulated everybody, especially C Battery' – and in the afternoon, since it was raining hard, Ommanney passed the time writing letters and doing office work.

Later he went out alone, for what would become, in effect, a valediction to the country of the Somme:

After tea walked over to Bazentin-le-Grand and had a look at High Wood and the old never-to-be-forgotten spots of 1916. I must go back there again if I have a chance and have a close look at my old positions. Today I failed to locate accurately my old O.P. on the Bazentin ridge. The trench along the top, in which it was, used to be a deep narrow revetted work, with fire steps, deep dugouts and everything complete. It was in fact the Boche 2nd line of defence which we captured on July 14 1916. It is now a thistle-grown shallow depression in which it is impossible to distinguish one particular spot, such as my O.P. was, from another. It leads one to hope that, such is the effect of nature, when the blasted trees have been cut down and a few houses built upon the land, the awful wilderness of the Somme battlefield will have regained some of the beauty of which the damnable war has robbed it – though there will always be the innumerable graves with their wooden crosses to remind us of the sacrifices which have been so gallantly made on this, the greatest of all battlefields.

So the fighting moved away from the Somme, after more than four years in which part of the region had been under harsh and repressive occupation, and during which the guns had rarely ceased to fire or the lists of casualties to increase.

Some weeks later as part of a relatively new operation called the 'Trouville Convoy', a unit of lady nurses based in Le Havre drove through the area in search of wounded, with a view to evacuating them from the casualty clearing stations to stationary hospitals far from the battle zone. On their return their senior member, Dorothy Seymour, recorded their findings in her diary: '*October 20th*. Cars got back late last night. Went without hitch – after passing Amiens, roads beautiful but no sign of a soul or a habitation. Albert and Bapaume and Cambrai flat and absolutely silent. No trees only short stumps and the whole war so passed on that no noise even of guns to be heard and no star shells to be seen.'

This peace would not be indefinite, for war would come again to the Somme a generation later, when in May–June 1940 Hitler's *Wehrmacht* swept through en route to a stunning victory which gave the Germans the extra fillip of a defeat avenged. It would then return in August–September 1944 when the Allies – in particular the British – fought their way eastwards through Amiens to the Franco-Belgian border as part of the great advance which would force the Germans back into their heartland; a feat which had not been achieved when Armistice put an end to the fighting in 1918. Yet compared with the campaigns of the First World War these were brief encounters with history; they would only, as it were, add a bar to the battle honours of the Somme of 1916 and 1918 – especially 1916.

*   *   *

'The greatest of all battlefields': it is an arresting phrase, and, despite rival claims that might be made for Verdun or Passchendaele (the popular name for the Third Battle of Ypres), one that was arguably very true when Lieutenant-Colonel Ommanney coined it in September 1918. The Second World War might offer other competitors such as Stalingrad or Normandy, while students of later wars might suggest Vietnam or the Iran–Iraq war of 1980–88. Yet in some ways the phrase still holds, for the Somme – and not only in British eyes – has come to stand for a kind of ultimate in modern warfare, and has therefore been adopted as a convenient metaphor for tenacious and sacrificial conflicts in areas far removed from the military. Thus the comment *'It's like the Somme!'* can convey an immediate and powerful meaning when applied to a whole range of situations, from a fierce dialogue between varying schools of intellectual thought or a hard-hitting parliamentary debate, to a no-holds-barred election campaign, a blood-on-the carpet board meeting, a brutal take-over battle, a management-union negotiation in some smoke-filled-room, even a stormy personal relationship or a failing marriage. A landscape of a particular war, 'the Somme' has become a landscape of the mind, a context ready and available in which to locate any high-risk, attritional struggle. Indeed, it has become part of the twentieth-century's vocabulary and of its heritage. Since it shows no sign even after eighty years of losing its potency there is every prospect that it will also be part of the twenty-first's.

CHAPTER EIGHTEEN

A PLACE OF LONG MEMORY

THE SOMME has for many years been a focus of pilgrimage. This was largely, of course, a product of the peace, which at last allowed free rein to an inevitable curiosity about a region which for so long had fascinated the public imagination. It also gave opportunity to those who wished to do so, and could afford the necessary time and money, to visit the area where relatives or friends had died. The railway and coach companies of Picardy saw rich touristic possibilities in this rising tide of interest, and were organizing battlefield visits to the Somme, and other war zones such as the Aisne, the Chemin des Dames and Verdun, soon after the fighting was over. The Michelin Company produced well-written and illustrated guides with accompanying road maps, beginning with the territory of the Marne and working their way through all the major sectors of France and Belgium, while Michelin Touring Offices offered information and advice from smart addresses both in Paris and London.

This was not the start of the process, however; there had been pilgrim visits while hostilities were still in progress and the Somme had much history still to come.

On 11 March 1918, ten days before the opening of the great German offensive, Colonel, Honorary Brigadier-General, W.R. Ludlow, former commanding officer of the 1/8th Battalion of the Royal Warwickshire Regiment, came to the Somme to look for the grave of his son. This was Captain Stratford Ludlow of the same battalion, who had gone into battle on 1 July as commander of C Company and was known to have been killed in action. As described in Chapter 4 (pages 72–3), the 1/8th Royal Warwicks, together with its sister battalion the 1/6th – 48th Division units temporarily attached to 4th Division – had taken part in the attack just south of Serre, towards the northern end of the Fourth Army Sector. With its high loss figure of 25 officers and 563 men – a total of 588 – it stands eighth in the list of battalions which suffered more than 500 casualties on the first day on the Somme.

After staying overnight in Amiens, Brigadier-General Ludlow, accompanied by an interpreter, left for Albert on a train packed with French women and children who were returning to their homes in Péronne. Arrived at Albert, where the statue of the Virgin and Child still hung above the devastated streets, he sought out the British military authorities. From the account of his journey which he subsequently had printed for private circulation later that year, it is evident that the work of reburying and commemorating the fallen of the Somme was already making substantial progress, even though much remained to be done:

> The corps headquarters placed every facility for my inspection on explaining my errand and showing the sketch of the spot where my son fell, and we were at once furnished with large-scale maps showing the line of the British and Hun trenches as they existed in 1916. From there we went to the Graves Registration Department and discussed the matter thoroughly with the officers in charge, who showed us maps on the wall over which they worked, covering a distance of about 18 miles long and 20 miles wide. This was shaded off into different areas showing the battle areas that had been cleared and the number of graves identified. It did not include the Serre and Beaumont Hamel areas and a good many others, but they had already located many thousand graves and made a large number of cemeteries.

Offered the assistance of a guide and a motor-car, they made their way beyond an area of normal cultivation to the old battlefield of Beaumont Hamel, Serre, Auchonvillers, Hébuterne, Fonquevillers and Gommecourt – 'only names upon the map,' Ludlow noted, 'as there is nothing to denote that they had ever been occupied as human habitation'. He particularly wanted to find Serre; having located it – no easy task since only the outside walls of a few houses remained standing – he worked his way back along the road to the point where it was crossed by the old British line of 1916:

The country was a complete waste, a series of rolling plains covered with thick coarse brown grass, every tree, hedge and pollard had disappeared, and only mounds covered with grass showed where villages had been. A few cabbages or broccoli struggled through the matted surface, and stumps of apple trees denoted what had once been gardens and flourishing orchards. The trenches were grown over or had fallen in, or filled with water in places, while the whole area was a mass of old shell holes. The high road from Mailly-Maillet was like a bright ribbon winding up and down the slopes, but every tree which formerly bordered it had vanished. It was here that the 8th Battalion consolidated the fourth line German trench. Several of the officers, including my son, were seen shouting out to their men, 'That's our objective,' smoking cigarettes, and waving them on.

The whole area had been so badly shelled, both in 1916 and during the 1917 withdrawal, that movement about was extremely difficult, while everywhere could be seen the pathetic detritus of war:

This part of the field had not been fully explored, and here and there one came across piles of equipment, coats and tunics, rusty rifles, bayonets and frogs, bully beef tins not opened, shells, hand grenades, and boxes of Mills bombs unopened, and all the usual debris of the battlefield. Along the line occupied by the 11th Brigade there were the remains of Huns' skulls, and bones, and shrapnel helmets, in all directions. A number of officers' tin hats were lying about, and one grave with a cross upon it and no inscription, had a tin hat attached to it. One grave was marked by a harrow, but the majority of them were hidden by the tall rank grass or were destroyed by subsequent shell fire.

The forerunner of many thousands who would come in later years to try and imagine the events of the first day of the great battle, Ludlow studied the terrain and found his mind filling with doubts and questions:

I sat on the edge of a shell hole opposite to the German position in No Man's Land, and I wondered how it was possible that any troops in the world could attack such a position in broad daylight on a lovely July morning. From careful investigation it was obvious that the wire had not been completely destroyed. There was not sufficient cover for a mouse, except that which was afforded by the shell holes in moving forward to the attack. Anyone would feel very proud and sad at the same time that two splendid battalions, which I once had the honour of commanding, should have behaved so splendidly and been attached to the immortal brigade of Regulars which formed the storming troops on that wonderful day. It was quite possible to realise and to understand, with the German artillery pounding No Man's Land, that the reserves were unable to come up and consolidate the position, and I regard it as a sheer impossibility, unless the same tactics were adopted as the Germans in moving on in massed formation, almost shoulder to shoulder.

He visited one of the military cemeteries, already established and named:

Within the old German lines is the Serre Road Cemetery No.1, a little square of about one acre, crowded with graves of our gallant regiments. A great number of these were nameless and inscribed to 'an unknown British officer' or 'an unknown British soldier,' but there were a great many names of old friends in the rank and file, although I could find very few officers. About 100 yards to the right of Serre Road Cemetery No.1 was a very fine stone obelisk with a bronze inscription and bronze chains and posts round it, bearing the following inscription in French: 'To the brave soldiers of the 242nd Regiment, who died for their country, June 15th, 1915,' and the thought ran through my mind that my friends in Birmingham might wish to see a similar suitable memorial to the 6th and 8th Battalions, which might be erected after the war. On a slight rise in the ground to the west of the cemetery was a wooden cross to an officer of the Somerset Light Infantry, bearing the following inscription: 'God buried him, and no man knoweth his sepulchre, 1st July, 1916.'

Sadly Ludlow found no sign of his son and decided to abandon his quest: 'On arrival again at Albert, the Graves Registration Staff promised to prosecute the search, but of course this is now impossible [Ludlow was writing after the area had been re-taken during the March offensive]. They also showed us a book of designs which the army are getting out for permanent tombstones to replace the wooden crosses, which were very simple and beautiful, and the cost will be kept down, so that people with very modest means may have a permanent memorial to their dear ones.'

No grave for Captain Stratford Ludlow would be found when, the hostilities having finally ceased on the Somme, the War Graves Commission continued its work in the vicinity of Serre. His name would join many others of his battalion on the Thiepval Memorial, but, the records show, not indefinitely; eventually his body was identified and he was buried in the companion cemetery to the one visited by his father in 1918, Serre Road No.2.

*   *   *

As for those who fought on the Somme and lived to come safe home, many would depart without a backward glance, wishing to shake the dust of it from their feet for ever. Or if they did look back it was to see the Somme, and indeed the whole war, as a warning, an incentive not to go down that same road again.

In 1920 or 21 former Captain Lionel Ferguson wrote out a fair copy of his diary, from enlistment in August 1914 to demobilization in March 1919. He added an emotive postscript, which while it does not specifically mention the Somme battles must have been strongly influenced by them, in that he was twice wounded on the Western Front, in 1916 and 1918, on each occasion during hard fighting 'on the Somme'. It was there, if anywhere, surely, that his postwar philosophy was formed:

> To those who in years to come, may ever read these notes: please remember, none of us regret our experience; but we have had our bad times. We have formed never to be forgotten friendships, thank God we can all look back on those happy days behind the line; but for the first time in our lives we have known the meaning of 'Hunger', 'Thirst', 'Dirt', 'Death' and other privations. We I think have all known the meaning of 'Fear' as we had never before seen it. Those who have never seen a barrage, those who have never seen death in all the awfulness of battle, will I fancy find it difficult to realize anything more fearful.
>
> Now, some two years later, we who went through it, know that those at home never did realize the work that 'The Soldier' was

asked to do. Those who talk of 'The Next War' are people who never 'suffered' in a front line trench; for never never again will those who have come back, advocate another War.

Yet for others the Somme would always have a strong attraction, almost a compulsion, enriched by a St Crispin's Day pride that they had been part of the great events which had happened there. Some felt this way even as early as 1916. Thus Captain Billy Lipscomb, who had raged against the incompetence of the opening offensive in which he had lost so many friends, and who had returned to serve on the Somme as a staff officer, could write on 30 December that year: 'If I survive this war, I should hate not to have known July 1, Thiepval, La Boisselle . . .'

Over the decades old memories would always be present in the minds of many survivors, ready to come into sharp focus at the slightest twitch upon the thread. A book, a photograph, a contact with a half-forgotten comrade, and the Somme would surge back, often more vivid than the events of later life.

In 1934 Arthur Dornam, who had been briefly involved in an early phase of the Battle of the Transloy Ridges, wrote a long letter to a former fellow-soldier whom he had not seen for many years but whose address he had been given following a chance meeting with the latter's father. After explaining the circumstances which had led him to his putting pen to paper, he stated: 'Naturally, when I am reminded of you, which I often am, I think chiefly of the period when we were much thrown together, and often wonder how the remaining ones of our Westminster and Ranger associates are going on. It so happened recently, that I picked up a book called *Her Privates We* by No. 123456 – a pseudonym for a jolly good writer, and he tells of the experiences of a chap who went through the Somme do. The place names that we knew so well, Mericourt and so on, Happy Valley etc. brought back recollections of our visit over the other side.'

In fact the pseudonym of the author in question, the Australian writer Frederic Manning, was 'Private 19022', but Dornam was certainly correct in suggesting that that book, first published in 1930 and already much reprinted, was a powerful evocation of the battle and territory of the Somme. He went on to evoke them most effectively himself, with an eye for telling detail and more than a dash of typical 'Tommy' humour. This letter of February 1934 has perhaps a special extra interest in that it offers an instructive contrast with Dornam's contemporary letter of October 1916, quoted in Chapter 11 (pages 212–13). In that account, largely covering the same events, a young man who had just emerged from a severe ordeal was writing what was basically a flat, down-to-earth report, without embroidery or bravado. In the later account there is the breezy nostalgia of the ex-soldier relishing shared experience with an old comrade, with distance lending, if not enchantment, certainly a softening of harsh outlines to the view. This is the Somme not of 'Lest we forget', but of 'Do you remember?'

After reminding his correspondent of their early training in England and first days in France, Dornam recalled their slow journey south in one of the notoriously laggard cattle-truck trains of French Railways:

> I have in mind one particular part of the trip Sommewards, when during a specially long interval everybody prepared to snatch a wash in a stream close by. Some were shaving – their steel pocket mirrors propped up on the footboard of the truck – when the train started to move. My – wasn't there a scramble. I had to run to catch up, and plenty of half shaved unfortunates ditto.
>
> And our first sight of the Obbo. Balloons at Mericourt, and the long drag up to Happy Valley. Do you remember that we turned off the track by error, and found ourselves among the French 75s, which were suddenly bombarded, and so colossal was our wind-up that we all ducked, and by the glare a long line of bottoms was seen. Then we started sleeping rough, and we fashioned that little bivvie to take three of us with Turnbull making himself comfortable under a bit of corrugated iron.
>
> And so on to Combles Sept. 25th. Receiving our little batch of bombs from a dugout along the valley, and really getting our first taste and smell of the real thing.
>
> And the journey up to the Trônes Wood. Do you remember a tin of pineapple chunks that we had there, I forget when I bought 'em, but they did in lieu of drink.
>
> Then we left for Lesboeufs – we had already walked over

Guillemont and Ginchy without knowing them. We were in that advanced trench on the left of the road for a day or two until the Friday night October 6th. And then we were told to clean our rifles, and keep those breech sticks handy, for we were going over the top at about 1 p.m. I seem to remember some lemonade powder that we ate while we were waiting, and I think we attempted to chirp a 'Dixie' song meantime.

When the whistle went, up we went, and after that handshake that was the last I saw of you for many a day. You went down at once I believe, but I never saw you go.

After trying to find cover from a rain of machine-gun bullets, I found myself in a shell hole with Cooper, and an old Welshman – can't think of his name – and one or two of the 4th London Fusiliers who were attacking with us. And there we had to stop until it was nearly dark. Then the Fusiliers crawled away, and Cooper tried to do so as well, but as a sniper had got us taped, he was caught and killed. The other chap and myself waited a bit longer, and then we risked it, and managed to gain the remnants of the Battn. who then occupied the same trench as they started from.

It was just dawn as we left the communication trench, over the other side of the road, and made our way to Lesboeufs, and for about one hundred yards we were in full view of the Jerries. Everybody pelted over that patch as fast as they could, and even then I saw the funny part of the blokes in front dodging about like rabbits, as though they could avoid anything that was coming to them.

In the sunken road in Lesboeufs, we had a real good drink, for all the rations and water was arriving – too late for many.

Then Trônes Wood again for the rest of Sunday, and in the middle of the night we were called again to return to the line, just to hold it.

We were in Rain Trench, and at first it seemed quiet until a Taube flew over, and just after that, we got it hot and strong. I clicked my packet in the arm and leg, and hobbled down to the stretcher-bearers, where I had to stop. Late that night the Batt. was relieved – the Division was moved to a different front. I was one of the last to leave, as I couldn't move easily, and the stretcher-bearers helped me out to the aid post.

* * *

As for actually returning to the Somme, that was not a feasible option for most old soldiers as they laboured through their working lives. But when older and retired, many expressed a wish, or were persuaded, to go back, especially when notable anniversaries offered an appropriate, and often highly publicized, occasion so to do. Soon veterans would be forming associations, travelling in groups across the Channel to pay visits to special points of the battlefield, or to hold services in cemeteries, saluting the names of dead friends and remembering them in life, as young and as keen to survive as they had been themselves. Their text, almost their benediction, spoken in these now sacred places, was the famous quatrain from Laurence Binyon's 'For the Fallen', written, far-sightedly, as early as 1914:

> They shall grow not old, as we that are left grow old,
> Age shall not weary them, nor the years condemn.
> At the going down of the sun and in the morning
> We will remember them.

Fifty-one years after first serving on the the Somme, Sidney Appleyard, former Private and Lance-Corporal of the Queen Victoria's Rifles, went back there, and subsequently added a final page to a transcription of the diary of which he had written the first entries in the summer of 1915.

1st July 1966 was the 50th anniversary of the commencement of the Battle of the Somme, and nostalgic ceremonies took place along the length of the battlefields – fireworks at one village, illumination of the old trenches at another, music at another. All over the Somme flags were put out as for a gigantic carnival. Village bands struggled with 'It's a Long Way to Tipperary', and suddenly all the villages were crowded with elderly English gentlemen, their lapels heavy with medals. Many wept at the Thiepval Memorial ceremony when Canadian planes flew low to scatter Flanders poppies over lines of troops of today and yesterday.

It is amazing how so many avoided death. On 1st July 1916 100,000 infantrymen attacked across these valleys, totally bare of cover. After four months the death-roll on both sides totalled nearly $1\frac{1}{4}$ million. We lost 600,000 to gain 45 villages, eight sizeable woods and an advance of nearly six miles. By military arithmetic it was a great victory.

The War Graves Commission have maintained immaculately the Somme memorial at Thiepval. This is the only place for miles where the flower beds don't have signs telling the public not to walk on them. As one of the war veterans said, 'They would be irrelevant here. I think everyone understands what this earth cost. The only people who really know about it are underneath. I think this anniversary will be the last. When it comes up to 75 years, we'll all be dead, too, and the Somme will seem as abstract as Waterloo.'

In the event, as can now be recognized, Appleyard's valediction was premature, in that the Somme has not yet become as abstract as Waterloo. Indeed, as time has passed, the territory of the old battlefield has inspired increasing interest, attracted more 'pilgrims', than ever before. Symptomatic of this continuing bond is the fact that in recent years certain parts of the actual ground of the Somme have become, legally, British possessions, such as the site of the great mine at La Boisselle, marking the beginning of the battle, or the Butte de Warlencourt, marking the end of it. Emotionally, of course, the sectors of the Somme had become part of the heritage of Britain, Canada, Australia, South Africa, New Zealand, Newfoundland, during the war itself. This was well understood by John Masefield who in 1919, at a time when the former belligerents were trying to come to terms with, and to justify, the scale of the sacrifice the war had entailed, wrote in an eloquent climax to a brief book about the battle:

The field of Gommecourt is heaped with the bodies of Londoners; the London Scottish lie at the Sixteen Poplars; the Yorkshires are outside Serre, the Warwicks in Serre itself; all the great hill of the Hawthorn Ridge is littered with the Middlesex; the Irish are at Hamel, the Kents on the Schwaben, and the Wilts and Dorset on the Leipzig. Men of all the towns and counties of England, Wales and Scotland lie scattered among the slopes from Ovillers to Maricourt. English dead pave the road to La Boisselle; the Welsh and Scotch are in Mametz. In gullies and sheltered places, where wounded could be brought during the fighting, there are little towns of the dead of all these places: 'Jolly young Fusiliers, too good to die.'

The places where they lie will be forgotten or changed, green things will grow, or have already grown, over their graves. It may be that all these dead will some day be removed to a National graveyard or Holy Field. There are three places, in that wilderness of the field, which should be marked by us. One is the slope of the Hawthorn Ridge, looking down the Y Ravine, where the New-foundland men attacked. Another is that slope in Delville Wood where the South Africans attacked. The third is all that great expanse from Sausage Valley to the windmill which the Australians won and held. Our own men lie as it was written for them. But over the graves on these places it should be graven, that these men came from many thousands of miles away to help their fellow-men in trouble, and that here they lie in the mud, as they chose.

Except that, as the writings quoted in this book show, these men of the Somme did not so choose. As Captain Bill Bland put it when writing to his wife on 29 June 1916: 'The conflict between communal duty and individual desire is never absolutely at rest in my heart. I want *both all* the time.' As the then Private Sidney Appleyard expressed it, somewhat more earthily, on his very first arrival on the Somme in the summer of 1915: 'We all have one great ambition, to see Germany smashed, and then have the time of our lives upon our return home.' For far too many this double ambition was not to be realized, but it was never the choice nor the intention of any who fought there, of any nationality, to join the ranks of what would later be categorized as – it was not a phrase that came readily to their lips – 'the glorious dead'.

Yet while recognizing their common humanity, the normality of their dreams and aspirations, it should still be acknowledged that the soldiers of the Somme faced a challenge special to their time and tackled it in their own special way. This book began with a quotation from a letter written in 1976 to the present author by a former participant in the battle, and it is fitting that it should end with the words of another: 'There can never be another war like the Great War, nor the comradeship and endurance we knew then. I think perhaps men are not like that now.'

Notes and References

For sources of quotations by named soldiers see Index of Contributors. For publication details of books referred to see Bibliography.

FOREWORD

page xix

'The Somme was just slaughter': letter to author by Major Bryant, 1976.

Charles Carrington quotation; from *A Subaltern's War*, (written under the pseudonym Charles Edmonds), pp. 114 and 116.

page xx

'Private letter' about the Second Battle of Ypres; quoted in my *Imperial War Museum Book of the Western Front*, pp. 177–8.

page xxi

Housman's 'blue remembered hills'; from *A Shropshire Lad*, poem XL; see also pages 298 and 357.

R.H. Tawney, quotations from 'Some Reflections of a Soldier', published in the *Nation*, October 1916.

page xxiv

Reference to 'the mud and the stars'; letter of 5 July 1916 by Second Lieutenant Edward Berrington-Behrens, RFA, quoted in *The Imperial War Museum Book of the Western Front*, pp. 265–6.

page xxv

'O Jesus, make it stop!'; from Siegfried Sassoon's poem 'Attack', written at Craiglockhart, Scotland, 1917; first published in the *Cambridge Magazine*, 20 October 1917.

pages xxvi, xxvii

Quotations by Sir Michael Howard; from his essay 'Europe on the Eve of the First World War, in *The Coming of the First World War*, edited by R.J.W. Evans and Hartmut Pogge von Strandmann; first quotation, p. 17, second quotation, pp. 12–13.

page xxvi

'Après la guerre'; see John Brophy and Eric Partridge, *The Long Trail*, p. 66.

page xxviii

Biography of General Maxse: John Baynes, *Far from a Donkey, The Life of General Sir Ivor Maxse KCB, CVO, DSO*, 1995.

Haig statements;

   of March 1915 ('We cannot hope to win until we have defeated the German Army'), Haig Diary, 28 March 1915, quoted by John Terraine, Foreword to *Sir Douglas Haig's Despatches*, edited by Lt-Col J.H. Boraston, p. viii;

   from Final Despatch ('It is in the great battles of 1916 and 1917 that we have to seek the secret of our victory in 1918.'), ibid., p. 327.

ONE A LANDSCAPE LIKE HOME

page 2

Raymond Asquith Letter of 4 August 1916, *Raymond Asquith: Life and Letters*, edited by John Jolliffe, p. 281.

Quotation by John Buchan: *The Battle of the Somme: First Phase*, 1916, p. 4.

Quotation by South African soldier, Private Willie Robins; see Index of Contributors.

Description by Second Lieutenant Charles Carrington: he was writing of Coulonvillers, the village where his battalion was out on rest. Letter to his mother of 30 July 1916, IWM Department of Documents. See Index of Contributors.

page 3

Comment on the Somme by Private Archie Surfleet, IWM Department of Documents, quoted Trevor Wilson, *The Myriad Faces of War*, p. 358. Surfleet is quoted extensively in Chapter 12; see Index of Contributors.

Comment by Ernst Jünger, *Storm of Steel*, p. 10

Comment by David Jones, from Preface to *In Parenthesis*, p. ix. An interesting contemporary use of the Somme as a historical and sociological watershed occurred in an article on English village life, 'England, Whose England?', in the *Independent on Sunday*, 29 October 1995. The author, Jonathan Glancey, described the Cotswold village of Salperton as possessing 'picture book, pre-Somme, forelock-tugging charms'.

Colonel Victor Stewart quotation, memoir, IWM Department of Documents, Ref: 66/144/1.

Comment by Paddy Griffith, *Battle Tactics of the Western Front*, 1994, p. 17.

Material on 1914 campaign, M. and M. Middlebrook, *The Somme Battlefields*, p. 48.

page 5

Haig quotation re barbed wire: *Sir Douglas Haig's Despatches*, edited by J.H. Boraston, p. 22.

pages 5–6

Creation of Third Army etc., and history of Albert basilica, M. and M. Middlebrook, op.cit., 48–9, 216–17.

page 8

Comparison of Butte de Warlencourt to Silbury Hill: Charles Carrington, *Soldier from the Wars Returning*, p. 143.

TWO BUILD-UP TO 'THE PUSH'

page 9

'Goalkeepers' joke; from a letter by Second Lieutenant Charles Carrington, 2 April 1916.

page 10

Details of and comment on 'minor operations' before the Somme; John Terraine, *Douglas Haig, The Educated Soldier*, p. 193.

page 18

The book of which Bland and Tawney were part-authors, with P.A. Brown, was entitled *English Economic History: Select Documents*, published by G. Bell & Sons.

A letter by Captain Bland to his wife written on 14 January 1916 (not reproduced here) has already been published in *Despatches from the Heart*, edited by Annette Tappert, Hamish Hamilton, 1984, and in *Forces Sweethearts*, edited by Joanna Lumley, Bloomsbury, 1993. Extracts from his letters have also appeared in Michael Stedman, *Manchester Pals*, published in 1994. Captain Charles May was quoted briefly in my *Imperial War Museum Book of the Western Front*.

page 19

'The old lie'; see Wilfred Owen's poem 'Dulce et Decorum Est', rightly considered one of the most potent anti-war poems of the First World War.

pages 23–4

Quotation re decision to attack on the Somme: see *Official History of the War: Military Operations, France and Belgium 1916*, Part I, pp. 30–31; this and subsequent volumes are hereafter referred to as *O.H. 1916 I, O.H. 1916 II* etc.; see Bibliography.

page 24

Lieutenant-General Rawlinson; usually referred to as General in Somme accounts but not promoted to full general in January 1917; see Robin Prior and Trevor Wilson, *Command on the Western Front*, p. 264; this was also the month in which Haig was promoted from General to Field Marshal.

pages 24–5

Details of British Armies; Prior and Wilson, op.cit., p. 137.

pages 25–6

Second Lieutenant Wollocombe would be wounded some weeks before the offensive began and so would not be with his battalion on 1 July, when, together with its sister battalion, the 8th Devons, it would suffer very heavily in the attack mounted from a point that would become famous on the Somme, Mansel Copse, opposite Mametz. The dead were buried in what had formerly been the battalion's front-line trench, in recognition of which a sign was erected shortly afterwards bearing the legend: 'The Devonshires held this trench, the Devonshires hold it still.' A memorial stone engraved with this moving quotation now stands at the entrance to the Devonshire cemetery.

Wollocombe returned to the Somme in August, serving again with the 9th Devons; he died of wounds, sustained during the fighting for Ginchy, on 10 September.

page 26ff

Sergeant Robert McKay's diary; see also my *Imperial War Museum Book of the Western Front*, where McKay is quoted on such subjects as the Third Battle of Ypres and Armistice Day 1918.

page 27

Two deserters shot; see Julian Putkowski and Julian Sykes, *Shot at Dawn*, pp. 74 and 317. McKay's information was correct; Putkowski and Sykes record the execution on the date given of a Rifleman McCracken and a Rifleman Templeton of the 15th Royal Irish Rifles; they add that desertion was the only crime for which soldiers were executed in the first quarter of 1916. One of the two had had three previous convictions, two involving unauthorized absence.

pages 29–30

Major-General Maxse's background and reputation; see Peter Simkins, *Kitchener's Army*, pp. 316, 306.

page 30

Maxse Somme report: from Maxse papers, IWM Department of Documents, file 23/1.

THREE COUNTDOWN TO ZERO

page 34

Comment on staff officer's performance in the Somme battle; *O.H. 1916 II*, p. 570.

Anthony Farrar-Hockley quotation; from his book *The Somme*, p. 62.

page 36

Cyril Falls on Kitchener's New Armies and the Territorial Force; from his book *The First World War*, pp. 166–7.

Winston Churchill quotation; from *The World Crisis 1916–1918*, 1927 edition, p. 195, two volume edition, 1938, p. 1091, NEL Mentor paperback edition, p. 749.

page 37

Maxse no donkey; see title of his 1995 biography, above, p. 344.

page 42

Soldier's comment on hearing of Lord Kitchener's death; Martin Middlebrook, *The First Day on the Somme*, p. 81.

page 46

'Thiepval as the key to the situation'; quotation from Captain D.P. Grant, *The 1/4th (Hallamshire) Battn., York and Lancaster Regiment, 1914–1919*, p. 37.

pages 48-9

German account of preliminary bombardment: from Stephen Westman, *Surgeon with the Kaiser's Army*, p. 94. See also Index of Contributors.

page 50

Official Historian on assurances that the opening attack on the Somme would face little or no resistance: *O.H. 1916 I*, p. 288.

page 51

Lt-Col Cordeaux's comment on swallows: his father, John Cordeaux, was a noted ornithologist, author of *Birds of the Humber District*.

page 52

Creeping barrage; details from David Fraser (General Sir David Fraser, GCB, OBE), *Alanbrooke*, pp. 72–3. Fraser states: 'The idea of such a barrage was French. In the preceding March Brooke had taken a French Colonel Herring round the 18th Division sector. The "creeping" or "rolling" barrage in exactly the form adopted was described to Brooke by Herring. It became, as he [Brooke] said, "famous and universal".' In this context see Bill Rawling, *Surviving Trench Warfare*, p. 77; discussing the use of the creeping barrage in the September attacks on the Somme, Rawling describes this as 'a refinement of the technique that had proved so useful for the British 18th Division on 1 July'.

page 56

Leutnant Busl's account; from Regimental History of the 6th Bavarian Infantry Regiment.

pages 57-8

Anonymous letter in a weekly newspaper; from the unpublished war diary of Mr F.A. Robinson, 29 July 1916; Robinson is quoted extensively in Chapter 13.

page 60

Lieutenant-Colonel E.T.F. Sandys' story was first told in Martin Middlebrook, *The First Day on the Somme*, published 1971.

page 62

'It was really a pity to have a war on July 1st, etc.'; from letter to author in 1976 by R.H. Locke, quoted in my TV documentary *The Battle of the Somme*.

FOUR THE FIRST DAY: THE FOURTH ARMY FRONT

page 67

Stephen Westman quotation; op.cit., pp. 94–5.

pages 67-8.

Anonymous 1/1st Welsh Heavy Battery account: IWM Department of Documents, Misc. 172/2641.

page 72

German regiment's description of attack at Hawthorn Ridge; quoted Nigel Cave, *Somme, Beaumont Hamel*, p. 30.

page 76

Comment by an artillery officer who walked the ground of the 10th Lincoln attack: *O.H. 1916 II* p. 381n.

page 77

R.H. Tawney quotation; if not to Bland, then the reference must be to May, as the only other captain of the battalion to be killed on 1 July.

pages 78

Details of casualties suffered by 22nd Manchesters and statement that 'they had ceased to exist in any recognizable form'; from Michael Stedman, *Manchester Pals*, p. 114. Mr Stedman's advice on matters relating to the 22nd Manchesters is gratefully acknowledged.

pages 83–4

Captain Spicer letter; quoted from his *Letters from France 1915–1918*, p. 55. For the origin of the famous pre-Somme toast, 'Gentlemen, when the barrage lifts', see Introduction to his *Letters*, pp. xvii-xviii.

page 86

Official History account of Green Howards attack, and of its discontinuance; *O.H. 1916 I*, pp. 363–4.

page 86ff

Captain Nevill's footballs, kicked into No Man's Land at zero hour, provided one of the great, mythic moments of 1 July 1916. Martin Middlebrook's *First Day on the Somme* republicized a story which had been widely admired (by the British), and as widely derided (by the enemy), in 1916 itself. Nevill's letters, now held in the IWM's Department of Documents, were published in 1991 in *Billie: The Nevill Letters, 1914–1916*, edited by Ruth Elwin Harris. Captain Nevill's grave can be found in the Commonwealth War Cemetery at Carnoy, though he is described as an officer of the East Yorkshire Regiment, in which he was commissioned, not of the 8th East Surreys, to which he was attached at the time of his death.

page 87

Re Private Cude's reference to 'Pioneers': One Pioneer (i.e. Labour) battalion was attached to each infantry division at this time.

page 89

Leutnant Busl's account; details as earlier extract quoted on p. 56.

page 91

French success on 1 July, and also the French role in the Somme battle; see pp. 256–9.

page 92

1 July casualty statistics: Peter Simkins, Introduction to Chris McCarthy, *The Somme: The Day-by-Day Account*, p. 8

FIVE THE FIRST DAY: THE THIRD ARMY FRONT

page 93

Comment on VII Corps attack at Gommecourt: John Terraine, *Douglas Haig, The Educated Soldier*, p. 207.

pages 95

Corporal Hubbard was one of many who were permanently affected by their experiences on the Somme. It is thought that the depressions from which he suffered as a result of his war service were instrumental in his taking his own life some years later.

pages 99–100

Report on the Defence of Gommecourt, translation of a German document; from the series of intelligence documents discussed, and quoted at length, in Chapter 9. The document was printed in an edition of the Royal United Service Institution *Journal* in 1917, and subsequently became the subject of a long analytical article in *The Spectator* (22 September 1917), which included this comment: 'We are not told how this document was obtained, but it was obviously not intended for Allied eyes, as it does justice, on the whole, to the skill and courage of the attackers and reveals the enemy's sense of keen relief at having been able to hold Gommecourt.' A copy of the *Spectator* article has been preserved with the papers of an officer who took part in the Gommecourt attack, Lieutenant A.F.D. Darlington.

page 102

Quotation by George Morgan; collage of sentences from my interview with former Private Morgan, also quoted in my *Tommy Goes to War*.

SIX THE SECOND DAY – AND AFTER

page 109

Brigadier-General Bertie Prowse's brother, Captain Cecil Prowse of the battle-cruiser HMS *Queen Mary*, had lost his life just a month earlier at the Battle of Jutland.

page 115

Psalm 15: Lee was presumably thinking of its opening verses: 'Lord, who shall abide in thy tabernacle? Who shall dwell in thy holy will? He that walketh uprightly, and worketh righteousness, and speaketh the truth in his heart.'

SEVEN TO PRESS THE ENEMY HARD

page 119

Haig quotations: *The Private Papers of Douglas Haig*, edited by Robert Blake, Eyre & Spottiswoode, 1952, p. 154, and John Terraine, *The First World War*, 1965, Papermac, 1984, p. 117.

Comment on casualties; Haig, *The Private Papers*, p. 154.

page 120

John Terraine comment on 'the true texture of the Somme'; see the chapter so-titled in his *The Smoke and the Fire*, pp. 111– 126.

page 121

C.E.W. Bean quotation; *From Anzac to Amiens*, p. 238.

Peter Simkins quotation; Introduction to Chris McCarthy, *The Somme: The Day-By-Day Account*, p. 10.

Gains and casualties; details from Prior and Wilson, op.cit, quoted P. Simkins, ibid., p. 10.

page 122

Official History's description of 17th Manchester and 9th Duke of Wellington's attack on 7 July; *O.H. 1916 II*, pp. 30–31.

page 127

Quotation by a young officer of 38th Division; from Wyn Griffith, *Up to Mametz*, p. 254.

page 130

John Terraine comment on 14 July assault; *Haig, The Educated Soldier*, p. 213.

page 137

Order to South African Brigade to take Delville Wood 'at all costs'; *O.H. 1916 II*, p. 92.

pages 137–8

'At all costs'; comment by General Sir Anthony Farrar-Hockley, *The Somme*, pp. 199–200. 'Congreve' was Lieutenant-General Sir Walter Congreve, GOC XIII Corps, of which the 9th (Scottish) Division, to which the South African Brigade was attached, formed part.

pages 138–9

Charles Carrington story; later told in his *A Subaltern's War*, pp. 62ff; also referred to in his *Soldier from the Wars Returning*, p. 135.

page 139

For the 'one line' reference in the Official History to Carrington's battalion's contribution to the seizure of Ovillers see *O.H. 1916 II*, p. 101. For recent high praise for Carrington, see Introduction (p.vii) by Paddy Griffith to new edition of Ernst Jünger's *Storm of Steel*, 1994.

page 144

Captain Reginald Gill is also quoted on the fighting for Pozières in my *Imperial War Museum Book of the Western Front*, pp. 119–20

'A later Australian historian'; Bill Gammage, *The Broken Years*, pp. 169–70.

page 145

Dr Bean quotation on Pozières; op.cit., p. 248.

New arrival's comment on the Somme in August; Private Edgar (Ted) Gale, 8th East Yorkshire Regiment, quoted pp. 156–7.

Death Valley: see M. and M. Middlebrook, *The Somme Battlefields*, p. 161.

pages 151–2

It is noteworthy that *1066 and All That* was first published in 1930, at the height of the 'disenchantment' vogue in military memoirs. In its breezy, scholastically flippant attitude to serious history it might be said to echo the 'school magazine' ethos of the trench journals discussed in Chapter 14.

page 155

'Johnsons and Coal Boxes; soldiers' slang for shells giving off black smoke; Jack Johnson was a famous negro pugilist.

page 160

Cavalry action, 14 July; Chris McCarthy op.cit. pp. 48/50.

page 167

'Comic Cuts' definition: Brophy and Partridge, *The Long Trail*, p. 86.

Haig Diary reference; *Britain and the Great War*, The Public Record Office and John Murray, 1994, p. 89.

page 167

On the dismissal of senior officers; see my *IWM Book of the Western Front*, '"Stellenbosched": Nightmare of a Brigadier-General', pp. 125–30. Haig once stated that he had dismissed more than 100 brigadier-generals; see Tim Travers, *The Killing Ground*, Allen & Unwin, 1989, p. 13.

pages 171–2

Translation from regimental history of German 66th Infantry Regiment.

page 172

German Students' War Letters, edited Dr Philip Witkop, translated A.F. Wedd, 1929. Since none of the students survived, this could be called a German equivalent of the famous British anthology, *War Letters of Fallen Englishmen*, published in 1930. A high-flown, sacrificial tone is common to both collections.

pages 176–7

Ernst Jünger quotation; from *Storm of Steel*, pp. 92–3.

page 178

Stephen Westman quotation: op.cit, p. 104.

page 179

Reference to 'this terrible milling at close quarters'; *O.H. 1917 I*, p. 4.

pages 179–80

Lieutenant-General Kiggell quotation: *O.H. 1916 II*, Appendix Volume, p. 60.

TEN TANKS – AND THE SEPTEMBER OFFENSIVES

page 181

GHQ Instruction re Tanks: *OH 1916 II*, Appendix Volume, pp. 39–40.

pages 182–3

Origin of the name 'tank': Swinton, *Eyewitness*, Hodder & Stoughton, 1932, p. 187.

Colonel Hankey on tanks; source, Lord Hankey, *The Supreme Command*, quoted Farrar-Hockley, op.cit., p. 226.

page 185

Solon (c.658–558 BC) was a great Athenian legislator, famous for his wisdom. His statement 'Call no man happy till he dies, he is at best but fortunate' is quoted in Herodotus, *Histories*, i.32.

page 186

Fourth Army Instructions for 15 September battle; *OH 1916 ii*, Appendix Volume, p. 63.

pages 186–7

Captain Sir Iain Colquhoun; see Malcolm Brown and Shirley Seaton, *Christmas Truce*, Papermac edition, pp. 204–6; *Raymond Asquith, Life and Letters*, p. 234.

pages 188–9

Colquhoun's distinguished role on 15 September; details from Lt. Col. the Rt. Hon. Sir F. Ponsonby, *The Grenadiers in the Great War*, p. 103ff; J. Jolliffe, op. cit., p. 296.

page 196

Dismissal of Major-General Barter; details from Terry Norman, *The Hell They Called High Wood*, pp. 235–7.

page 198

'Not half'; Brophy and Partridge, op.cit. p. 125.

pages 201ff

Account by Lieutenant Geoffrey Fildes; a later, more impersonal account of the attack on Lesboeufs was included in his 1918 volume *Iron Times with the Guards*, published under the pseudonym 'An "O.E"' (i.e. an Old Etonian).

pages 206–7

Details of 18th Division's preparation for Thiepval attack from Captain G.H.F. Nichols, *The 18th Division in the Great War*, Chapter 6; also from 18th Division

Report on the Battle of Thiepval, IWM Department of Documents, Maxse Papers 28/2.
page 207
Ref to 18th Division 'in fine fettle'; *O.H. 1916 II*, p. 394.

ELEVEN 'THE PITILESS SOMME'

page 206
The War the Infantry Knew; first published without naming its editor, Captain J.C. Dunn, in 1938; reissued in new edition acknowledging his editorship in 1987. The 'pitiless Somme' reference occurs on p. 302.
Earl of Cavan's protest re November attack; details from Prior and Wilson, op.cit., pp. 256–8.
page 209
Quotation on Haig's strategy in continuing the campaign; Charles Carrington, *Soldier from the War Returning*, p. 143.
'Valley of humiliation' quotation: see also Carrington's *A Subaltern's War*, p. 132, where he uses the same phrase – from Bunyan's *Pilgrim's Progress* – in relation to the Third Battle of Ypres. It is noteworthy that it was in the Valley of Humiliation that Bunyan's hero, Christian, fought his 'battle' with the arch-enemy Apollyon. 'This sore combat', writes Bunyan, 'lasted for above half a day, even till Christian was almost quite spent. For you must know, that Christian, by reason of his wounds, must needs go weaker and weaker.' A fair description, as Carrington was doubtless well aware, of an attritional encounter.
His description of the Butte de Warlencourt is also from *Soldier from the Wars Returning*, p. 143.
Official History's description of the Butte de Warlencourt: *O.H. 1916 II*, 433n.
page 210
George Harbottle's description of the Butte; *Civilian Soldier 1914–1919*, privately published memoir, pp. 61–2.
page 211
Quotation re 47th Division's attack: *O.H. 1916 II*, p. 437.
page 213
Reference to the 'Rangers' 7 October attack: *O.H. II*, p. 434. A notable casualty of this attack was Sergeant Leslie Coulson, former Reuters' correspondent and poet, who served by choice in the ranks; he died on 8 October of wounds received in the previous day's fighting. Among his possessions after his death was found a poem, 'Who Made the Law?', that has become famous as an icon of contemporary protest against the brutality of the Western Front war, of which these ar the opening lines:

> Who made the Law that men should die in meadows?
> Who spake the word that blood should splash in lanes?

Who gave it forth that gardens should be bone-yards?
Who spread the hills with flesh, and blood, and brains?
Who made the Law?

For details of Coulson's career and writings see Anne Powell, *A Deep Cry*, Aberporth, Palladour Books, 1993.

page 215

Quotation by Sidney Rogerson; from his book *Twelve Days*, p. 92.

page 232

Affectionate portrait of a Western Front estaminet; Brophy and Partridge, op.cit., pp. 96–7.

TWELVE THE ANCRE – AND CLOSEDOWN

page 233

One of the Somme's striking memorials; 51st (Highland) Division Memorial at Y Ravine, Beaumont Hamel. It might be said that the statue of the caribou overlooking the ground across which the Newfoundlanders made their disastrous attack on 1 July, and the Highlander's statue marking the seizure of this same bitterly contested sector in mid-November, fairly sum up both the tragedy and the achievement of the Somme of 1916.

pages 237–8

Historian of 63rd (Royal Naval) Division; Douglas Jerrold, adjutant of Hawke Battalion. The extract is from *The Great War – I Was There*, 1935, part 22, p. 887, quoted Leonard Sellers, *The Hood Battalion*, p. 180. Jerrold also wrote the division's official history, *The Royal Naval Division*, Hutchinson, 1928.

51st Division history written in 1918; Captain Robert B. Ross, *The Fifty-First in France*, p. 233.

Haig's statement: 'nothing is so costly as failure'; from Peter Simkins, *IWM Review*, No.9, 1994, *Somme Footnote: the Battle of the Ancre and the struggle for Frankfort Trench, November 1916*, pp. 91–2.

List of Divisions involved in Ancre battle; Leonard Sellers, *The Hood Battalion*, p. 174.

page 242

Edmund Blunden quotation on Beaumont Hamel; *Undertones of War*, p. 88.

page 243

51st Division gains and casualties; Nigel Cave, *Somme, Beaumont Hamel*, p. 97.

page 248

The 'sinister ruins of Serre', Farrar-Hockley, *The Somme*, p. 244; the quotation is from C.R.M.F. Crutwell, *A History of the Great War 1914–1918*, p. 275.

31st Division's failure; C. McCarthy, op.cit., p. 156.

page 251

Weather details for last day of fighting; from C. McCarthy, op. cit., p. 162.

page 252

Official History's statement that Haig had contemplated a further development of the Ancre offensive; *O.H. II*, p. 523.

French reaction to British calling off the campaign; *O.H. II*, pp. 553–4.

Description of Somme battle by the Prime Minister, Herbert Asquith; quoted Christopher Martin, *The Battle of the Somme*, p. 98. Asquith's third son, Arthur, a Lieutenant-Commander in the 63rd (Naval) Brigade, had been transferred to a non-combatant role at Corps Headquarters on the eve of the Ancre battle.

pages 252–3

Haig Despatch: *The Times*, 30 December 1916; reprinted in *Sir Douglas Haig's Despatches*, pp. 20 and 51.

page 253

Hindenburg quotation: *O.H. 1916 II*, p. 555.

page 254

Ludendorff quotation, *My War Memories, 1914–1918*, pp. 276–7.

C.E.W. Bean comment; from his *Anzac to Amiens*, p. 268.

A.J.P. Taylor quotation; *The First World War: An Illustrated History*, 1963, p. 140.

page 255

Quotation by Captain von Hentig of the General Staff of the Guard Reserve Division; *O.H. 1916 I*, p. 494.

Churchill quotation; *The World Crisis, 1916–1918*, 1927 Edition, pp. 195–6, NEL Mentor Edition, 1968, p. 750.

pages 255–6

Peter Simkins quotation; Introduction to C. McCarthy, op.cit., p. 13.

page 256

Cyril Falls quotation: *The First World War*, p. 170.

John Terraine quotation; *The Smoke and the Fire*, p. 126.

Trevor Wilson quotation; *The Myriad Faces of War*, p. 325.

page 257

Alistair Horne on the first phase of the Somme; *The Price of Glory*, p. 293.

page 258

Villages taken by the French in September/October 1916, and quotation by Pierre Loti; *The Somme*, Comité Departemental du Tourisme de la Somme, 21, rue Ernest Cauvin – 80000 Amiens, France.

page 259

Territory gained by the Germans at Verdun and quotation by the German Crown Prince; Alistair Horne, op. cit., p. 331.

THIRTEEN   CIVILIANS AND THE SOMME

page 260

Newspaper reports in London, 1 July; Vera Brittain, *Testament of Youth*, Gollancz, 1933, pp. 275–6.

page 261ff

F.A. Robinson is also quoted briefly in my *Imperial War Museum Book of the First World War*, pp. 8 and 228–9.

pages 265–6

1916 film *The Battle of the Somme*: for full details, background and viewing guide to this film, and its successor about the final stage of the battle and the advance of the tanks, see *The Battles of the Somme and the Ancre*, edited by Roger Smither, published in association with DD Video by the Department of Film, Imperial War Museum, 1993. See also my *IWM Book of the First World War*, pp. 236–9.

pages 269–70

For the full text of Haig's Final Despatch, see *Sir Douglas Haig's Despatches*, edited J.H. Boraston, pp. 311–57.

pages 272

Major R.S. Cockburn's document; written May 1918. From its unfinished state it would seem that it has not been previously published; extracts from his excellent account of his personal experiences during the war, also held in the IWM, have appeared both in my own *Tommy Goes to War* and in Peter Simkins' *Kitchener's Army*. Sentiments very akin to Cockburn's were also expressed by R.H. Tawney in the article quoted in the Foreword (p. xix), originally published in the *Nation* in October 1916 and reprinted in *The Attack, and other papers*, p. 25.

'[We] are depicted as merry assassins, rejoicing in the opportunity of a "scrap" in which we know that more than half our friends will be maimed and killed, exulting in the duty of turning human beings into lumps of disfigured clay, light-hearted as children who shoot at sparrows with a new air-gun and clap their hands when they fall, charmed from the transient melancholy of childhood by a game of football or a packet of cigarettes.'

FOURTEEN   'SOMMEWHERE IN FRANCE'

page 274

The Siegfried Sassoon quotation is from his poem 'Suicide in the Trenches', first published in the *Cambridge Magazine*, 23 February 1918. The quatrain in which it appears is particularly relevant to themes discussed in this and the previous chapter:

> You smug-faced crowds with kindling eye
> Who cheer when soldier lads march by,

> Sneak home and pray you'll never know
> The hell where youth and laughter go.

A variant on the last two lines is quoted by Winston Churchill as epigraph to his chapter on the Somme in his book *The World Crisis*.

Concert parties in France during the early phase of the Somme battle: referred to in *The Sphere*, 8 July 1916.

page 275

The reference by Lieutenant E.F. Chapman to 'all the good B.E.F. songs' is from his letter of 26 March 1917.

All editions of the *Wipers Times* and its variants have been published in facsimile; for details see Bibliography.

page 279

Fighting in which 1/4th Gloucestershire was involved on 23 July 1916; details from *O.H. 1916 II*, p. 144.

page 281

Second Lieutenant F.W. Harvey's *A Gloucestershire Lad at Home and Abroad* was published by Sidgwick & Jackson, which also published four further volumes by Harvey over the next five years, including an account of his time as a prisoner of war under the title *Comrades in Captivity*.

page 285

Charles Carrington comment on humane treatment by Germans on 1 July 1916; extract from unpublished essay, 'The Defence of the Gommecourt Salient', 1926.

FIFTEEN 'GERMANS GONE AWAY'

page 286

Fragments of 'unfinished business'; e.g. see Leonard Sellers, *The Hood Battalion*, Chapter 20, describing a minor action in the Puisieux sector.

page 296

Captain Christopher Carrington is buried in the Guards Cemetery, Lesboeufs.

page 297

William Orpen quotations; from *An Onlooker in France*, pp. 36 and 49.

page 298

A.E. Housman's *A Shropshire Lad*, originally published in 1896 at the author's own expense, became extremely popular during the First World War, which gave a special resonance to Housman's recurring, fatalistic theme of doomed lads dying young. As Robert Lowell has written: 'One feels Housman foresaw the Somme.' The lines quoted are from poem XXIII, beginning 'The lads in their hundreds to Ludlow come in for the fair'.

The comment on the Promenade Concert performance of Butterworth's *A Shropshire Lad* is from a report entitled 'Butterworth's Rhapsody at Queen's Hall' in *The Times*, 7 September 1917.

SIXTEEN THE SOMME 1918: THE RETREAT

page 305

Quotation re fate of General Gough's Fifth Army: *O.H. 1918 II*, p. 119.

page 317

Fate of the Leaning Virgin statue on the Albert basilica; Rose E.B. Coombs, *Before Endeavours Fade*, p. 81.

SEVENTEEN THE SOMME 1918: THE ADVANCE

page 318

Ludendorff quotation; Ludendorff, *My War Memories 1914–1918*, Vol II, pp. 679 and 684, quoted John Terraine, *To Win a War*, p. 114.

pages 318–19

British Army 1918 improvements; Prior and Wilson, op.cit., p. 290ff.

page 319

'Keep your mouth shut' notice; *O.H. 1918 Vol IV*, p. 16, footnote 2; copy in papers of Lieutenant Clifford Carter, Dept of Docs, IWM.

page 320

Haig comment on being entrusted with the direction of Anglo-French operations; Terraine, *To Win a War*, p. 106.

Australian advance; Dr C.E.W. Bean, *From Anzac to Amiens*, p. 472.

page 321

Dummy radio traffic before Amiens offensive; Terraine, *To Win a War*, pp. 106ff.

Ludendorff and Haig quotations re German defeat; from John Terraine, *The First World War*, p. 175.

pages 323–4

Battle nomenclature; *O.H. 1918, Vol IV*, p. 179n. The footnote adds 'and the Battle of Albert did not end until the 29th August'.

pages 324–5

Attack by 15th Brigade, 5th Division; *O.H. 1918 IV*, pp. 190–91.

pages 330–31

On the subject of the Somme, Verdun and Third Ypres as the supreme battlefields of the First World War, see this evocative comment by Modris Ecksteins in his *Rites of Spring*, p. 145:

'The battles of Verdun, the Somme, and Ypres embody the logic, the meaning, the essence of the Great War. Two out of every three *poilus* were funnelled through Verdun in 1916; most British soldiers saw action at the Somme or Ypres or both; and most German units were in Flanders or at Verdun at some point. They also constituted the crucial battle areas of the war. And the standard imagery that we have of the Great War – the deafening, enervating artillery barrages, the attacks in which long lines of men moved forward as if in slow motion over a moonscape of craters and mud, only to confront machine-guns, uncut barbed wire, and grenades – comes from these battles rather than those of the first or last year of the war.'

The Somme as an ultimate in modern warfare; cf., for example, John Keegan's 1976 best-seller *The Face of Battle*, in which (p. 280) he discussed 'the revelation', resulting form the Somme battle, 'that war could threaten with death the young manhood of a whole nation ... [a] realization [which] was to have important political after-effects during the Second World War'. He described an occasion when the American General George Marshall was in England, offering powerful arguments in favour of a prompt invasion of occupied Europe. 'Lord Cherwell remarked to him. "It's no use – you are arguing against the casualties on the Somme."' Keegan added: 'The same realization was to colour British strategic thinking, both official and academic, about what sort of wars she should fight.' For a recent instance, it was widely assumed that fears of a Somme-type battle significantly affected British, and indeed American, strategic thinking during the Gulf War in 1991.

EIGHTEEN   A PLACE OF LONG MEMORY

pages 332–6

Account by Brigadier-General W.R. Ludlow CB; from a pamphlet entitled *A Short Description of the Battle of Beaumont-Hamel, July 1st 1916*, produced for private circulation in July 1918. Copy in IWM Department of Documents in papers of Sidney Williamson, formerly 1/8th Battalion, Royal Warwickshire Regiment.

page 334

1/8th Royal Warwickshire's 1 July casualties; Martin Middlebrook, *The First Day on the Somme*, p. 331–2.

pages 341–2

John Masefield quotation; from his book *The Battle of the Somme*, p. 94.

page 342

Final quotation; letter to author by W.R. Chittendon, quoted in TV Documentary *The Battle of the Somme*, 1976.

BIBLIOGRAPHY

All books published in London unless otherwise stated.

Raymond Asquith: Life and Letters, edited by John Jolliffe, Collins, 1980

John Baynes, *Far from a Donkey, The Life of General Sir Ivor Maxse KCB, CVO, DSO*, Brassey's, 1995

C.E.W. Bean, *From Anzac to Amiens*, Canberra, Australian War Memorial, 1946

Billie: The Nevill Letters, edited by Ruth Elwin Harris, Julia MacRae Books, 1991

Edmund Blunden, *Undertones of War*, Cobden-Sanderson, 1928, Penguin Modern Classics, 1982

Anthony Boden, *F.W. Harvey, Soldier, Poet*, Gloucester, Alan Sutton Publishing, 1988

Vera Brittain, *Testament of Youth*, Gollancz, 1933, Virago, 1978

John Brophy and Eric Partridge, *The Long Trail*, André Deutsch 1965, Sphere Books, 1969

Malcolm Brown, *Tommy Goes to War*, J. M. Dent, 1978, Everyman paperback, 1981, 1986; *IWM Book of the First World War*, Sidgwick & Jackson, 1991, paperback edition, 1993; *IWM Book of the Western Front*, Sidgwick & Jackson, 1993, paperback edition, 1994

Malcolm Brown and Shirley Seaton, *Christmas Truce*, Leo Cooper/Secker & Warburg, 1984; expanded edition, Papermac, 1994

Peter Bryant, *Grimsby Chums, The Story of the 10th Lincolnshires in the Great War*, Hull, Humberside Leisure Services, 1990

John Buchan, *The Battle of the Somme: First Phase*, Nelson, 1916; *Second Phase*, Nelson, 1917

Charles Carrington (as Charles Edmonds) *A Subaltern's War*, Peter Davies, 1929, reprinted Bath, Cedric Chivers, 1966; *Soldier from the Wars Returning*, Hutchinson, 1965, Arrow Books, 1970

Nigel Cave, *Somme, Beaumont Hamel*, Leo Cooper, 1994

Winston Churchill, *The World Crisis*, 1916–1918, Thornton Butterworth,1927, two-volume edition, Odhams Press, 1938, NEL Mentor paperback edition, 1968

The Coming of the First World War, edited by R.J.W. Evans and Hartmut Pogge von Strandmann, Oxford, The Clarendon Press, 1988, OUP paperback, 1995

Rose E.B. Coombs, *Before Endeavours Fade*, After the Battle Publications, 1976, revised edition, 1994

C.R.M.F. Crutwell, *A History of the Great War 1914–1918*, Oxford University Press, 1935

Modris Ecksteins, *Rites of Spring*, Bantam Press, 1989

Cyril Falls, *The First World War*, Longmans, 1960

General Sir Anthony Farrar-Hockley, *The Somme*, Batsford, 1954, Pan Books, 1966

G.P. Fildes (under the pseudonym 'An "O.E"'), *Iron Times with the Guards*, John Murray, 1918

General Sir David Fraser, *Alanbrooke*, Collins 1982, Hamlyn Paperback, 1983

Bill Gammage, *The Broken Years, Australian Soldiers in the Great War*, Canberra, Australian National University Press, 1974, Penguin Books Australia, 1975

German Regimental Histories:
> 6th Bavarian Reserve Infantry Regiment (*Das Königlich Bayerische Reserve-Infanterie Regiment Nr 6*), compiled Dr Oskar Bezzell, Munich, Max Schenk, 1938
>
> 66th Infantry Regiment (*Das 3 Magdeburgische Infanterie-Regiment Nr 66 in Weltkriege*), compiled Dr Otto Korfes, Berlin, Wilhelm Kolk, 1930

German Students' War Letters, edited by Dr Philip Witkop, Munich, 1928, translated A.F. Wedd, Methuen, 1929

Captain D.P. Grant, *The 1/4th (Hallamshire) Battn., York and Lancaster Regiment, 1914–1919*, Arden Press, [1931]

Paddy Griffith, *Battle Tactics of the Western Front*, New Haven and London, Yale, 1994

Wyn Griffith, *Up to Mametz*, Faber & Faber, 1931, Norwich, Gliddon Books, with introduction by Colin Hughes, 1988

Sir Douglas Haig's Despatches, edited by J.H. Boraston, 1919, J.M. Dent, 1979

The Private Papers of Douglas Haig, edited by Robert Blake, Eyre & Spottiswoode, 1952

George Harbottle, *Civilian Soldier 1914–1919: a period relived*, Newcastle upon Tyne, Carlis Print, *c.* 1980

Alistair Horne, *The Price of Glory, Verdun 1916*, Macmillan, 1962, new edition Penguin Books, 1993

Douglas Jerrold, *The Royal Naval Division*, Hutchinson, 1928

David Jones, *In Parenthesis*, Faber & Faber, 1937

Ernst Jünger, *Storm of Steel*, first English edition, Chatto and Windus, 1929, new edition, with an introduction by Paddy Griffith, Constable, 1994

John Keegan, *The Face of Battle*, Jonathan Cape, 1976

Erich von Ludendorff, *My War Memories 1914–1918*, Hutchinson, 1919

Chris McCarthy, *The Somme: The Day-By-Day Account*, with introduction by Peter Simkins, Arms and Armour Press, 1993

Lyn Macdonald, *Somme*, Michael Joseph, 1983

Christopher Martin, *The Battle of the Somme*, Wayland Publishers, 1973

John Masefield, *The Battle of the Somme*, Heinemann, 1919, Bath, Cedric Chivers, 1968

Michelin Guides:

The Somme, The First Battle of the Somme (1916–1917)
The Somme, The Second Battle of the Somme (1918)
published just after the First World War and recently republished in facsimile editions by G.H. Smith & Son, Easingwold, North Yorkshire, with introductions by Dr A.J. Peacock

Martin Middlebrook, *The First Day on the Somme*, Allen Lane, 1971, Penguin, 1984; *The Kaiser's Battle*, Allen Lane, 1978, Penguin, 1983

Martin and Mary Middlebrook, *The Somme Battlefields*, Viking, 1991, Penguin, 1994

Captain G.H.F. Nichols, *The 18th Division in the Great War*, London and Edinburgh, William Blackwood, 1922

Terry Norman, *The Hell They Called High Wood*, William Kimber, 1984

Official History of the War:

Military Operations, France and Belgium, 1916, Vol I, 1932
Military Operations, France and Belgium, 1916, Vol II, 1938
Military Operations, France and Belgium, 1918, Vol I, 1935
Military Operations, France and Belgium, 1918, Vol IV, 1947
Military Operations, France and Belgium, 1916, Vol I: Appendices, 1932
Military Operations, France and Belgium, 1916, Vol II, Maps & Appendices, 1938
All volumes originally published by Macmillan, recently republished in facsimile editions jointly by the Imperial War Museum and the Battery Press, Nashville, Tennessee, USA

William Orpen, *An Onlooker in France*, Williams and Norgate, 1924, Dublin, Parkgate Books, 1996

Lieutenant-Colonel the Rt. Hon. Sir F. Ponsonby, *The Grenadiers in the Great War*, Macmillan, 1920

Robin Prior and Trevor Wilson, *Command on the Western Front*, Blackwell, 1992

Julian Putkowski and Julian Sykes, *Shot at Dawn*, Barnsley, Wharncliffe Publishing Ltd, 1989

Bill Rawling, *Surviving Trench Warfare*, Toronto, University of Toronto Press, 1992

Sidney Rogerson, *Twelve Days*, Arthur Barker, 1930, Norwich, Gliddon Books, 1988

Captain Robert B. Ross, *The Fifty-First in France*, Hodder and Stoughton, 1918

Leonard Sellers, *The Hood Battalion*, Leo Cooper, 1995

Peter Simkins, *Kitchener's Army*, Manchester, Manchester University Press, 1988

The Somme and the Butte de Warlencourt, edited by A.H.G. Stephenson, Western Front Association, 1990

Lancelot Dykes Spicer, *Letters from France, 1915–1918*, Robert York, 1979

Michael Stedman, *Manchester Pals*, Leo Cooper, 1994

Major-General Sir Ernest Swinton, *Eyewitness*, Hodder and Stoughton, 1932

R.H. Tawney, *The Attack, and other papers*, Allen and Unwin, 1953

A.J.P. Taylor, *The First World War: An Illustrated History*, Hamish Hamilton, 1963, Penguin, 1966

John Terraine, *Haig, the Educated Soldier*, Hutchinson, 1963; *To Win a War*, Sidgwick & Jackson, 1978; *The Smoke and the Fire*, Sidgwick & Jackson, 1980; *The First World War*, Papermac, 1984

[Captain J.C. Dunn], *The War the Infantry Knew*, P.S. King, 1938; reissued in new edition with an introduction by Keith Simpson, Jane's Publishing Company, 1987, Cardinal (Sphere Books), 1989

Stephen Westman, *Surgeon with the Kaiser's Army*, William Kimber, 1968

Trevor Wilson, *The Myriad Faces of War*, Blackwell, 1986, Polity Press Cambridge in association with Blackwell, 1988

The Wipers Times, Facsimile Edition, Peter Davies, 1973

INDEX OF CONTRIBUTORS

Ranks of soldiers are given as they were at the time of the experiences described. Decorations are not shown. TF indicates a division of the Territorial Force. In the case of fatalities, the date and cause of death, and the place of burial or commemoration, are given in square brackets. The help of the Commonwealth War Graves Commission in supplying these details is gratefully acknowledged. The names of copyright holders or donors, where known, are given in round brackets. Every effort has been made to trace such copyright holders; the Museum would be grateful for any information which might help to trace those whose identities or addresses are not known. Figures in italics refer to illustrations.

GENERAL INDEX

Figures in italics refer to illustrations. For sources of personal evidence from IWM archives see Index of Contributors.